THE PHILOSOPHY OF

# JEAN-PAUL SARTRE

# THE PHILOSOPHY OF

# JEAN-PAUL SARTRE

### EDITED AND INTRODUCED BY
## ROBERT DENOON CUMMING

## VINTAGE BOOKS
### A DIVISION OF RANDOM HOUSE, NEW YORK

Library of Congress Cataloging in Publication Data
Sartre, Jean-Paul, 1905-
    The philosophy of Jean-Paul Sartre.
    Translations of extracts from the author's works.
    1. Philosophy—Collected works. I. Title.
[B2430. S32E53 1972]    194    72-632
ISBN 0-394-71808-9

Manufactured in the United States of America
VINTAGE BOOKS EDITION, September 1972

# ACKNOWLEDGMENTS

*For permission to reprint selections from the works of Jean-Paul Sartre, the editor wishes to thank:*

*Farrar, Straus and Giroux, Inc., for* The Transcendence of the Ego, *translated by Forrest Williams and Robert Kirkpatrick, copyright © 1957 by The Noonday Press, Inc.*

*New Directions, Publishers, for* Nausea, *translated by Lloyd Alexander, copyright 1949, all rights reserved.*

*Philosophical Library, Inc., for* The Emotions, *copyright 1954;* The Psychology of the Imagination, *copyright 1948;* Being and Nothingness, *translated by Hazel Barnes, copyright © 1956; and* Literature and Existentialism [What is Literature?], *translated by Bernard Frechtman, copyright 1952.*

*Alfred A. Knopf, Inc., for* No Exit and Three Other Plays, *Vintage Edition, translated by Stuart Gilbert, copyright 1946 by Stuart Gilbert, and in Great Britain under the title* The Flies *and* In Camera *by Hamish Hamilton Ltd.;* Search for a Method, *translated by Hazel Barnes, copyright © 1963 by Alfred A. Knopf, Inc., and in Great Britain under the title* The Problem of Method *by Methuen and Company Ltd.; a brief portion of* Critique de la Raison Dialectique, *translated for this volume by Starr and James B. Atkinson and* The Condemned of Altona, *translated by Sylvia and George Leeson, copyright © 1960 by Hamish Hamilton Ltd., and in Great Britain by Hamish Hamilton, Ltd.*

*Editions Gallimard,* Situations III, *copyright 1949 by Editions Gallimard.*

*George Braziller, Inc., for* Saint Genet, Actor and Martyr, *translated by Bernard Frechtman, copyright © 1963 by George Braziller, Inc., and in Great Britain by W. H. Allen & Company.*

# Contents

# CONSCIOUSNESS AND BEING

# CONSCIOUSNESS AND THE OTHER

# CONSCIOUSNESS AND ACTION

# CONSCIOUSNESS AND ACTION *(Cont.)*

# CONSCIOUSNESS AND LITERATURE

# CONSCIOUSNESS AND SOCIETY

# CONSCIOUSNESS AND SOCIETY *(Cont.)*

# THE PHILOSOPHY OF JEAN-PAUL SARTRE

# INTRODUCTION

Joe laid out a couple of frogs and was backing off towards the door, when he saw in the mirror that a big guy in a blouse was bringing down a bottle on his head held with both hands. He tried to swing around but he didn't have time. The bottle crashed his skull and he was out.

In August, 1938, Jean-Paul Sartre cited this description from *U.S.A.* of the death of the American Joe in a French café, and went on to reach the verdict, "Dos Passos is the greatest novelist of our time." The verdict may now seem preposterous, but it reminds us that one important formative influence on Sartre, who published his first novel in 1938, was the "technical revolution in the art of telling a story," which he credited to American novelists. This influence might provide an initial point of contact between our American experience and Sartre's intellectual career. Some point of contact is desperately needed, for Sartre has remained entirely indifferent to the techniques of contemporary Anglo-American philosophy—he admits he prefers detective stories to Wittgenstein. And we have been almost as indifferent to his philosophical writings. Can we ease our way into an understanding of Sartre's philosophy by taking advantage of his debt to the techniques of American novelists? Sartre's novels and plays have attained considerable recognition in the United States, and some selections from these works are included in this anthology. But if we are to approach his philosophy by way of his literary works, we eventually shall have to face the complicated philosophical question of the relation between his literary works and his philosophy.

Unfortunately there are other complications, which we had better not shirk. For Sartre's affection for things American has weakened since 1938, and he has recently commented on his sense of remoteness from us, by complaining that Americans are "too full of oversimplifications."

The first item difficult to pin down in any simple fashion is Sartre's inheritance. This novelist-philosopher is doubly a hybrid: if he began his career as a novelist with enthusiasm for the contemporary American novel, he began his career as a philosopher with enthusiasm for contemporary German philosophy. Indeed it is fashionable to regard Sartre's philosophy as really German rather than French, because Germans are supposed to be romantic, turbulent, and confused, while Frenchmen since Descartes are supposed to be rationalistic, clear, and distinct. German influences were in fact present from Sartre's birth in 1905 in Paris, for his mother's family were German-speaking exiles from Alsace. Sartre even favors German names for his heroes—Schneider, Hoederer, Goetz. But the most recent of these heroes is Franz, whose German name suggests that his role in the play is somehow French.

Indeed we shall see that what is most striking with regard to any influence on Sartre he has himself recollected is some equivocal complication. His French father, a naval engineer, died of tropical fever while Sartre was still a baby, so that he enjoyed without challenge the "peaceful possession" of his mother, and feels that he may have been spared an Oedipus complex. But this delightful simplification of his relationship with his mother was complicated by the child's thinking of her as an older sister. (After her husband's death she had resumed her place as the daughter of the family, and Sartre took his place beside her as her infant brother.) If Sartre could not see himself in the role of Oedipus, he could still turn to Greek myth for the plot of his first play and find a particular fascination in the relationship between Orestes and Electra. An incestuous brother-sister relationship is still featured in his last play, and he admits, "Even today, this is the only form of relationship which I have any feeling for." We shall see that hybrid, equivocal, and ultimately frustrating relationships are at the focus of his philosophy.

That incest tantalizes Sartre is due less, he suspects, to its sexual attractiveness than to the fact that the sexual consummation is frustrated by a prohibition. But the only prohibition Sartre ascribes to his dying father was the injunction, "Don't let him join the navy." Thus the bereaved child was not properly equippéd (a psychoanalyst has reported) with a superego. He has taken full advantage of this inadequacy, mocking the piety of his generation as a generation of "Aeneases with their Anchiseses mounted on their backs." His lack of respect for the prohibitions of any higher tribunal extends to the Puritan conscience of his German forebears and its American equivalent. Nothing is sacred for Sartre, not even the Freudian theory of the superego.

Why then has he remained so tantalized by frustrating prohibitions? It has been suggested that Sartre's grandfather compensated for the loss of Sartre's father, by equipping him with a super-superego. Grandfather dominated the family by staging, in the most grandiloquent Victorian style, patriarchal performances which assigned the child his role in life. Grandfather had received the academic reward meted out to educated exiles from Alsace: he taught German in French schools. He also taught his grandson to hate the Germans who had "taken Alsace and all the clocks in the house"—although there was still one, which had been given by grateful German students to whom he had taught French, and "the family always wondered where they had stolen it." Sartre recalls that "at the age of seventy," grandfather was "still entranced with French, because he had had a difficult time learning it, and never felt it was quite his." Thus he attempted to dedicate his grandson to French literature. But the youthful Sartre preferred Nick Carter, Buffalo Bill, and Michael Strogoff. Grandfather also attempted to dedicate him to an academic career. "In my person," Sartre explains, "martyred Alsace would enter the École Normale Supérieure, pass the finals brilliantly, and emerge that prince among men—a professor of literature." But the child detected something equivocal in his grandfather's devotion to French authors: "On the pretext of worshipping them, . . . he cut them up to transport them more easily from one language to another."

He who would translate and anthologize Sartre has been duly warned.

In 1929 Sartre emerged from the École Normale, but having failed his finals on the first trial, and as a professor of philosophy. During the next ten years he taught in various *lycées*, except for the academic year 1933-34, which he spent in Berlin studying German phenomenology. The trip was prompted by news of this movement brought back by Raymond Aron. At the news Sartre reportedly turned "almost pale with excitement." Here was his emancipation from the French philosophical tradition in which he had been indoctrinated at the Sorbonne and the École Normale. His excitement, a few years later, over the revolutionary techniques of American novelists was similarly excitement over the prospect of his emancipation from the French literary tradition. Emancipation itself will become the theme of both Sartre's philosophical and his literary works. Thus Sartre apparently did inherit a sense of mission from the patriarch dedicated to the emancipation of Alsace. But Sartre himself (characteristically, as we shall see) has accented the negative—the loss of Alsace in 1871: "I am a grandson of the defeat." To "this shame I did not suffer," he has attributed "a certain spirit of revenge" that lent epic scope to his aspirations as a youngster. It may be that this spirit has continued to animate such aggressive *prises de position* as the attack on French literature implicit in Sartre's peremptory verdict that an American is "the greatest of living novelists."

In any case, truculent *prises de position* have punctuated Sartre's career, rupturing his relations with such former friends and collaborators as Aron and Camus, and encouraging the impression that he is unpredictable and outrageous. Thus a question posed by the first anthology to present his thought from his earliest to his latest philosophical work is whether or not this is a development in which some continuity can be traced. I have just suggested the theme of emancipation. But there are complications in his treatment of this theme. I shall try to unravel some of them in this introduction. It is not an essay on Sartre which can be read or understood independently of the selections, and the headings in this introduction anticipate some of those which will be used for the selections themselves. Page references to the selections are supplied in brackets. In order to indicate the chronology of Sartre's development, the dates given in parentheses after the English titles of Sartre's works are the original French publication dates.

## CONSCIOUSNESS

Since the selections from Sartre's earliest philosophical work are followed by selections from his earliest novel, the first step in dealing with the question of continuity is to examine the relationship between Sartre's philosophical and literary preoccupations. It is not simply a question of his adopting a literary form to sugar-coat the bitter pill of philosophical argument. Later we shall see that in Sartre's philosophy it is not possible to separate form from content, technique from substance. We shall find that there are substantive philosophical reasons why Sartre resorts to literature, and that the particular literary forms and techniques he employs are philosophically significant.

If we begin by asking ourselves why Sartre "knows of nothing more impressive" in literature than Dos Passos' description of the death of Joe, we shall soon discover how difficult it is to separate the American novelist in Sartre from the German philosopher. The technique that most obviously appeals to Sartre here is Dos Passos' use of the mirror. For it is not just one technique among others; it is storytelling itself. Sartre has begun his essay on Dos Passos with the announcement, "A novel is a looking glass." No analogy seems more harmlessly traditional than that of art mirroring life, but Sartre adds a revolutionary implication. The analogy appeals to him, because a mirror is a surface. It lacks depth. Dos Passos' art of storytelling is superficial in the sense that a looking glass is merely "reflective"; all that is disclosed by his descriptions is a succession of appearances—"inexplicable tumults of color, noises, and passions." But reflection in the traditional French novel was a different and a more profound undertaking, which Sartre is employing the mirror analogy to discredit. (We shall see in a moment that Proust's *À la recherche du temps perdu* is the discreditable novel Sartre has primarily in mind.) In this tradition reflection is explanatory: individuals in the novel pause to reflect and explain what they are doing, by reference to their characters. And insofar as their explanations are incomplete, they allow themselves to be further explained by the reflections of the novelist. They, or the novelist, intervene in the succession of appearances, go behind what they appear to be doing, and discover that their souls have depths wherein reside the causes that explain what they are really doing. The succession of appearances is no longer inexplicable, but predetermined. Everything ultimately finds its place in the novel. The "tumults" themselves turn out in retrospect to have been only superficial disturbances; the "noises" and the "passions" are finally stilled by being explained.

Sartre's denial that the novelist has any right to intervene in his novel and reflect on what is happening roused a critical protest in the United States. What was overlooked was the congruity of Sartre's doctrine of the "authorless novel" with his doctrine of characterless characters, and the fact that the literary Sartre, who dislodges the novelist from the novel and character as a principle of explanation in the novel, is a philosopher who dislodges the self from consciousness as an explanation of its structure. What we see, in the "mirror" provided by Dos Passos' novel, is what is mirrored, for example, by Joe's own consciousness. In other words, I am suggesting that one reason Sartre "knows of nothing more impressive" in literature than Dos Passos' description of the death of Joe, is that consciousness for Sartre as a philosopher is fundamentally analogous to Joe's final glimpse in the mirror, when he is merely conscious of what is happening. Now Sartre is not denying that we do reflect, in the deeper, traditional sense, and explain what we do by reference to our characters. What he is asserting is that the self or character of which we then become conscious, is an outcome of this process of reflection; it is not an antecedent structure which, when disclosed by reflection, will provide a causal explanation of why I am doing what I am doing. He is further asserting that to the extent that I construe as an explanatory principle the self or character of which I become conscious through reflection, my self-consciousness is self-deception.

Sartre's attack on the traditional novel's reflective structure is an attack on the reflective structure of consciousness in the French philosophical tradition. The threat of deception in this tradition had come from outside consciousness: things might not conform to our sensory impressions—to what we are conscious of when we perceive them. But this external threat seemed to have been outmaneuvered as soon as Descartes had recognized it by doubting the existence of these things. For he could not then also doubt his own doubting—*i.e.*, that this process of reflection presupposed his own existence. He thus became conscious of himself as a deeper reality, a "sub-stance"—something underlying and sustaining the process of reflection—to which could be attributed what appeared during this process, even if the appearances have no direct reference to external things. This maneuver of reflective self-enclosure, when consciousness concludes that the self of which it has become reflexively conscious is impregnable to deception, is for Sartre the characteristic maneuver of self-deception—and of the French philosophical tradition, from Descartes' *cogito* to Bergson's *moi profond*. This entire tradition Sartre lumps together as "subjective idealism."

Sartre's literary techniques and his philosophical approach are alike designed to emancipate us from this self-deception. They subvert the Cartesian distinction between my indirect experience of external things and the immediate experience of myself, and restore and reinforce as my immediate experience my pre-reflective consciousness of things, and of my involvement with things, so that what we see reflected in the "mirror" of pre-reflective consciousness is recognized to be presupposed by the operations of reflection. The philosophical task of restoration is complicated by the fact that Sartre's philosophical procedure is itself reflective. He will therefore face the methodological problem of insuring that philosophical reflection actually reflects—mirrors—what appears in the "mirror" of the pre-reflective consciousness.

I have been drawing attention to Sartre's use of an analogy, because his philosophy will develop by traveling along a network of analogies. Although other analogies will soon become more important, I have been drawing attention to the analogy of a mirror in order to circumvent a serious difficulty, which could not be resolved in the translations themselves. This is the difficulty of dealing with the levels of reflection in Sartre and the distinction between reliable and distorting reflection. "Reflection" implies etymologically a reversal in the direction of a movement, but this reversal can be instanced either by an optical reflection in a mirror (and in this instance the reflection is immediate in the sense that no movement is visible) or by the visible movement of a physical body (for which French has the term *réflexion*). Sartre will rely on reflection in the sense suggested by the instance of the mirror (*i.e.*, on the reflective consciousness, insofar as it *immediately* reflects what appears to the pre-reflective consciousness) in order to expose the distortions in the structure of consciousness which we shall see are introduced by the *movement* of reflection in the second sense. I ordinarily employ the term "reflection" in this second sense, and I have brought in the analogy of the mirror to have it available when I need to distinguish "reflection" in the first sense. To indicate the reflexive character of reflection in both senses, Sartre takes full advantage of the French language, which is well stocked with reflexive verbal forms. English is not. I have overworked the adjective "reflexive" in this introduction; in the translations it is necessary to rely on circumlocutions, so that at times it sounds as if Sartre were being elaborately metaphysical, when he is only being French. Furthermore, the reflexive form "oneself" is stilted in English, so I have to resort (as I did in the last paragraph) to the too personal form "myself," so that at times it sounds as if Sartre were being unnecessarily existential, when his approach is merely phenomenological.

## SELF-CONSCIOUSNESS

Sartre adapted his phenomenological approach from Husserl, who had promulgated the program, turn "back [from subjective idealism] to things themselves." Husserl was proposing to describe any act of consciousness by reflecting on what we are (pre-reflectively) conscious of in performing this act. Take, by way of an example, Husserl's reflective description of the act of perception. When we perceive something, we are conscious of what we perceive as not appearing completely in this particular act of perception or in any succeeding acts of perception we might perform. (Husserl's description is summarized by Sartre [p. 77], and Sartre's concrete illustrations may help prepare the uninitiated reader for the difficult methodological argument that now follows from this description.) The conclusion that perceptual experience is a succession of uncertain and indefinitely corrigible appearances had been a traditional philosophical argument for disregarding these appearances as cognitively unreliable, and for seeking knowledge of the reality that lies behind these appearances. The knowledge sought usually took the form of some explanation of these appearances as the effects of causal factors (brain traces, etc.) of which we are not conscious when we perceive something. But instead of disregarding perceptual appearances, Husserl focused his reflection upon the structure a perceptual appearance must necessarily have for us to be conscious of it as a perceptual appearance. To recognize the uncertainty and indefinite corrigibility of a perception is to transcend reflexively these limitations of a perception; for the uncertainty and indefinite corrigibility are recognized to be certain, final, and incorrigible characteristics of perception itself. Husserl makes a further reflexive move: such immediate recognition is itself to be recognized as a more fundamental form of knowledge than the scientific linking of effects to causes.

Among the intrinsic characteristics of an act of perception —and indeed of any act of consciousness—the most striking for Husserl was the fact that it is a recognitional act whereby we are immediately "conscious *of something*." For this characteristic justified Husserl's reflective procedure of turning "back to things themselves," by recognizing that we recognize something when we are conscious of it. Husserl employed the terms "intentional" and "meaning-endowing" to describe this immediate reference of consciousness to what it is consciousness of—to what it "aims at," is "directed toward." An act of consciousness "intends" what it is consciousness of, and endows it with meaning, by recognizing it, identifying it, as "something." Since we are not conscious of this intentional relationship as a cause-effect relationship, meanings are not reducible to psychological occurrences, which are amenable to explanation in empirical psychology. Such psychological occurrences, for example, as sensory impressions are only subjective raw materials for the process of perception; they have to be structured and unified by the intentional acts which supply the identifying and objectifying reference to the thing itself. It is not these sensory impressions that the subject is immediately conscious of: what he recognizes is some object.

We note that Husserl's distinction between his method of reflective description and scientific explanation has been carried over by Sartre into literature, to become the distinction with which he commends Dos Passos' description as mirroring the succession of appearances that appear in the "mirror" of consciousness, and disdains the intrusions of character as a causal factor which is alleged to explain what occurs in the traditional novel.

There was one crucial difficulty which Husserl faced in applying his reflective method, and which Sartre inherits, as we have already anticipated. Husserl had to insure that he does recognize what appears to the pre-reflective consciousness. Immediate recognition was not immediately feasible; for preconceived, habitual explanations of what appears to consciousness had to be prevented from encroaching on and distorting what actually appears. To preclude these distortions, a particular reflective posture on the part of consciousness had to be strenuously maintained—the "phenomenological reduction" or *epoché*. This posture is roughly comparable to Cartesian doubt: the things which really exist, corresponding to what I am conscious of, are to be "bracketed" and "put out of reach," so that we no longer pay any attention to such problems as whether or not, and by what sequence of psychological and physical causes, perception provides us with knowledge of the external world. By reflecting then on what still remains within the scope of our investigation, I recognize, according to Husserl, that I, as a psychophysical organism, could perform neither the meaning-endowing acts themselves nor this reduction by which they are being segregated as a subject-matter for reflective investigation. In other words, the individual as he really exists, as well as the things that really exist, must be "bracketed." But the subject-matter under investigation still retains an internally connected and unified structure as my experience. This subjective structure is attributed by Husserl to the agency of a Transcendental Ego.

Husserl's reflective procedure is subtler than this bald summary suggests, but we are only concerned here with Sartre's first philosophical work, *The Transcendence of the Ego* (1936). In our selections [pp. 51-57] Sartre disposes of Husserl's Transcendental Ego as a relapse into Cartesian idealism. Husserl, Sartre claims, has allowed the reflexive movement of reflection to distort the intentional structure of consciousness. A more rigorous reflective description would disclose, according to Sartre, that when I become self-conscious, I am reflecting upon my pre-reflective consciousness of something else, and that the self (the ego) of which I become conscious is not the subject performing this act of reflection, but its intentional object, which has emerged in retrospect from the pre-reflective consciousness I am reflecting upon. The intentional relationship of consciousness to its object cannot be relaxed in favor of self-consciousness, or reversed by reflection's "turning back" and converted into the "centripetal" relationship to a subject, which is the structure of self-consciousness in the idealistic tradition.

Since we have already watched Sartre carry over into literature the implications of Husserl's philosophical program, we would anticipate that more than a technical philosophical error is at stake for Sartre in Husserl's relapse into Cartesian idealism.

The intellectual villain or traitor that Sartre is stalking with his own reflective description is, not Descartes or Husserl, but self-consciousness, which attempts, in effect, to secure for the self the privileged function, which it performs in Descartes and Husserl, of transcending my experiences by providing them with a necessary, predetermined structure, so that I can become conscious of these experiences as attributes of myself, and of myself as enjoying higher status than these experiences. Self-consciousness is thereby actually attempting to obscure the merely derivative status of the self; it is distorting its own intentional structure in order to avoid remaining conscious of the self as an object that has emerged in retrospect from my pre-reflective consciousness of something else.

Thus Sartre's repudiation of the doctrine of the Transcendental Ego is the discovery of the obliquity self-consciousness betrays in fostering this doctrine. "One senses," Sartre will later proclaim (when he generalizes this discovery so that it applies to social as well as epistemological relationships), "one's true relation to oneself and to others, because one flees it." This proclamation will forbid that frequent oversimplification of Sartre's philosophy which confuses it with a romantic philosophy of life. There are tame versions of existentialism that do take the form of some design for living, flaunt the writer's sense of destiny, and compose some sort of *Bildungsroman*. But in the more virulent forms of existentialism, such as Sartre's, the significant orientation is not any simple sense of direction, but the sense that one is already going in the wrong direction. Romantic philosophies of life often celebrate the straightforward claims of unreflective experience, emancipated from the transcendental evasions of reflection; for Sartre, too, as a phenomenologist, it is impossible for reflection to go beyond experience and discover the reality that lies behind what appears in the "mirror" of consciousness. But consciousness in Sartre continues to risk this impossible evasion and to distort its own "mirror."

## STORYTELLING

It is Sartre's repudiation of the Transcendental Ego which promotes "the technical revolution in the art of telling a story," which he credits to American novelists. The way the story of Joe's death is told may not have seemed a very impressive piece of evidence for the verdict, "Dos Passos is the greatest novelist of our time." But we may have missed Sartre's philosophical excitement. We have now seen that in his philosophy the attempt by consciousness to "reflect," in the sense of "turning back" and reversing its own movement so that this movement emanates from a self, is frustrated and condemned to obliquity by the intentional direction of this movement. We shall soon recognize a further impediment: the intentional movement of consciousness in Sartre (in contrast with Descartes' disembodied and instantaneous *cogito*) is embodied in an intentional action that takes time. To the analogies between the mirror and storytelling, and between the mirror and consciousness, can be added another detail of the death of Joe which may have appealed to Sartre—the frustration of Joe's action, when he sees in the mirror the bottle coming down on his head: "He tried to swing around (*Il essaya de se retourner*, in the French translation Sartre read) but he didn't have time."

We have not yet reached Sartre's analysis of the symbolism of intentional actions. But if detecting Sartre's philosophical critique of traditional reflection implicit in his appraisal of an action in a novel seems fanciful exegesis, I can plead that it obtains its plausibility from the fact that Sartre himself turns novelist at this juncture in his philosophy where reflection is unable to turn back on the intentional movement of consciousness and reconstitute it as a self-conscious, "centripetal" movement. I am not simply pleading that Sartre's first novel, *Nausea* (1938), rehashes in another genre the philosophical arguments of the *Transcendence of the Ego* against the privileged status of the self. It is the fact that *Nausea* is a novel—that Sartre as a philosopher is concerned to argue by telling a story—that illustrates the frustration in his philosophy of the traditional reflexive method of transcendental idealism. Husserl regarded his investigation of transcendental consciousness as yielding self-knowledge, and he labeled this investigation an "Egology." But with Sartre's repudiation of the Transcendental Ego, self-consciousness no longer yields self-knowledge. Reflection can no longer achieve what the reflexive method traditionally requires—the instantaneous coincidence of the subject performing the act of reflection (the Cartesian "I think") with the object that it is directed toward (the Cartesian "I am"). To become conscious of the "I" as subject a further act of reflection must be performed, separated from the first in time. This predicament of reflection has been noted by Sartre's collaborator, Simone de Beauvoir, *"On ne peut jamais se connaître, mais seulement se raconter."* Self-consciousness is not knowledge but a story one tells about oneself, for in contrast with the structure of knowledge, the structure of a story is temporal. Thus at the juncture in his philosophy where Sartre turns novelist, he finds it indispensable to distinguish his undertaking from Proust's *À la recherche du temps perdu.*

The structure of the story *Nausea* reproduces the reflexive aspiration of consciousness in Sartre's philosophy: *Nausea* is a novel (at the higher, reflective level) about the pre-reflective experiences that led up to the writing of the novel. Proust's novel has a comparable structure. But in Proust (as in Husserl) experience is recaptured in its necessary structure by the reflective movement which transcends experience. Thus Proust's *recherche* is successfully completed in his terminal volume, *Le temps retrouvé*. But Sartre has his ostensible protagonist in *Nausea*, Roquentin, tell a story to show that one cannot in fact "catch time by the tail" [p. 59]. Furthermore, the true protagonist, nausea itself, is (in one of its manifestations) the reflexive experience of the discrepancy between the necessary structure of the story as told (as a work of art) and the sense of contingency —of the indeterminacy of the future—which is the experience of the sloppiness of living one's life that one seeks to alleviate by telling the story about it. This discrepancy, which self-consciousness (as well as Proust and the literary tradition) obscures by its loquacity, is preserved in *Nausea*. The novel is not completed within the novel, which ends with Roquentin's aspiration to regain his past experience by writing the novel, but with his actual future left dangling [p. 73].

Within the novel *Nausea* the analogue for the novel is "Some of These Days." Sartre's selection of this jazz lyric doubtless parodies Proust's use of *la petite phrase* from the Vinteuil Sonata to confront the novelist with his vocation as an artist. But the story Sartre tells of his own vocation is worth noting. As we have already seen, his sense of vocation was supplied initially by his grandfather, but it took shape as a sense of the structure of the work of art Sartre acquired from the musical accompaniment of the silent movies, to which he was addicted as a child:

When everything seemed tranquil in the castle, sinister chords warned of the presence of the assassin. How fortunate they were—the cowboys, the musketeers, the cops: their future was present in this premonitory music, determining what was happening. An uninterrupted melody blended with their lives, drawing them on towards victory or death by its advance towards its own consummation. They were awaited: by the girl in peril, by the general, by the traitor hidden in the forest, by the pal tied near a keg of powder, grimly watching the flame run along the fuse. The progress of the flame, the desperate struggle of the virgin against her attacker, the galloping of the hero across the prairie—all these images, all these movements intermingled, and presiding over them "The Ride to the Abyss," an orchestral piece adapted for the piano from the "Damnation of Faust": all became one—Destiny. The hero jumped down from his horse, stamped out the flame, the traitor threw himself on him, . . . but the contingencies of their duel participated in the rigorous necessity of the musical development: these were false contingencies which barely concealed the universal order. What delight when the last thrust of the knife coincided with the final chord! I was fulfilled, I had found the world where I aspired to live, I had reached the absolute. How disconcerting it was when the lamps came on again.

The disconcerting sense that all was no longer one is the nauseous sense of discrepancy between the necessary structure, the predetermined development of the work of art, and the contingent, shapeless vagueness of going on living [p. 96].

While, in Sartre's recollection, the musical accompaniment is assigned the function of structuring a transcendent world, the visual imagery of the movie is assigned the correlative function of dissolving the structure of the real world. The "flow" of images was "a restlessness at work undermining the wall" on which they were being projected. In the same manner "they relieved the solids [of which they were the images] of the embarrassing massiveness which encumbered me in my body, and my youthful idealism rejoiced in this infinite contraction." The correlative functions of the two senses are, we note, the two sides of the idealistic reduction effected by Husserl. The youthful moviegoer was a phenomenologist. Visual consciousness for Sartre is at once cinematic and idealistic—a flickering flow of successive appearances which undermine the real world of things they mirror. But if souls have no depth in Sartre, things are profound. Visual consciousness is too superficial a rendering of experience, and the visual analogy of the "mirror" of consciousness will require rectification.

## CONTINGENCY

"It took me thirty years," Sartre will comment in 1963, "to get rid of my idealism." This is the intellectual emancipation which is illustrated by the selections in this anthology, beginning with his attack on the Transcendental Ego and continuing with the anti-novel *Nausea*. The idealistic tradition that culminates in Husserl's phenomenological reduction is a tradition in which visual perception is not only the primary form of pre-reflective experience, but also the model for the reflective procedure the philosopher employs in analyzing experience. Thus when Husserl in his *Ideas* proposes the method of reduction, he enjoins us to "set aside all previous habits of thought, and see through . . . the mental barriers which these habits have set along the horizon of our thinking." We must "learn to see what stands before our eyes"—*i.e.*, what appears immediately to consciousness. Husserl's recurrent behest to philosophical reflection is to "look and see."

It seems to have occurred to Sartre that there was one habit of thought Husserl was not seeing through—the habit of visualizing thought as analogous to visual perception. Sartre assaults this final mental barrier. What appears immediately to consciousness, when I see something, cannot be the thing as it really exists, since I can only see it—and am conscious of seeing it—from a distance, out of reach. Thus it is visual consciousness which encourages reflection to undermine the real world by "bracketing" the thing as it really exists. Sartre sets consciousness to work to undermine this visionary aspiration in turn, pitting a reduction of his own against Husserl's. Thankless as may be the task of analyzing a mystical vision [p. 60], we should at least recognize the respect in which the mysticism of Sartre's reduction is not a "vision." When he discredits visual consciousness as "abstract" and "cleaned up" [p. 64], he is disturbing the traditional co-ordination of the senses, by appealing from visual perception to tactile perception. Deluded by his visual analogy, Husserl failed in his effort to get "back to things themselves." But when I touch something, I am conscious of reaching the thing as it is—massive, solid, resisting my effort. The fascination of tactile experience, its mysticism, is the achievement, at the pre-reflective level, of this immediate contact of subject with object, which frustratingly eludes the grasp of reflection.

Hands and their analogues (*e.g.*, crabs) keep turning up in Sartre. The hands are often soiled by their contact with things. In *Nausea* itself, the misgiving that visual experience is "cleaned up" probably taunts Husserl's claim that his reduction "purifies" experience, but in Sartre's later writings (*e.g.*, in *Dirty Hands*) contamination becomes a statement of his activist politics. When I see something, I am not conscious of the transaction taking place between my eye and what is seen; but when I handle something, I am not just perceiving but perceiving by acting, and I am affected by the action. (Sartre's distinction between visual experience and tactile experience seems to have been inspired by Heidegger's distinction between *Vorhandenheit*—the mode of being, recognized by Husserl, of something confronting us—and *Zuhandenheit*—the mode of being of something we are putting to use without visualizing what it is.) Thus tactile experience will provide Sartre with phenomenological evidence that Husserl's idealistic phenomenology is visionary, contemplative, esthetic. But at the same time, Sartre is substituting a different conception of esthetic experience itself, as we have already observed by following out the comparison with Proust that is implicit in *Nausea*. In Sartre's later works, it is Flaubert's estheticism which receives the brunt of Sartre's attack, and Sartre may well have in mind Flaubert's edict, "Art is a luxury, it requires calm, white hands."

In *Nausea* itself, the problem of action is barely delineated, and the theme of contamination is largely epistemological. Sartre not only re-orients (at the pre-reflective level) visual consciousness toward the object of tactile consciousness, but also deals (at the reflective level) with the idealistic reduction as dissolving the object into the subjectivity of self-consciousness. This reflexive maneuver he mocks by giving it an additional twist: the primary object of which Roquentin is conscious in the "vision" is a root, which is the analogue not only of a clutching hand, but also of a digestive apparatus. Idealists have often

*Introduction*

supplemented their visual analogies with biological analogies that instill confidence in the reflective efficacy of consciousness. Just as Sartre counters their visual analogies with the tactile sense of the object's resistance, so he counters their biological analogies with the subject's sense of revulsion. Nausea is the subject's inability to digest its experience by reflecting on it. The disgust in the "vision," with vegetation, vitality, and any impulse from the vernal wood, is not just Sartre's urban "allergy to cholorophyll," which Simone de Beauvoir has diagnosed. It is disgust with the complacent good digestion that is idealism's dialectical apparatus: "The spider draws things into its web, coats them with its own drivel, and slowly swallows, reducing them to its own nature." Thus consciousness "assimilates" things to itself; their solid structure is "dissolved" into items of consciousness—whether these be visualized as ideas, or felt as manifestations of a will to power or of an *élan vital.*

Here again we have to recognize that Sartre is not disgusted with idealism simply as a philosophy. Its visionary aspiration is the aspiration of consciousness itself; and it is the experience of living, not any plainly philosophical argument, that frustrates reflection in Sartre and transforms its facile movement into a sense of revulsion. This nausea cannot be eluded, for consciousness can never finally release its visionary aspiration from a sense of its own embodiment: consciousness is muddied; its meaning-endowing movement is clogged as it becomes consciousness of the flabbiness and sluggishness of the flesh. In *Nausea* the social structure is equally structureless. Roquentin finds nothing so sickening as "the communion of souls," and he feels himself mired in *Bouville* (Mucktown). This feeling is doubtless commentary on Sartre's own experience of being stuck in a provincial city. Sartre taught school in Le Havre and in Laon, before he finally obtained a position in Paris in 1937.

This swamping of the aspiration of consciousness to transcend experience may remind us of the Slough of Despond that impeded the *Pilgrim's Progress from This World to that Which is to Come.* Only in Sartre, in contrast with Bunyan, the transcendent world never comes; despondency can never finally be overcome. But if Sartre's nauseous "vision" seems closer to traditional Puritanism than to the philosophical tradition, he is still a philosopher writing a novel, and we can trace the philosophical implications of an esthetic experience in which touch

19

and taste express distrust of transcendental aspiration as visionary. For these are the senses which have traditionally been dis-
missed by idealism as "non-esthetic." Touch lacks the transcendental dimension of sight: "By the sense of touch," Hegel
explains, "the individual merely comes into contact with some
particular thing, its material resistance, but a work of art is
not merely a sensuous thing, but the ideal manifested through a
sensuous medium." In Sartre, however, the artist requires the
resistance of a recalcitrant material to create a work of art, and
Sartre interprets sculpture, for example, not as a purely visual
art, but as the esthetic experience of "the only being who can
touch other beings." Sight for Hegel is a distinctively esthetic
or "ideal" sense, since its object is "free and independent as the
object of an appetiteless vision." In contrast, for Hegel, "taste
is unable to leave the object in its free independence but is concerned with it in the wholly active way of consuming it." In
Sartre, however, no vision, not even esthetic vision, is appetiteless; consciousness is concerned with all objects in an active
way. Sartre therefore disdains visual imagery, and resorts instead to the clumsier and murkier imagery of manipulation and
digestion, in order to discredit the visual illusion of esthetic distance.

## EMOTIONAL AND IMAGINATIVE CONSCIOUSNESS

Frustrating impediments are for Sartre a distinctive feature of
appetitive behavior. In *Theory of the Emotions* (1939), he deals,
in effect, not with the emotions traditionally characterized as
"appetitive," but with those which were distinguished as "iras-
cible," on the ground that impediments between the subject
and the object of his appetite were their immediate occasion.
This one portion of the traditional theory takes on general significance in Sartre: emotional consciousness is not simply sometimes consciousness of the resistance of specific things and of
specific human prohibitions, but is perpetually consciousness of
its inability to satisfy its own aspiration to reach the transcendental. Sartre had not worked out his theory of symbolism in
1939, but we can detect his disparagement of transcendental
aspiration in his selecting, as a typical quiver of emotion, the
experience of sour grapes, when one sees from a distance an object which is frustratingly out of reach: "I stretch out my hand

to pick a bunch of grapes" but "I cannot reach it," so I shrug my shoulders, drop my hand, muttering, "They are too green" [p. 75].

In this situation I could not really act. I accordingly resorted to play-acting—to an action at a distance which "brackets" and transcends the real world of action. My intentional consciousness of the grapes is still embodied, but my body, instead of serving as the instrument of the action of picking the grapes, plays a role in the meaning-endowing act whereby I identify the grapes as "too green" to be picked. The shrugging of my shoulders and the setting of my teeth on edge not only transforms the intentional object (the bunch of grapes) but also operates reflexively to half obscure from my consciousness the fact that this transformation is self-deception. The grapes have not been transformed, but I am no longer perceiving them as ripe enough to be picked; I am imagining them to be "too green."

In *The Psychology of the Imagination* (1940), Sartre analyzes the distinction between perceiving and imagining, incorporating in this analysis the distinction of *Nausea* between living and storytelling, and the distinction of *The Theory of the Emotions* between acting and play-acting. Since it is not the real world of perceptual experience, as in Husserl's reduction, but the transcendental that has receded "out of reach" in Sartre, the attempt of consciousness to reach it becomes imaginative. The distinction of level, which Husserl had drawn between the really existing thing perceived and the "ideal" or "unreal" object of my intention, survives in Sartre as a distinction between the act of perception, whereby I am conscious of something as really existing there, in front of me, and the act of imagination whereby I become conscious of something as not existing there. Sartre uses the example of a portrait: to perceive a portrait is to be conscious of a certain distribution of colors, etc. (including, of course, the tactile quality of the color [p. 92]); to imagine the object portrayed is to "bracket" the portrait as a really existing thing, so that the distribution of colors, etc., becomes material the imagination endows with transcendent meanings as embodying aspects of this object. The indispensability of such material embodiment to art indicates that the realm of the imagination does not enjoy the autonomy in Sartre that the transcendental region enjoyed in Husserl, and that esthetic experience is not for Sartre the "manifestation" of a higher reality that it was for idealistic esthetics [p. 81]. Instead it is the sense of unreality that is heightened in Sartre when the material support is weakened, as it is in the case of the mental image as contrasted with the artistic image; and this sense of unreality reaches its frustrating climax when Sartre finally arrives reflexively at the self-portrayal, the self-impersonation, implicit in the attempt to live the equivocal life of the imagination:

> The object of an image is something unreal. . . . It is out of reach. I cannot touch it, change its place, or rather I can indeed do so, but on condition that I do it unreally, by not using my own hands, but phantom hands which administer unreal blows to this face. To act upon these unreal objects, I must double myself, make myself unreal [p. 88].

In the progress of Sartre's analysis from the portrait to this self-portrayal, the crucial intervening example is that of a portrayal of Maurice Chevalier by an impersonator [p. 81]. The bodily movements of the impersonator still provide, as in the instance of the portrait, perceptual materials for the act of the imagination, but what Sartre stresses is the recalcitrance of these materials; for in much the same way that he pitted tactile perception against visual perception in the "vision" of *Nausea*, in order to weaken the structure of meaning consciousness ordinarily attributes to our experiences, so he now plays perception and imagination off against each other:

> The difference between the consciousness of a portrayal and the consciousness of a portrait derives from the materials. The material of the portrait itself solicits the spectator to carry out the synthesis, inasmuch as the painter endowed it with a perfect resemblance to its model. The material of the impersonation is a human body. It is rigid, and resists the imitation. The impersonator is small, plump, and dark-haired; a woman who is imitating a man. . . . The object which she produces by means of her body is a weak form which can always be interpreted in two distinct ways: I am always free to see Maurice Chevalier as an image or a small woman making faces. . . . Only a definite act of will can keep consciousness from sliding from the level of the image to that of perception. Even so, this sliding usually oc-

curs at one moment or another. . . . A hybrid state develops, which is neither entirely perceptive nor entirely
imaginative. . . . This unstable and transitory state is obviously what is most entertaining for the spectator in an
impersonation. [pp. 82-86]

In Sartre's later works we shall be able to push beyond what
is obvious here. The reason this sliding consciousness of an
equivocal object is entertaining rather than merely frustrating
is that all consciousness is equivocal, unstable, and transitory,
and is frustrated by the fact that it therefore cannot become reflexively an object for itself. In other words it is "consciousness
of something," but it cannot become conscious of itself as
something; and it can find some relief from this predicament
by becoming conscious of something which is almost as unstable and transitory, and thus objectifies and symbolizes characteristics it would have if it could become an object for itself
and if an object could have these characteristics. This inability
of consciousness to stabilize and consolidate itself as self-consciousness will undergo further investigation in Sartre's next
work, in which he will analyze reflection as "the drama of the
being who cannot be an object for himself." But he will finally
leave us with the consolation that consciousness can take in
"sliding," which symbolizes the transitoriness of its own movement.

## CONSCIOUSNESS AND BEING

Under this heading are included selecticns from the first part of
*Being and Nothingness* (1943). Here Sartre converts the phenomenological approach of his earlier writings, which we have
been examining, into a "phenomenological ontology." In these
earlier writings Husserl's "consciousness of something" had already become, as it were, consciousness of some thing—*i.e.*, of
the actual, tangible existing thing that Husserl had "bracketed."
What Sartre had followed Husserl in analyzing phenomenologi-
cally as the intentional activity of identifying what something is,
now involves the recognition of the principle of identity as an
ontological principle: I am conscious of a thing as being what
it is.

The identifying activity of consciousness Sartre analyzes in

Gestalt fashion, as an articulative operation in which a figure emerges from a ground. But Sartre repudiates Gestalt psychology to the extent that it is a causal explanation: the emergence of the figure in Sartre is the spontaneous movement of our consciousness; by recognizing what this figure is, consciousness transcends whatever circumstances might be alleged to explain its occurrence as a response to their stimulus. Sartre's analysis, moreover, is reflexive in that he is less concerned with the emergence of the figure than with this transcending movement which is the emergence of consciousness itself.

In analyzing the emergence of consciousness, Sartre combines Husserl's phenomenological analysis of the structure of consciousness with Heidegger's ontology, in which the structure of a "world" is articulated by man's emergence—by his *"ex-sistence* in the world." Sartre effects the combination by construing human existence in Heidegger as conscious existence, and by converting into a dialectic the transcending movement with which consciousness *ex-sists.* What Husserl and the early Sartre had distinguished as levels of consciousness are set in motion as *stages* in the development of consciousness. This conversion is feasible in Sartre, since consciousness is not anchored to a Transcendental Ego, and the resulting analysis of consciousness in Sartre is perhaps somewhat closer to Hegel's *Phenomenology* than to Husserl's. However the conversion is not complete, since consciousness, which earlier was incapable of reaching the transcendental level, is now incapable of arriving at the final stage of synthesis where Spirit is Absolute. What Sartre takes over from Hegel is the antithetical moment in the dialectic, when "Spirit is the Negative." Since no later moment of synthesis supervenes, the energy of the antithetical moment is promptly expended in a limping, equivocal dialectic, in which (in contrast with Hegel's progressive dialectic) the onward and upward movement of human aspiration continually comes to grief.

The vehemence of Sartre's own *prises de position*—and of his repudiations of positions—may betray, as I noted earlier, a certain inherited "spirit of revenge," but this vehemence also finds a philosophical rendering in Sartre's accent on the antithetical and the negative. Consciousness for Sartre is not simply unstable and transitory; at each moment its emergence is a revolutionary *prise de position*—and an *arrachement* which is the repudiation by consciousness of what already is. We have

recognized particular acts of consciousness which are revolutionary (*e.g.*, the visual undermining of the real world, the tactile undermining of visual experience, the emotional revulsion
of nausea, the imaginative transformation of the grapes), but
Sartre is generalizing in *Being and Nothingness* and assigning
to consciousness as such a revolutionary role as the continual
restructuring of our experience. Revolutionary techniques,
whether those of the American novel or of German philosophy,
are thus not merely formal procedures but serve to implement
this role. (This revolutionary role of consciousness prepares the
way for Sartre's later commitment to revolutionizing the social
structure.)

To summarize the influences on Sartre I have mentioned and
put them together to compose his own analysis of consciousness:
Husserl's "consciousness of something" articulates as a Gestalt
Heidegger's "world"; and the articulation involves negation—
*i.e.*, "consciousness of something" is consciousness of it as this
thing and not that thing. To what can be attributed to these influences, Sartre adds an analysis of the negative relationship of consciousness to itself: "Consciousness is not what it is and is what
it is not." This double-dealing yields a dialectical version of his
earlier distinction between self-consciousness and "consciousness of something": the aspiration of consciousness to self-
consciousness is its attempt to achieve the self-identity of a
thing, but this is an attempt by consciousness to become other
than itself.

## CONSCIOUSNESS AND THE OTHER

Self-identity has been the problem frustrating self-consciousness ever since Sartre expelled "characters" from novels and the
Transcendental Ego from philosophy. This problem is reformu-
lated dialectically in the next set of selections from *Being and
Nothingness*. Sartre now resorts, in effect, to a Transcendental
*Alter Ego*. Self-consciousness is consciousness of myself as
something of which the other is conscious but of which I cannot
become conscious. His consciousness of me transcends my consciousness, because I have become for him the object that I can
never become for myself. When he looks at me I am conscious of
his consciousness identifying me as having this or that character; I cannot pass comparable value judgments on myself, ex-

cept by attempting the impossible—to look at myself with another's eyes.

The methodological potency ascribed by Sartre to the look of
the other may be a continuing debt to Husserl's method of "looking and seeing." But in Husserl the Transcendental Ego provided
reflection with a fixed source of insight into the structure of consciousness. When the other looks at me in Sartre, his insight and
its source are beyond my control. I am no longer master of the
phenomenological situation; it is his consciousness which endows my actions with their meanings. To regain control, my
consciousness cannot simply reflect—"turn back" upon itself.
To elude the self the other is conscious of as mine, my consciousness must detour, turn upon him, and alter his consciousness of me. Thus we have a more complicated "flight" than we
anticipated earlier.

My flight from the self he is conscious of and my pursuit of the
self I would have him conscious of become a game of hide and
seek, in which the successive alterations in the structure of my
consciousness can only be traced dialectically as altered relationships between my consciousness and his. Thus we are offered
a truncated version of the Hegelian master-slave dialectic, in
which Sartre denies that reflection can transcend this antithesis
which is established at the pre-reflective level of looking and
seeing. Further, we already know that looking and seeing are
not for Sartre methodologically privileged forms of experience,
but are vitiated by their aloofness. It is only because my intentions are embodied in overt actions that I am exposed to the
other's look; and the dialectic of my relation with him does not
remain a duel at a visible distance, but culminates in tactile
forms of self-aggrandizement and humiliation, in which my
body changes sides in the dialectic, and my consciousness of myself as something embodied participates in my alienation by the
caress, which embodies the other's tactile consciousness of me.
[pp. 215-223].

## CONSCIOUSNESS AND ACTION

Since the problem of self-identity cannot be resolved by reflection it becomes explicitly a problem of action in the next set of
selections from *Being and Nothingness*. This conversion of
Sartre's phenomenological ontology into what has come to be

known as "phenomenological existentialism" is associated, of course, with his experience of the German Occupation and the French Resistance. I have accordingly included selections from his description of the German Occupation, as an encounter with the other which alienated Frenchmen from themselves, and from his Resistance play *The Flies*, in which Orestes advances beyond the inconclusive experience of reflection (comparable to Roquentin's experience in *Nausea*) and arrives at an "irreparable action" with which he must identify himself. But the environmental determinants of Sartre's existentialism should not be stressed (as they are when Sartre's philosophy is assumed to be simply a by-product of the war) to the extent of forgetting that his analysis of the other's consciousness of me is grafted on his earlier phenomenological analysis of "consciousness of something." Thus Sartre describes Frenchmen's alienation from themselves during the Occupation as the experience of "a certain way things had of being less ours, more alien, colder, somehow more public, as if an alien look had violated the intimacy of our hearths." The problem of self-alienation Orestes faces is similarly the experience that there is nothing with which he can identify himself as his own: he *sees* things which should have been his but are not, because he has never put them to any use in *action* [p. 236]. We should not forget that tactile experience of the resistance of a thing was a delineation of the problem of action in Sartre's early phenomenological writings. Their having been written before the French Resistance, serves to illustrate the phenomenological argument Sartre now offers against determinism: "The environment can only act on the subject to the extent that he understands it; that is, transforms it into a situation" [p. 301].

But just because the process of understanding in Sartre is phenomenological, the environment cannot be overlooked. The things of which the subject is conscious are features of his environment. Consciousness transcends its circumstances in one sense, but only as consciousness of these circumstances. Thus the concept of freedom Sartre opposes to determinism should not be confused (as it sometimes is) with the Kantian conception. The transformation in Sartre of circumstances into a situation is their articulation by consciousness; the articulation is selective, and thus involves an implicit, pre-reflective but free decision as to their meaning. In Kant reflection lifts the decision out of the phenomenal region of the particular circumstances of which the individual is conscious; he decides, not as an individual, but as a legislator for a noumenal society of rational agents. In Sartre the decision remains phenomenal [p. 268]. There is no higher tribunal. The agent is not in a position to legislate morally for others, and Sartre analyzes moral decisions as analogous, not to legislative decisions, which are general in their scope, but to the creative decisions embodied in particular works of art.

In order to follow Sartre's analysis it is more helpful to recall Husserl than Kant, even though Sartre has criticized the transcendental and subjective orientation of Husserl's idealism as a failure to face the problem of action. Husserl had refurbished the idealistic idiom of construction by describing intentional acts as "constitutive"—*i.e.*, as structuring their sensory materials by their reference to something. When Sartre repudiated Husserl's phenomenology as transcendental, this idiom acquired esthetic implications: Husserl's constructive acts of consciousness became, in Sartre's *Psychology of the Imagination*, acts of imaginative consciousness. When Sartre repudiated Husserl's phenomenology as subjective, actual existing things replaced Husserl's sense-impressions as materials for these constructive acts of imaginative consciousness. Sartre now, in effect, remedies Husserl's failure to face the problem of action, by finding these constructive acts of imaginative consciousness embodied in overt actions. Assisted by the equivocal use of the French *faire* to cover both doing and making [p. 305]. Sartre treats actions as hybrid phenomena, at once esthetic and moral. Thus it is no accident that the example with which Sartre begins his analysis of actions [p. 243] is Constantine's construction of Constantinople, with the intention of providing the Roman Empire with a Christian capital rivaling pagan Rome. Constantine's overt construction embodies an imaginative reconstruction which brackets, transcends, and thereby confers meaning on his environment, so that in the light of his intention, the actual capital, Rome, is identified as "not sufficiently secure from invasion" and as "too corrupt in its morals," to be a Christian capital. (The example also gathers together other influences on Sartre besides Husserl's: the restructuring reminds us of the articulation of a Gestalt; the world-wide empire at stake, of Heidegger's characterization of the human situation as "being-in-a-world"; the rivalry between the two capitals and the negative identification of Rome, of the antithetical, negative moment that Sartre's dialectic of consciousness retains from Hegel.)

The distinction between the esthetic and the moral that survives in Sartre is the phenomenological distinction between intentional "consciousness of something" and the self-consciousness that is reflexively implicit in "consciousness of something": the structure of the work of art embodies what the artist is conscious of, but since his consciousness has been inherently articulative and selective in its constructive activity, the structure of the work of art is also a structure of decisions, whose interrelationship composes the artist's "choice of himself." To this extent the succession of examples which we noted in *The Psychology of the Imagination* can become stages in the dialectical analysis of the same action: the work of art is implicitly a self-portrait.

Thus Sartre's preferred idiom for what the agent does when he acts is that he is making something of himself, and the example he favors of a significant moral choice is that made by an artist, who has made something of himself (in a moral sense) by making something (in the esthetic sense). Sartre accordingly finds moral intentions implicit in the writings of Flaubert, Baudelaire, Genet, *et al.* The phenomenological warrant for this privileged role of the artist in Sartre's moral analysis is that it is impossible, in Sartre's analysis of consciousness as intentional, to satisfy directly the reflective aspiration of consciousness to become itself identifiable as something. Consciousness is condemned to obliquity, and the pursuit of a self therefore takes the form of self-expression; self-consciousness secures symbolic expression in something (the work of art) which embodies one's intentional consciousness of something else. Symbolism for Sartre, as for Freud, is the result of frustration, but the frustrating experience for Sartre is that of reflection. At this juncture his phenomenological existentialism becomes existential psychoanalysis; the individual's intentions can be deciphered only by interpreting what his actions indicate he is conscious of, and can be deciphered readily only when these actions are the creation of a work of art in which these intentions are symbolically exhibited.

## EXISTENTIAL PSYCHOANALYSIS

Sartre's analysis of the symbolism of artistic actions extends to all actions, for since the intentional activity of any consciousness is constructive any agent is an artist and the facts of his situation are artifacts. Even the other, who originally entered Sartre's analysis as a spectator, becomes in his turn an artist, since his look is the vehicle of the constructive activity of his consciousness: "The other's look shapes my body . . . , sculptures it, makes it." By thus making something of me, "he possesses me, and this possession is nothing other than the consciousness of possessing me" [p. 209]. The interchangeable use in English of such expressions as "making a woman" and "having a woman" may facilitate our understanding of this final extension of the range of "artistic" activity. Yet it is more prudent to expect that Sartre may seem his most capricious or obsessed in his analysis of the "appropriative" relationship of possession. We should perhaps pause to recognize again that despite the transitions we have been tracing from acting to making to having, Sartre's entire analysis is still geared to his original distinction between the intentional movement and the reflexive aspiration of consciousness: "consciousness of something" is not only the "construction" of what it is consciousness of, but it is also implicitly the aspiration to *be* something itself; it therefore takes the further form of aspiring to make something of oneself by making something (of what one is conscious of), but this aspiration to make something only displays its reflexive significance as the aspiration to make something one's *own*.

This dialectical juggling provides Sartre's existential psychoanalysis with three categories—Being, Doing-Making, and Having. Lest the juggling seem entirely arbitrary, it is worth discerning, however remotely, the three traditional categories of *situs*, *actio*, and *habitus*, which are older than Aristotelianism and can be found embedded in primitive forms of language. With Sartre's analysis of "situation" (which he adapts from Heidegger's analysis of the *Dasein*) he has in effect restored that concrete and rudimentary sense (which Being had before philosophical reflection began its enterprise of idealistic abstraction) whereby something is, if it occupies a place. We have already watched Sartre exploit the equivocation of *faire* in order to strengthen the sense in which doing something is creative. He is similarly reinvigorating "having" (*avoir*) by recourse, in effect, to its primitive sense as a verb of action referring to something one holds in one's hand. *Nausea* has prepared us for analogies to tactile experience. But Sartre is now developing a reflexive analysis of human behavior as a whole, in which he is restoring, in effect, the original reference of the English be-havior to the self-possession of actively upholding oneself.

In this reflexive analysis, the consciousness of myself implicit in my intentional consciousness of something becomes dialectical, insofar as it becomes consciousness of the discrepancy between its own transparent fluidity as consciousness and the opaque inertia of the resistant thing which it is consciousness of. This dialectic is triggered, is set in motion, whenever consciousness becomes consciousness of something whose characteristics are hybrid and equivocal in meaning, because they are transitional between these antithetical states of transparent fluidity and opaque inertia, for consciousness then feels that the transparency and fluidity which are distinctive of its characterlessness as "consciousness of . . ." are compromised by what it is consciousness of. Thus when consciousness becomes consciousness of something thickening, of something becoming sluggish, or (conversely) of something resistant and inert which is softening and dissolving—*e.g.*, of something slimy, creepy, soggy, sticky, etc.—its tactile sense of these characteristics is (reflexively) the moral sense of contamination and revulsion, which menaced our equanimity in *Nausea*. Now that "consciousness of" has become possessive—*i.e.*, now that the meaning-endowing activity of consciousness has become the aspiration to make something mine—the impediment that menaces its constructive movement is the prospect of being possessed, of being "had," by something equivocal, because I can make nothing of it, because it is not quite a thing but is almost structureless [p. 345].

In *Nausea* Roquentin's consciousness coped with the sloppiness of his existence and the sluggishness of his flesh by making something of himself: he told a story. Sartre has similarly analyzed the prospect of transformation that provided the reflexive dimension of his own vocation as an artist: "My loquacious consciousness would flow into letters of bronze, the sounds of my life would be replaced by indelible inscriptions, my flesh with a style, the soft spirals of time by eternity."

With the assimilation of doing to making in *Being and Nothingness*, other modes of human activity besides the artistic are dramatized as symbolic. Just as consciousness feels menaced when its freedom and ease of movement are impeded and compromised by what it is consciousness of, so it feels its movement facilitated and enhanced when it becomes conscious of something smooth (*lisse*)—of a surface that yields to the caressing, shaping movement of the hand. But we have noted that there is one ultimate impediment that never yields to the reflexive aspiration of consciousness—its own intentional movement toward its object. Thus objective symbols of this movement, and of its reflexive aspiration to "recuperate" this movement, are indispensable to consciousness. Sartre's final symbol for the way the intentional movement prevails is a slippery slope (*pente glissante*) [p. 353]; consciousness cannot hold itself back reflexively from becoming intentional "consciousness of something." The performance, which is still available to consciousness and which is peculiarly exhilarating, is embodied in and symbolized by the *glissement* of the skier; his free and easy movement does not sink into the sticky snow (congealed fluidity), but appropriates and shapes it as he slides down the slope, upheld by the track he is himself making out of the snow [p. 314]. The moral implications of the skier's sense of exhilaration are brought out by the injunction, *Glissez, mortels, n'appuyez pas!* Skiing symbolizes the emancipation of consciousness from the menace in *Nausea* of taking root in the damp, nourishing soil or of becoming stuck in the muck of bourgeois Bouville.

## CONSCIOUSNESS AND LITERATURE

The existential psychoanalysis of *Being and Nothingness* culminates in this "psychoanalysis of things." The label indicates that Sartre is still committed to Husserl's original phenomenological program of turning "back to things," and to analyzing self-consciousness as implicit in "consciousness of something" in order to avoid Husserl's relapse into idealism. What Sartre largely neglects in this psychoanalysis is his more complicated preceding analysis in *Being and Nothingness* of self-consciousness as consciousness of the self as something of which the other is conscious. He remedies this neglect in *What Is Literature?* (1947) and *Saint Genet* (1952).

# Introduction

Since Sartre's existential psychonalysis has assimilated the intentional structure of consciousness to the structure of a work of art, which embodies symbolically the intentions of the artist, it is hardly surprising that he should turn around and answer the question "What Is Literature?" by analyzing the literary work as structured by our consciousness of it. His earlier discovery that one cannot become conscious of oneself as something he converts into the discovery that the novelist cannot become conscious of his novel as something—*i.e.*, as an objective work of art. Objectivity is reserved for the other—his readers. Since the writer accordingly must solicit the active co-operation of his readers' consciousnesses in constructing the work of art, the only subject-matter for the novel consistent with its structure is the freedom of others—social freedom. But since the actual structure of society is oppressive, the novelist can only point out to his readers roads to freedom.

*Roads to Freedom* is, in fact, the general title of a sequence of novels (1945, 1949) which Sartre began, before finishing *Being and Nothingness*, in order to deal with problems of the other, action, and emancipation that had emerged during World War II. His model for this undertaking we have already anticipated—Dos Passos' treatment in *U.S.A.* of World War I and its aftermath. But Sartre doubtless was encouraged also by the analogies which he was himself drawing to the structure of a work of art in treating these problems in *Being and Nothingness*. Thus he was tempted philosophically, not only to impose these problems (as we have just noted) on the structure of a work of art in *What Is Literature?* but also to impose the structure of a work of art on these problems in *Roads to Freedom*. But he seems to have been mistaken as to the literary genre which afforded the appropriate structure. He never completed the fourth and final novel in this sequence, but I have been able to set the stage for his treatment of these problems in *Being and Nothingness* by borrowing selections from his plays.

Sartre's abandonment of *Roads to Freedom* he has himself explained by the fact that the problem of action took a different form after the war. But he has made even this point in a play: *Dirty Hands* (1948) introduces a contrast between the grimy hands of sustained proletarian action and the "red gloves" ("the bloody gloves") that display and protect the aristocratic, myth-making gesture of a modern Orestes; individualistic acts of glorious violence have lost the plausibility they enjoyed during the period of the Resistance. What I am suggesting is that Sartre's abandonment of the novel itself in favor of the drama as a genre, can be construed as his finding a more suitable vehicle for the "drama of the being who cannot be an object for himself" but only for the other, and only as the result of an action performed in the presence of the other. Although *What Is Literature?* argues that the novel must be a novel of social action, one need not look far for a notable exception: *Nausea* is a novel of individual reflection. While the reader of a novel is also an individual reflecting by himself, the theater audience composes a social group; the "action" of a novel is merely imagined by the reader, but in a play the "action" is actually embodied in the actions of the actors, and the actor identifies himself by his actions with the other (the character he is impersonating) of whom others (the audience) are conscious.

Novelists before Sartre had conducted their reflections in a hall of mirrors, but no playwright has ever played so much with the problems of the other and of play-acting in the presence of the other. Shakespeare possibly. But Sartre harnesses Shakespeare in the play *Kean* (1954). Sartre wrote this play for another (the actor Pierre Brasseur); it is a rewrite of another play Alexandre Dumas wrote for another actor (whom Brasseur had already played the part of in the movie *Les enfants du paradis*); the hero, Kean, is himself an actor who would emancipate himself from play-acting by performing a real action, but much of the action of the play is pieced together out of the plays of Shakespeare in which Kean is acting, so that episodes from these plays become episodes in his real relations with others in the audience.

Less involuted illustrations can be found of the decisive role the other has played for Sartre. There is the closeness of his collaboration since student days with Simone de Beauvoir; there is his readiness to write prefaces, not only to other writers' works, but also for the exhibitions of artists and for editions reproducing their works. Some of these prefaces have been collected together in *Situations IV* (1964) under the subtitle *Portraits*. No philosopher since Plato has provided so extensive a gallery of his contemporaries, but Plato in his later dialogues apparently lost interest in portraying his contemporaries, while Sartre's portraits of others are among his most recent essays.

The extent to which Sartre has placed his literary performance at the disposal of others is most strikingly illustrated by the huge volume, *Saint Genet, comédien et martyr* (1952), which Sartre has written as an introduction to Jean Genet's collected works. For Genet's discovery of his vocation as a writer is analyzed by Sartre in much greater detail than he has ever analyzed his discovery of his own vocation. This analysis, however, does advance the development of Sartre's own philosophy; since the road to freedom which this play-actor (*comédien*) had followed in becoming a playwright was the career of a thief and homosexual, Sartre is able to interweave the two analyses which he elaborated independently of each other in *Being and Nothingness*—the analysis of the appropriative relationship of consciousness to things with the analysis of self-consciousness as consciousness of one's alienation by the other's consciousness. Nothing belonged to Genet, the illegitimate child who belonged to no one. During his childhood he sought to make something his own, but society was already alert to the threat to the established order embodied in an illegitimate child: perhaps his hand entered an open drawer; taken by surprise by the look of the other, he became conscious of himself as something others identify as a thief [p. 379]. His gesture of appropriation was countered by society, which appropriated him to play an exemplary role as a scapegoat who would legitimize and sanctify its property-owning structure.

Genet's vulnerability to the look of the other and to the "vertiginous word"—"thief"—is interpreted by Sartre as the equivocal experience of the inaccessibility and irresistible proximity of the self of which the other is conscious. The inability of consciousness to "turn back" and reach this self was embodied and symbolized by the fact that the look of the other took Genet by surprise from behind; the proximity of this self, by the fact that the look was not for Genet the visual experience of a look from a distance, but the experience of being raped—of actual physical contact and violation. Thus Genet became conscious of himself, not only as vulnerable from behind to the look of the other in all his subsequent acts of theft, but also as vulnerable from behind in all his subsequent amorous relations with others. His thievery and his passive homosexuality were alike reflexive maneuvers to become conscious of the self that others were conscious of—from behind him.

Genet's career involved other forms of play-acting besides these re-enactments of his original martyrdom. The thief must pose as an honest man to his victim; the passive homosexual adopts the role and gestures of a woman. These undertakings implement the idealistic aspiration of consciousness to dematerialize objects, even one's physical organs, and to divert them from their practical or biological function. This idealistic aspiration finds its consummation in Genet's vocation as a writer.

Although Sartre has analyzed Genet's vocation in much greater detail than his own, he also clearly feels a sense of identification with Genet. He has in fact identified himself (as he has identified the self) with lack of identity. Long before he became conscious in *Nausea* of the contingent as that which has no legitimate place in the scheme of things, Sartre felt himself committed to illegitimacy. He was a "false bastard," although he adopted this interpretation of his father's demise partly by way of repudiating the theological interpretation lavished by his doting family, which made of him a "miracle," a "gift of heaven." As a child he too felt propertyless: his mother admonished him to keep quiet because they were living in a house that was not their own. Sartre has also recalled his first encounter with the other, and recognition of "another truth" to challenge the private daydreams he cherished in the bosom of his family. His first encounter with "my true judges, my contemporaries, my peers," occurred when his mother took the diminutive Sartre to the Luxembourg Gardens. No other child would play with him. It was from this "indifference" of his contemporaries that he was rescued by the play-acting in which he indulged in his grandfather's presence, and by the literary vocation this role thrust on him as a child.

The sanctity of Genet's vocation requires further reference to Sartre. More is at stake than a wretched pun (Seins-Genet) on Genet's equivocal femininity, more than an erudite recollection that Saint Genet was a Roman actor who was baptized on the stage and became the patron saint of actors. The surreptitious procedures and poses of the writer may warrant the analogy to a thief, writing may be as sterile as homosexuality, but the discreditable feature for Sartre of the vocation of the writer is that it is clerical. "Atheism" has been for Sartre "a cruel and prolonged enterprise" which coincides with his effort to emancipate himself, not only from philosophical idealism, but also from his idealistic sense of his own vocation as a writer.

## Introduction

In Sartre's early writings, the aspiration of self-consciousness to perform the phenomenological function of stabilizing and synthesizing experience was, in effect, an idealistic aspiration to become a Transcendental Ego. Once Sartre's phenomenological approach was converted, in *Being and Nothingness*, into an ontology, this aspiration could be redescribed as the aspiration to "become God"—*i.e.*, to confer a necessary structure on my experience by becoming ontologically the transcendent source af all its meanings. The aspiration to become a writer takes the same reflexive form. Thus Sartre admits today that he exhibited in Roquentin "the fabric of my life without complacency." But he adds, "At the same time, I was *myself*, the elect, the annalist of hell, the photomicroscope of glass and steel, bent over my own protoplasmic distillations." However Sartre cannot entirely repudiate his early writings, for this repudiation is only the final stage in their discrediting of the reflexive maneuver of self-consciousness.

The development which has taken place in Sartre's latest writings is that "culture" has become as sanctimonious a withdrawal from experience, as much of a distortion obscuring the actual social structure, as the "self" or "character" was of the actual structure of consciousness in his early writings. The sense of vocation Sartre had inherited from his grandfather was equivocal: grandfather himself had been intended by his father to become a pastor, and when he became a professor instead, he had continued to worship "culture," as the descent among men of the "Holy Spirit"—the "patron of art and letters," who imposes on "the elect" the duty of fabricating artistic and literary works to serve as "relics" for future professors to worship.

Sartre has not yet told the story of his final emancipation. But he has continued to write. For even if culture is not salvation, it is still "a human product," and it is still a "mirror," which "presents to man his image." Thus Sartre still reflects, but having finally discredited the reflexive attempt by consciousness to consolidate and consecrate a self (or an *oeuvre* that is one's own to serve as a cultural surrogate for a self), he has finally become convinced of his lack of identity—that he is *n'importe qui*. Thus he has prescribed a humbler task for his reflections, by retrieving the analogy of the "mirror" with which we began this introduction.

A change has taken place in Sartre's philosophy to the extent
that the individual's lack of identity is no longer simply ontological but sociological. When Sartre now reflects and recognizes
that he is "no one in particular," he is recognizing that the distorting movement of reflection with which he, as a bourgeois
intellectual, has "turned back" on himself, has merely twisted
certain threads in the social fabric; he can therefore also recognize that he is "everyman." Thus Sartre's emancipation from
membership in "the elect" has become preoccupation with un-
raveling and reforming the social fabric. But here an American
is likely to perceive a flaw in the mirror Sartre holds up to mankind. *Being and Nothingness* could be interpreted as an existential document of the Occupation and Resistance, and its strenu-
ous and contorted argumentation could be pardoned by those
who had lived through a more sheltered war. When irreparable
actions went out of fashion in the postwar world, and politics and
life became matters for negotiation, existential psychoanalysis
could retain a certain vogue, for the existential component lent
a twinge of moral vigor to psychoanalytic adjustments and to
the symbols literary critics were employing psychoanalysis to
track down; thus *Saint Genet* has commanded attention. But in
the meantime Sartre himself had taken off in a new and disconcerting direction.

Sartre had become a fellow traveler. Fellow travelers had
been in step with Dos Passos' America of the thirties, but they
had long since rediscovered America and the beneficence of
capitalism, so that the thirty years Sartre today admits having
spent in emancipating himself from idealism only put him
thirty years behind them in their chronology. Nor was Sartre's
fellow-traveling apparently restricted to politics. We cannot
weigh here the alarming implications of Philip Thody's observation (in the most detailed survey in English of Sartre's literary
works) that there is only one character anywhere in Sartre's
voluminous writings who enjoys making love, and he is "a good,
reliable party member." But it sometimes is said that the only
general pattern discernible in Sartre's recent writings is a
frantic effort to follow, from a not always safe distance, the
twistings and turnings of the Party line. And it is now com-

monly believed that the Sartre of the *Critique of Dialectical Reason* (1960) has repudiated existentialism in favor of Marxism. He himself almost says so.

Despite the repudiations entailed by Sartre's successive *prises de position* a continuity can be traced from his earliest to his latest philosophical work, which is the continuity of his phenomenological analysis, employed as the instrument of his emancipation from idealism. His original phenomenological analysis having become dialectical in *Being and Nothingness,* his later works can be recognized to continue and complete this analysis dialectically. A review of Sartre's dialectical development is now relevant, for although Sartre in the *Critique* rarely refers to his previous writings, he does characterize any dialectical development as a "totalizing" activity, in which the preceding moments are particular and incomplete relationships within the whole, which dialectical reason undertakes to grasp. In his early phenomenological writings, Sartre analyzed particular forms of "consciousness of something"—perception, imagination, emotion—and the self-consciousness that is reflexively implicit in these forms. In *Being and Nothingness* he moved on from these particular forms to human behavior as a whole. For he recognized that consciousness of oneself as something is only a particular and dialectically incomplete moment in one's relationship to the other and that consciousness itself is only a particular and dialectically incomplete moment in the course of the action in which it is embodied. Thus having analyzed the relationship between consciousness and the body, he went on to analyze action as consciousness of making something and thereby appropriating it as one's own. Sartre next grasped in *Saint Genet* the interrelationship between Genet's relation to the other and his relation to the things he appropriated as a thief, analyzing this interrelationship in terms of analogies between the operations of consciousness and the making of a work of art, which was the aspiration of Genet's (and Sartre's) own consciousness.

In these terms Sartre has been able to explore only certain pockets in the social structure. The social group that entered Sartre's dialectic in *What Is Literature?* and attended his plays was bourgeois. The sanctions exercised against the youthful Genet were those of a small, cohesive farming community, where the rights of property were sacred; as an adult, Genet par-

ticipated only in the unproductive activities of a thief, homosexual, and writer. Genet (and Sartre) had little experience of
an industrial environment where the worker does not make
something his own by making it. Thus consciousness of something practical, which has been made by the work of the other,
has still to be analyzed by Sartre if he is to expand his original
analysis of the structure of consciousness into an analysis of the
structure of society as a whole, and take into account the extent
to which relations to the other and property relations are based
on relationships of production.

This transition from an existentialist analysis of acting and
making to a Marxist analysis of *praxis*, is illustrated by the
elementary example of a phenomenological analysis Sartre offered in *Search for a Method* (1957), which he has republished
as a preface to the *Critique*. Someone does something—*e.g.*,
crosses a room to open a window [p. 416]. His intentional consciousness, which endows his circumstances with the meaning
"too warm," is embodied in this action. But this action not only
defines the agent's situation but also the agent himself: he has
crossed the room deliberately, before settling down to work,
and his action thereby expresses his intention of being orderly.
It will be noted that the distinction (of the early phenomenological writings) between consciousness of something and the reflexive consciousness implicit in consciousness of something,
has been retained, and that these two forms of consciousness are
still embodied in an action in the way they were in *Being and
Nothingness*. But the window introduces a new set of relations
for analysis. The window itself is the product of an intentional
action: just as the agent's action has structured the situation
as "too warm," so the structure of the window indicates that the
worker who made it was conscious of it as something to be
pushed up or down or to be swung out. The difference between
the agent-artist (of *Being and Nothingness*) and the worker is
that the latter's action is anonymous: he did not make the
window his own; its structure does not express his own intentions. Thus Sartre's analysis is still phenomenological, but it is
also transformed by the new subject-matter requiring analysis.

Having repudiated the Transcendental Ego, Sartre discovered
in the "vision" of *Nausea* how superficial was the structure of
meaning, which our successive acts of "consciousness of something"—of this thing, of that thing, etc.—articulate as an or-

dered world in which these things all find their place: "The meaning of things, the way things are to be used" vanished as nothing more than "the feeble points of reference which men have traced on their surface [p. 59]." Even when consciousness repudiated visionary aspiration to the extent of seeking the actual contact of tactile experience, the resistance of the thing was experienced as simply its massiveness, its solidity; and consciousness still preferred the caress, which "slides" over the surface without "bearing down," and felt menaced whenever it became consciousness of something too shapeless, too soft to present a surface distinguishable from its own movement. But in the *Critique* experience has become rougher, harder, and technological. Artifacts are encountered, which are "heavy" with meaning; "consciousness of something," as consciousness of the use to which it is to be put, is now its deeply "incised" structure.

The reflexive forms of consciousness Sartre finds implicit in "consciousness of something" undergo a corresponding materialization in the *Critique*. Once the cosmological superstructure, in which everything had its meaningful place articulated by consciousness, "melted" in *Nausea*, consciousness was reduced to consciousness of something (and reflexively of myself) as not necessarily there—to consciousness of the contingency and superfluousness of its existence and my existence. Social superstructures, in which everything and everyone ostensibly have a place, are similarly undermined in the *Critique*, to expose as the fundamental fact of human existence—economic scarcity. Consciousness of something as not necessarily there, is now consciousness of something as "scarce." The reflexive consciousness of the contingency of my existence is still, as in *Nausea*, consciousness of myself as *de trop*. But this superfluousness is no longer the meaningless, nauseous proliferation of shapeless existences, overflowing my consciousness of them. I am now conscious of my existence as rendered superfluous (*excédentaire*) by the scarcity of the things on which it depends. Instead of the metaphor of indigestion in *Nausea*, we are faced with actual hunger.

Sartre went on from the phenomenological "vision" of *Nausea* to present in *Being and Nothingness* an ontological version of the contingency of the self as its lacking something—value—to be itself [p. 176]; my consciousness that I ought to be something, which I was not, to be myself was the idealistic aspiration which rendered self-consciousness dialectical. But the other intervened in the dialectic by passing value judgments on my action, alienating me from myself: I could only become conscious of myself as something he was conscious of. In the *Critique* the fact that what is lacking and valuable is something scarce, imposes a materialistic dialectic in which the technological mode of production is basic, and some anonymous material product intervenes as the alienating factor that determines my relation to myself as well as to others. Sartre's elementary example is the way a Paris bus structures the bus queue, as a certain portion of the urban environment [p. 456]. Waiting for the bus, I am conscious, not only of it, but also of its making me something other than myself: I become an anonymous individual who has taken his place in a quantitative "series," whose inert members are only passively and externally related to each other, by means of the bus for which we are waiting. My interest in the bus is identical with the other's interest, and therefore antithetical, since the "scarcity" of places in the bus may render me *de trop;* and the decision as to who finds a place is reached by a numerical sequence that requires no reference to the personal values for which I wrestled with the other in *Being and Nothingness.*

Here Sartre's dialectic of course overlaps the Marxist dialectic, in which the mode of production is basic to the social structure, capitalistic society is disintegrating, and the individual is atomized and alienated as "the product of his product." But the two dialectics are geared differently. The fact that things are scarce, which renders the mode of production basic and the Marxist dialectic valid for Sartre, was a fact whose significance was emphasized by British political economists (as later by Social Darwinians); but Marx himself emphasized overproduction as a factor in the disintegration of capitalism. Sartre's readjustment of the Marxist dialectic is perhaps less a matter of his harking back to dead economic theories, or of his lively concern with the new problems of underdeveloped countries, than it is the continuing negative accent of his dialectic. Furthermore, since what is accentuated by scarcity is our consciousness of the thing which is scarce, Sartre's analysis remains phenomenological; and since scarcity is for Sartre the fundamental fact of all human existence, this phenomenological analysis holds for all social history, from the most primitive technology to any future communist society we can anticipate as the outcome of social history.

The more positive outcome, which Marx anticipated, was consistent with the optimism of his emphasis on overproduction rather than scarcity. But his anticipation itself assumed the guise of a scientific prediction. In taking the mode of production as basic to his dialectic, he considered that he was achieving a causal explanation in which the development of mechanical techniques of production would produce in turn predictable social forces. Sartre not only refuses to predict the outcome of social history, but he also denounces Engels and Stalinism for distorting the dialectic of social history into mechanical relationships between social forces. His denunciation of this distortion as the "petrification," "ossification," etc., of Marxism indicates that the distortion is the confusion he has always denounced as a phenomenologist—the confusion of the relationships which hold within the field of consciousness with the external causal relationships which hold between inert things. But at the same time this "petrification" of Marxism is itself for Sartre an historical development that illustrates the passivity and inertness to which man is condemned in his thinking as well as in his other activities (*e.g.*, as a member of a bus queue) when he becomes "the product of his product." This formula is Marxist. But in Marxism it points up the worker's predicament under capitalism. Sartre's generalization of this formula so that it applies to all social history, including the development of Marxism as a theory of social history, betrays his continuing preoccupation with the reflexive moment in the dialectic and its distortion of the dialectic.

The two moments that Sartre does in fact distinguish in analyzing social structures are the intentional and the reflexive moments which he has always distinguished in analyzing the structures of consciousness. Under the pressure of some external threat of which we are mutually conscious, I undertake an action which is the same as the action of others, and this concerted action is the "fusion" of a "series" (for example, the proletariat) into a "group" [p. 470]. The structure of this group is as unstable as the structure of consciousness in *Being and Nothingness*. When the threat has been removed, the effort to keep the group together (*i.e.*, to keep it from disintegrating into a "series") takes the reflexive form of a group consciousness and an action of the group upon itself (for example, by the party apparatus), which substitutes mutual fear for the external threat that has become remote [p. 474]. But just as the self of which one becomes reflexively conscious was the distortion into something of the fluid movement of consciousness, so the group that is now the product of the action of the group upon itself no longer retains the dynamic structure of the concerted action but becomes something as inert and institutionalized as, for example, the French Communist Party.

## THE VERDICT OF HISTORY

This sequence of moments composes a merely formal analysis of social structures. The historical episodes, which Sartre introduces to illustrate this sequence, are not assigned, as they would be by Marx, to historical stages. We are no longer sustained dialectically by Marxist confidence in history. This confidence derived from the fact that proletarian aspirations in the present historical stage are to be fulfilled in the future on a higher level at the final stage of history. But the instability and equivocations of phenomenological consciousness are not overcome by Sartre's converting it into historical consciousness. (Sartre provides a familiar example of the instability of historical consciousness. World War I was an equivocal episode; it was identified as a victory by the French and a defeat by the Germans; but young Frenchmen did not remain conscious of the war as a victory; it became something due to the folly of their fathers, and they "transcended" the victory toward a dream of universal peace, while young Germans "transcended" their fathers' defeat toward the Nazi prospect of revenge.) By refusing to predict any final outcome, superseding our present experience, Sartre lends finality to the immediate significance of the present. Even its uncertainty as to the future is accorded a final significance, which may be warranted technologically by the prospect of atomic weapons depriving us of the future, but which we are tempted to defer (as the orientation of Marxism toward the future illustrates), since technological development itself is progressive in its effects.

However, the equivocations of historical experience in Sartre are not fundamentally technological but phenomenological. The

way in which he confers final significance on present experience
—on the indecisiveness of days of decision—reminds us un-
mistakably of the original reflexive maneuver with which Husserl instituted his phenomenological program. The uncertainty
and indefiniteness characteristic of perceptual experience had
encouraged the philosophical tradition to "transcend" perceptual
experience, but Husserl discovered that uncertainty and indefiniteness were immediate and certain characteristics that
define perceptual experience. In Sartre the reflexive maneuver
itself becomes historical. For what further defines our present
experience, besides its uncertainty and indefiniteness, and distinguishes it from past history is the reflexivity (instanced by
the reflexive movement of the *Critique* itself) of our historical
consciousness: we are conscious, as no past epoch has been, of
our place in history. But our historical consciousness is equivocal. For we are certain that our epoch will be "transcended," in
the phenomenological sense that it will be identified in the
future differently than it is by ourselves—*i.e.*, that our actions
will be endowed with a meaning that is not the meaning we
ourselves are presently conscious of in undertaking them. But
we are hopelessly uncertain, not only that there will be in fact a
future to judge us, but also as to what its verdict might be.
Thus our sense of our time, of our historical identity, is heightened by the extent to which it eludes us, in the same dialectical
fashion in which the individual's self-consciousness is heightened, as consciousness of the inaccessibility of the self which
he is, but which only the other can be conscious of.

This equivocal predicament of our historical self-consciousness supplies the epilogue of Sartre's last play, *The Condemned
of Altona* (1956). Sartre's spokesman is Franz, a Nazi torturer
who refuses to transcend the experience of German defeat and
live on as the heir of capitalistic enterprise, now prospering in
Germany; for this prosperity deprives his earlier ruthlessness of
the justification it seemed to have, so long as the prospective
outcome was Germany's and capitalism's destruction. But his
equivocal name indicates that he is to be re-identified by the
audience with France, now (*i.e.*, in 1956) at war and now torturing in Algeria and also without the justification alleged, since
an *Algérie française* will not be the outcome of this war.
Franz finally appeals from his sense of the guilt of his period to
the higher tribunal of history. But the appeal goes unanswered

and he is left with the experience of the contingency of history, for the place in history of the twentieth century remains undecided. Condemned as guilty, yet too indefinite to be formally indicted, and with no higher tribunal to press the charges, our century leaves in his mouth a "taste" which is "rancid" in the bitterness of its guilt, yet "insipid" in its tastelessness. This period flavor is a shudder of revulsion, which confers on our present historical experience an immediacy ordinarily lacking, since we ordinarily conceive our historical experience as relative to what came before and to what will follow. And this immediacy is conferred in the same phenomenological fashion in which it was conferred in the "vision" of *Nausea* on the contingent, indefinite meaning of individual experience.

To claim, in retrospect, that Sartre is the greatest philosopher of our time would be as preposterous as his own claim, in his essay of August, 1938, that "Dos Passos is the greatest novelist of our time." After all, one of the great accomplishments of Anglo-American philosophy in our time is supposed to have been disabusing us of the historicism that has enticed Continental philosophers ever since Hegel suspected that history was "going on behind our backs." A more plausible verdict thus might be the claim that Sartre is the only philosopher *of our time.* Sartre discovered for himself, in September, 1938, that history had been going on behind his back and was therefore a further impediment, besides the intentional movement of consciousness, to reflection's "turning back" on experience and transcending it. And he has become the only noteworthy philosopher in our time, whose final preoccupation is the uncertain significance of our time. Sartre's own claim on his behalf could be Franz's last words: "I have been! I, Franz von Gerlach, . . . have taken the century upon my shoulders and have said: 'I will answer for it. This day and forever'" [p. 484].

But to trace, as I have tried in this introduction, the continuity of Sartre's development up to this final dramatic outcome, may override his own sense of historical contingency. Sartre warns us that to read the history of a writer in terms of his development is to leave out the history: the uncertainties he faced at each moment, the indefiniteness of each moment. We are distorting his experience by creating a cultural "relic," as his grandfather attempted to do—as our culture tempts professors to do. We are indulging the idealistic illusion that experience can be recaptured—the illusion Sartre denounced in *Nausea* as the retrospective effort of the storyteller to "catch time by the tail." In recalling, as we are doing, his earlier writings and reflecting on his development, we constitute ourselves a higher tribunal, reaching our verdict in the light of the outcome he did not himself foresee. What was to be the future work of the writer or artist was once not his, but because we believe that culture is the fulfillment and consecration of experience—the descent among men of the Holy Spirit—our introduction to his work short-circuits and falsifies his experience by anticipating his final vision. In other words, Sartre explains, we tell a story:

A certain Sanzio was terribly anxious to see the pope; he made such a fuss that they took him to the public square the day the Holy Father would pass; the child turned pale, his eyes opened wide. At last they asked, "You must be satisfied now, Raphael? Did you get a good look at our Holy Father?" . . . "What Holy Father? All I saw were colors."

———————

The most difficult of Sartre's works to translate is the *Critique of Dialectical Reason,* and the translations are a tribute to the conscientiousness and skill of Starr and Jim Atkinson, who also helped to compile the bibliography. I have revised all the translations and tried to secure uniformity in the English terminology. Sartre's own use of italics and capital letters has usually been respected. In order to make it easier for the reader to locate Sartre's discussion of specific topics, I have often inserted headings of my own. The omission in the translation of passages in the original French is always indicated. At the end of each of the selections page numbers are supplied, which refer to the original English translations. (In the case of selections from the *Critique,* these numbers refer to the original French.) In the bibliography at the end of the book the numbers after the English translations refer to the pages in this book, so that the selections from any work of Sartre's may easily be located.

Angela Macintosh typed the translations and made useful suggestions. My wife helped with the introduction. Morris Philipson was constantly encouraging and overcame many difficulties.

# CONSCIOUSNESS

# I

---

*Self-Consciousness*

## 1 CONSCIOUSNESS AND REFLECTION

The mode of existence of consciousness is to be conscious of itself. And consciousness is consciousness of itself *insofar as it is consciousness of a transcendent object.*\* All is therefore clear and lucid in consciousness. The object with its characteristic opacity is in front of consciousness, but consciousness is purely and simply consciousness of being consciousness of that object; this is the law of its existence.

Further, this consciousness of consciousness—except in the case of reflective consciousness to be dealt with later—is not *positional*—*i.e.*, consciousness is not for itself its own object.† Its object is by nature outside of it, and this is why consciousness *posits* and *grasps* the object in the same act. Consciousness only knows itself as absolute inwardness. Such a consciousness we shall call primary or *unreflected consciousness*. . . .

A pure consciousness is an absolute simply because it is consciousness of itself. It remains accordingly a "phenomenon" in the very special sense in which "to be" and "to appear" are one. It is entirely lightness, entirely translucence. This is the difference between Husserl's *cogito* and Descartes'. But if the I were a necessary structure of consciousness, this opaque I would at once be raised to the rank of an absolute. We would then be in the presence of a monad. And this, indeed, is un-

---

\* The term "transcendent" must not be confused with "transcendental." The object of an "intentional" act of consciousness "transcends" this act in that I am conscious of it as not an "immanent" or subjective component of the act itself. "Transcendental" designates that region of consciousness which survives, and is opened up for investigation, by the phenomenological reduction.—Ed.
† An act of consciousness is "positional" or "thetic," when it asserts the existence of its object.—Ed.

fortunately the orientation of the new thought of Husserl (see his *Cartesian Meditations**). Consciousness is loaded down; it has lost that character which rendered it the absolute existent by virtue of its non-existence [*inexistence*]. It is heavy, *weighty*. All the accomplishments of phenomenology are in danger of crumbling, if the I is not, in the same manner as the world, a relative existent—*i.e.*, an object *for* consciousness. . . .

All those who have described the *cogito* have presented it as a reflective operation—*i.e.*, as a secondary operation at a higher level. This *cogito* is performed by a consciousness which is oriented toward a consciousness, by a consciousness which takes consciousness as an object. It must be understood that the certitude of the *cogito* is absolute, for (as Husserl states) there is an indissoluble unity of the reflecting consciousness and the consciousness reflected upon, to the extent that the reflecting consciousness could not exist without the reflected consciousness. But the fact remains that we are in the presence of a synthesis of two consciousnesses, one of which is consciousness *of* the other. Thus the essential principle of phenomenology, "all consciousness is consciousness of something," is preserved. Now my reflecting consciousness does not take itself for its object when I effect the *cogito*. What it affirms concerns the reflected consciousness. Insofar as my reflecting consciousness is consciousness of itself, it is *non-positional* consciousness. It becomes positional only as directed upon the reflected consciousness, which itself, before being thus reflected upon, was not a positional consciousness of itself. Thus the consciousness which states "I think" is not the consciousness which thinks. Or rather it is not *its own* thought which it posits by this thetic act. We are accordingly justified in inquiring if the I which thinks is common to the two superimposed consciousnesses, or if it is not rather the I of the reflected consciousness. No reflecting consciousness reflects upon itself; it remains unreflected upon until a third act of consciousness at a higher level posits it. But

---

* In the first edition (1900-1901) of the *Logische Untersuchungen*, in which Edmund Husserl initiated his phenomenological program, he was "utterly unable to find" the transcendental ego which Neo-Kantians claimed was "a necessary center of conscious reference." In the *Ideen* (original German edition, 1913; translated into English as *Ideas*, Collier Books edition, 1962, p. 156) Husserl reversed himself. He reiterated the doctrine of the transcendental ego in the *Cartesianische Meditationen* (first published in a French translation in 1931; English translation, Nijhoff, 1960, pp. 65f.)—Ed.

there is no infinite regress here, since a consciousness does not need a reflecting consciousness to reflect upon it, in order to be conscious of itself. It simply is conscious of itself without positing itself as its object.

Is it not the reflective act which brings the Me to birth in the reflected consciousness? This would explain how every thought apprehended by intuition possesses an I, without our running into the difficulties previously noted. Husserl would be the first to recognize that an unreflected thought undergoes a radical modification as soon as it is reflected upon. But need this modification amount only to a loss of "naïveté"? Would not the appearance of the I be essential to this change?

Here we should obviously appeal to concrete experience. This may seem impossible, since the form of experience we are concerned with is reflective—*i.e.*, equipped with an I. But every unreflected consciousness, being non-positional consciousness of itself, leaves behind a non-positional memory which one can consult. To do so, we need only try to reconstruct the complete moment when this unreflecting consciousness appeared, and this by definition it is always possible to do. For example, I was absorbed a moment ago in reading. I am now trying to recall the circumstances of my reading, my attitude, the lines that I was reading. What I am going to revive are not only those external details but also a certain density [*épaisseur*] of unreflected consciousness, since the objects revived could only have been perceived *by* this consciousness and remain relative to it. This consciousness must not be posited as an object of my reflection; I must instead direct my attention to the objects I am reviving, but *without losing sight* of the unreflected consciousness. I must conspire with it and draw out an inventory of its content in a non-positional fashion. The outcome of this experiment is obvious: so long as I was reading, there was consciousness *of* the book, *of* the hero of the novel, but the I was not inhabiting this consciousness. It was only consciousness of the object and non-positional consciousness of itself. These a-thetically apprehended results I can now make the object of a thesis, and announce, there was no I in the unreflected consciousness. . . .

When I run after a streetcar, when I look at the time, when I am absorbed in looking at a portrait, no I is present. There is consciousness of the streetcar-having-to-be-caught, etc., and non-positional consciousness of that consciousness. On these occasions I am immersed in the world of objects; they constitute the unity of my consciousnesses; they present themselves with values, with qualities that attract or repel—but I have disappeared, I am nothing. There is no place for Me at this level of consciousness. This is not accidental, it is not due to a temporary lapse of attention, but to the structure of consciousness itself.*

*The Transcendence of the Ego, 40–42, 44–49.*

## 2 THE VERTIGO OF CONSCIOUSNESS

Transcendental consciousness is an impersonal spontaneity. It determines its existence at each moment, without anything *before* it being conceivable. Thus each moment of our conscious life reveals to us a creation *ex nihilo.* Not a new *arrangement,* but a new existence. There is something anguishing for each of us, to experience directly this tireless creation of an existence of which *we* are not the creators. At this level man has the impression of ceaselessly escaping from himself, of overflowing himself, of an abundance always unexpected taking him by surprise. And he saddles the unconscious with the task of accounting for this transcending† of the Me by consciousness. The Me cannot in fact cope with this spontaneity, for *the will is an object which itself is constituted for and by this spontaneity.* The will orients itself toward states of consciousness, emotions, or things, but it never turns back upon consciousness. We are well aware of this from the occasions on which we try to *will* a consciousness (I *will* fall asleep, I *will* no longer think about that, etc.). In these various cases, it is essentially necessary that the will be maintained and preserved *by the consciousness which is radically opposed* to the consciousness the will would bring about (if I *will* to fall asleep, I stay awake; if I *will* not to think about this or that, I *thereby* think about it).

It seems to me that this monstrous spontaneity is at the

* For Sartre's later analysis of the reflective consciousness see below, pp. 178f. —Ed.

† Sartre often employs the colloquial expressions *surpasser* and *dépasser* and their derivatives to designate the transcending movement of consciousness. In translating I use "transcend" and its derivatives, since "surpass," "go beyond," "exceed," etc., carry misleading connotations.—Ed.

source of numerous psychasthenic disturbances. Consciousness is terrified of its own spontaneity, because it feels this spontaneity as *beyond* freedom. This can be clearly seen in an example from Janet. A young wife was in terror, when her husband left her alone, of sitting at the window and soliciting the passers-by like a prostitute. Nothing in her education, in her past, or character could explain such a fear. It seems to me that a negligible circumstance (reading, conversation, etc.) had produced what might be called "a vertigo of possibility." She found herself monstrously free, and this vertiginous freedom appeared to her as the occasion for this gesture which she was afraid of making. But this vertigo is understandable only in terms of consciousness suddenly appearing to itself as infinitely overflowing in its possibilities the I which ordinarily serves as its unity.

Perhaps in fact the essential function of the ego is less theoretical than practical. We have observed indeed that it does not draw phenomena together into a unity, . . . that their real and concrete unity has already been secured. But perhaps the essential role of the ego is to mask from consciousness its very spontaneity. . . . Everything happens as if consciousness constituted the ego as a false representation of itself, as if consciousness hypnotized itself with this ego it has constituted, absorbing itself in the ego, as if to make the ego its guardian and its law. It is thanks to the ego in fact that a distinction can be made between the possible and the real, between appearance and being, between the willed and the undergone.

But it can happen that consciousness suddenly produces itself on the pure reflective level. Not perhaps without the ego, yet as escaping from the ego on all sides, dominating and maintaining the ego by a continuous creation. On this level there is no longer any distinction between the possible and the real, since the appearance is the absolute. There are no longer any barriers or limits, nothing to conceal consciousness from itself. Then consciousness recognizes what could be called the fatality of its spontaneity, and is suddenly anguished.

It is this anguish, absolute and without remedy, this fear of itself, which seems to me constitutive of pure consciousness and which holds the key to the psychological disturbance referred to above. If the I of the "I think" is the primary structure of consciousness, this anguish is impossible. If, on the other hand, my point of view is adopted, we have not only a coherent explanation of this disturbance, but also a permanent motive for carrying out the phenomenological reduction. Fink admits, not without melancholy, that so long as one remains in the "natural" attitude, there is *no reason,* no "motive" for exercising the *epoché.** In fact this natural attitude is entirely coherent and does not yield any of those contradictions which lead the philosopher, according to Plato, to undertake a philosophical conversion. Thus the *epoché* appears in the phenomenology of Husserl as a miracle. Husserl himself, in the *Cartesian Meditations,* alludes vaguely to certain psychological motives, which would lead one to undertaking the reduction. But these motives seem hardly adequate. Moreover the operation of the reduction seems possible only after prolonged investigation. It seems a *learned* operation, which confers on it a sort of arbitrariness. But if the "natural" attitude appears entirely as an effort consciousness makes to escape from itself by projecting itself into the Me and becoming absorbed there, if this effort is never completely rewarded, and if a simple act of reflection is enough for consciousness in its spontaneity to break abruptly away from the I and be given as independent—then the *epoché* is no longer a miracle, an intellectual method, a learned procedure. It is an anguish which is imposed on us and which we cannot avoid. It is at one and the same time a pure event of transcendental origin and an ever possible accident of our daily life.† . . .

If the I becomes an object, it participates in all the vicissitudes of the world. It is not an absolute; it has not created the universe; it is suspended like other existents, by the *epoché,* solipsism becomes inconceivable now that the I no longer enjoys privileged status. Instead of the formulation, "I alone exist as absolute," it should be asserted, "Absolute consciousness alone exists as absolute"—which is obviously a truism. My I, in fact, is not more certain for consciousness than the I of other men. It is only more intimate.

Theorists of the extreme left have sometimes reproached phenomenology for being an idealism and for drowning reality

* The term *epoché* was used by the Greek skeptics for abstention from judgment. It is taken over by Husserl to characterize the phenomenological reduction. Eugen Fink was Husserl's authorized spokesman in the article to which Sartre is referring, "Die Phänomenologische Philosophie Edmund Husserls in der Gegenwärtigen Kritik," *Kantstudien,* xxxviii (1933) pp. 356f., 381.—Ed.
† For Sartre's later analysis of anguish see below, pp. 115–123.—Ed.

in the stream of ideas. But if idealism is the philosophy without evil of Brunschvicg, if it is a philosophy in which the effort of spiritual assimilation never meets external resistance, in which suffering hunger, and war are diluted in a slow process of the unification of ideas, nothing is more unfair than to call phenomenologists "idealists." On the contrary, for centuries we have not felt in philosophy so realistic a trend. The phenomenologists have plunged man back in the world, have given full weight to his anguish, his sufferings, and to his revolts. Unfortunately, as long as the I remains a structure of absolute consciousness, phenomenology can still be reproached for providing an escapist doctrine, for drawing a piece of man out of the world, and thereby turning our attention away from real problems. It seems to me that this reproach no longer has any justification, if the Me is made an existent strictly contemporaneous with the world, whose existence has the same essential characteristics as the world. I have always thought that a working hypothesis as fruitful as historical materialism never required for its foundation the absurdity which is metaphysical materialism. In fact it is not necessary for the *object* to precede the *subject* for spiritual pseudo-values to vanish and for ethics to find its foundation in reality. It is sufficient that the Me be contemporary with the World and that the subject-object dualism, which is purely logical, finally disappear from the preoccupations of philosophers. The World has not created the Me, the Me has not created the World. They are two objects for the absolute, impersonal consciousness, and it is by this consciousness that they are linked together. This absolute consciousness, when it is purified of the I, no longer has anything of a *subject*. It is no longer a collection of representations. It is quite simply a primary condition and absolute source of existence. And the relation of interdependence established by this absolute consciousness between the Me and the World is sufficient for the Me to appear as "in jeopardy" before the World, for the Me . . . to draw the whole of its content from the world. No more is needed in the way of a philosophical foundation for an ethics and a politics which are absolutely positive.

*The Transcendence of the Ego, 98–106.*

57

# II

·

## *Consciousness of Existence*

For the most trivial event to become an adventure, all you have
to do is to start telling about it. This is what deceives people: a
man is always a teller of stories, he lives surrounded by his
stories and the stories of others, he sees everything which happens to him through these stories; and he tries to live his life
as if it were a story he was telling.

But you have to choose: live or tell. For example, when I was
in Hamburg, with that Erna girl I didn't trust, I was leading a
crazy life. But I was on the inside of it, I didn't think about it.
And then one evening, in a little café in San Pauli, she left me to
go to the toilet. I was alone, there was a phonograph playing
"Blue Sky." I began to tell myself what had happened since I
landed. I said to myself, "The third evening, as I was going into a
dance hall called La Grotte Bleue, I noticed a tall woman half-
drunk. And that woman is the one I am waiting for now, listening to 'Blue Sky,' the woman who is going to come back, sit
down beside me, and put her arms around my neck." Then I had
the violent feeling that I was having an adventure. But Erna
came back, she sat down beside me, she put her arms around my
neck and I hated her without quite knowing why. I understand
now: I had to begin living again and the feeling of an adventure
was fading.

While you live, nothing happens. The scenery changes, people
come in and go out, that's all. There are no beginnings. Days add
on to days without rhyme or reason, an interminable and monotonous addition. . . . But when you tell about a life, everything changes; only it's a change that nobody notices: the proof
is that people talk about true stories. As if there could be true
stories; events take place in one direction, and we tell about

58

them in the opposite direction. You seem to start at the beginning: "It was a fine autumn evening in 1922. I was a notary's clerk in Marommes." But in reality you have begun at the end. It is there, invisible and present, it lends these few words the pomp and value of a beginning. "I was out walking, I had left the town without realizing it, I was thinking about my money troubles." This sentence, taken simply for what it is, means that the fellow was absorbed, morose, a hundred miles from an adventure, exactly in the mood to let things happen without noticing them. But the end is there, transforming everything. For us, the fellow is already the hero of the story. His moroseness, his money troubles are much more precious than ours, they are golden with the light of future passions. The story is going on backwards: moments have stopped piling themselves happy-go-luckily one on top of the other, they are caught up by the end of the story which draws them on and each one of them in turn the previous moment: "It was night, the street was deserted." The sentence is tossed off carelessly, it seems inconsequential; but we are not taken in, we put it to one side: it's a piece of information whose value we shall appreciate later on. And we have the feeling that the hero has lived all the details of this night as annunciations, as promises, or even that he lived only those that were promises, blind and deaf to all that did not herald adventure. We forget that the future was not yet there; the fellow was walking in a night without premonitions, a night which offered him without discrimination its monotonous abundance and he did not choose.

I wanted the moments of my life to follow each other and order themselves like those of a life remembered. I might as well try to catch time by the tail.

*Nausea, 56–59.*

## 2 CONTINGENCY

All at once the veil is torn away, I have understood, I have *seen.* . . . The roots of the chestnut tree sank into the ground just beneath my bench. I couldn't remember it was a root anymore. Words had vanished and with them the meaning of things, the ways things are to be used, the feeble points of reference which men have traced on their surface. I was sitting, stooping over, head bowed, alone in front of this black, knotty lump, entirely raw, frightening me. Then I had this vision.

It took my breath away. Never, up until these last few days, had I suspected the meaning of "existence." I was like the others, like the ones walking along the seashore, wearing their spring clothes. I said, like them, "The sea *is* green; that white speck up there *is* a seagull," but I didn't feel that it existed or that the seagull was an "existing seagull"; usually existence conceals itself. It is there, around us, in us, it is *us*, you can't say two words without mentioning it, but you can never touch it. When I believed I was thinking about it, I was thinking nothing, my head was empty, or there was just one word in my head, the word "being." Or else I was thinking—how can I put it? I was thinking of *properties*. I was telling myself that the sea belonged to the class of green objects, or that green was one of the qualities of the sea. Even when I looked at things, I was miles from dreaming that they existed: they looked like scenery to me. I picked them up in my hands, they served me as tools, I foresaw their resistance. But that all happened on the surface. If anyone had asked me what existence was, I would have answered in good faith, that it was nothing, simply an empty form added to things from the outside, without changing anything in their nature. And then all at once, there it was, clear as day: existence had suddenly unveiled itself. It had lost the harmless look of an abstract category: it was the dough out of which things were made, this root was kneaded into existence. Or rather the root, the park gates, the bench, the patches of grass, all that had vanished: the diversity of things, their individuality, were only an appearance, a veneer. This veneer had melted, leaving soft, monstrous lumps, in disorder—naked, with a frightful and obscene nakedness.

I kept myself from making the slightest movement, but I didn't need to move in order to see, behind the trees, the blue columns and the lampposts of the bandstand and the Velleda, in the middle of a clump of laurel. All these objects—how can I put it? They made me uncomfortable. I would have liked them to exist less forcefully, more dryly, more abstractly, with more reserve. The chestnut tree pressed itself against my eyes. Green blight covered it halfway up; the bark, black and swollen, looked like boiled leather. The sound of the water in the Masqueret Fountain trickled in my ears, made a nest there, filled them with sighs; my nostrils overflowed with a green, putrid odor. All things, gently, tenderly, were letting themselves exist like weary women giving way to laughter, saying, "It's good to laugh," in a damp voice; they were sprawling in front of each other, abjectly confessing their existence. I realized there was no mean between non-existence and this swooning abundance. If you existed, you had to exist to excess, to the point of moldiness, bloatedness, obscenity. In another world, circles, musical themes keep their pure and rigid lines. But existence is a yielding. Trees, pillars blue as night, the happy gurgling of a fountain, living smells, little mists of heat floating in the cold air, a red-haired man digesting on a bench: all these somnolences, all these digestings taken together, had their vaguely funny side. Funny—no: not quite that, nothing that exists can be funny; it was like a floating, almost entirely elusive analogy, to certain situations in vaudeville. We were a heap of existences, uncomfortable, embarrassed at ourselves, we hadn't the slightest reason to be there, none of us, each one confused, vaguely alarmed, felt superfluous in relation to the others. *Superfluous* [*de trop*]:* it was the only relationship I could establish between these trees, these gates, these stones. In vain I tried to *count* the chestnut trees, to *locate* them by their relationship to the Velleda, to compare their height with the height of the plane trees: each of them eluded the relations in which I tried to enclose it, isolated itself, and overflowed. Of these relations (which I obstinately maintained in order to delay the collapse of the human world, of measurements, quantities, directions) I felt the arbitrariness of these relations; they no longer bit into things. *Superfluous,* the chestnut tree there, in front of me, a little to the left. *Superfluous,* the Velleda.

And I myself—soft, weak, obscene, digesting, juggling with dismal thoughts—*I, too, was superfluous.* Fortunately, I didn't feel it, rather it was a matter of understanding it; but I was uncomfortable because I was afraid of feeling it (even now I'm afraid—afraid that it might catch me behind my head and lift me up like a wave from the depths). I dreamed vaguely of kill-

---

* *De trop* ("too much," "in excess") is a colloquial expression which Sartre frequently employs for the contingent. I translate "superfluous," since in Sartre's phenomenological version of the stream of consciousness, the metaphor of "overflowing" is often used in rendering the sense of contingency as consciousness of something as "exceeding" (*i.e.,* transcending) our consciousness of it.—Ed.

ing myself to wipe out at least one of these superfluous existences. But even my death would have been *superfluous*. *Su-*
*perfluous,* my corpse, my blood on these stones, between these
plants, at the bottom of this smiling garden. And the gnawed
flesh would have been *superfluous* in the earth which would
receive my bones, at last, cleaned, peeled, as clean as teeth, it
would have been *superfluous:* I was *superfluous* for eternity.

The word Absurdity is emerging under my pen; a little while
ago, in the garden, I couldn't find it, but neither was I looking for
it, I didn't need it: I thought without words, *on* things, *with*
things. Absurdity was not an idea in my head, or the breath of a
voice, only this long serpent dead at my feet, this serpent of
wood. Serpent or claw or root or vulture's talon, what difference
does it make. And without formulating anything clearly, I understood that I had found the clue to existence, the clue to my
nauseas, to my own life. In fact, all I could grasp beyond that
comes down to this fundamental absurdity. Absurdity: another
word. I struggle against words; beneath me there I touched the
thing. But I wanted to fix the absolute character of this absurdity.
A movement, an event in the tiny colored world of men is only
relatively absurd—in relation to the accompanying circumstances. A madman's ravings, for example, are absurd in relation to the situation in which he is, but not in relation to his own
delirium. But a little while ago I made an experiment with the
absolute or the absurd. This root—there was nothing in relation
to which it was absurd. How can I pin it down with words?
Absurd: in relation to the stones, the tufts of yellow grass, the
dry mud, the tree, the sky, the green benches. Absurd, irreducible; nothing—not even a profound, secret delirium of nature—
could explain it. Obviously I did not know everything, I had
not seen the seeds sprout, or the tree grow. But faced with this
great wrinkled paw, neither ignorance nor knowledge was important: the world of explanations and reasons is not the world
of existence. A circle is not absurd, it is clearly explained by the
rotation of the segment of a straight line around one of its
extremities. But neither does a circle exist. This root, in contrast,
existed in such a way that I could not explain it. Knotty, inert,
nameless, it fascinated me, filled my eyes, brought me back un-
ceasingly to its own existence. In vain I repeated, "This is a
root"—it didn't take hold any more. I saw clearly that you
could not pass from its function as a root, as a suction pump, *to*

*that,* to that hard and thick skin of a sea lion, to this oily, callous, stubborn look. The function explained nothing: it allowed you to understand in general what a root was, but not at all *that one there.* That root, with its color, shape, its congealed movement, was—beneath all explanation. Each of its qualities escaped it a little, flowed out of it, half solidified, almost became a thing; each one was *superfluous* in the root and the whole stump now gave me the impression of uncoiling out of itself a little, denying itself, losing itself in a frenzied excess. I scraped my heel against this black claw: I wanted to peel off some of the bark. For no reason at all, out of defiance, to make the bare pink of a scratch appear absurd on the tanned leather: to *play* with the absurdity of the world. But, when I drew my heel back, I saw that the bark was still black.

Black? I felt the word deflating, emptying of meaning with extraordinary rapidity. Black? The root *was not* black, there was no black on this piece of wood—there was something else: black, like the circle, did not exist. I looked at the root: was it *more than* black or *almost* black? But I soon stopped questioning myself because I had the feeling of knowing what the score was. Yes, I had already scrutinized innumerable objects, with deep uneasiness. I had already tried—in vain—to think something *about* them: and I had already felt their cold, inert qualities elude me, slip through my fingers. . . . Weird [*louche*]:* that's what they were, the sounds, the smells, the tastes. When they ran quickly under your nose like startled hares and you didn't pay too much attention, you might believe them to be simple and reassuring, you might believe that there was real blue in the world, real red, a real perfume of almonds or violets. But as soon as you held on to them for an instant, this feeling of comfort and security gave way to a deep uneasiness: colors, tastes, and smells were never real, never themselves and nothing but themselves. The simplest, most unanalyzable quality had too much content for itself, was superfluous at heart. That black against my foot, it didn't look like black, but rather the confused effort to imagine black by someone who had never seen black, and who wouldn't know where to stop, who would have imagined an ambiguous being beyond colors. It *looked*

* *Louche* is a favorite expression of Sartre's. Its literal meaning is "squinting." Its figurative meaning of "suspicious-looking" takes on in Sartre the philosophical implication of "equivocal."—Ed.

*like* a color, but also—like a bruise or a secretion, like an oozing—and like something else, a smell, for example, it melted into the smell of damp earth, warm moist wood, into a black smell that spread like varnish over this nervous wood, in a flavor of chewed, sweet fiber. I did not simply *see* this black: sight is an abstract invention, an idea that has been cleaned up, simplified, one of man's ideas. That black there, amorphous, weakly presence, overflowed sight, smell, and taste. But this exuberance became confusion and finally it was no longer anything because it was too much.

This moment was extraordinary. I was there, motionless, paralyzed, plunged in a horrible ecstasy. But at the heart of this ecstasy, something new had just appeared; I understood the nausea, I possessed it. To tell the truth, I did not formulate my discoveries to myself. But I think it would be easy for me to put them in words now. The essential point is contingency. I mean that by definition existence is not necessity. To exist is simply *to be there*;* existences appear, let themselves be *encountered,* but you can never *deduce* them. Some people, I think, have understood this. Only they tried to overcome this contingency by inventing a being that was necessary and self-caused. But no necessary being can explain existence: contingency is not a delusion, an appearance which can be dissipated; it is the absolute, and, therefore, perfectly gratuitous. Everything is gratuitous, this park, this city, and myself. When you realize this, your heart turns over and everything begins to float. . . .

How long will this fascination last? I *was* the root of the chestnut tree. Or rather I was entirely conscious of its existence. Still detached from it—since I was conscious of it—yet lost in it, nothing but it. A consciousness which was uneasy but nevertheless let itself fall with all its overhanging weight on this piece of inert wood. Time had stopped: a small black pool at my feet; it was impossible for something to come *after* this moment. I would have liked to tear myself away from that atrocious joy, but I did not even imagine it would be possible. I was inside; the black stump did *not* move, it stayed there, in my eyes, as a lump of food sticks in the windpipe. I could neither accept nor refuse it. What effort it took to raise my eyes! Did I raise them? Rather did I not obliterate myself for a moment in

* *Cf.*, Martin Heidegger's elucidation of the *Da-sein* in *Being and Time*, esp. p. 56.—Ed.

order to be reborn in the following moment with my head thrown back and my eyes raised upward? In fact, I was not even conscious of the transition. But suddenly it became impossible for me to think of the existence of the root. It was wiped out, I could repeat in vain, it exists, it is still there, under the bench, against my right foot. It no longer meant anything. Existence is not something which lets itself be thought of from a distance; it must invade you suddenly, master you, weigh heavily on your heart like a great motionless beast.—Or else there is nothing more at all.

There was nothing more, my eyes were empty and I was spellbound by my deliverance. Then suddenly it began to move before my eyes in light, uncertain motions; the wind was shaking the top of the tree.

It did not displease me to see something move; it was a change from these motionless existences who watched me like staring eyes. I told myself, as I followed the swinging of the branches: movements never quite exist, they are processes, transitions between two existences, moments of weakness. I expected to see them come out of nothingness, ripen by stages, blossom; at last I was going to surprise existences in the process of being born.

No more than three seconds and all my hopes were swept away. Viewing these hesitant branches groping around like blind men, I could not succeed in grasping the process of coming into existence. This idea of process was a human invention. An idea too clear. All these trifling agitations, each of them, asserted themselves. They overflowed the leaves and branches everywhere. They whirled around these dry hands, enveloped them with tiny whirlwinds. Of course a movement was something different from a tree. But it was still an absolute. A thing. My eyes only encountered fullness. The tips of the branches were seething with existences which unremittingly renewed themselves and which were never born. The wind existing had just lighted on the tree like a huge fly, and the tree was shuddering. But the shudder was not an emerging quality, a process from potentiality to actuality; it was a thing; a shudder-thing flowed into the tree, took possession of it, shook it, and suddenly abandoned it, going further on to twist about itself. All was fullness and all was active, there was no weak moment in time; all, even the most imperceptible stirring, was mode of existence.

And all these existents which bustled around this tree came from nowhere and were going nowhere. All at once they existed, then all at once they existed no longer. Existence is without memory; of the vanished it retains nothing—not even a memory. Existence everywhere, to infinity, in excess, forever and everywhere; existence—which is limited only by existence. I let myself sink down on the bench, dazed, overwhelmed by this profusion of beings without beginnings. Everywhere blossomings, bloomings, my ears buzzed with existence, my flesh itself throbbed and opened, abandoned itself to the universal burgeoning. It was revolting. Why, I thought, why so many existences, since they all look alike? What good are so many trees, so much the same? So many existences that don't come off, obstinately begun again, and again muffed—like the awkward efforts of an insect fallen on its back? (I was one of those efforts.) Such abundance did not give the impression of generosity; quite the opposite. It was dismal, ailing, embarrassed at itself. Those trees, those great clumsy bodies. I began to laugh because I suddenly thought of the formidable springtimes described in books, full of crackings, burstings, gigantic explosions. There were idiots who would tell you about the will to power and the struggle for survival. Hadn't they ever seen a beast or a tree? This plane tree with its scaling bark, this half-rotten oak, I was supposed to take them for rugged, youthful endeavor surging toward the sky. And that root? I was undoubtedly supposed to see it as a voracious claw tearing at the earth, devouring its food.

Impossible to see things that way. Softnesses, weaknesses, yes. The trees were floating. Gushing toward the sky? Rather collapsing. At any moment I expected to see the tree trunks shrivel up, like weary penises, crumple up, fall on the ground, softly folded in a black heap. *They didn't want* to exist, only they could not help themselves. That's it. So they quietly minded their own business; the sap rose up slowly through the ducts, half reluctant, and the roots sank slowly into the earth. But at each moment they seemed about to leave everything there and come to nothing. Tired and old, they kept on existing, reluctantly, simply because they were too weak to die, because death could only come to them from the outside. Only notes of music can proudly carry their own death in themselves as an internal necessity; only they don't exist. Every existing thing is born without reason, goes on living out of weakness, and dies by accident. I leaped back and closed my eyes. But the images, forewarned, leaped up and filled my closed eyes with existences: existence is a fullness from which man can never get away.

Strange images. They represented a multitude of things. Not real things; other things which looked like real things. Wooden objects which looked like chairs, shoes, other objects which looked like plants. And then two faces: the couple who were eating opposite me last Sunday in the Brasserie Vézélize. Fat, warm, sensual, absurd, with red ears. I could see the woman's neck and shoulders. Naked existence. That pair—it suddenly horrified me—that pair were still existing somewhere in Bouville; somewhere—in the midst of what smells? That soft bosom still gently rubbing up against clean fabric, nestling in lace, and the woman still feeling her bosom existing under her blouse, thinking, "My titties, my lovely fruits," smiling mysteriously, attentive to the blooming of her swelling breasts, tickling her.—Then I shouted, and found myself with my eyes wide open.

Had I dreamed this enormous presence? It was there, deposited on the garden, tumbling down in the trees, all soft, sticky, soiling everything, all thick, a jelly. And I, was I inside, with the garden? I was frightened, furious, I thought it was so stupid, so out of place. I hated this ignoble messiness. Piling up to the sky, spilling over, filling everything with its gelatinous slither, and I could see depths upon depths of it reaching far beyond the limits of the garden, the houses, and Bouville, as far as the eye could reach. I was no longer in Bouville; I was nowhere, I was floating. I was not surprised, I knew it was the World, the naked World revealing itself all at once, and I choked with rage at this gross absurd being. You couldn't even ask where all this came from, or how it was that a world existed, rather than nothingness. It didn't have any meaning, the world was present everywhere, before, behind. There had been nothing *before* it. Nothing. There had never been a moment in which it could not have existed. That was what bothered me; of course there was *no reason* for its existing, this flowing larva. But it was not possible for it not to exist. It was unthinkable: to imagine nothingness you had to be there already, in the midst of the World, eyes wide open and alive; nothingness was only an idea in my head, an existing idea floating in this immensity; this nothingness had not come *before* existence, it was an existence like any other and ap-

peared after many others. I shouted, What filth, what filth! And
I shook myself to get rid of this sticky filth, but it held and there
was so much, tons and tons of existence, endless. I suffocated
at the bottom of this immense weariness. And then, all at once,
the park emptied as through a great hole. The world disappeared
as it had come, or else I woke up—anyway I saw no more of it;
nothing was left but the yellow earth around me, out of which
dead branches rose upward.

I got up and went out of the park. Once at the gate, I turned
around. Then the garden smiled at me. I leaned against the gate
and watched for a long time. The smile of the trees, of the
clump of laurel, *meant* something: that was the real secret of
existence. I remembered one Sunday, not more than three weeks
ago. I had already detected everywhere a sort of conniving
mood. Was it addressed to me? I felt with weariness that I had
no way of understanding. No way. Yet it was there, waiting, a
sort of look. It was there on the trunk of the chestnut tree—it was
*the* chestnut tree. Things—one might have said thoughts—
which halted halfway, which were forgotten, which forgot what
they wanted to think and which stayed like that, hanging around
with an odd little meaning which was beyond them. That little
meaning annoyed me. I *could not* understand it, even if I had
stayed leaning against the gate for a century. I had learned all I
could know about existence.

*Nausea, 170–182.*

## 3  THE WORK OF ART

To think that there are fools who find consolation in the arts.
Like my Aunt Bigeois: "Chopin's Preludes were such a help to me
when your poor uncle died." And the concert halls overflow
with the humiliated, the outraged, their eyes shut, seeking to
transform their pale faces into receiving antennae. They imagine
that the sounds can be inveigled and will flow into them, sweet
and nourishing sounds, and that their sufferings become music,
like Werther's; they suppose that beauty is compassionate toward them. What jerks they are!

I'd like them to tell me if they find this music compassionate.
Just now I was far from swimming in beatitude. On the surface
I was figuring out my expenses, mechanically. Down below stag-

nated all those unpleasant thoughts—the unformulated questions, mute astonishments—which leave me neither day nor night. Thoughts of Anny, of my wasted life. And then, still further down, nausea, timid as dawn. But there was no music then, I was morose and calm. All the things around me were made of the same material as I, a sort of sloppy suffering. . . .

But now there is this song of the saxophone. And I'm ashamed. A glorious little suffering has just been born, an exemplary suffering. Four notes on the saxophone. They come and are gone, they seem to say: "Do as we do, suffer in rhythm [*en mesure*]." That's it. Of course I'd like to suffer that way, rhythmically, without complacency, without self-pity, with an arid purity. But is it my fault if the beer at the bottom of my glass is warm, if there are brown stains on the mirror, if I am superfluous, if the most sincere of my sufferings, the driest, drags and weighs down, with too much flesh, and the skin too slack as well, like a sea elephant, with bulging eyes, damp and appealing, but so ugly? No, they certainly can't tell me it's compassionate, this little pain of diamond, turning around above the record and dazzling me. Not even ironic: it turns gaily, completely taken up with itself; like a scythe it has cut through the tasteless intimacy of the world, and now it turns, and all of us . . . who were abandoning ourselves to existence, because we were together, confiding together, it has caught us unawares, while we were living our sloppy, easygoing lives. I'm ashamed of myself and of what exists in the presence of this music.

It does not exist. This is annoying. If I were to get up, rip this record from its support, and break it in two, I wouldn't reach it. *It* is beyond—always beyond something, a voice, a violin note. Through thicknesses and thicknesses of existence, it unveils itself, slender and steady, and when you want to grasp it, you meet only with existents, bump into existents devoid of meaning. It is behind them: I don't even hear it. I hear the sounds, the vibrations of the air which unveil it. It does not exist, since there is nothing superfluous about it: it is; everything else is superfluous in relation to it. It *is*.

And I too, I wanted *to be*. That's all I wanted; that sums up my life: at the bottom of all those endeavors which seemed unconnected, I find the same desire: to drive existence out of me, to empty the passing moments of their fat, to wring them dry, to purify myself, harden myself, so that I might give at last the

clear, sharp sound of a saxophone note. That might even make a
story with a moral: there was once a poor fellow who got lost in
the wrong world. He existed, just like other people, in the world
of public gardens, bars, commercial towns, and he wanted to
convince himself that he lived elsewhere, behind the canvas of
paintings, with the doges of Tintoretto, with the gallant Floren-
tines of Gozzoli, behind the pages of books, with Fabricio del
Dongo and Julien Sorel, behind the phonograph records, with
the long dry laments of jazz. And then, after having made a
complete fool of himself, he understood, he woke up, he saw
that it was all a big mistake. He was in a bar, and nowhere
else, in front of a glass of warm beer. He continued sitting overwhelmed on the bench; he thought: I'm a fool. And at that very
moment, from the other side of existence, in that other world
which one can glimpse from afar, but without ever approaching, a little melody began to dance, to sing: "Do as I do, suffer in
rhythm."

The voice sings:

> *Some of these days,*
> *You'll miss me, honey.*

There must be a scratch on the record there, for it makes a
funny noise. And that's something which clutches the heart:
the melody is absolutely untouched by this tiny coughing of the
needle on the record. It is so far—so far behind. This too, I understand: the record is scratched and wearing out, the singer is
perhaps dead; I, I'm about to leave, I'm going to take my train.
But behind the existent who tumbles from one present moment
to another, without past, without future, behind these sounds
which decompose from day to day, are chipped away, and slide
toward death, the melody remains the same, young and steady,
like a witness without pity.

The voice is silent. The record scrapes a little, then stops.
Released from an importunate dream, the café ruminates, chews
over the pleasure of existing. . . . In fifteen minutes I shall be
on the train, but I am not thinking about that. I am thinking
about a clean-shaven American, with thick black eyebrows,
suffocating with heat, on the twentieth floor of a New York
skyscraper. Above New York the sky burns, the blue of the sky
is inflamed, enormous yellow flames come and lick the roofs;

the Brooklyn kids are going to put on bathing suits and play under the water of the fire hoses. The dim room on the twentieth floor is boiling hot. The American with black eyebrows sighs, pants, the sweat rolls down his cheeks. He is sitting, in shirt sleeves, in front of his piano. He has a taste of smoke in his mouth and, vaguely, a ghost of a tune in his head. "Some of these days." Tom will turn up in an hour with his hip flask; then they will collapse into leather armchairs and drink brimming glasses of whiskey and the fire of the sky will come and inflame their throats, they will feel the weight of an immense torrid slumber. But first the tune must be put down: "Some of these days." The damp hand picks the pencil off the piano. "Some of these days, You'll miss me, honey."

That's the way it happened. That way or some other way, it makes little difference. That's how it was born. It is the worn-out body of this Jew with coal-black brows that it chose for its birth. He held his pencil limply and the sweat dropped from his ringed fingers onto the paper. And why not I? Why should it have to be this fat pig in particular, full of stale beer and whiskey, for the miracle to be consummated?

"Madeleine, would you put the record back on? Just once again, before I leave."

Madeleine starts to laugh. She turns the crank and there it is beginning again. But I am no longer thinking of myself. I am thinking of that fellow far away who composed this tune, one day in July, in the black heat of his room. I tried to think of him *through* the melody, through the white, acid-sour sounds of the saxophone. He made this. He had his troubles, everything didn't work out for him the way it should have: bills to be paid—and then there must have been somewhere a woman who wasn't thinking about him the way he would have liked her to—and then there was this frightful heat wave which transformed men into puddles of melting fat. There is nothing very pretty or glorious in all that. But when I hear the song and think that he made it, I find his suffering and his perspiration moving. He was lucky. He wouldn't have realized it though. He would have thought: with a little luck, this thing will bring in fifty bucks! Well, this is the first time in years that a man has seemed moving to me. I'd like to know something about him. It would be interesting to find out what sort of troubles he had, if he had a woman, or if he lived alone. Not at all out of concern with hu-

manity; quite the reverse. But because he had made this. I have
no desire to get to know him—anyway perhaps he's dead. Just a
little information about him and to be able to think about him,
from time to time, when I am listening to this record. I don't
suppose it would make any difference to him if he were told
that in the seventh largest city of France, near the station,
someone is thinking about him. But I'd be happy, if I were in his
place: I envy him. I have to leave. I get up, but I hesitate for a
moment, I'd like to hear the Negress sing. For the last time.

She sings. So two are saved: the Jew and the Negress. Saved.
Perhaps they thought themselves lost forever, drowned in existence. Yet no one could think of me as I think of them, with such
gentleness. No one, not even Anny. They are a little like the
dead for me, a little like the heroes of a novel; they have washed
themselves of the sin of existing. Not completely, of course—
but so far as any man can. This idea suddenly threw me into a
turmoil, because I was not even hoping for that anymore. I feel
something brush timidly against me and I dare not move because I'm afraid it will go away. Something I no longer knew: a
sort of joy.

The Negress sings. Then one can justify his existence? To
some slight extent? I feel extraordinarily intimidated. It isn't
because I have much hope. But I am like someone completely
frozen after a trip through the snow, who suddenly comes into
a warm room. I think he would stay near the door, without
moving, still cold, shuddering.

> *Some of these days,*
> *You'll miss me, honey.*

Couldn't I try? Of course, it wouldn't be a piece of music—
but couldn't I, in another medium? It would have to be a book.
. . . I don't quite know which kind—but one would have to be
able to suspect, behind the printed words, behind the pages,
something which did not exist, which would be above existence. It would have to be beautiful and hard as steel and make
people ashamed of their existence.

I, I feel myself vacillating. I dare not make a decision. If I were
sure I had talent. But never—never had I written anything of
that sort. Historical articles, yes—lots of them. A book. A novel.
And there would be people who would read this novel and say:

"It was Antoine Roquentin who wrote it, a red-headed fellow who hung around cafés," and they would think about my life as I think about the Negress's: as something precious and almost legendary. A book. Of course, at first it would be boring and tiresome work, and that would not keep me from existing or from feeling that I exist. But a time would come when the book would be written, would be behind me and I think that a little of its clarity would fall on my past. Then perhaps I could, through it, recall my life without revulsion. Perhaps some day, thinking of this very moment now, of this gloomy hour when I am waiting, hunched up, until it's time to climb aboard the train, perhaps I shall feel my heart beat faster and say to myself: "That was the day, that was the hour, when it all began." And I might succeed, with the past, and only with the past—in accepting myself.

*Nausea, 232–238.*

# III

———•———

*Emotional Consciousness*

An emotion is a transformation of the world. When the routes previously marked out become too difficult to follow, or when we do not see any route, we can no longer remain in a world which is so urgent.* The routes are blocked, but we must act. We then attempt to change the world—*i.e.*, to experience it as if the relations of things to their potentialities were not controlled by set procedures but by magic. We are not just playacting. We are cornered, and we throw ourselves into our new attitude with all the strength at our command. But this attempt is not self-conscious, for it would then be the object of reflection. Primarily it is becoming conscious of new relationships and new requirements. Our consciousness of an object being impossible, or generating a tension which is unbearable, we become conscious of it, or try to become conscious of it, in some other way. In order to transform the object, consciousness transforms itself.

Such a change in the orientation of consciousness is nothing unusual. A thousand examples can be found in the course of our activities and in the processes of perception. To try to find, for example, a feature hidden in the lines of a puzzle-picture ("Where is the gun?") is to behave perceptually in front of the picture in a new fashion—is to behave in front of the branches of a tree, telegraph poles, which are found in the picture, as if we were confronted by a gun—is to realize those movements of the eyes which we would make in front of a gun. But we are not conscious of these movements as such. Through them an intention which transcends them, and of which they constitute the material, is oriented toward the trees and the poles which

* For Sartre's conception of the "world," see Heidegger's analysis in *Being and Time* of the *Umwelt*, esp. pp. 67f.—Ed.

74

are experienced as "possible guns," until suddenly the perception crystallizes and the gun appears. Thus through a change of intention, as with a change of behavior, we apprehend a new object, or an old object in a new way. It is not necessary for us to place ourselves first on the reflective level. The instruction accompanying the puzzle provides our motivation directly. We try to find the gun without leaving the unreflecting level. In other words, a potential gun appears, vaguely localized in the picture. The change in intention and behavior which is characteristic of an emotion is similar. The impossibility of finding a solution to the problem is apprehended objectively as a quality of the world, and provides the motivation for a new unreflecting consciousness, which now experiences the world differently. The new aspect of the world and new behavior required—through which this aspect is experienced—provides the material for the new intention.

But emotional behavior is not on the same level as ordinary behavior, it is not *effective*. Its purpose is not to act really on the object as such by utilizing particular means. Emotional behavior tries to confer on the object, without modifying it in its real structure, another quality, a diminished existence, or a diminished presence (or an enlarged existence, etc.). The body, oriented by consciousness, changes its relationships to the world, in order to change the qualities of the world. Emotion may be play-acting but it is a play in which we believe. One simple example will clarify this structure of an emotion. I stretch out my hand to pick a bunch of grapes. I cannot reach it; it is beyond my grasp. I shrug my shoulders, drop my hand, muttering, "They are too green," and I go away. All these gestures, these words, this behavior I am not conscious of as such. It is a little drama which I am acting out under the grapevine, in order to confer on the grapes this quality of "too green." This drama is a substitute for the action which I could not carry through. I was initially conscious of the grapes as "something to be picked." But this demanding quality soon becomes unbearable, since it is a potentiality that cannot be realized. This tension becomes unbearable in its turn, and a motive for becoming conscious of a new quality of the grapes—the quality "too green," which will resolve the conflict and suppress the tension. But this quality I cannot confer chemically on the grapes; I cannot act by the ordinary routes on the grapes. Thus I become conscious of this bitter taste of grapes which are too green, through an acting out of disgust. I confer magically on the grapes the quality I desire. In this instance the play-acting is only partly sincere. Were the situation more demanding, the incantatory behavior would be carried out more seriously. We would then be dealing with an emotion.

*The Emotions, 58–62.*

# IV

---•---

## *Imaginative Consciousness*

### 1 PERCEPTION AND IMAGINATION

When I form the image of Peter, it is Peter who is the object of my actual consciousness. As long as this consciousness remains unaltered, I can give a description of the object as it appears to me in imagination, but not of the image as such. To specify the properties of the image as an image, I must resort to a new act of consciousness: I must *reflect*. Thus the image as image can be described only by a higher-order act of consciousness in which attention is diverted from the object and directed to the way in which the object is given. . . .

To perceive, to conceive, to imagine: these are the three modes of consciousness by which the same object can be given.

When I am perceiving. I am *observing* objects. The object, although it enters entirely into my perception, is only given from one side at a time. Take the example of a cube: I cannot know that it is a cube until I have apprehended its six sides, but of these I can see only three at a time, never more. I must therefore apprehend them successively. And when I make the transition, for example, from sides ABC to sides BCD, there always remains a possibility that side A has disappeared during my change of position. The existence of the cube therefore remains doubtful. Note too that when I see three sides of the cube at the same time, these three sides never present themselves to me as squares: their angles become obtuse, and starting from these appearances I must reconstruct their character as square. This has all been said a hundred times: it is characteristic of perception that the object appears only in a series of profiles, of aspects. The cube is certainly present to me, I can touch it, see it; but I always see it only in a certain way which solicits and excludes at one and the same time an infinite number of other points of view. We must *learn* about objects—*i.e.*, multiply possible points of view toward them. The object itself is the synthesis of all these appearances. . . .

When, in contrast, I conceive of a cube, I think of its six sides and its eight angles all at once. I think that its angles are right angles, its sides square. I am at the center of my idea, I grasp all of it immediately. . . . There is no learning process, no apprenticeship to serve. This is beyond doubt the clearest difference between thought and perception. This is why we can never perceive a thought nor think a perception. The two phenomena are radically distinct. . . .

What about the image? Is it apprenticeship or knowledge? Note first that it seems to fall on the side of perception. In both cases the object is given by profiles, by aspects, by what the Germans designate by the apt term *Abschattungen*. Only we don't have to tour around it: the cube when imagined is given immediately as what it is. When I say, "The object that I perceive is a cube," I am making an hypothesis which the further progress of my perceptions may force me to reject. When I say, "The object which I am at this moment imagining is a cube," my judgment is conclusive. It is absolutely certain that the object I am imagining is a cube.

This is not all. Consider this piece of paper on the table. The longer I look at it, the more it discloses its particular features. Each new orientation of my attention, of my analysis, discloses a new detail: the upper edge of the sheet is slightly warped; the end of the third line is dotted. But no matter how long I may contemplate an image, I shall never find anything in it but what I have put there. This is of central importance for distinguishing between an image and a perception. In the world of perception nothing can appear without entertaining an infinite number of relations with other things. Rather it is this infinite number of relationships—as well as the infinite number of relationships between the elements of this thing—which constitute the essence of a thing. There is accordingly something *overflowing* about the world of "things." There is always, at each moment, infinitely *more* than we can see; to exhaust the abundance of my actual perception, would require infinite time. This way of "overflowing" constitutes the very nature of objects. When we say, "No object can exist without having definite individuality," we must be understood to mean "without having an infinite number of specific relationships with an infinite number of other objects."

Now the image, in contrast, suffers from a sort of essential poverty. The different elements of an image have no relationship with the rest of the world, while among themselves they have but two or three relationships—either those that I have been able to ascertain, or those it is important for me at the moment to retain. It must not be said that other relationships exist covertly, that they wait for a bright light to be focused on them. They do not exist at all. Two colors, for example, which would clash in reality, can exist together in an image without any sort of relationship between them. . . .

The image presents its object all in one piece. No risk, no expectation; instead a certainty. My perception can deceive me, but not my image. Our attitude toward the object of the image could be called "quasi-observation." Our attitude is indeed that of observation, but it is an observation from which nothing is learned. If I imagine the page of a book, I am adopting the attitude of a reader, I *look* at the printed pages. But I am not reading. And in fact I am not even looking, since I already *know* what is written there.

*The Psychology of the Imagination, 3, 9–13.*

## 2 MENTAL AND MATERIAL IMAGES

I wish to recall the face of my friend Peter. I make an effort and I produce a certain imaginative consciousness of Peter. The object is very imperfectly rendered: certain details are lacking, others are doubtful, the whole is rather vague. There is a certain feeling of sympathy and pleasantness which I wanted to revive when confronted by this face, but which has not been recovered. I do not give up, I get up and take a photograph from a drawer. It is a fine photograph of Peter, I retrieve all the details of his face, even some which had eluded me. But the photograph lacks life: it is a perfect rendering of the external traits of his face, but it does not give his expression. Fortunately I own a carefully drawn caricature. Here the relations between the different features of his face are deliberately distorted, the nose is much too long, the cheekbones are too prominent, etc. Nevertheless, something which was missing in the photograph

—vitality, expression—is clearly evident in this drawing. I have found Peter again.

Mental representation, photograph, caricature: these three very different realities appeared in our example as three stages of the same process, three moments of a single act. From the beginning to the end, the intention remains the same: to represent [*rendre présent*] the face of Peter, who is not there. But it is only the subjective representation that psychology terms an image. Is this legitimate?

Consider our example again. We have used three procedures to recall the face of Peter. In all three we found an "intention" and this intention envisages the same object. This object is neither the representation, nor the photograph, nor the caricature: it is my friend Peter. Furthermore, in the three cases, I envisaged the object in the same way: I want to make the face of Peter appear as a perception, I want to "make him present" to myself. And since I cannot make this perception emerge directly, I have recourse to a certain material which acts as an *analogue*, as an equivalent for the perception.

In the first two cases, at least, the material can be perceived for its own sake, though it is not its own nature that it should function as the material for the image. The photo, taken by itself, is a *thing:* I can try to ascertain its exposure time by its color, the chemical used to tone it and fix it, etc. The caricature is a *thing,* I can take pleasure in investigating its lines and colors, without reflecting that they have the function of representing something. . . .

It is obvious that the mental image must also have a material, and a material which derives its meaning solely from the intention that animates it. To recognize this, all I need do is compare my initial empty intention with my mental image of Peter, which is something that emerged and arrived to fill my intention. The three cases are thus strictly parallel. They are three situations with the same form, but with material that varies. . . .

We can conclude that the act of imagining envisages an absent or non-existent object in its corporality, through a physical or psychical content, which is given not for its own sake, but only as an analogical representative of the object envisaged. The species of this genus depend on the material, since the informing intention remains the same. We shall therefore distinguish between images whose material is derived from the world of things (engravings, photos, caricatures, actors' impersonations, etc.) and those whose material is derived from the mental world (consciousness of movements, feelings, etc.). There are intermediary types which present us with syntheses of external elements and of psychical elements, as when we see a face in a flame, in the arabesques of a tapestry, or in the case of hypnagogic images, which are constructed . . . on the basis of entoptic lights.

The mental image cannot be investigated by itself. There is not a world of images and a world of objects. Every object, whether it is presented by an outward or an inner perception, can function either as a present reality or as an image, depending on what center of reference has been chosen. The two worlds, real and imaginary, are composed of the same objects: only the grouping and the interpretation of these objects vary.

*The Psychology of the Imagination,* 22–24, 26–27.

### 3  FROM THE SIGN TO THE IMAGE

On the stage of the music hall, Franconay is doing some impersonations. I recognize the person she is imitating; it is Maurice Chevalier. I appraise the imitation: "That really is Maurice Chevalier," or "It doesn't come off." What is going on in my consciousness?

Only, some will say, an association by resemblance, followed by a comparison: the imitation has produced in my consciousness an image of Maurice Chevalier; I then compare the two. This view is unacceptable. We have completely succumbed to the illusion of immanence. William James' objection, moreover, carries its full weight here: what is this resemblance which goes in search of images in the unconscious—this resemblance which precedes the consciousness we have of it?

We might attempt to retain this view by introducing several corrections. We might discard the resemblance and resort instead to contiguity. The name "Maurice Chevalier" calls forth in us an image by contiguity. Will the explanation hold for the numerous instances where the impersonator suggests without supplying the name? There are a large number of signs comparable to a name: Franconay, without naming Chevalier, might suddenly put on a straw hat. Posters, newspapers, caricatures, have gradually built up a whole arsenal of signs. They need only be borrowed.

It is true that imitations employ signs which are recognized as such by the spectator. But the relationship of the sign to the image, if this is to be understood as an associative link, does not exist. One reason is that consciousness of imitation, which is itself an imaginative form of consciousness, does not involve a mental image. Another reason is that the image, like the sign, is a consciousness, and there can be no external link between these two consciousnesses. A consciousness does not have an opaque and unconscious surface by which it can be grasped and attached to another consciousness. Between two consciousnesses there cannot be any relationship of cause to effect. A consciousness is entirely synthesis, carried out entirely within itself: only from within this synthesis can a consciousness join itself, by an act of retention or of protention, to a preceding or succeeding consciousness. In other words, if one consciousness is to act on another consciousness, it has to be retained and re-created by the consciousness on which it is to act. There are no passivities, only internal integrations and disintegrations, at the heart of an intentional synthesis which is transparent to itself. One consciousness is not the cause of another consciousness, but is its motivation.

This brings us to the real problem. The consciousness of imitation is a temporal form—*i.e.*, it develops its structures in time. It is a consciousness of meaning [*signification*]. But a meaning-endowing consciousness of a special kind which knows beforehand that it is going to become the consciousness of an image. It then becomes an imaginative consciousness, but one which retains in itself what was essential in the consciousness of the sign. The synthetic unity of these consciousnesses is an act of a certain duration, in which the consciousness of sign and that of image are in the relation of means to end. The essential problem is to describe these structures: to show how the consciousness of sign serves as a *motivation* for the consciousness of the image, how the latter involves the former in a new synthesis, how there takes place, at the same time, a functional transformation of the perceived object, which passes from the state when its material functions as a sign to a state when its material is representative.

The difference between the consciousness of an impersonation and the consciousness of a portrait derives from the materials. The material of the portrait itself solicits the spectator to carry out the synthesis, inasmuch as the painter endowed it with a perfect resemblance to its model. The material of the impersonation is a human body. It is rigid, and resists the imitation. The impersonator is small, plump, and dark-haired; a woman who is imitating a man. The result is that the imitation can only be approximate. The object which Franconay produces by means of her body is a weak form which can always be interpreted in two distinct ways: I am always free to see Maurice Chevalier as an image or a small woman making faces. Hence the essential role of signs in clarifying and guiding consciousness.

Consciousness is first oriented toward the general situation: it is disposed to interpret everything as an imitation. But it remains empty; it is only a question (Whom is she going to imitate?), only an oriented anticipation. From the outset it is oriented, through the imitator, toward an indeterminate person, conceived as the object X of the imitation.* Consciousness undertakes a double assignment: to determine the object X in accordance with the signs provided by the imitator; and to realize the object as an image through the person who is imitating it.

The impersonator appears. She is wearing a straw hat; she is sticking out her lower lip, she is keeping her head forward. I stop perceiving, I *read*—*i.e.*, I carry through a synthesis involving these signs. The straw hat is at first a simple sign, just as the cap and the foulard of a real singer are signs that he is about to sing an apache song. In other words, I do not at first perceive Chevalier's hat *through* the straw hat; I recognize that the hat of the impersonator *refers* to Chevalier, just as the cap refers to the *"milieu apache."* To decipher the signs is to produce the concept "Chevalier." At the same time I am making the judgment, "She is imitating Chevalier." With this judgment the structure of my consciousness is transformed. Now its theme is Chevalier. In virtue of its crucial intention, my consciousness is imaginative, my knowledge is realized in the intuitive material furnished me.

This intuitive material is very poor; the imitation reproduces

* Of course what we are considering here is only the ideal case, where all the phases of consciousness are sharply distinct. An impersonation can be as close a resemblance as a portrait—*e.g.*, when the impersonator employs make-up.

only a few elements—relationships, which are only minimally intuitive: the rakish angle of the straw hat and the angle formed by the neck and chin. In addition, certain of these relationships are deliberately altered: the angle of the straw hat is exaggerated, since this is the principal sign which must strike us first and around which all the others are ordered. A portrait is a faithful rendering of its model in all its complexity, and imposes on us, as life does, an effort of simplification, if we would abstract characteristic traits; but an imitation presents characteristic traits as such from the very outset. A portrait is in some respect, at least in appearance, something natural. An imitation is already a model that has been thought through and reduced to formulae, to schemata. Into these conventional formulae, consciousness wants an imaginative intuition to flow. But these arid schemata—so arid, so abstract that they could be read a moment ago as signs—are engulfed in a mass of details which seem to get in the way of this intuition. How is Maurice Chevalier to be discovered in these plump painted cheeks, this dark hair, this female body, these female clothes?

We should recall here a famous passage from *Matter and Memory:*

> *A priori* . . . it does seem that the sharp distinction between individual objects is a luxury of perception. . . . It does seem that we set out neither from the perception of the individual, nor from the conception of the genus, but from some intermediate form of knowledge—from a confused sense of a striking quality or resemblance.*

That dark hair we do not see as dark; that body we do not perceive as a female body, we do not see its prominent curves. Nevertheless, since it is a matter of descending to the level of intuition, we employ the sensory content with respect to its most general traits. The hair, the body are perceived as vague masses, as filled spaces. They have sensory opacity; beyond this they are but a *setting*. For the first time in our description of imaginative consciousnesses, we see appear—and at the heart of perception—a fundamental indeterminacy. . . . These qualities which are so vague and which are perceived only with respect to their general traits, have no value in themselves: they are in-

* Henri Bergson, *Matière et Mémoire*, p. 172.

tegrated into the imaginative synthesis. They represent the indeterminate body, the indeterminate hair of Maurice Chevalier.

These elements are not sufficient. Positive specifications must be realized. It is not a matter of constituting, with the body of the impersonator Franconay, a perfect *analogue* of the body of Chevalier. All I have available are a few elements which were functioning just now as signs. Since I do not have a complete equivalent of the person imitated, I have to realize in the intuition a certain *expressive nature*, the essence, as it were, of Chevalier presented to intuition.

First I must lend life to these arid schemata. But we have to be careful: if I perceive them for their own sake, if I notice the edges of the lips, the color of the straw of the hat, the consciousness of the image vanishes. I must carry through the movement of perception in reverse, starting out with knowledge and determining the intuition as a function of this knowledge. That lip was just now a sign; I make an image of it. But it is an image only to the extent to which it was a sign. I see it only as a "large protruding lip." Here we meet again an essential characteristic of the mental image—the phenomenon of quasi-observation. What I perceive is what I know; I cannot learn anything from the object, and the intuition is only knowledge which has been weighed down and degraded. At the same time, these differentiated features are joined together by vaguely intuited zones: the cheeks, the ears, the neck of the impersonator function as an indeterminate connective tissue. Here too, it is knowledge which is primary: what is perceived corresponds to the vague knowledge that Maurice Chevalier has cheeks, ears, a neck. The details fade away, and what cannot disappear resists the imaginative synthesis.

But these different intuitive elements are insufficient to realize the expressive nature. Here a new factor emerges—feeling.

Two principles are to be recognized:

1   Any perception is accompanied by an affective reaction.*

2   Any feeling is a feeling of something, that is, it envisages its object in a certain fashion and projects upon it a certain quality. To have sympathy for Peter is to be conscious of Peter as sympathetic.

* *Cf.* Abramowski, *Le subconscient normal.*

Now the role of feeling in the consciousness of imitation can be understood. When I see Maurice Chevalier, this perception involves a certain affective reaction. I project on the physiognomy of Maurice Chevalier a certain indefinable quality which might be called his meaning [*sens*]. In the consciousness of imitation, the knowledge intended, on the basis of the signs and the commencement of the intuitive realization, awakens this affective reaction, which becomes incorporated into the intentional synthesis. Correlatively, the affective meaning of the face of Chevalier begins to appear on the face of Franconay. It is this affective meaning which realizes the synthetic union of the various signs, animating their rigid aridity and giving them a certain life and density. It is this affective meaning which endows the isolated elements of the imitation with an indefinable meaning and the unity of an object and which functions as the real intuitive material of the consciousness of the imitation. Finally, it is this object as an image which we contemplate on the body of the impersonator: the signs reunited by an affective meaning—*i.e.*, the *expressive nature*. This is the first occasion, but not the last, that we see feeling take the place of the strictly intuitive elements of perception in order to realize the object as an image.

The imaginative synthesis is accompanied by a vigorous consciousness of spontaneity—we might even say, of freedom. This is because, in the last analysis, only a definite act of will can keep consciousness from sliding from the level of the image to that of perception. Even so, this sliding usually occurs at one moment or another. It often happens that the synthesis is not completely carried out: the face and body of the impersonator do not lose all of their individuality; but the expressive something "Maurice Chevalier" nevertheless appears on this face, on this female body. A hybrid state develops, which is neither entirely perceptive nor entirely imaginative, and which would be well worth describing for its own sake. This unstable and transitory state is obviously what is most entertaining for the spectator in an impersonation.

*The Psychology of the Imagination, 34–40.*

Always ready to bog down in the materiality of an image, thought escapes by flowing into another image, and from it to still another. But in most cases this distrust, which is like a memory of reflection, does not appear. In these cases the laws of development that are native to the image are often confused with the laws of the essence under consideration. . . . The dangers of this substitution are illustrated by the following example: "I wanted to convince myself of the idea that every oppressed individual or group derives from its oppression the strength needed to shake off its oppressors. But I had the definite impression that such a theory was arbitrary and I felt a certain uneasiness. I made a new effort of thought: now there emerged the image of a compressed spring. At the same time I felt in my muscles the latent force of the spring. It would expand the more violently, the more it had been compressed. For a moment I felt with complete evidence the necessity of the idea which I could not convince myself of before."

We see what is involved. The oppressed *is* the spring. *On* the compressed spring can already be observed as evident the force with which it will expand; but a compressed force clearly represents potential energy, and this potential energy is that of the oppressed, since the oppressed *is* the spring. Here we see clearly the contamination between the laws of the image and those of the essence represented. This idea of potential energy which increases in proportion to the force exercised, it is the spring which *presents* it; it can be apprehended on the spring. Change the term of comparison and substitute for the spring an organism, for example, and you will have an entirely opposed intuition—something which could be expressed by saying, "Oppression demeans and degrades those who suffer it." But the image of the spring, left to itself and envisaged purely and simply as the image of a spring, would not be sufficient to carry conviction. No doubt the spring accumulates force. But never enough to throw off the weight, since the force accumulated in the spring is always less than that compressing the spring. The conclusion that then would be drawn from the image would be that the oppressed gains in strength and value from the very fact of its oppression, but it will never succeed in throwing off its yoke.

In fact, . . . more is involved. The image is falsified by the meaning: the energy which accumulates in the compressed spring, is not felt as stored up purely passively, but as a living force which will increase with the passage of *time*. Here the image of the spring is no longer a simple image of a spring. It is also something indefinable: an image of a living spring. Here there is no doubt a contradiction, but there is . . . no image without inherent contradiction. It is in and by this very contradiction that the impression of evidence is constituted. Thus the image carries within itself a power to convince which is spurious and which comes from the ambiguity of its nature.

*The Psychology of the Imagination, 170–171.*

## 5 FEELING AND IMAGINATION

The object as an image is something unreal [*irréel*]. It is no doubt present, but at the same time it is out of reach. I cannot touch it, change its place; or rather I can indeed do so, but on condition that I do it unreally, by not using my own hands but phantom hands which administer unreal blows to this face. To act upon these unreal objects, I must double myself, make myself *unreal*. But then none of these objects require me to act, to do anything. They are neither heavy, nor demanding, nor compelling: they are purely passive, they wait. The feeble life that we breathe into them comes from us, from our own spontaneity. If we turn away from them, they vanish into nothing. . . .

This passive object, kept artificially alive, but about to vanish at any moment, cannot fulfill our desires. But it is not entirely pointless: to constitute an unreal object is a way of deceiving for a moment our desires, if only to aggravate them later, somewhat like the effect of sea water on thirst. If I desire to see a friend I make him appear unreally. This is a way of playing at satisfying my desire. But the satisfaction is only play-acting, for in fact my friend is not really there. What is more, it is the desire which constitutes the object for the most part. To the extent that it projects the unreal object before it, the desire specifies itself as desire. At first it is only Peter that I desire to see. But my desire becomes desire for that smile, for that look. It thus becomes limited and aggravated at the same time, and the unreal object—at any rate so far as its affective aspect is concerned—is precisely the limitation and the aggravation of this desire. It is but a mirage; in the imaginative act desire feeds on itself. To be more exact, the object as an image is a *specific lack;* it is hollow. . . .

In organizing itself with knowledge into an imaginative form, desire becomes precise and concentrated. Enlightened by this knowledge, the desire projects outside itself its object. It thereby becomes conscious of itself. The act by which a feeling becomes conscious of its exact nature, limits and defines itself—this act is one and the same as the act by which it presents itself with a transcendent object. . . . It is impossible for the image to link itself to desire from the outside; for this would involve a desire which is natively anonymous and entirely indifferent to the object on which it will finally fix itself. Instead the affective state, *being consciousness*, cannot exist without a transcendent correlative.

When feeling is oriented toward something real, actually perceived, the thing, like a reflector, returns the light it has received from it. As a result of this continual interaction, the feeling is continually enriched at the same time as the object soaks up affective qualities.* The feeling thus obtains its own particular depth and richness. The affective state follows the progress of attention, it develops with each new discovery of perception, it assimilates all the features of the object; as a result its development is unpredictable, since it is subordinate to the development of its real correlative, even while it remains spontaneous. At each moment perception overflows it and sustains it, and its density and depth come from its being confused with the perceived object: each affective quality is so deeply incorporated in the object that it is impossible to distinguish between what is felt and what is perceived.

In the constitution of the unreal object, knowledge plays the role of perception; it is with it that the feeling is incorporated. Thus the unreal object emerges. . . . Feeling then behaves in the face of the unreal as in the face of the real. It seeks to fuse with it, to adapt itself to its contours, to feed on it. Only this unreal, so well specified and defined, is empty; or rather it is the simple reflection of the feeling.

* Such as gracious, troubling, congenial, light, heavy, refined, disturbing, horrible, repulsive, etc.

To prefer to the real the imaginary is not only to prefer to a mediocre present a richness, a beauty, a splendor which are imaginary, *in spite of* the fact that they are unreal. It is also to adopt feelings and behavior which are imaginary *because* they are imaginary. It is not this or that image alone that is chosen, but the imaginary state with all its implications, it is not just an escape from features of reality (poverty, frustrated love, failure of our undertakings, etc.) that is sought, but from the form itself of reality, its character of *presence*, the responsiveness it demands of us, the subordination of our actions to their object, the inexhaustibility of our perceptions, their independence, the very way our feelings have of developing. This artificial, congealed, formalized life in slow motion, which is for most of us but a makeshift, is exactly what a schizophrenic desires. The morbid dreamer who imagines he is a king, would not adjust himself to a real throne, nor even to a tyranny where all his desires would be granted. A desire is in fact never literally granted because of the abyss which separates the real from the imaginary. The object which I desired, can indeed be given to me, but only on another level of existence to which I must adapt myself. Here it is now in front of me. If I did not have to act at once, I would hesitate for a long time, surprised, not able to recognize this reality so full and rich in consequences. I would ask myself: "Is it really *this* I wanted?" The morbid dreamer will not hesitate; it is not *this* which he wanted. More than any other consideration is the fact that the present requires an adaptation which he is no longer able to muster; a sort of indeterminacy on the part of our feelings is needed, a real plasticity, for the real is always new, always *unpredictable*. I wanted Anny to come; but the Anny I desired was only the correlative of my desires. Here she is, but she overflows my desire on all sides; I must begin my apprenticeship all over again. In contrast the feelings of the morbid dreamer are solemn and congealed; they keep recurring with the same forms and the same labels. He has taken his time in constructing them; nothing has been left to chance; they will not tolerate the slightest deviation. The traits of the unreal objects corresponding to their feelings have been correlatively fixed for ever. Thus the dreamer can choose from the storeroom of accessories the feelings he wishes to put on and the objects that go with these feelings, as an actor chooses his costumes. Today it is ambition, tomorrow sexual love. Only objects as images with their "essential poverty" can submissively minister to his feeling, without ever taking it by surprise, deceiving it, or guiding it. Only unreal objects can vanish into nothingness when the caprice of the dreamer is over, since they are only its reflection; only unreal objects have no other consequences than those he wants to draw from them. It is therefore a mistake to look upon the world of the schizophrenic as a torrent of images with a richness and a glitter which compensate for the monotony of reality. His world is poor and meticulous, where the same scenes keep on tirelessly recurring to the slightest detail, accompanied by the same ceremonial, where everything is regulated in advance, foreseen—where above all, nothing can escape, resist, or surprise. In short, if the schizophrenic imagines so many amorous scenes, it is not just because his real love has been frustrated, it is rather because he is no longer capable of love.

*The Psychology of the Imagination,*
*177–179, 199–200, 210–212.*

## 6 ART AND EXISTENCE

The "beautiful" is not something which can be perceived; by its very nature, it is isolated from the world. . . . A painting, for example, cannot be illumined by projecting a beam of light on the canvas; it is the canvas that is illumined, not the painting. The fact of the matter is that the painter has not *realized* his mental image at all; he has simply constituted a material analogue of such a kind that anyone can experience the image provided he looks at the analogue. But the image thus provided with an external analogue remains an image. There is no realization of the imaginary, nor can we speak of its *objectification.* Each stroke of the brush was not make for its own sake, nor even to constitute a coherent real whole [*ensemble*], in the sense in which a certain lever in a machine can be said to have been conceived for the whole and not for its own sake. The brush stroke was made in relation to an unreal synthetic whole, and the aim of the artist was to constitute a whole of *real* colors which would enable this unreal to disclose itself. The painting should then be conceived as the *visitation* of a material thing now and again (whenever the spectator adopts the imaginative attitude) by an unreal which is the object painted. What misleads us here is the real, sensory pleasure given by certain real colors on the canvas. Some of the reds of Matisse, for example, stimulate a sensory pleasure in those who see them. But it must be understood that this sensory pleasure, if considered in isolation—for example, if stimulated by a color in nature—has nothing esthetic about it. It is simply a pleasure of the senses. But when the red of the painting is experienced, it is experienced nonetheless as a part of an unreal whole, and it is in the setting of this whole that it is beautiful. It is, for example, the red of a rug by a table. But it is never pure color. Even if the artist is concerned solely with the sensory relationships between forms and colors, he chooses for that very reason a rug in order to increase the sensory value of the red: tactile elements, for example, must be intended through the red; it is a *woolly* red, because the rug is made of wool. Without this woolliness of the color something would be lost. And surely the rug is painted there *for the sake of the red* which it justifies, not the red for the sake of the rug. If Matisse chose a rug rather than a sheet of dry, glazed paper, it is because of the voluptuous mixture of the color, the thickness, and the tactile quality of the wool. Consequently the red can truly be enjoyed only when it is experienced as the *red of the rug* and so as unreal. The powerful contrast with the green of the wall would have been weakened, if the green were not completely stiff and glazed, because it is the green of wallpaper. Thus it is in the unreal that the relationship of colors and forms takes on its true meaning. And even when the objects delineated have their usual meaning reduced to a minimum, as in the paintings of the cubists, at least the painting is not flat. The forms we see are certainly not the forms of a rug, a table, nor of anything else we see in the world. Nevertheless, they do have thickness, matter, depth, and exhibit spatial relationships with each other. They are *things*. And it is precisely to the extent to which they are things that they are unreal. Cubism has introduced the fashion of claiming that a painting should not represent or imitate reality but should constitute an object in itself. As an esthetic doctrine such a program is perfectly defensible, and to it we are indebted for numerous masterpieces. But we must be clear as to what is at stake. To claim that the painting, although entirely without objective meaning, nevertheless is a *real* object, would be a serious mistake. Cer-

tainly it carries no reference to Nature. The real object no
longer functions as an analogue of a bouquet of flowers or of a
forest glade. But when I "contemplate" it, I am nonetheless not
adopting a realizing attitude. The painting is still an *analogue*.
Only what is disclosed through it is an unreal assemblage of
*novel things*—of objects I have never seen, never will see, but
which are no less objects, even though they do not exist *in the
painting*, nor anywhere in the world, and yet disclose themselves through the canvas, having in some sense taken possession of it. It is the assemblage of these unreal objects that I characterize as *beautiful*. The esthetic enjoyment is real, but it is not
experienced for its own sake, as produced by a real color; it is
but a way of apprehending the unreal object, and far from being
oriented toward the real painting, it serves to constitute the
imaginary object through the real canvas. This is the ground of
the celebrated disinterestedness of esthetic experience. This is
why Kant could say that it does not matter whether the beautiful object, insofar as it is experienced as beautiful, exists or
not. This is why Schopenhauer could speak of a kind of suspension of the Will to Power. This is not due to some mysterious
way of apprehending the real, which we are able to employ occasionally. What happens is that the esthetic object is constituted and apprehended by an imaginative consciousness which
posits it as unreal.

What we have just shown regarding painting can easily be
extended to the art of fiction, poetry, and drama, too. It is obvious that the novelist, the poet and the dramatist constitute an
unreal object by means of verbal analogues; it is also obvious
that the actor who plays Hamlet makes use of himself, of his
whole body, as an analogue of the imaginary person. Even the
famous dispute about the paradox of the actor can be resolved.
Some have argued that the actor *does not believe* in the character he plays, while others cite extensive testimony that shows
that the actor becomes involved in some way with the character. To my mind these two views are not mutually exclusive.
If by "belief" is meant actual realization, it is obvious that the
actor does not actually suppose himself to be Hamlet. But this
does not mean that he does not "mobilize" himself to produce
Hamlet. He uses all his feelings, all his strength, all his gestures
as analogues of the feelings and behavior of Hamlet. But by this
very fact he deprives them of their reality. *He lives entirely in*

*an unreal way.* It matters little that he is *really* weeping, when
carried away by his role. These tears . . . he himself experiences (and his audience with him) as the tears of Hamlet—*i.e.*,
as the analogue of unreal tears. . . . The actor is completely
caught up, inspired, by the unreal. It is not the character who
becomes real in the actor; it is the actor who *becomes unreal* in
the character.*

But are there not some arts whose objects seem to escape
unreality by their very nature? A melody, for example, carries no
reference to anything besides itself. Is a cathedral anything
more than a mass of *real* stone which dominates the surrounding housetops? But let us take a closer look. I listen to a symphony orchestra, for example, playing the Beethoven Seventh
Symphony. Let us disregard exceptional cases which are marginal cases of esthetic contemplation, as when I go primarily "to
hear Toscanini" interpret the Seventh Symphony in his own way.
Usually what draws me to the concert is the desire "to hear the
Seventh Symphony." Of course I have some objection to hearing
an amateur orchestra, and prefer this or that conductor. But
this is due to my desire to hear the symphony "played perfectly," because the symphony will then be *perfectly itself*. The
shortcomings of a poor orchestra which plays "too fast" or "too
slow," "in the wrong tempo," etc., seem to me to rob, to "betray"
the work it is interpreting. At best the orchestra effaces itself
before the work performed, and, provided I can trust the per-
formers and their conductor, I am confronted by the symphony
itself as it actually is. This everyone will concede. But now, what
is the Seventh Symphony itself? Obviously it is a *thing*, that is
something which confronts me, which resists, which endures.
Of course there is no need to show that this thing is a synthetic
whole, which does not exist as notes but as thematic configura-
tions. But is this "thing" real or unreal? Above all keep in mind
that I am listening to the Seventh Symphony. For me this "Seventh Symphony" does not exist in time. I do not experience it
as an occurrence with a date, as an artistic disclosure which is
unfolding itself in the Châtelet auditorium on the 17th of November, 1938. If I hear Furtwängler tomorrow, or eight days

---

* It is in this sense that an inexperienced actress can claim that her stage fright
helped her represent the timidity of Ophelia. If it did, it is because she suddenly
converted it into an unreal—*i.e.*, because she ceased to apprehend it for its own
sake and experienced it as an *analogue* for the timidity of Ophelia.

later, conduct another orchestra performing the same symphony, I am in the presence of the same symphony again. Only it is being played either better or worse. Let us now see *how* I hear the symphony. Some people shut their eyes. In this case they detach themselves from the visual and dated occurrence of this particular interpretation; they surrender to the pure sounds. Others watch the orchestra or the back of the conductor. But they do not see what they are looking at. This is what Revault d'Allonnes calls reflection with auxiliary fascination. The auditorium, the conductor, and even the orchestra have disappeared. I am then confronted by the Seventh Symphony, but on the condition of hearing it *not anywhere*, of no longer thinking of the occurrence as actual and dated, and on the condition that I listen to the succession of themes as an absolute succession and not as real succession which is unfolding itself, for example, at the same time that Peter paid a visit to this or that friend. To the extent to which I hear the symphony it is *not here*, between these walls, at the tip of the violin bows. Nor is it "past" as if I thought, this is the work that matured in the mind of Beethoven on such a date. It is completely outside the real. It has its own time—*i.e.*, it has an inner time, which flows from the first note of the allegro to the last note of the finale. But this time does not succeed a preceding time, which happened "before" the beginning of the allegro; nor is it followed by a time which will come "after" the finale. The Seventh Symphony is in no way *in time*. It therefore escapes entirely from the real. It appears actually present, but as absent, as being out of reach. I cannot act upon it, change a single note of it, or slow down its movement. But it depends for its appearance on the real: on the conductor's not fainting, on a fire in the hall not bringing the performance to a halt. The conclusion is not that *the* Seventh Symphony has been interrupted; only that its *performance* has been interrupted. Does this not show that the performance of the symphony is its *analogue*? It can only disclose itself through analogues which are dated and unfold in our time. But to experience it through these analogues an imaginative reduction must be carried out—*i.e.*, the real sounds must be apprehended as analogues. The symphony accordingly appears as a perpetual elsewhere, as a perpetual absence. We must not think of it (as Spandrell does in Huxley's *Point Counter Point* and as so many Platonists do) as existing in another world, in an intelligible heaven. It is not only outside of time and space (as are essences, for example), but is also outside of the *real*, outside of existence. I do not hear it really, I hear it imaginatively. This explains the marked difficulty we always experience in passing from the "world" of the theater or of music into that of our ordinary preoccupations. Actually there is no transition from one world to another, but only a transition from the imaginative attitude to an attitude of realization. Esthetic contemplation is an induced dream, and the transition to reality is a genuine awakening. The disappointment that accompanies the return to reality has often been noted. But this sense of discomfort occurs even after attending a realistic, cruel play, when the return to reality should be experienced as reassuring. The sense of discomfort is in fact merely that of the dreamer awakened; a fascinated consciousness, engulfed in the imaginary, is suddenly emancipated by the sudden ending of the play or symphony, and regains contact with existence. Nothing more is needed to provoke the nauseous sense of revulsion that characterizes the consciousness of reality.

From these few observations, we can reach the conclusion that the real is never beautiful. Beauty is a value which applies only to the imaginary and which entails the negation of the world in its essential structure. For this reason it is stupid to confuse the moral and the esthetic. The values of the Good presuppose being-in-the-world; they concern behavior in the real world and are entirely subject to the essential absurdity of existence. To adopt an esthetic attitude toward life is constantly to confuse the real and the imaginary. It does happen, however, that we adopt the attitude of esthetic contemplation when confronted with events or real objects. In such cases anyone can observe in himself a kind of withdrawal in relation to the object contemplated which itself slides into nothingness. From this moment on, it is no longer *perceived;* it functions as an analogue of itself—*i.e.*, as an unreal image of what it is appears to us through its actual presence. This image can be purely and simply the object itself, neutralized, negated, as when I contemplate a beautiful woman or death at a bullfight. It can also be the imperfect and confused appearance of what it *might* be, through what it is, as when the painter becomes aware of the harmony of two very violent and vivid colors through the real patches of color which he finds on a wall. At once the object appears as *behind* itself, becomes untouchable, beyond our reach; hence a sort of painful disinterestedness in relation to it. It is in this sense that one can say that the extreme beauty of a woman kills desire for her. In fact we cannot at the same time place ourselves on the level of the esthetic, where there appears this unreal "herself" we admire, and on the realistic level of physical possession. To desire her we must forget that she is beautiful, for desire is a plunge into the heart of existence, into what is most contingent and absurd. Esthetic contemplation of real objects is of the same structure as paramnesia, in which the real object functions as an analogue of itself in the past. But in the one case there is negation and in the other a relegation of the thing to the past. Paramnesia differs from the esthetic attitude as memory differs from imagination.

*The Psychology of the Imagination*, 275–282.

# CONSCIOUSNESS
# AND BEING

# I

---•---

## *The Pursuit of Being*

### 1 CONSCIOUSNESS OF SOMETHING

All consciousness, as Husserl has shown, is consciousness *of* something. This means that there is no consciousness which is not a *positing* of a transcendent object, or if you prefer, that consciousness has no "content." We must renounce those neutral "givens" which, according to the system of reference chosen, find their place either "in the world" or "in the psyche." A table is not *in* consciousness—not even as a representation. A table is *in* space, beside the window, etc. The existence of the table in fact is a center of opacity for consciousness; it would require an infinite process to inventory the total contents of a thing. To introduce this opacity into consciousness would be to refer to infinity the inventory which it can make of itself, to make consciousness a thing, and to deny the *cogito*. The first procedure of a philosophy ought to be to expel things from consciousness and to re-establish its true connection with the world, *i.e.,* as a positional consciousness *of* the world. All consciousness is positional in that it transcends itself in order to reach an object, and it exhausts itself in this same positing. All that there is of *intention* in my actual consciousness is directed toward the outside, toward the table; all my judgments or practical activities, all my present inclinations transcend themselves; they aim at the table and are absorbed in it. Not all consciousness is knowledge (there are states of affective consciousness, for example), but all knowing consciousness can be knowledge only of its object.

However, the necessary and sufficient condition for a knowing consciousness to be knowledge *of* its object, is that it be consciousness of itself as being that knowledge. This is a necessary condition, for if my consciousness were not consciousness of being consciousness of the table, it would then be consciousness of that table without consciousness of being so. In other words, it would be a consciousness ignorant of itself, an unconscious—which is absurd. This is a sufficient condition, for my being conscious of being conscious of that table suffices in fact for me to be conscious of it. That is of course not sufficient to permit me to affirm that this table exists *in itself*—but rather that it exists *for me*.

What is this consciousness of consciousness? We suffer to such an extent from the illusion of the primacy of knowledge that we are immediately ready to make of the consciousness of consciousness an *idea ideae* in the manner of Spinoza; that is, a knowledge of knowledge. Alain, wanting to express the obvious "To know is to be conscious of knowing," interprets it in these terms: "To know is to know that one knows." In this way we should have defined *reflection* or positional consciousness of consciousness, or better yet *knowledge of consciousness*. This would be a complete consciousness directed toward something which is not it; that is, toward consciousness as object of reflection. It would then transcend itself and like the positional consciousness *of* the world would be exhausted in aiming at its object. But that object would be itself a consciousness.

It does not seem possible for us to accept this interpretation of the consciousness of consciousness. The reduction of consciousness to knowledge in fact involves our introducing into consciousness the subject-object dualism which is typical of knowledge. But if we accept the law of the knower-known dyad, then a third term will be necessary in order for the knower to become known in turn, and we will be faced with this dilemma: either we stop at any one term of the series—the known, the knower known, the knower known by the knower, etc. In this case the totality of the phenomenon falls into the unknown; that is, we always bump up against a non-self-conscious reflection and a final term. Or else we affirm the necessity of an infinite regress (*idea ideae ideae*, etc.), which is absurd. Thus to the necessity of ontologically establishing consciousness we would add a new necessity: that of establishing it epistemologically. Are we obliged after all to introduce the law of this dyad into consciousness? Consciousness of self is not dual. If we wish to avoid an infinite regress, there must be an immediate, non-cognitive relation of the self to itself.

Furthermore the reflecting consciousness posits the consciousness reflected-on, as its object. In the act of reflecting I pass judgment on the consciousness reflected-on; I am ashamed of it, I am proud of it, I will it, I deny it, etc. The immediate consciousness which I have of perceiving does not permit me either to judge or to will or to be ashamed. It does not *know* my perception, does not *posit* it; all that there is of intention in my actual consciousness is directed toward the outside, toward the world. In turn, this spontaneous consciousness of my perception is *constitutive* of my perceptive consciousness. In other words, every positional consciousness of an object is at the same time a non-positional consciousness of itself. If I count the cigarettes which are in that case, I have the impression of revealing an objective property of this collection of cigarettes: *they are a dozen.* This property appears to my consciousness as a property existing in the world. It is very possible that I have no positional consciousness of counting them. Then I do not know myself as counting. Proof of this is that children who are capable of making an addition spontaneously cannot *explain* subsequently how they set about it. Piaget's tests, which show this, constitute an excellent refutation of the formula of Alain—To know is to know that one knows. Yet at the moment when these cigarettes are revealed to me as a dozen, I have a non-thetic consciousness of my adding activity. If anyone questioned me, indeed, if anyone should ask, "What are you doing there?" I should reply at once, "I am counting." This reply aims not only at the instantaneous consciousness which I can reach by reflection but at those fleeting consciousnesses which have passed without being reflected-on, those which are forever not-reflected-on in my immediate past. Thus reflection has no kind of primacy over the consciousness reflected-on. It is not reflection which reveals the consciousness reflected-on to itself. Quite the contrary, it is the non-reflective consciousness which renders the reflection possible; there is a pre-reflective *cogito* which is the condition of the Cartesian *cogito*. At the same time it is the non-thetic consciousness of counting which is the very condition of my act of adding. If it were otherwise, how would the addition be the unifying theme of my consciousnesses? In order that this theme should preside over a whole series of syntheses of unifications and recognitions, it must be present to itself, not as a thing but as an operative intention which can exist only as the revealing-revealed (*révélante-révélée*), to use an expression of Heidegger's. Thus in order to count, it is necessary to be conscious of counting.

Of course, someone may say, but this makes a circle. For is it not necessary that I count *in fact* in order to *be conscious* of counting? That is true. However there is no circle, or if you like, it is the very nature of consciousness to exist "in a circle." The idea can be expressed in these terms: every conscious existence exists as consciousness of existing. We understand now why the first consciousness of consciousness is not positional; it is because it is one with the consciousness of which it is consciousness. With one move it determines itself as consciousness of perception and as perception. . . . (Henceforth we shall put the "of" inside parentheses to show that it merely satisfies a grammatical convention.)

This self-consciousness we ought to consider not as a new consciousness, but as *the only mode of existence which is possible for a consciousness of something.* Just as an extended object has to exist according to three dimensions, so an intention, a pleasure, a grief can exist only as immediate self-consciousness. If the intention is not a thing in consciousness, then the being of the intention can be only consciousness. It is not necessary to understand by this that on the one hand, some external cause (an organic disturbance, an unconscious impulse, another *Erlebnis*) could determine that a psychic event—a pleasure, for example—occurs, and that on the other hand, this event so determined in its material structure should have to occur as self-consciousness. This would be to make the non-thetic consciousness a *quality* of the positional consciousness (in the sense that the perception, positional consciousness of that table, would have as addition the quality of self-consciousness) and would thus fall back into the illusion of the theoretical primacy of knowledge. This would be moreover to make the psychic event a thing and to *qualify* it with "conscious" just as I can qualify this blotter with "red." Pleasure cannot be distinguished—even logically—from consciousness of pleasure. Consciousness (of) pleasure is constitutive of the pleasure as the very mode of its own existence, as the material of which it is made, and not as a form which is imposed afterwards upon a hedonic material. Pleasure cannot exist "before" consciousness of pleasure —not even in the form of potentiality. . . . A potential pleasure can exist only as consciousness (of) being potential. Potentialities of consciousness exist only as consciousness of potentialities.

Conversely, as I showed earlier, we must avoid defining pleasure by the consciousness which I have of it. This would be to fall into an idealism of consciousness which would bring us back by a devious route to the primacy of knowledge. Pleasure must not disappear behind its own self-consciousness; it is not a representation, it is a concrete event, full and absolute. It is no more a quality of self-consciousness than self-consciousness is a quality of pleasure. There is no more first a consciousness which receives *subsequently* the affect "pleasure" like water which one stains, than there is first a pleasure (unconscious or psychological) which receives subsequently the quality of "conscious" like a ray of light. There is an indivisible, indissoluble being—definitely not a substance supporting its qualities like particles of being, but a being which is existence through and through. Pleasure is the being of self-consciousness and this self-consciousness is the law of being of pleasure. This is what Heidegger expressed very well when he wrote (though speaking of *Dasein*, not of consciousness): "The 'how' (*essentia*) of this being, so far as it is possible to speak of it generally, must be conceived in terms of its existence (*existentia*)." This means that consciousness is not produced as a particular instance of an abstract possibility but that in emerging* at the center of being, it creates and supports its essence—that is, the synthetic ordering of its possibilities.

This means also that the type of being of consciousness is the opposite of that which the ontological proof reveals to us. Since consciousness is not *possible* before being, but since its being is the source and condition of all possibility, its existence implies its essence. Husserl expresses this aptly in speaking of the "necessity of fact." In order for there to be an essence of pleasure, there must be first the *fact* of a consciousness (of) this pleasure. It is futile to try to invoke pretended *laws* of conscious-

* Sartre's use of the term *surgir* (which I translate "emerge") and its derivatives, blends the phenomenological meaning which "appear" has in Husserl with one of the ontological meanings which Heidegger lends the etymology of his corresponding term *ex-sistere*. As an alternative to *surgissement*, Sartre sometimes employs the more energetic *jaillissement* (translated as "upsurge"), which incorporates his own phenomenological metaphor of the stream of consciousness.—Ed.

ness of which the articulated whole would constitute the essence. A law is a transcendent object of knowledge; there can be consciousness of a law, not a law of consciousness. For the same reasons it is impossible to assign to a consciousness a motivation other than itself. Otherwise it would be necessary to conceive that consciousness to the degree to which it is an effect, is not conscious (of) itself. It would be necessary in some manner that it should be without being conscious (of) being. We should fall into that too common illusion which makes consciousness semi-conscious or a passivity. But consciousness is consciousness through and through. It can be limited only by itelf.

This self-determination of consciousness must not be conceived as a genesis, as a becoming, for that would force us to suppose that consciousness is prior to its own existence. Neither is it necessary to conceive of this self-creation as an act, for in that case consciousness would be conscious (of) itself as an act, which it is not. Consciousness is a plenum of existence, and this determination of itself by itself is an essential characteristic. It would even be wise not to misuse the expression "cause of self," which allows us to suppose a progression, a relation of self-cause to self-effect. It would be more exact to say very simply: The existence of consciousness comes from consciousness itself. By that we need not understand that consciousness "derives from nothingness." There cannot be "nothingness of consciousness" *before* consciousness. "Before" consciousness one can conceive only of a plenum of being of which no element can refer to an absent consciousness. If there is to be nothingness of consciousness, there must be a consciousness which has been and which is no more and a witnessing consciousness which poses the nothingness of the first consciousness for a synthesis of recognition. Consciousness is prior to nothingness and "is derived" from being.*

One will perhaps have some difficulty in accepting these conclusions. But considered more carefully, they will appear perfectly clear. The paradox is not that there are "self-activated" existences but that there is no other kind. What is truly unthinkable is passive existence; that is, existence which perpetu-

---

* That certainly does not mean that consciousness is the foundation of its being. On the contrary, as we shall see later, there is a full contingency of the being of consciousness. We wish only to show (1) that *nothing* is the cause of consciousness, (2) that consciousness is the cause of its own way of being.

ates itself without having the force either to produce itself or to preserve itself. From this point of view there is nothing more incomprehensible than the principle of inertia. Indeed where would consciousness "come" from if it did "come" from something? From the limbo of the unconscious or of the physiological. But if we ask ourselves how this limbo in its turn can exist and where it derives its existence, we find ourselves faced with the concept of passive existence; that is, we can no more absolutely understand how this non-conscious given (unconscious or physiological) which does not derive its existence from itself, can nevertheless perpetuate this existence and find in addition the ability to produce a consciousness. Evidence of this is the great favor which the proof *a contingentia mundi* has enjoyed.

Thus by abandoning the primacy of knowledge, we have discovered the *being* of the *knower* and encountered the absolute, that same absolute which the rationalists of the seventeenth century had defined and logically constituted as an object of knowledge. But precisely because the question concerns an absolute of existence and not of knowledge, it is not subject to that famous objection according to which a known absolute is no longer an absolute because it becomes relative to the knowledge which one has of it. In fact the absolute here is not the result of a logical construction on the ground of knowledge but the subject of the most concrete of experiences. And it is not at all *relative* to this experience because it *is* this experience. Likewise it is a non-substantial absolute. The ontological error of Cartesian rationalism is not to have seen that if the absolute is defined by the primacy of existence over essence, it cannot be conceived as a substance. Consciousness has nothing substantial, it is pure "appearance" in the sense that it exists only to the degree to which it appears. But it is precisely because consciousness is pure appearance, because it is total emptiness (since the entire world is outside it)—it is because of this identity of appearance and existence within it that it can be considered as the absolute. . . .

## 2  THE ONTOLOGICAL PROOF

Consciousness is consciousness *of* something. This means that transcendence is the constitutive structure of consciousness; that is that consciousness emerges *supported by* a being which

is not itself. This is what we call the ontological proof. No doubt
someone will reply that the existence of a requirement of consciousness does not prove that this requirement must be satisfied. But this objection cannot hold up against an analysis of
what Husserl calls intentionality, though, to be sure, he misunderstood its essential character. To say that consciousness is
consciousness of something means that for consciousness there
is no being outside of that precise obligation to be a revealing
intuition of something—*i.e.*, of a transcendent being. Not only
does pure subjectivity, if initially given, fail to transcend itself to posit the objective; but it would also lose its purity.
What can properly be called subjectivity is consciousness (of)
consciousness. But this consciousness (of being) consciousness
must be qualified in some way, and it can be qualified only as
revealing intuition or it is nothing. Now a revealing intuition
implies something revealed. Absolute subjectivity can be established only in the face of something revealed; immanence can
be defined only within the apprehension of a transcendent. It
might appear that there is an echo here of Kant's refutation of
problematical idealism. But we ought rather to think of Descartes. We are here on the ground of being, not of knowledge. It
is not a question of showing that the phenomena of inner sense
imply the existence of objective spatial phenomena, but that
consciousness implies in its being a non-conscious and transphenomenal being. In particular there is no point in replying
that in fact subjectivity implies objectivity and that it constitutes
iself in constituting the objective; we have seen that subjectivity is powerless to constitute the objective. To say that consciousness is consciousness of something is to say that it
must occur as a revealed-revelation of a being which is not it
and which gives itself as already existing when consciousness
reveals it.

Thus we have left pure appearance and have arrived at full
being. Consciousness is a being whose existence posits its essence, and inversely it is consciousness of a being, whose essence implies its existence; that is, in which appearance lays
claim to *being*. Being is everywhere. Certainly we could apply
to consciousness the definition which Heidegger reserves for
*Dasein* and say that it is a being such that in its being, its being
is in question. But it would be necessary to complete the definition and formulate it more like this: *consciousness is a being*

*such that in its being, its being is in question insofar as this being implies a being other than itself.*

We must understand that this being is no other than the transphenomenal being of phenomena and not a noumenal being which is hidden behind them. It is the being of this table, of this package of tobacco, of the lamp, more generally the being of the world which is implied by consciousness. It requires simply that the being of that which *appears* does not exist *only* insofar as it appears. The transphenomenal being of what exists *for consciousness* is itself in itself (*lui-même en soi*). . . .

*Being and Nothingness, liii–lviii, lxiii–lxiv.*

# II

———•———

## *The Encounter with Nothingness*

### 1 THE QUESTION

Consciousness is an abstraction since it conceals within itself its ontological origin in the region of the in-itself; conversely the phenomenon is likewise an abstraction since it must "appear" to consciousness. The concrete can be only the synthetic totality of which consciousness, like the phenomenon, constitutes only moments. The concrete is man within the world in that specific union of man with the world which Heidegger, for example, calls "being-in-the-world." We deliberately begin with the abstract if we question "experience" as Kant does, inquiring into the conditions of its possibility—or if we effect a phenomenological reduction like Husserl, who would reduce the world to the state of the noematic-correlate of consciousness. But we will no more succeed in restoring the concrete by the addition or organization of the elements which we have abstracted from it than Spinoza could reach substance by the infinite summation of its modes. . . .

It is enough now to open our eyes and question without prejudice this totality which is man-in-the-world. It is by the description of this totality that we shall be able to reply to these two questions: (1) What is the synthetic relation which we call being-in-the-world? (2) What must man and the world be in order for a relation between them to be possible? In truth, the two questions are interdependent, and we cannot hope to reply to them separately. But each type of human behavior, being the behavior of man-in-the-world, can present to us at one and the same time man, the world, and the relation which unites them, provided we envisage these forms of behavior as realities objectively apprehensible, and not as subjective impressions which disclose themselves only when reflected upon.

## The Encounter with Nothingness

We shall not limit ourselves to the study of a single mode of behavior. We shall try on the contrary to describe several, and proceeding from one kind of behavior to another, attempt to penetrate into the profound meaning of the relation "man-world." But first of all we should choose a single example, which can serve us as a guiding thread in our inquiry.

Now this very inquiry furnishes us with the example we need: this man that *I am*—if I apprehend him such as he is at this moment in the world, I recognize that he stands before being with a questioning attitude. At the very moment when I ask, "Is there any mode of behavior which can reveal to me the relation of man with the world?" I pose a question. This question I can consider objectively, for it matters little whether the questioner is myself or the reader who reads my work and who is questioning along with me. But on the other hand, the question is not simply the objective totality of the words printed on this page; it is indifferent to the symbols which express it. In a word, it is a human attitude filled with meaning. What does this attitude reveal to us?

In every question we stand before a being which we are questioning. Every question presupposes a being who questions and a being which is questioned. This is not the original relation of man to being-in-itself, but rather it stands within the limitations of this relation and takes it for granted. On the other hand, this being which we question, we question *about* something. That *about which* I question the being participates in the transcendence of being. I question being about its modes of being or about its being. From this point of view the question is a kind of expectation; I expect a reply from the being questioned. That is, on the basis of a pre-interrogative familiarity with being, I expect from this being a revelation of its being or of its way of being. The reply will be a "yes" or a "no." It is the existence of these two equally objective and contradictory possibilities which on principle distinguishes the question from affirmation or negation. There are questions which on the surface do not permit a negative reply—like, for example, the one which we put earlier, "What does this attitude reveal to us?" But actually we see that it is always possible with questions of this type to reply, "Nothing" or "Nobody" or "Never." Thus at the moment when I ask, "Is there any behavior which can reveal to me the relation of man with the world?" I admit *on principle* the possibility of a negative reply such as, "No, such behavior does not exist." This means that we admit to being faced with the transcendent fact of the non-existence of such behavior. . . .

It is obvious that non-being always appears within the limits of a human expectation. It is because I expect to find fifteen hundred francs that I find *only* thirteen hundred. It is because a physicist *expects* a certain verification of his hypothesis that nature can tell him no. It would be in vain to deny that negation appears on the original basis of a relation of man to the world. The world does not disclose its non-beings to one who has not first posited them as possibilities. But is this to say that these non-beings are reducible to pure subjectivity?

We need only consider an example of negative judgment and ask whether it makes non-being appear in the midst of being or merely defines a previous discovery. I have an appointment with Peter at four o'clock. I arrive at the café a quarter of an hour late. Peter is always punctual. Will he have waited for me? I look at the room, the patrons, and I say, "He is not here." Is there an intuition of Peter's absence, or does negation indeed enter in only with judgment? At first sight it seems absurd to speak here of intuition since to be exact there could not be an intuition of *nothing* and since the absence of Peter is this nothing. Common sense, however, bears witness to this intuition. Do we not say, for example, "I suddenly saw that he was not there." Is this just a matter of misplacing the negation? Let us look a little closer.

It is certain that the café by itself with its patrons, its tables, its booths, its mirrors, its light, its smoky atmosphere, and the sounds of voices, rattling saucers, and footsteps which fill it —the café is a fullness of being. And all the intuitions of detail which I can have are filled by these odors, these sounds, these colors—all phenomena which have a transphenomenal being. Similarly Peter's actual presence in a place which I do not know is also a plenitude of being. We seem to have found fullness everywhere. But we must observe that in perception there is always the construction of a figure on a ground. No one object, no group of objects is specifically designed to be organized as either ground or figure; all depends on the direction of my attention. When I enter this café to search for Peter, there is formed a synthetic organization of all the objects in the café, as the ground on which Peter is given as about to appear.

This organization of the café as the ground is an original nihilation. Each element of the setting, a person, a table, a chair, attempts to isolate itself, to lift itself upon the ground constituted
by the totality of the other objects, only to fall back once more
into the undifferentiation of this ground; it melts into the
ground. For the ground is that which is seen only as the object
of a purely marginal attention. Thus the original nihilation of
all the figures which appear and are swallowed up in the total
neutrality of a *ground* is the necessary condition for the appearance of the principal figure, which is here the person of Peter.
This nihilation is given to my intuition; I am witness to the successive disappearance of all the objects which I look at—in particular of the faces, which detain me for an instant (Could this be
Peter?) and which as quickly decompose precisely because they
"are not" the face of Peter. Nevertheless if I should finally discover Peter, my intuition would be filled by a solid element, I
should be suddenly halted by his face and the whole café would
organize itself around him as a distinct person.

But now Peter is not here. This does not mean that I discover
his absence in some particular spot in the establishment. In fact
Peter is absent from the *whole* café; his absence congeals the
café in its evanescence; the café remains *ground;* it persists in
offering itself as an undifferentiated totality to my only marginal attention; it slips [*glisse*] into the background; it pursues
its nihilation. Only it makes itself ground for a determined figure; it carries the figure everywhere in front of it, presents
the figure everywhere to me. This figure which slips constantly
between my look and the solid, real objects of the café is precisely a perpetual evanescence; it is Peter emerging as nothingness on the ground of the nihilation of the café. So that what is
offered to intuition is a flickering of nothingness; it is the nothingness of the ground, the nihilation of which summons and demands the appearance of the figure, and it is the figure—the
nothingness which slips as a *nothing* onto the surface of the
ground. It serves as foundation for the judgment—"Peter is
not here." It is in fact the intuitive apprehension of a double
nihilation. To be sure, Peter's absence supposes an original relation between me and this café; there are an infinite number of
people who are without any relation with this café for want of a
real expectation which ascertains their absence. But, to be exact, I myself expected to see Peter, and my expectation has

brought about the occurrence of Peter's absence as a real event concerning this café. It is an objective fact at present that I have *discovered* this absence, and it presents itself as a synthetic relation between Peter and the setting in which I am looking for him. Peter absent haunts this café and is the condition of its self-nihilating organization as ground. By contrast, judgments which I can make subsequently to amuse myself, such as, "Wellington is not in this café, Paul Valéry is no longer here, etc."— these have a purely abstract meaning; they are pure applications of the principle of negation without real foundation or any effect and they never succeed in establishing a *real* relation between the café and Wellington or Valéry. Here the relation "is not" is merely *thought*. This example is sufficient to show that non-being does not come to things by a negative judgment; it is the negative judgment, on the contrary, which is conditioned and supported by non-being. . . .

But where does nothingness come from? If it is the original condition of the questioning attitude and more generally of all philosophical or scientific inquiry, what is the original relation of the human being to nothingness? What is the original nihilating conduct? . . .

We shall be helped in our inquiry by a more complete examination of the behavior which served us as a point of departure. We must return to the question. We have seen, it may be recalled, that every question in essence posits the possibility of a negative reply. In a question we question a being about its being or its way of being. This way of being or this being is veiled; there always remains the possibility that it may unveil itself as a nothingness. But from the very fact that we presume that an existent can always be revealed as *nothing*, every question supposes that we realize a nihilating withdrawal [*recul*] in relation to the given, which becomes a simple *presentation*, fluctuating between being and nothingness.

It is essential therefore that the questioner have the permanent possibility of detaching himself from the causal series which constitutes being and which can only produce being. If we admitted that the question is determined in the questioner by universal determinism, the question would thereby become unintelligible and even inconceivable. A real cause, in fact, produces a real effect and the caused being is wholly engaged by the cause in what is; to the extent that its being depends on the cause, it cannot have within itself the tiniest germ of nothingness. Thus insofar as the questioner must be able to effect in relation to the questioned a kind of nihilating withdrawal, he is not subject to the causal order of the world; he unsticks [*désenglue*] himself from being. This means that by a double movement of nihilation, he nihilates the thing questioned in relation to himself by placing it in a *neutral* state, between being and non-being—and that he nihilates himself in relation to the thing questioned by wrenching himself away from being in order to be able to bring out of himself the possibility of a non-being. Thus in posing a question, a certain negative element is introduced into the world. We see nothingness making the world iridescent, casting a shimmer over things. But at the same time the question emanates from a questioner who in order to motivate himself in his being as one who questions, disengages himself from being. This disengagement is then by definition a human process. Man presents himself at least in this instance as a being who introduces nothingness into the world, inasmuch as he himself is affected with non-being for this purpose. . . .

## 2 ANGUISH

The condition on which human reality* can deny [*nier*] all or part of the world is that human reality carry nothingness within itself as the *nothing* which separates its present from all its past. But this is still not all, for the *nothing* envisaged would not yet have the sense of nothingness; a suspension of being which would remain unnamed, which would not be consciousness of suspending being would come from outside consciousness and by reintroducing opacity into the heart of this absolute lucidity, would have the effect of cutting [consciousness] in two. Furthermore this nothing would by no means be negative. Nothingness, as we have seen above, is the ground of the negation because it conceals the negation within itself, because it is the negation as being. It is necessary then that conscious being constitute itself in relation to its past as separated from this past by a nothingness. It must necessarily be conscious of this cleavage in being, but not as a phenomenon which it experiences, rather as a structure of consciousness which it is.

* *Réalité humaine* is Sartre's translation of Heidegger's *Dasein.*—Ed.

Freedom is the human being putting his past out of play by secreting his own nothingness. It must be clearly understood that this original necessity of being its own nothingness does not belong to consciousness intermittently and on the occasion of particular negations. This does not happen just at a particular moment in psychic life when negative or interrogative attitudes appear; consciousness continually experiences itself as the nihilation of its past being.

But someone doubtless will believe that he can use against us here an objection which we have frequently raised ourselves: if the nihilating consciousness exists only as consciousness of nihilation, we ought to be able to define and describe a constant mode of consciousness, present *qua* consciousness, which would be consciousness of nihilation. Does this consciousness exist? Thus a new question has been raised: if freedom is the being of consciousness, consciousness ought to exist as consciousness of freedom. What form does this consciousness of freedom assume? In freedom the human being *is* his own past (as also his own future) in the form of nihilation. If our analysis has not led us astray, there ought to exist for the human being, insofar as he is conscious of being, a certain mode of standing opposite his past and his future, as being both this past and this future and as not being them. We shall be able immediately to . . . reply to this question: it is in anguish that man becomes the consciousness of his freedom, or if you prefer, anguish is the mode of being of freedom as consciousness of being; it is in anguish that freedom is, in its being, in question for itself.

Kierkegaard describing anguish before sin characterizes it as anguish in the face of freedom. But Heidegger, who is known to have been greatly influenced by Kierkegaard,* considers anguish instead as the apprehension of nothingness. These two descriptions of anguish do not appear to us contradictory; on the contrary the one implies the other.

First we must acknowledge that Kierkegaard is right; anguish is distinguished from fear in that fear is fear of beings-in-the-world whereas anguish is anguish before myself. Vertigo is anguish to the extent that I am afraid not of falling over the precipice, but of throwing myself over. A situation provokes fear if there is a possibility of my life being changed from without; my being provokes anguish to the extent that I distrust my-

* Jean Wahl: *Études Kierkegaardiennes*, Kierkegaard et Heidegger.

self and my own reactions in that situation. The artillery preparation which precedes the attack can provoke fear in the soldier who undergoes the bombardment, but his anguish begins when he tries to foresee the conduct with which he will face the bombardment, when he asks himself if he is going to be able to "hold out." Similarly the recruit who reports for active duty at the beginning of the war can in some instances be afraid of death, but more often he is "afraid of being afraid"; that is, he is filled with anguish before himself. Most of the time dangerous or threatening situations present themselves in different perspectives; they will be apprehended through a feeling of fear or of anguish according to whether we envisage the situation as acting on the man or the man as acting on the situation. The man who has just received a hard blow—for example, losing a great part of his wealth in a crash—can have the fear of threatening poverty. He will experience anguish a moment later when nervously wringing his hands (a symbolic reaction to the action which has occurred but which remains still wholly indeterminate), he exclaims to himself: "What am I going to do? But what am I going to do?" In this sense fear and anguish are mutually exclusive since fear is unreflective apprehension of the transcendent and anguish is reflective apprehension of the self; the one emerges from the destruction of the other. The normal process in the case which I have just cited is a constant transition from the one to the other. But there also exist situations where anguish appears pure; that is, without being preceded or followed by fear. If, for example, I have been raised to a new status and entrusted with a delicate and flattering mission, I can feel anguish at the thought that I will not be capable perhaps of fulfilling it, and yet I will not have the least fear in the world of the consequences of my possible failure.

What is the meaning of anguish in the various examples which I have just given? Let us take up again the example of vertigo. Vertigo announces itself through fear; I am on a narrow path—without a guardrail—which goes along a precipice. The precipice presents itself to me as *to be avoided;* it represents a danger of death. At the same time I conceive of a certain number of causes, originating in universal determinism, which can transform that threat of death into reality; I can slip on a stone and fall into the abyss; the crumbling earth of the path can give way under my steps. Through these various anticipations, I am given to myself as a thing; I am passive in relation to these possibilities; they come to me from without; insofar as I am also an object in the world, subject to gravitation, they are *my* possibilities. At this moment *fear* appears, which in terms of the situation is the apprehension of myself as a destructible transcendent in the midst of transcendents, as an object which does not contain in itself the origin of its future disappearance. My reaction will be of the reflective order; I will pay attention to the stones in the road; I will keep myself as far as possible from the edge of the path. I realize myself as repudiating the threatening situation with all my strength, and I project before myself a certain number of future actions destined to keep the threats of the world at a distance from me. These actions are *my* possibilities. I escape fear by the very fact that I am placing myself on a plane where *my own* possibilities are substituted for the transcendent probabilities where human action had no place.

But these actions, precisely because they are *my* possibilities, do not appear to me as determined by alien causes. Not only is it not strictly certain that they will be effective; but also it is not strictly certain that they will be adopted, for they do not have sufficient existence in themselves. We could say, altering the expression of Berkeley, that their "being is a sustained-being" and that their "possibility of being is only an ought-to-be-sustained." Due to this fact their possibility has as a necessary condition the possibility of contradictory actions (*not* to pay attention to the stones in the road, to run, to think of something else) and the possibility of the contrary action (to throw myself over the precipice). The possibility which I make *my* concrete possibility can appear as my possibility only by emerging on the ground of the totality of the logical possibilities which the situation allows. But these rejected possibles in turn have no other being than their "sustained-being"; it is I who sustain them in being, and inversely, their present non-being is an "ought-not-to-be-sustained." No external cause will remove them. I alone am the permanent source of their non-being, I engage myself in them; in order to cause *my* possibility to appear, I posit the other possibilities so as to nihilate them. This would not produce anguish if I could apprehend myself in my relations with these possibles as a cause producing its effects. In this case the effect defined as my possibility *would be strictly* determined. But then it would cease to be *possible;* it would become simply "due-to-happen [*à-venir*]." If then I wished to avoid anguish and vertigo, it would be enough if I were to consider the motives (instinct of self-preservation, prior fear, etc.), which make me reject the situation envisaged, as *determining* my prior activity in the same way that the presence at a determined point of one given mass determines the trajectories followed by other masses; it would be necessary, in other words, that I apprehend in myself a strict psychological determinism. But I am in anguish precisely because any action on my part is only *possible*, and this means that while constituting a set of motives *for* repudiating that situation, I at the same moment apprehend these motives as not sufficiently effective. At the very moment when I apprehend my being as *horror* of the precipice, I am conscious of that horror as *non* determining in relation to my possible conduct. In one sense that horror calls for prudent action, and it is in itself an adumbration of that action; in another sense, it only posits the final evolution of that action as possible, precisely because I do not apprehend it as the *cause* of this final evolution but as a demand, an appeal, etc.

Now as we have seen, consciousness of being is the being of consciousness. There is no question here of contemplating afterwards a horror already constituted; it is the very being of horror to appear to itself as "not being the cause" of the conduct it calls for. In short, to avoid fear, which reveals to me a transcendent future strictly determined, I take refuge in reflection, but the latter has only an undetermined future to offer. This means that in establishing a certain action as a possibility and precisely because it is *my* possibility, I am aware that *nothing* can compel me to adopt that action. Yet I am indeed already there in the future; it is for the sake of that being which I will soon be at the turning of the path that I now exert all my strength, and in this sense there is already a relation between my future being and my present being. But a nothingness has slipped into the heart of this relation; I *am* not the self which I will be. First I am not that self because time separates me from it. Secondly, I am not that self because what I am is not the foundation of what I will be. Finally I am not that self because no actual existent can determine strictly what I am going to be. Yet as I am already what I will be (otherwise I would not be interested in being this rather than that), *I am the self which I will be, in the mode of not being it.* It is through my horror that

I am carried toward the future, and the horror nihilates itself in that it constitutes the future as possible. Anguish is precisely my consciousness of being my own future, in the mode of not-being. To be exact, the nihilation of horror as a *motive*, which has the effect of reinforcing horror as a *state*, has as its positive counterpart the appearance of other forms of conduct (in particular that which consists in throwing myself over the precipice) as *my* possible *possibilities*. If *nothing* compels me to save my life, *nothing* prevents me from throwing myself into the abyss. The decisive conduct will emanate from a self which I am not yet. Thus the self which I am depends on the self which I am not yet to the exact extent that the self which I am not yet does not depend on the self which I am. Vertigo appears as the apprehension of this dependence. I approach the abyss, and it is myself that I am looking for in its depths. At this moment, I am playing with my possibilities. My eyes, surveying the abyss from top to bottom, imitate my possible fall and realize it symbolically; at the same time suicide, from the fact that it becomes a *possibility* possible for *me*, now provides possible motives for adopting it (suicide would make my anguish cease). Fortunately these motives in their turn, from the sole fact that they are motives for a possible action, present themselves as ineffective, as non-determining; they can no more *produce* the suicide than my horror of the fall can *determine me* to avoid it. It is this counter-anguish which generally puts an end to anguish by transmuting it into indecision. Indecision, in its turn, calls for decision. I abruptly get away from the edge of the precipice and resume my way.

The example which we have just analyzed has shown us what we could call "anguish in the face of the future." There exists another: anguish in the face of the past. It is that of the gambler [*joueur*] who has freely and sincerely decided not to gamble anymore and who, when he approaches the gaming table, suddenly sees all his resolutions melt away. This phenomenon has often been described as if the sight of the gaming table reawakened in us a tendency which entered into conflict with our former resolution and ended by drawing us in spite of it. Such a description is a description of things and peoples the mind with opposing forces (there is, for example, the moralists' famous "struggle of reason with the passions"). Furthermore, it does not account for the facts. In reality—the letters of Dostoevsky bear witness to this—there is nothing in us which resembles an inner *debate* as if we had to weigh motives and incentives before deciding. The earlier resolution of "not playing any more" is always *there*, and in the majority of cases the gambler, when in the presence of the gaming table, turns toward it as if to ask it for help; for he does not wish to play, or rather having taken his resolution the day before, he thinks of himself still as not wishing to play anymore; he believes in the effectiveness of this resolution. But what he apprehends then in anguish is precisely the total inefficacy of the past resolution. It is there doubtless but congealed, ineffectual, transcended by the very fact that I am conscious *of* it. The resolution is still *me* to the extent that I realize constantly my identity with myself across the temporal flux, but it is no longer *me*—due to the fact that it has become an object *for* my consciousness. I am not subject to it, it fails in the mission which I have given it. The resolution is there still, I *am* it in the mode of not-being. What the gambler apprehends at this instant is again the permanent rupture with determinism; it is nothingness which separates him from himself; I should have liked so much not to gamble any more; yesterday I even had a synthetic apprehension of the situation (threatening ruin, disappointment of my relatives) as *forbidding me* to play. It seemed to me that I had established a *real barrier* between gambling and myself, and now I suddenly perceive that my former understanding of the situation is no more than a memory of an idea, a memory of a feeling. In order for it to come to my aid once more, I must remake it *ex nihilo* and freely. The not-gambling is only one of my possibilities, as the fact of gambling is another of them, neither more nor less. *I must rediscover* the fear of financial ruin or of disappointing my family, etc., I must re-create it as experienced fear. It stands behind me like a boneless phantom. It depends on me alone to lend it my flesh. I am alone and naked before temptation as I was the day before. After having patiently built up dams and walls, after enclosing myself in the magic circle of a resolution, I perceive with anguish that *nothing* prevents me from gambling. The anguish *is me* since by the very fact of taking my position in existence as consciousness of being, I make myself *not to be* the past of good resolutions *which I am*.

It would be vain to object that the sole condition of this anguish is ignorance of the underlying psychological determinism. According to such a view my anxiety would come from lack of knowing the real and effective incentives which in the darkness of the unconscious determine my action. In reply we shall point out first that anguish has not appeared to us as a *proof* of human freedom; the latter was given to us as the necessary condition for the question. We wished only to show that there exists a specific consciousness of freedom, and we wished to show that this consciousness is anguish. This means that we wished to establish anguish in its essential structure as consciousness of freedom. Now from this point of view the existence of a psychological determinism could not invalidate the results of our description. Either anguish is actually an ignorance (of which we are ignorant) of this determinism—and then anguish apprehends itself in fact as freedom—or else one may claim that anguish is consciousness of being ignorant of the real causes of our acts. In the latter case anguish would come from a presentiment, hidden deep within ourselves, of monstrous motives which would suddenly trigger guilty acts. But in this case we should suddenly appear to ourselves as *things-in-the-world;* we should be to ourselves our own transcendent situation. Then anguish would disappear to give way to *fear,* for fear is a synthetic apprehension of the transcendent as threatening.

This freedom which reveals itself to us in anguish can be characterized by the existence of that *nothing* which insinuates itself between motives and act. It is not *because* I am free that my act is not subject to the determination of motives; on the contrary, the structure of motives as ineffective is the condition of my freedom. If someone asks what this *nothing* is which provides a foundation for freedom, we shall reply that we cannot describe it since it *is not,* but we can at least suggest its meaning by saying that this nothing is made-to-be by the human being in his relation with himself. The nothing here corresponds to the necessity for the motive to appear as motive only as a correlate of a consciousness of motive. In short, as soon as we abandon the hypothesis of the contents of consciousness, we must recognize that there is never a motive *in* consciousness; motives are only *for* consciousness. And due to the very fact that the motive can emerge only as appearance, it constitutes itself as ineffective. Of course it does not have the externality of a temporal-spatial thing; it always belongs to subjectivity and it is apprehended as *mine.* But it is by nature transcendence in immanence, and consciousness escapes it because of the very fact that consciousness posits it; for consciousness has now the task of conferring on the motive its meaning and its importance. Thus the *nothing* which separates the motive from consciousness characterizes itself as transcendence in immanence. It is by producing itself as immanence that consciousness nihilates the nothing which makes consciousness exist for itself as transcendence. But we see that the nothingness which is the condition of all transcendent negation can be elucidated only in terms of two other original nihilations: (1) Consciousness *is not* its own motive inasmuch as it is *empty* of all content. This refers us to a nihilating structure of the pre-reflective *cogito*. (2) Consciousness confronts its past and its future as facing a self which it is in the mode of not-being. This involves a nihilating structure of temporality. . . .

### 3 POSSIBILITY

Freedom, manifesting itself through anguish, is characterized by a constantly renewed obligation to remake the *self* which designates the free being. As a matter of fact, when we showed earlier that my possibilities were agonizing because it depended on *me* alone to sustain them in their existence, that did not mean that they derived from a *Me* which to itself, at least, would first be given and would then pass in the temporal flux from one consciousness to another consciousness. The gambler who must realize anew the synthetic apperception of a *situation* which would forbid him to play, must re-invent at the same time the *self* which can evaluate that situation, which "is in situation." This *self* with its *a priori* and historical content is the essence of man. Anguish as the manifestation of freedom in the face of self means that man is always separated by a nothingness from his essence. We should refer here to Hegel's statement: *"Wesen ist was gewesen ist."* Essence is what has been. Essence is everything in the human being which we can indicate by the words—that is. Due to this fact it is the totality of characteristics which *explain* the act. But the act is always beyond that essence; it is a human act only insofar as it transcends every explanation which we can give of it, precisely because everything about man that can be designated by the formula "that is"—has been. Man continually carries with him a pre-judicative comprehension of his essence, but due to this very fact he is separated from it by a nothingness. Essence is all that human reality apprehends in itself as *having been*. It is here that anguish appears as an apprehension of self insofar as the self exists in the perpetual mode of wrenching away from what is; or rather, insofar as it makes itself exist as such. For we can never apprehend an *Erlebnis* as a living consequence of the *nature* which is ours. The flowing of our consciousness progressively constitutes this nature, but this nature remains always behind us and it dwells in us as the permanent object of our retrospective comprehension. It is insofar as this nature is a requirement without being a recourse that it is apprehended in anguish.

In anguish freedom is anguished before itself inasmuch as it is prompted and hampered by nothing. Someone will say, freedom has just been defined as a permanent structure of the human being; if anguish manifests it, then anguish ought to be a permanent state of my affectivity. But, on the contrary, it is exceptional. How can we explain the rarity of the phenomenon of anguish?

We must note first of all that the most common situations of our life, those in which we apprehend our possibilities as such by actively realizing them, do not manifest themselves to us through anguish, because their very structure excludes anguished apprehension. Anguish in fact is the recognition of a possibility as *my* possibility; that is, it is constituted when consciousness sees itself cut off from its essence by nothingness or separated from the future by its very freedom. This means that a nihilating nothing removes from me all excuse and that at the same time what I project as my future being is always nihilated and reduced to the rank of simple possibility because the future which I am remains out of my reach. But we ought to note that in these various instances we have to do with a temporal form where I await myself in the future, where I "make an appointment with myself on the other side of that hour, of that day, or of that month." Anguish is the fear of not finding myself at that appointment, of no longer even wishing to be there. But I can also find myself engaged in acts which reveal my possibilities to me at the very instant when they are realized. In lighting this cigarette I learn my concrete possibility, or if you prefer, my desire of smoking. It is by the very act of drawing toward me this paper and this pen that I give to myself as my most immediate possibility the act of working at this book; here I am involved, and I discover my involvement at the very moment when I am already throwing myself into it. At that moment, to be sure, it remains my possibility, since I can at each moment turn myself away from my work, push away the notebook, put the cap on my fountain pen. But this possibility of interrupting the action is rejected on a second level by the fact that the action which discovers itself to me through my act tends to crystallize as a transcendent, relatively independent form. The consciousness of man *in action* is non-reflective consciousness. It is consciousness *of* something, and the transcendent which discloses itself to this consciousness is of a particular nature; it is a *structure* of requiredness [*exigence*] in the world, and the world correlatively discloses in this structure complex relations of instrumentality.* In the act of tracing the letters which I am writing, the whole sentence, still unachieved, is revealed as a passive requirement that it be written. It is the very meaning of the letters which I form, and its appeal is not put into question, precisely because I cannot write the words without transcending them toward the sentence and because I discover it as the necessary condition for the meaning of the words which I am writing. At the same time in the very framework of the act a referential complex of instruments reveals itself and organizes itself (pen-ink-paper-lines-margin, etc.), a complex which cannot be apprehended for itself but which emerges at the heart of the transcendence which discloses to me as a passive requirement the sentence to be written. Thus in the quasi-generality of everyday acts, I am involved, I have ventured, and I discover my possibilities by realizing them and in the very act of realizing them as requirements, urgencies, instrumentalities.

Of course in every act of this kind, there remains the possibility of putting this act into question—insofar as it refers to more distant, more essential ends—as its ultimate meanings and my essential possibilities. For example, the sentence which I write is the meaning of the letters which I trace, but the whole work which I wish to produce is the meaning of the sentence. And this work is a possibility with respect to which I can feel anguish; it is truly *my* possibility, and I do not know whether I will continue it tomorrow; tomorrow in relation to it my freedom can exercise its nihilating power. But that anguish implies

* *Cf. Being and Time*, pp. 68f.—Ed.

the apprehension of the work as such as *my* possibility. I must place myself directly opposite it and realize my relation to it. This means that I ought not only to raise with reference to it objective questions such as, "Is it necessary to write this work?" for these questions refer me simply to wider objective significations, such as, "Is it opportune to write it *at this moment*? Isn't this just a repetition of another such book? Is its material of sufficient interest? Has it been sufficiently thought through?" etc.—all significations which remain transcendent and present themselves as a multitude of requirements in the world.

In order for my freedom to be anguished in connection with the book which I am writing, this book must appear in its relation with me. On the one hand, I must discover my essence as *what I have been*—I have been "wanting to write this book," I have conceived it, I have believed that it would be interesting to write it, and I have constituted myself in such a way that it is not possible *to understand me* without taking into account the fact that this book *has been* my essential possibility. On the other hand, I must discover the nothingness which separates my freedom from this essence: *I have been* "wanting to write," but *nothing*, not even what I have been, can compel me to write it. Finally, I must discover the nothingness which separates me from what I shall be: I discover that the permanent possibility of abandoning the book is the very condition of the possibility of writing it and the very meaning of my freedom. It is necessary that in the very constitution of the book as my possibility, I apprehend my freedom as being the possible destroyer in the present and in the future of what I am. That is, I must place myself on the plane of reflection. So long as I remain on the plane of action, the book to be written is only the distant and presupposed meaning of the act which reveals my possibilities to me. The book is only the implication of the action; it is not made an object and posited for itself; it does not "raise the question"; it is conceived neither as necessary nor contingent. It is only the pemanent, remote meaning in terms of which I can understand what I am writing in the present, and hence, it is conceived as *being;* that is, only by positing the book as *the existing basis* on which my present, existing sentence emerges, can I confer a determined meaning upon my sentence.

Now at each moment we are thrust into the world and involved there. This means that we act before positing our possibilities and that these possibilities, which are disclosed as realized or in process of being realized, refer to meanings which can only be put into question by special acts. The alarm which rings in the morning refers to the possibility of my going to work, which is *my* possibility. But to apprehend the summons of the alarm as a summons is to get up. Therefore the very act of getting up is reassuring, for it eludes the question, "Is work *my* possibility?" Consequently it does not put me in a position to apprehend the possibility of quietism, of refusing to work, and ultimately the possibility of refusing the world and the possibility of death. In short, to the extent that I apprehend the meaning of the ringing, I am already up at its summons; this apprehension guarantees me against the anguished intuition that it is I who confer on the alarm its requiredness—I and I alone.

In the same way, what we might call everyday morality excludes ethical anguish. There is ethical anguish when I consider myself in my original relation to values. Values actually are requirements which demand a foundation. But this foundation can in no way be *being*, for every value which would found its ideal nature on its being would thereby cease even to be a value and would realize the heteronomy of my will. Value derives its being from its requiredness and not its requiredness from its being. It does not offer itself to a contemplative intuition which would apprehend it as *being* value and thereby would remove from it its right over my freedom. On the contrary, it can be revealed only to an active freedom which makes it exist as value by the sole fact of recognizing it as such. It follows that my freedom is the unique foundation of values and that *nothing*, absolutely nothing, justifies me in adopting this or that particular value, this or that particular scale of values. As a being by whom values exist, I am unjustifiable. My freedom is anguished at being the foundation of values while itself without foundation. It is anguished in addition because values, due to the fact that they are essentially revealed to a freedom, cannot disclose themselves without being at the same time "put into question," for the possibility of overturning the scale of values appears complementarily as *my* possibility. Anguish before values is the recognition of the ideality of values.

Ordinarily, however, my attitude with respect to values is eminently reassuring. In fact I am involved in a world of values.

The anguished apperception of values as sustained in being by my freedom is a secondary and mediated phenomenon. The immediate is the world with its urgency; and in this world where I engage myself, my acts make values spring up like partridges. My indignation has given to me the anti-value "baseness," my admiration has given the positive value "greatness." Above all my obedience, which is real, to a multitude of tabus reveals these tabus to me as existing in fact. The bourgeois who call themselves "respectable citizens" do not become respectable as the result of contemplating moral values. Rather from the moment of their emerging in the world they are thrown into a pattern of behavior the meaning of which is respectability. Thus respectability acquires a being; it is not put into question. Values are sown on my path as thousands of little real requirements, like the signs which order us to keep off the grass.

Thus in what we shall call the world of the immediate, which presents itself to our unreflective consciousness, we do not first appear to ourselves, to be later thrown into undertakings. Our being is immediately "in situation"; that is, it arises in undertakings and knows itself first insofar as it is reflected in those undertakings. We discover ourselves then in a world peopled with requirements, in the heart of projects "in the course of realization." I write. I am going to smoke. I have an appointment this evening with Peter. I must not forget to reply to Simon. I do not have the right to conceal the truth any longer from Claude. All these trivial passive expectations of the real, all these commonplace, everyday values, derive their meaning from an original projection of myself which is my choice of myself in the world. But to be exact, this projection of myself toward an original possibility, which brings into existence values, appeals, expectations, and in general a world, appears to me only beyond the world as the meaning and the abstract, logical signification of my undertakings. Furthermore, there exist concretely alarm clocks, signs, tax forms, policemen—so many guardrails against anguish. But as soon as the undertaking is held at a distance from me, as soon as I am referred to myself because I must await myself in the future, then I discover myself suddenly as the one who gives its meaning to the alarm clock, the one who by a sign forbids himself to walk on a flower bed or on the lawn, the one from whom the boss's order borrows its urgency, the one who decides the interest of the book which he is writing, the one finally who makes the values exist in order to determine his action by their requirements. I emerge alone and in anguish, confronting the unique and original project which constitutes my being; all the barriers, all the guardrails collapse, nihilated by the consciousness of my freedom. I do not have nor can I have recourse to any value against the fact that it is I who sustain values in being. Nothing can ensure me against myself, cut off from the world and from my essence by this nothingness which I *am*. I have to realize the meaning of the world and of my essence; I make my decision concerning them—without justification and without excuse.

Anguish then is the reflective apprehension of freedom by itself. In this sense it is mediation, for although it is immediate consciousness of itself, it arises from the negation of the appeals of the world. It appears at the moment that I disengage myself from the world where I had been involved—in order to apprehend myself as a consciousness which possesses a preontological comprehension of its essence and pre-judicative sense of its possibilities. Anguish is opposed to the spirit of seriousness which apprehends values starting from the world, and which rests in the reassuring, substantiation of values as things. In this spirit I define myself starting from the object by leaving aside *a priori* as impossible all undertakings in which I am not involved at the moment; the meaning which my freedom has given to the world, I apprehend as coming from the world and constituting my obligations. In anguish I apprehend myself at once as totally free and as not being able to derive the meaning of the world except as coming from myself.

#### 4 FLIGHT

We should not however conclude that being brought up to the reflective level and envisaging one's distant or immediate possibilities suffice to apprehend oneself in *pure* anguish. In each instance of reflection anguish emerges as a structure of the reflective consciousness insofar as the latter considers consciousness as an object of reflection; but it still remains possible for me to maintain various modes of behavior with respect to my own anguish—in particular, modes of flight.* Everything takes place, in fact, as if our essential and immediate behavior with

* Cf. *Being and Time*, p. 184.—Ed.

respect to anguish is flight. Psychological determinism, before being a theoretical conception, is first an attitude of excuse, or if you prefer, the basis of all attitudes of excuse. It is reflective conduct with respect to anguish; it asserts that there are within us antagonistic forces whose type of existence is comparable to that of things. It attempts to fill the void which encircles us, to re-establish the links between past and present, between present and future. It provides us with a *nature* productive of our acts, and these very acts it makes transcendent; it assigns to them a foundation in something other than themselves by endowing them with an inertia and externality eminently reassuring because they constitute a permanent game of *excuses*. Psychological determinism denies that transcendence of human reality which makes it emerge in anguish beyond its own essence. At the same time by reducing us to *never being anything but what we are*, it re-introduces in us the absolute positivity of being-in-itself and thereby reinstates us at the heart of being.

But this determinism, a reflective defense against anguish, is not given as a reflective *intuition*. It avails nothing against the *evidence* of freedom; hence it is given as a faith to take refuge in, as the ideal end toward which we can flee to escape anguish. That is made evident on the philosophical plane by the fact that deterministic psychologists do not claim to found their thesis on the pure givens of introspection. They present it as a satisfactory hypothesis, the value of which comes from the fact that it accounts for the facts—or as a necessary postulate for establishing all psychology. They admit the existence of an immediate consciousness of freedom, which their opponents uphold against them under the name of "proof by intuition of the inner sense." They merely focus the debate on the *value* of this inner revelation. Thus the intuition which makes us apprehend ourselves as the original cause of our states and our acts has been discussed by nobody. It is within the reach of each of us to try to mediate anguish by rising above it and *judging* it as an illusion due to the mistaken belief that we are the real causes of our acts. The problem which presents itself then is that of the degree of faith in this mediation. Is anguish disarmed by being judged? Obviously not. However here a new phenomenon emerges, a process of "distraction" in relation to anguish which, once again, supposes within it a nihilating power.

By itself determinism would not suffice to establish distraction since determinism is only a postulate or an hypothesis. This process of distraction is a more complete activity of flight which operates on the very level of reflection. It is first an attempt at distraction in relation to the possibles opposed to *my* possible. When I constitute myself as the comprehension of a possible as *my* possible, I must recognize its existence at the end of my project and apprehend it as myself, waiting for me over there in the future and separated from me by a nothingness. In this sense I apprehend myself as the original source of my possibility, and it is this which ordinarily we call the consciousness of freedom. It is this structure of consciousness and this alone that the proponents of free-will have in mind when they speak of the intuition of the inner sense. But it happens that I force myself at the same time to *be distracted* from the constitution of other possibilities which contradict *my* possibility. In truth I cannot avoid positing their existence by the same movement which generates the chosen possibility as mine. I cannot help constituting them as *living* possibilities; that is, as *having the possibility of becoming my possibilities*. But I force myself to see them as endowed with a transcendent, purely logical being, in short, as things. If on the reflective level I envisage the possibility of writing this book as *my* possibility, then between this possibility and my consciousness I introduce a nothingness of being which constitutes the writing of the book as a possibility and which I apprehend precisely in the permanent possibility that the possibility of not writing the book is *my* possibility. But I attempt to place myself on the other side of the possibility of not writing it as I might do with respect to an observable object, and I let myself be penetrated with what I wish to see there; I try to apprehend the possibility of not writing as needing to be mentioned merely as a reminder, as something which does not concern me. It must be an external possibility in relation to me, like movement in relation to the motionless billiard ball. If I could succeed in this, the possibilities hostile to *my* possibility would be constituted as logical entities and would lose their effectiveness. They would no longer be threatening since they would be "outsiders," since they would surround my possible as purely *conceivable* eventualities; that is, fundamentally, conceivable *by* another or as *possibles of another who might find himself in the same situation*. They would belong to the objective situation as a transcendent structure, or if you prefer (to utilize

Heidegger's terminology)—*I* shall write this book but *one* could also not write it. Thus I should hide from myself the fact that the possibles are *myself* and that they are immanent conditions of the possibility of my possible. They would preserve just enough being to preserve for my possible its character as gratuitous, as a free possibility for a free being, but they would be disarmed of their threatening character. They would not *interest* me; the chosen possible would appear—as a result of its having been chosen—as my only concrete possible, and consequently the nothingness which separates me from it and which actually confers on it its possibility would be filled up.

But flight before anguish is not only an effort at distraction before the future; it attempts also to disarm the past of its threat. What I attempt to flee here is my very transcendence insofar as it sustains and transcends my essence. I assert that I *am* my essence in the mode of being of the in-itself. At the same time I always refuse to consider that essence as being historically constituted and as implying my action as a circle implies its properties. I apprehend it, or at least I try to apprehend it as the original beginning of my possible, and I do not admit at all that it has in itself a beginning. I assert then that an act is free when it exactly reflects my essence. However this freedom which would disturb me if it confronted me, I attempt to bring back to the heart of my essence—*i.e.*, of my self. It is a matter of envisaging the self as a little God which inhabits me and which possesses my freedom as a metaphysical faculty. It would be no longer my being which would be free *qua* being but my self which would be free in the heart of my consciousness. It is a fiction eminently reassuring since freedom has been thrust down into the heart of an opaque being; to the extent that my essence is not translucency, that it is transcendent in immanence, freedom would become one of its properties. In short, it is a matter of apprehending my freedom in my self as the freedom of another.* We see the principal themes of this fiction: My self becomes the origin of its acts, as the Other is of his, by virtue of a personality already constituted. To be sure, he (myself) lives and transforms himself; we will admit even that each of his acts can contribute to transforming him. But these harmonious, continued transformations are conceived as if they were biological. They resemble those which I can observe in my friend Peter when I see him after a separa-

* See below, p. 200.—Ed.

tion. Bergson expressly satisfied these demands for reassurance when he conceived his theory of the profound self which endures and organizes itself, which is constantly contemporary with the consciousness which I have of it and which cannot be transcended by consciousness, which is found at the origin of my acts not as a cataclysmic power but as a father begets his children, in such a way that the act without following from the essence as a strict consequence, without even being foreseeable, enters into a reassuring relation with it, a family resemblance. The act goes farther than the self but along the same road; it preserves, to be sure, a certain irreducibility, but we recognize ourselves in it, and we find ourselves in it as a father can recognize himself and find himself in the son who continues his work. Thus by a projection of freedom—which we apprehend in ourselves—into a psychic object which is the self, Bergson has helped disguise our anguish, but it is at the expense of consciousness itself. What he has established and described in this manner is not our freedom as it appears to itself; *it is the freedom of the Other*.

Such then is the set of processes by which we try to hide anguish from ourselves; we apprehend our particular possible by avoiding considering all other possibles, which we make the possibles of an undifferentiated Other. The chosen possible we do not wish to see as sustained in being by a pure nihilating freedom, and so we attempt to apprehend it as engendered by an object already constituted, which is no other than our self, envisaged and described as if it were another person. We should like to preserve from the original intuition what it reveals to us as our independence and our responsibility but we tone down all the original nihilation in it; moreover we are always ready to take refuge in a belief in determinism if this freedom weighs upon us or if we need an excuse. Thus we flee from anguish by attempting to apprehend ourselves from without as an Other or as *a thing*. What we are accustomed to call a revelation of the inner sense or an original intuition of our freedom contains nothing original; it is an already constructed process, expressly designed to hide from ourselves anguish, the veritable immediate "given" of our freedom.

Do these various constructions succeed in stifling or hiding our anguish? It is certain that we cannot overcome anguish, for we *are* anguish. As for veiling it, aside from the fact that the very nature of consciousness and its translucency forbid us to take the expression literally, we must note the particular type of behavior which it indicates. We can hide an external object because it exists independently of us. For the same reason we can turn our look or our attention away from it—that is, very simply, fix our eyes on some other object; henceforth each reality—mine and that of the object—resumes its own life, and the accidental relation which united consciousness to the thing disappears without thereby altering either existence. But if I *am* what I wish to veil, the question takes on quite another aspect. I can in fact wish "not to see" a certain aspect of my being only if I am aware of the aspect which I do not wish to see. This means that in my being I must refer to this aspect in order to be able to turn myself away from it; or rather, I must think of it constantly in order to take care not to think of it. In this connection it must be understood not only that I must of necessity perpetually carry within me what I wish to flee, but also that I must aim at the object of my flight in order to flee it. This means that anguish, the intentional aim of anguish, and a flight from anguish toward reassuring myths must all be given in the unity of the same consciousness. In a word, I flee in order not to know, but I cannot avoid knowing that I am fleeing; and the flight from anguish is only a mode of becoming conscious of anguish. Thus anguish, properly speaking, can be neither hidden nor avoided.

Yet to flee anguish and to be anguish cannot be exactly the same thing. The fact that I am my anguish in order to flee it presupposes that I can decenter myself in relation to what I am, that I can be anguish in the form of "not-being it," that I can dispose of a nihilating power at the heart of anguish itself. This nihilating power nihilates anguish insofar as I flee it and nihilates itself insofar as *I am anguish in order to flee it*. This attitude is what we call *bad faith*. There is then no question of expelling anguish from consciousness nor of constituting it as an unconscious psychic phenomenon; very simply I can make myself guilty of bad faith while apprehending the anguish which I am, and this bad faith, intended to fill up the nothingness which I *am* in my relation to myself, precisely implies the nothingness which it suppresses.

We are now at the end of our first description. The examination of the negation cannot lead us farther. It has revealed to us the existence of a particular type of conduct: conduct in the face of non-being, which supposes a special transcendence needing separate study. We find ourselves then in the presence of two human *ekstases:** the *ekstasis* which throws us into being-in-itself and the *ekstasis* which involves us in non-being. It seems that our original problem, which concerned only the relations of man to being, is now considerably complicated. But in pushing to its conclusion our analysis of transcendence toward non-being, it is possible for us to get valuable information for the understanding of *all* transcendence. Furthermore the problem of nothingness cannot be excluded from our inquiry. If man adopts any particular behavior in the face of being-in-itself—and our philosophical question is a type of such behavior—it is because he *is not* this being. We rediscover non-being as a condition of the transcendence toward being. We must then get hold of the problem of nothingness and not let it go before its complete elucidation.

However the examination of the question and of the negation has given us all that it can. We have been referred by it to empirical freedom as the nihilation of man in the heart of temporality and as the necessary condition for the transcending apprehension of negations. It remains to found this empirical freedom. It cannot be both the original nihilation and the ground of all nihilation. Actually it contributes to constituting transcendences in immanence which condition all negative transcendences. But the very fact that the transcendences of empirical freedom are constituted in immanence as *transcendences* shows us that we are dealing with secondary nihilations which suppose the existence of an original nothingness. They are only a stage in the analytical regression which leads us from the examples of transcendence called "negations" to the being which is its own nothingness. Obviously it is necessary to find the foundation of all negation in a nihilation which is exercised *in the very heart of immanence;* in absolute immanence, in the pure subjectivity of the instantaneous *cogito* we must discover the original act by which man is to himself his own nothingness. What must be consciousness in its being, for man as consciousness to emerge in the world as the being who is his own nothingness and by whom nothingness comes into the world?

We seem to lack here the instrument to permit us to resolve this new problem; negation directly involves only freedom. We

* *Cf. Being and Time,* p. 329.—Ed.

must find in freedom itself the mode of behavior which will permit us to push further. Now this mode of behavior, which will lead us to the threshold of immanence and which remains still sufficiently objective so that we can objectively disengage its conditions of possibility—this we have already encountered. Have we not remarked earlier that in bad faith, we are-anguish-in-order-to-flee-anguish within the unity of a single consciousness? If bad faith is to be possible, we should be able within the same consciousness to meet with the unity of being and non-being—the being-in-order-not-to-be. Bad faith is going to be the next object of our investigation. For man to be able to question, he must be capable of being his own nothingness; that is, he can be at the origin of non-being in being only if his being—in himself and by himself—is transfixed with nothingness. Thus the transcendences of past and future appear in the temporal being of human reality. But bad faith is instantaneous. What then are we to say that consciousness must be in the instantaneity of the pre-reflective *cogito*—if the human being is to be capable of bad faith?

*Being and Nothingness*, 3–5, 7, 9–12,
23, 25–45.

# III

———•———

*Self-Negation*

## 1  BAD FAITH

The human being is not only the being by whom negations are
disclosed in the world; he is also the being who can take negative
attitudes toward himself. In our introduction we defined consciousness as "a being such that in its being, its being is in question insofar as this being implies a being other than itself." But
now that we have examined questioning behavior we can also
write the formula thus: "Consciousness is a being, the nature of
which is to be conscious of the nothingness of its being." In a
prohibition or a veto, for example, the human being denies a future transcendence. But this negation is not a matter of observation. My consciousness is not restricted to envisaging a negation. It constitutes itself in its own flesh as the nihilation of a
possibility which another human reality projects as its possibility. For that reason it must arise in the world as a *No:* it is as a
No that the slave first apprehends the master, or that the prisoner
who is trying to escape sees the guard who is watching him.
There are even men (*e.g.*, caretakers, overseers, jailers), whose
social reality is entirely that of the No, who will live and die,
having forever been only a No upon the earth. Others so as to
make the No a part of their very subjectivity, establish their human personality as a perpetual negation. This is the meaning
and function of what Scheler calls "the man of resentment"—
the man who is a No. But there are subtler modes of behavior, the
description of which will lead us further into the inwardness of
consciousness. Irony is one of these. In irony a man nihilates
what he posits within one and the same act; he leads us to believe
in order not to be believed; he affirms to deny and denies to affirm; he creates a positive object but it has no being other than
its nothingness. Thus attitudes of negation toward the self per-

mit us to raise a new question: What are we to say is the being of man who has the possibility of denying himself? But it is out of the question to discuss the attitude of "self-negation" generally. The kinds of behavior which can be ranked under this heading are too diverse, we risk retaining only the abstract form of them. It is best to choose and to examine one specific attitude which is essential to human reality and which is such that consciousness instead of directing its negation outward turns it toward itself. This attitude, it seems to me, is *bad faith* [*mauvaise foi*].

Frequently this is identified with falsehood. We say indifferently of a person that he is guilty of bad faith or that he lies to himself. We shall willingly grant that bad faith is a lie to oneself, on condition that we distinguish the lie to oneself from lying in general. Lying is a negative attitude, anyone will agree. But this negation does not bear on consciousness itself; it aims only at the transcendent. The essence of the lie implies in fact that the liar actually is in complete possession of the truth which he is hiding. A man does not lie about what he is ignorant of; he does not lie when he spreads an error of which he himself is the dupe; he does not lie when he is mistaken. The ideal case of the liar would be a cynical consciousness, affirming truth within himself, denying it in his words, and denying the denial to himself. Now this doubly negative attitude refers to the transcendent; the fact expressed is transcendent since it does not exist, and the original negation refers to a *truth;* that is, to a particular type of transcendence. As for the inner negation which I effect correlatively with the affirmation for myself of the truth, this refers to words; that is, to an event in the world. Furthermore the inner disposition of the liar is positive; it could be the object of an affirmative judgment. The liar intends to deceive and he does not seek to hide this intention from himself nor to disguise the translucency of consciousness; on the contrary, he has recourse to it when there is a question of deciding secondary behavior. It explicitly exercises a regulatory control over all attitudes. As for his flaunted intention of telling the truth ("I'd never want to deceive you! This it true! I swear it!")—all this, of course, is the object of an inner negation, but also it is not recognized by the liar as his intention. It is played, impersonated, it is the intention of the character which he plays in the eyes of his questioner, but this character, precisely because he *does not exist,* is a transcendent. Thus the lie does not involve the inner structure of present consciousness; all the negations which constitute it refer to objects which as such are removed from consciousness. The lie then does not require special ontological foundation, and the explanations which the existence of negation in general requires hold without alteration in the case of deceit. Of course we have described the ideal lie; doubtless it happens often enough that the liar is more or less the victim of his lie, that he half persuades himself of it. But these common popular forms of the lie are also degenerate aspects of it; they represent intermediaries between falsehood and bad faith. The lie is a behavior of transcendence.

The lie is also a normal phenomenon of what Heidegger calls the *"Mit-sein."* * It presupposes my existence, the existence of the *Other,* my existence *for* the Other, and the existence of the Other *for* me. Thus there is no difficulty in holding that the liar must make the project of the lie in entire clarity and that he must possess a complete comprehension of the lie and of the truth which he is altering. It is sufficient that an overall opacity hide his intentions from the *Other;* it is sufficient that the Other can take the lie for truth. By the lie consciousness affirms that it exists by nature as *hidden from the Other;* it utilizes for its own profit the ontological duality of myself and myself in the eyes of the Other.

The situation cannot be the same for bad faith if this, as we have said, is indeed a lie to oneself. To be sure, the one who practices bad faith is hiding a displeasing truth or presenting as truth a pleasing untruth. Bad faith then has in appearance the structure of falsehood. Only what changes everything is the fact that in bad faith it is from myself that I am hiding the truth. Thus the duality of the deceiver and the deceived does not exist here. Bad faith on the contrary implies in essence the unity of a *single* consciousness. This does not mean that it cannot be conditioned by the *Mit-sein* like all other phenomena of human reality, but the *Mit-sein* can only solicit bad faith by presenting itself as a *situation* which bad faith permits transcending; bad faith does not come from outside to human reality. One does not undergo his bad faith; one is not infected with it; it is not a *state.* But consciousness affects itself with bad faith. There must be an original intention and a project of bad faith; this project implies a comprehension of bad faith as such and a pre-reflective appre-

* A "being-with" others in the world.—Trans.

hension (of) consciousness as affecting itself with bad faith. It follows first that the one to whom the lie is told and the one who lies are one and the same person, which means that I must know in my capacity as deceiver the truth which is hidden from me in my capacity as the one deceived. Or rather, I must know what the truth is exactly *in order* to conceal it more carefully—and this not at two different moments, which at a pinch would allow us to re-establish a semblance of duality—but in the unitary structure of a single project. How then can the lie subsist if the duality which conditions it is suppressed?

To this difficulty is added another which is derived from the total translucency of consciousness. That which affects itself with bad faith must be conscious (of) its bad faith since the being of consciousness is consciousness of being. It appears then that I must be in good faith, at least to the extent that I am conscious of my bad faith. But then this whole psychic system is annihilated. We must agree in fact that if I deliberately and cynically attempt to lie to myself, I fail completely in this undertaking; the lie falls back and collapses under my look; it is ruined *from behind* by the very consciousness of lying to myself which pitilessly constitutes itself within my project as its very condition. We have here an *evanescent* phenomenon which exists only in and through its own differentiation. To be sure, these phenomena are frequent and we shall see that there is in fact an "evanescence" of bad faith, which, it is obvious, vacillates continually between good faith and cynicism: Even though the existence of bad faith is very precarious, and though it belongs to the kind of psychic structures which we might call "metastable," * it presents nonetheless an autonomous and durable form. It can even be the normal aspect of life for a very great number of people. A person can *live* in bad faith, which does not mean that he does not have abrupt awakenings to cynicism or to good faith, but which implies a constant and particular style of life. Our embarrassment then appears extreme since we can neither reject nor comprehend bad faith.

## 2 THE UNCONSCIOUS

To escape from these difficulties some have recourse to the unconscious. In the psychoanalytical interpretation, for example,

* Sartre's own word, meaning subject to sudden changes or transitions.—Trans.

they use the hypothesis of a censor, conceived as a line of de-marcation with customs, passport division, currency control, etc., to re-establish the duality of the deceiver and the deceived. Here instinct or, if you prefer, original drives and complexes of drives constituted by our individual history, make up *reality*. An instinct is neither *true* nor *false* since it does not *exist for it-self*. It simply *is*, exactly like this table, which is neither true nor false in *itself* but simply *real*. As for the conscious symbols of the instinct, this interpretation takes them not for appearances but for real psychic facts. Fear, lapses of memory, dreams really exist as concrete facts of consciousness in the same way as the words and the attitudes of the liar are concrete, really existing patterns of behavior. The subject has the same relation to these phenomena as the deceived to the behavior of the deceiver. He observes them in their reality and must interpret them. There is a *truth* in the activities of the deceiver; if the deceived could re-attach them to the situation which the deceiver is in and to his project of the lie, they would become integral parts of truth, by virtue of being lying behavior. Similarly there is a truth in the symbolic acts; it is what the psychoanalyst discovers when he re-attaches them to the historical situation of the patient, to the unconscious complexes which they express, to the blocking of the censor. Thus the subject deceives himself about the *mean-ing* of his behavior, he apprehends it in its concrete existence but not in its *truth*, simply because he cannot derive it from an original situation and from a psychic constitution which remain alien to him.

By the distinction between the "id" and the "ego," Freud has cut the psychic whole into two. I *am* the ego but I *am not* the id. I hold no privileged position in relation to my unconscious psyche. I *am* my own psychic phenomena insofar as I observe them in their conscious reality. For example I am the impulse to steal this or that book from this bookstall. I co-operate with the im-puse; I clarify it, and I decide in terms of it to commit the theft. But I *am* not those psychic facts, insofar as I receive them pas-sively and am obliged to resort to hypotheses about their origin and their true meaning, just as the scientist makes conjectures about the nature and essence of an external phenomenon. This theft, for example, which I interpret as an immediate impulse determined by the rarity, the interest, or the price of the vol-ume which I am going to steal—it is in truth a process derived from self-punishment, which is attached more or less directly to an Oedipus complex. The impulse toward the theft contains a truth which can be reached only by more or less probable hypotheses. The criterion of this truth will be the number of conscious psychic facts which it explains; from a more pragmatic point of view it will be also the success of the psychiatric cure which it allows. Finally the discovery of this truth will necessitate the co-operation of the psychoanalyst, who appears as the *mediator* between my unconscious drives and my conscious life. The Other appears as being able to effect the synthesis between the unconscious thesis and the conscious antithesis. I can know myself only through the mediation of the other, which means that I am in relation to *my* "id," in the position of the *Other*. If I have a little knowledge of psychoanalysis, I can, under circumstances particularly favorable, try to psychoanalyze myself. But this attempt can succeed only if I distrust every kind of intuition, only if I apply to my case *from the outside*, abstract schemes and rules already learned. As for the results, whether they are obtained by my efforts alone or with the co-operation of a professional psychoanalyist, they will never have the certainty which intuition confers; they will possess simply the always increasing probability of scientific hypotheses. The hypothesis of the Oedipus complex, like the atomic theory, is nothing but an "experimental idea"; as Peirce said, it is not to be distinguished from the set of experiments which it allows to be performed and the results which it enables us to predict. Thus psychoanalysis substitutes for the notion of bad faith, the idea of a lie without a liar; it allows me to understand how it is possible for me to be lied to without lying to myself since it places me in the same relation to myself that the Other is in respect to me; it replaces the duality of the deceiver and the deceived, the essential condition of the lie, by that of the "id" and the "ego." It introduces into my subjectivity the deepest intersubjective structure of the *Mitsein*. Can this explanation satisfy us?

Considered more closely the psychoanalytic theory is not as simple as it first appears. It is not accurate to hold that the "id" is presented as a thing in relation to the hypothesis of the psychoanalyst, for a thing is indifferent to the conjectures which we make concerning it, while the "id" in contrast is sensitive to them when we approach the truth. Freud in fact reports resistance when at the end of the first period the doctor is approaching the truth. This resistance is objective behavior apprehended from without: the patient shows defiance, refuses to speak, gives fantastic accounts of his dreams, sometimes even removes himself completely from the psychoanalytic treatment. It is a fair question to ask what part of himself can thus resist. It cannot be the "ego," envisaged as a psychic totality of the facts of consciousness; this could not suspect that the psychiatrist is approaching the goal since the ego's relation to the *meaning* of its own reactions is exactly like that of the psychiatrist himself. At the very most it is possible for the ego to appreciate objectively the degree of probability in the hypotheses set forth, as a witness of the psychoanalysis might be able to do, according to the number of subjective facts which they explain. Furthermore, this probability would appear to the ego to border on certainty, which he could not take offense at, since most of the time it is the ego who is committed by a *conscious* decision to the psychoanalytic therapy. Are we to say that the patient is disturbed by the daily revelations which the psychoanalyst makes to him and that he seeks to remove himself, at the same time pretending in his own eyes to wish to continue the treatment? In this case it is no longer possible to resort to the unconscious to explain bad faith; it is there in full consciousness, with all its contradictions. But this is not the way that the psychoanalyst means to explain this resistance; for him it is secret and deep, it comes from afar; it has its roots in the very thing which the psychoanalyst is trying to make clear.

Furthermore it is equally impossible to explain the resistance as emanating from the complex which the psychoanalyst wishes to bring to light. The complex as such is rather the collaborator of the psychoanalyst since it aims at expressing itself in clear consciousness, since it plays tricks on the censor and seeks to elude it. The only level on which we can locate the refusal of the subject is that of the censor. It alone can comprehend the questions or the revelations of the psychoanalyst as approaching more or less near to the real drives which it strives to repress—it alone because it alone *knows* what it is repressing.

If we reject the language and the materialistic mythology of psychoanalysis, we perceive that the censor in order to apply its activity with discernment must know what it is repressing. In fact if we abandon all the metaphors representing the repression as the impact of blind forces, we have to admit that the censor must choose and in order to choose must be aware of so doing. How could it happen otherwise that the censor allows licit sexual impulses to pass through, that it permits needs (hunger, thirst, sleep) to be expressed in clear consciousness? And how are we to explain that it can relax its surveillance, that it can even be deceived by the disguises of the instinct? But it is not sufficient that it discern the condemned drives; it must also apprehend them *as to be repressed*, which implies in it at the very least an awareness of its activity. In a word, how could the censor discern the impulses needing to be repressed without being conscious of discerning them? How can we conceive of a knowledge which is ignorant of itself? To know is to know that one knows, said Alain. Let us say rather: All knowing is consciousness of knowing. Thus the resistance of the patient implies on the level of the censor an awareness of the thing repressed as such, a comprehension of the goal toward which the questions of the psychoanalyst are leading, and an act of synthetic connection by which it compares the *truth* of the repressed complex to the psychoanalytic hypothesis which aims at it. These various operations in their turn imply that the censor is conscious (of) itself. But what type of self-consciousness can the censor have? It must be the consciousness (of) being conscious of the drive to be repressed, but precisely *in order not to be conscious of it*. What does this mean if not that the censor is in bad faith?

Psychoanalysis has not gained anything for us since in order to overcome bad faith, it has established between the unconscious and consciousness an autonomous consciousness in bad faith. The effort to establish a veritable duality, and even a trinity (*Es, Ich,* and *Überich* expressing itself through the censor) has resulted in a mere verbal terminology. The very essence of the reflexive idea of hiding something from oneself implies the unity of one and the same psychic structure and consequently a double activity within unity, tending on the one hand to maintain and locate the thing to be concealed and on the other hand to repress and disguise it. Each of the two aspects of this activity is complementary to the other; that is, it implies the other in its being. By separating consciousness from the unconscious by means of the censor, psychoanalysis has not succeeded in dissociating the two phases of the act, since the libido is a blind conatus toward conscious expression and since the conscious phenomenon is a passive, doctored result. Psychoanalysis has merely localized this double activity of repulsion and attraction on the level of the censor.

Furthermore the problem still remains of accounting for the unity of the total phenomenon (repression of the drive which disguises itself and passes over into symbolic form), of establishing comprehensible connections among its different phases. How can the repressed drive "disguise itself" if it does not include (1) the consciousness of being repressed, (2) the consciousness of having been repressed because it is what it is, (3) a project of disguise? No mechanistic theory of condensation or of transference can explain these modifications by which the drive itself is affected, for the description of the process of disguise implies a veiled appeal to finality. And similarly how are we to account for the pleasure or the anguish which accompanies the symbolic and conscious satisfaction of the drive if consciousness does not include—beyond the censor—an obscure comprehension of the goal to be attained as simultaneously desired and forbidden. By rejecting the conscious unity of the psyche, Freud is obliged to imply everywhere a magic unity linking distant phenomena across obstacles, just as sympathetic magic unites the bewitched person and the wax image fashioned in his likeness. The unconscious drive (*Trieb*) through magic is endowed with the character "repressed" or "condemned," which completely pervades it, colors it, and magically provokes its symbolism. Similarly the conscious phenomenon is entirely colored by its symbolic meaning although it cannot apprehend this meaning by itself in clear consciousness.

Aside from its inferiority in principle, the explanation by magic does not avoid the coexistence—on the level of the unconscious, on that of the censor, and on that of consciousness—of two contradictory, complementary structures which reciprocally imply and destroy each other. Proponents of the theory have hypostasized and "reified" bad faith; they have not escaped it. This is what has inspired a Viennese psychiatrist, Steckel, to depart from the psychoanalytical tradition and to write in *The Frigid Woman*: "Every time that I have been able to carry my investigations far enough, I have established that the core of the psychosis was conscious." Moreover the cases which he reports in his work bear witness to a pathological bad faith which the Freudian doctrine cannot account for. There is the question, for example, of women whom marital disappointment has made frigid; that is, they succeed in hiding from themselves, not complexes deeply sunk in half physiological darkness, but modes of behavior which are objectively discoverable, which they cannot fail to recognize at the moment they perform them. Frequently in fact the husband reveals to Steckel that his wife has given objective signs of pleasure, but the woman when questioned will fiercely deny them. Here we find a pattern of *distraction*. Admissions which Steckel was able to draw out inform us that these pathologically frigid women apply themselves to becoming distracted in advance from the pleasure which they dread; many for example at the time of the sexual act, turn their thoughts away toward their daily occupations, make up their household accounts. Will anyone speak of an unconscious here? Yet if the frigid woman thus distracts her consciousness from the pleasure which she experiences, it is by no means cynically and in full agreement with herself; *it is in order to prove to herself* that she is frigid. We have in fact to deal with a phenomenon of bad faith since the efforts taken in order not to be present to the experienced pleasure imply the recognition that the pleasure is experienced; they imply it *in order to deny it*. But we are no longer on the ground of psychoanalysis. Thus on the one hand the explanation by means of the unconscious, due to the fact that it breaks the psychic unity, cannot account for the facts which at first sight it appeared to explain. And on the other hand, there exists an infinite number of types of behavior in bad faith which explicitly rebuff this kind of explanation because their essence implies that they can appear only in the translucency of consciousness. We find that the problem which we had attempted to resolve is still untouched.

### 3 PLAY-ACTING

If we wish to get out of our difficulties, we should examine more closely the patterns of bad faith and attempt a description of them. This description will permit us perhaps to define more precisely the conditions under which bad faith is possible; that is, to reply to the question we raised at the outset: "What must be the being of man if he is to be capable of bad faith?"

Take the example of a young woman who has consented to go out with a particular man for the first time. She knows very well the intentions which the man who is speaking to her cherishes regarding her. She knows also that it will be necessary sooner or later for her to make a decision. But she does not want to feel the urgency; she concerns herself only with what is respectful and discreet in the attitude of her companion. She does not apprehend this conduct as an attempt to make what we call "the first advances"; that is, she does not want to see possibilities of temporal development which his conduct presents. She restricts this behavior to what is in the present; she does not wish to read in the phrases which he addresses to her anything other than their explicit meaning. If he says to her, "I find you so attractive!" she disarms this phrase of its sexual implications; she attaches to the conversation and to the behavior of the speaker the immediate meanings which she imagines as objective qualities. The man who is speaking to her appears to her sincere and respectful as the table is round or square, as the wall coloring is blue or gray. The qualities thus attached to the person she is listening to are in this way congealed in a permanence like that of things, which is no other than the projection of the strict present of the qualities into the temporal flux. This is because she does not quite know what she wants. She is profoundly aware of the desire which she inspires, but the desire cruel and naked would humiliate and horrify her. Yet she would find no charm in a respect which would be only respect. In order to satisfy her, there must be a feeling which is addressed wholly to her *personality*—i.e., to her full freedom—and which would be a recognition of her freedom. But at the same time this feeling must be wholly desire; that is, it must address itself to her body as object. This time, then, she refuses to apprehend the desire for what it is; she does not even give it a name; she recognizes it only to the extent that it transcends itself toward admiration, esteem, respect and that it is wholly absorbed in the more refined forms which it produces, to the extent of no longer retaining any prominence except as a sort of warmth and density. But then suppose he takes her hand. This act of her companion risks changing the situation by calling for an immediate decision. To leave the hand there is to consent in herself to flirt, to involve herself. To withdraw it is to break the troubled and unstable harmony which gives the hour its charm. Her aim is to postpone the moment of decision as long as possible. We know what happens next; the young woman leaves her hand there, but she *does not notice* that she is leaving it. She does not notice because it happens by chance that she is at this moment wholly spiritual. She draws her companion up to the most lofty regions of senti-mental speculation; she speaks of Life, of her life, she shows herself in her essential aspect—a personality, a consciousness. And during this time the divorce of the body from the soul is ac-complished; the hand rests inert between the warm hands of her companion—neither consenting nor resisting—a thing.

We shall say that this woman is in bad faith. But we see im-mediately that she uses various procedures in order to maintain herself in this bad faith. She has disarmed the actions of her companion by reducing them to being only what they are; that is, to existing in the mode of the in-itself. But she permits herself to enjoy his desire, to the extent that she will apprehend it as not being what it is, will recognize its transcendence. Finally while feeling profoundly the presence of her own body—to the extent of being excited perhaps—she realizes herself as *not being* her own body, and she contemplates it as though from above as a passive object to which events can *happen* but which can neither provoke them nor avoid them because all its possibilities are outside of it. What unity do we find in these various aspects of bad faith? It is a certain art of forming contradictory concepts which unite in themselves both an idea and the negation of that idea. The basic concept which is thus engendered, utilizes the double property of the human being, who is at once a *facticity* and a *transcendence*. These two aspects of human reality are and ought to be capable of a valid co-ordination. But bad faith does not wish either to co-ordinate them or to surmount them in a synthesis. Bad faith seeks to affirm their identity while preserv-ing their differences. It must affirm facticity as *being* transcend-ence and transcendence as *being* facticity, in such a way that at the instant when a person apprehends the one, he can find him-self abruptly faced with the other.

We can find the prototype of formulae of bad faith in certain famous expressions which have been rightly conceived to pro-duce their whole effect in a spirit of bad faith. Take for example the title of a work by Jacques Chardonne, *Love Is Much More than Love* [*L'amour, c'est beaucoup plus que l'amour*]. We see here how unity is established between *present* love in its facticity —"the contact of two epidermises," sensuality, egoism, Proust's mechanism of jealousy, Adler's battle of the sexes, etc.—and love as transcendence—Mauriac's "river of fire," the longing for the infinite, Plato's *eros*, Lawrence's deep cosmic intuition, etc. Here we leave facticity to find ourselves suddenly beyond the present and the factual condition of man, beyond the psychological, in the heart of metaphysics. On the other hand, the title of a play by Sarment, *I Am Too Great for Myself* [*Je suis trop grand pour moi*], which also presents characters in bad faith, throws us first into full transcendence in order suddenly to imprison us within the narrow limits of our actual essence. We find this structure again in the famous sentence: "He has become what he was [*Il est devenu ce qu'il était*]," or in its no less famous opposite: "Eternity at last changes each man into himself [*Tel qu'en lui-même enfin l'éternité le change*]." Of course these various formulae have only the appearance of bad faith; they have been conceived in this paradoxical form explicitly to shock the mind and discountenance it by an enigma. But it is precisely this appearance which is of concern to us. What counts here is that the formulae do not constitute new, solidly structured ideas; on the contrary, they are formed so as to remain in perpetual disintegration and so that we may slide at any moment from naturalistic present to transcendence and vice versa.

We can see the use which bad faith can make of these judgments which all aim at establishing that I am not what I am. If I were only what I *am*, I could, for example, seriously consider an adverse criticism which someone makes of me, question myself scrupulously, and perhaps be compelled to recognize the truth in it. But thanks to transcendence, I escape all that I am. I do not even have to discuss the justice of the reproach. As Susannah says to Figaro, "To prove that I am right would be to recognize that I can be wrong." I am on a plane where no reproach can touch me since what I really am is my transcendence. I flee from myself, I escape myself, I leave my tattered garment in the hands of the fault-finder. But the ambiguity necessary for bad faith comes from the fact that I affirm here that I *am* my transcendence in the mode of being of a thing. It is only thus, in fact, that I can feel that I escape all reproaches. It is in the sense that our young woman purifies the desire of anything humiliating by being willing to consider it only as pure transcendence, which she avoids even naming. But conversely "I Am Too Great for Myself," while showing our transcendence changed into facticity, is the source of an infinity of excuses for our fail-

ures or our weaknesses. Similarly our young woman flirting
maintains transcendence to the extent that the respect, the esteem manifested by the actions of her admirer are already on
the plane of the transcendent. But she arrests this transcendence, she glues [*empâte*] it down with all the facticity of the
present; respect is nothing other than respect, it is an arrested
transcending which no longer transcends itself toward anything.

But although this *metastable* concept of "transcendence-fac-
ticity" is one of the most basic instruments of bad faith, it is not
the only one of its kind. We can equally well use another kind
of duplicity derived from human reality which we will express
roughly by saying that its being-for-itself implies correlatively a
being-for-others. Upon any one of my actions it is always possible for two looks to converge, mine and that of the Other. The
action will not present exactly the same structure in each
case. But as we shall see later, as everyone feels, there is between
these two aspects of my being, no difference between appearance
and being—as if I were to myself the truth of myself and as if
the Other possessed only a deformed image of me. The equal
dignity of being, possessed by my being-for-others and by my
being-for-myself permits a perpetually ·disintegrating synthesis
and a perpetual game of escape from the for-itself to the for-
others and from the for-others to the for-itself. We have seen also
the use which our young woman made of our being-in-the-midst-
of-the-world—*i.e.*, of our inert presence as a passive object
among other objects—in order to relieve herself suddenly from
the functions of her being-in-the-world—that is, from the being
which makes there to be a world by projecting itself beyond the
world toward its own possibilities. Let us note finally the confusing syntheses which play on the nihilating ambiguity of these
temporal *ekstases*, affirming at once that I am what I have been
(the man who deliberately *arrests himself* at one period in his
life and refuses to take into consideration the later changes)
and that I am not what I have been (the man who in the face of
reproaches or rancor dissociates himself from his past by insist-
ing on his freedom and on his perpetual re-creation). In all these
concepts, which have only a transitive role in the reasoning and
which are eliminated from the conclusion (like imaginary
numbers in the calculations of physicists), we find again the
same structure. We have to deal with human reality as a being
which is what it is not and which is not what it is.

But what exactly is necessary in order for these concepts of disintegration to be able to receive even a pretense of existence, in order for them to be able to appear for a moment to consciousness, even in a process of evanescence? A quick examination of the idea of sincerity, the antithesis of bad faith, will be very instructive in this connection. Actually sincerity presents itself as a requirement and consequently is not a *state*. Now what is the ideal to be attained in this case? It is necessary that a man be *for himself* only what he *is*. But is this not precisely the definition of the in-itself—or if you prefer—the principle of identity? To posit as an ideal the being of things, is this not to assert at the same time that this being does not belong to human reality and that the principle of identity, far from being a universal axiom universally applied, is only a synthetic principle enjoying a merely regional universality? Thus in order that the concepts of bad faith can delude us at least for a moment, in order that the candor of "pure hearts" (*cf.* Gide, Kessel) can have validity for human reality as an ideal, the principle of identity must not represent a constitutive principle of human reality and human reality must not be necessarily what it is but must be able to be what it is not. What does this mean?

If man is what he is, bad faith is forever impossible and candor ceases to be his ideal and becomes instead his being. But is man what he is? And more generally, how can he *be* what he is when he exists as consciousness of being? If candor or sincerity is a universal value, it is evident that the maxim "one must be what one is" does not serve solely as a regulative principle for judgments and concepts by which I express what I am. It posits not merely an ideal of knowing but an ideal of *being;* it proposes to us an absolute conforming of being with itself as a prototype of being. In this sense it is necessary that we *make ourselves* what we are. But what *are we* then if we have the constant obligation to make ourselves what we are, if our mode of being is having the obligation to be what we are?

Take, for example, this waiter in the café. His movement is quick and studied, a little too precise, a little too rapid. He comes toward the patrons with a step a little too quick. He bends forward a little too eagerly; his voice, his eyes express an interest a little too solicitous for the order of the customer. Finally there he returns, trying to imitate in his walk the inflexible stiffness of some kind of automaton while carrying his tray with the recklessness of a tightrope walker by putting it in a perpetually unstable, perpetually broken equilibrium which he perpetually re-establishes by a light movement of the arm and hand. All his behavior seems to us a game. He is trying to link his movements together as if they were mechanisms, the one regulating the other; his gestures and even his voice seem to be mechanisms; he is imitating the quickness and pitiless rapidity of things. He is playing with himself. But what is he playing? We need not watch long before we can explain it: he is playing *at being* a waiter in a café. There is nothing there to surprise us. A game is a kind of investigation in which one gets one's bearings. The child plays with his body in order to explore it, to take inventory of it; the waiter in the café plays with his condition in order to *realize* it. This obligation is not different from that which is imposed on all tradesmen. Their condition is wholly one of ceremony. The public demands of them that they realize it as a ceremony; there is the dance of the grocer, of the tailor, of the auctioneer, by which they endeavor to persuade their clientele that they are nothing but a grocer, an auctioneer, a tailor. A grocer who dreams is offensive to the buyer, because such a grocer is not wholly a grocer. Etiquette requires that he limit himself to his function as a grocer, just as the soldier at attention makes himself into a soldier-thing with a look straight in front of him, which does not see at all, which is no longer meant to see, since it is the regulation and not the interest of the moment which determines the point on which he must fix his eyes (the look "fixed at ten paces"). There are indeed many precautions to imprison a man in what he is, as if we lived in perpetual fear that he might escape from it, that he might overflow and suddenly elude his condition.

At the same time, from the point of view of his own consciousness, the waiter in the café cannot be immediately a café waiter in the sense that this inkwell *is* an inkwell, or the glass *is* a glass. It is not that he cannot form reflective judgments or concepts concerning his condition. He knows well what it "means": the obligation of getting up at five o'clock, of sweeping the floor of the shop before the restaurant opens, of starting the coffee pot going, etc. He knows the rights which it allows: the right to the tips, the right to belong to a union, etc. But all these concepts, all these judgments refer to the transcendent. It is a matter of abstract possibilities, of rights and duties conferred on a "person possessing rights." And it is precisely this person *whom I have to be* (let us assume that I am the waiter in question) and who I am not. It is not that I do not wish to be this person or that I want this person to be different. But rather there is no common measure between his being and mine. It is a performance [*representation*] for others and for myself, which means that I can be the waiter only by "acting his part." But if I so represent myself, I am not he; I am separated from him as the object from the subject, separated *by nothing*, but this nothing isolates me from him. I cannot be he, I can only play *at being* him; that is, imagine to myself that I am he. And thereby I affect him with nothingness. In vain do I fulfill the functions of a café waiter. I can be the waiter only in the neutralized mode, as the actor is Hamlet, by mechanically making the *typical gestures* of my state and by aiming at myself as an imaginary café waiter through those gestures taken as an "analogue."* What I attempt to realize is a being-in-itself of the café waiter, as if it were not just in my power to confer their value and their urgency upon my duties and the rights of my position, as if it were not my free choice to get up each morning at five o'clock or to remain in bed, even though it meant getting fired. As if from the very fact that I sustain this role in existence I did not transcend it on every side, as if I did not constitute myself as one *beyond* my condition. Yet there is no doubt that I *am* in a sense a café waiter—otherwise could I not just as well call myself a diplomat or a reporter? But if I am one, this cannot be in the mode of being-in-itself. I am a waiter in the mode of *being what I am not*.

Furthermore we are dealing with more than mere social positions; I am never any one of my attitudes, any one of my actions. The good speaker is the one who *plays* at speaking, because he cannot *be speaking*. The attentive pupil who wishes to *be* attentive, his eyes riveted on the teacher, his ears open wide, so exhausts himself in playing the attentive role that he ends up by no longer hearing anything. Perpetually absent to my body, to my acts, I am despite myself that "divine absence" of which Valéry speaks. I cannot say either that I *am* here or that I *am* not here, in the sense that we say "that box of matches *is* on the table"; this would be to confuse my "being-in-the world" with a "being-in the midst of the world." Nor that I *am* standing, nor that I *am* seated; this would be to confuse my body with the idio-

* Cf. above, p. 80.—Ed.

syncratic totality of which it is only one of the structures. On all sides I escape being and yet—I am.

But take a mode of being which concerns only myself: I am sad. One might think that surely I am the sadness in the mode of being what I am. What is the sadness, however, if not the intentional unity which comes to reassemble and animate the totality of my conduct? It is the meaning of this dull look with which I view the world, of my bowed shoulders, of my lowered head, of the listlessness in my whole body. But at the very moment when I adopt each of these modes of behavior, do I not know that I can also not adopt it? Let a stranger suddenly appear and I will lift up my head, I will assume a lively cheerfulness. What will remain of my sadness except that I complacently promise it an appointment for later after the departure of the visitor? Moreover is not this sadness itself a mode of behavior? Is it not consciousness which affects itself with sadness as a magical recourse against a situation which is too urgent?* And in this case even, should we not say that being sad means first to make oneself sad? That may be, someone will say, but after all doesn't giving oneself the being of sadness mean to *receive* this being? It makes no difference from where I receive it. The fact is that a consciousness which affects itself with sadness *is* sad precisely for this reason. But it is difficult to comprehend the nature of consciousness; the being-sad is not a ready-made being which I give to myself as I can give this book to my friend. I do not possess the property of *affecting myself with being*. If I make myself sad, I must continue to make myself sad from beginning to end. I cannot take advantage of the impetus already acquired and allow it to go on its way without re-creating it, nor can I carry it in the manner of an inert body which continues its movement after the initial shock. There is no inertia in consciousness. If I make myself sad, it is because I *am* not sad—the being of the sadness escapes me by and in the very act by which I affect myself with it. The being-in-itself of sadness perpetually haunts my consciousness (of) being sad, but it is as a value which I cannot realize; it stands as a regulative meaning of my sadness, not as its constitutive modality.

Someone may say that my consciousness at least *is*, whatever may be the object or the state of which it makes itself conscious-ness. But how do we distinguish my consciousness (of) being

* *Cf.* above, p. 74.—Ed.

sad from sadness? Is it not all one? It is true in a way that my consciousness *is*, if one means by this that for another it is a part of the totality of being on which judgments can be brought to bear. But it should be noted, as Husserl clearly understood, that my consciousness appears originally to the Other as an absence. It is the object always present as the *meaning* of all my attitudes and all my conduct—and always absent, for it gives itself to the intuition of another as a perpetual question—still better, as a perpetual freedom. When Peter looks at me, I know of course that he is looking at me. His eyes, things in the world, are fixed on my body, a thing in the world—that is the objective fact of which I can say: it *is*. But it is also a fact *in the world*. The meaning of this look is not a fact in the world, and this is what makes me uncomfortable. Although I smile, promise, threaten, nothing I do can get hold of the approbation, the free judgment which I seek; I know that it is always beyond. I feel it in my actions themselves, which are no longer operations directed toward things. To the extent that they are linked with the other, they are for myself merely *presentations* which await being constituted as graceful or uncouth, sincere or insincere, etc., by an apprehension which is always beyond my efforts to provoke, an apprehension which will be provoked by my efforts only if of itself it lends them force (that is, only insofar as the apprehension allows itself to be provoked from the outside), and *is its own mediator with the transcendent*. Thus the objective fact of the being-in-itself of the consciousness of the Other is posited in order to disappear in negativity and in freedom: consciousness of the Other is as not-being; its being-in-itself "here and now" is not-to-be.

*Consciousness of the Other is what it is not.*

Furthermore the being of my own consciousness does not appear to me as the consciousness of the Other. It *is* because it makes itself, since its being is consciousness of being. But this means that making sustains being; consciousness has to be its own being, it is never sustained by being; it sustains being in the heart of subjectivity, which means once again that it is inhabited by being but that it is not being: *consciousness is not what it is.*

## 4 SINCERITY

Under these conditions what can be the significance of the ideal of sincerity except as a task impossible to achieve, of which the very meaning is in contradiction with the structure of my consciousness. To be sincere, we said, is to be what one is. That supposes that I am not originally what I am. But here naturally Kant's "You ought, therefore you can" is implicitly understood. I can *become* sincere; this is what my duty and my effort to achieve sincerity imply. But here we observe that the original structure of "not being what one is" renders impossible in advance all movement toward being in itself or "being what one is." And this impossibility is not hidden from consciousness; on the contrary, it is the very stuff of consciousness; it is the discomfort which we constantly experience; it is our very incapacity to recognize ourselves, to constitute ourselves as being what we are. It is this necessity which means that, as soon as we posit ourselves as a certain being, by a legitimate judgment based on inner experience or correctly deduced from *a priori* or empirical premises, then by that very positing we transcend this being—and that not toward another being but toward emptiness, toward *nothing*.

How then can we blame another for not being sincere or rejoice in our own sincerity since this sincerity appears to us at the same time to be impossible? How can we in conversation, in confession, in introspection, even attempt to be sincere since the attempt will by its very nature be doomed to failure and since at the very time when we announce it we have a pre-judicative comprehension of its futility? In introspection I try to determine exactly what I am, to make up my mind to be my true self without delay—even though it means consequently to set about searching for ways to change myself. But what does this mean if not that I am constituting myself as a thing? Shall I determine the set of purposes and motivations which have impelled me to do this or that action? But this is already to postulate a causal determinism which constitutes the flow of my states of consciousness as a succession of physical states. Shall I uncover in myself "drives," even though it be to affirm them in shame But is this not deliberately to forget that these drives are realized with my consent, that they are not forces of nature but that I lend them their efficacy by a perpetually renewed decision concerning their value. Shall I pass judgment on my character, on my nature? Is this not to veil from myself at that moment what I know only too well, that I thus judge a past to which by definition my present is not subject? The proof of this is that the same man who in sincerity posits that he is what in actuality he was, is indignant at the reproach of another and tries to disarm it by asserting that he can no longer be what he was. We are readily astonished and upset when the penalties of the court affect a man who in his new freedom *is no longer* the guilty person he was. But at the same time we require of this man that he recognize himself as *being* this guilty one. What then is sincerity except precisely a phenomenon of bad faith? Have we not shown indeed that in bad faith human reality is constituted as a being which is what it is not and which is not what it is?

Let us take an example: A homosexual frequently has an intolerable feeling of guilt, and his whole existence is determined in relation to this feeling. One will readily foresee that he is in bad faith. In fact it frequently happens that this man, while recognizing his homosexual inclination, while avowing each and every particular misdeed which he has committed, refuses with all his strength to consider himself *"a pederast."* His case is always "different," peculiar; there enters into it something of a game, of chance, of bad luck; the mistakes are all in the past; they are explained by a certain conception of the beautiful which women cannot satisfy; we should see in them the results of a restless search, rather than the manifestations of a deeply rooted tendency, etc., etc. Here is assuredly a man in bad faith who borders on the comic since, acknowledging all the facts which are imputed to him, he refuses to draw from them the inevitable conclusion. His friend, who is his most severe critic, becomes irritated with this duplicity. This critic asks only one thing— and perhaps then will be indulgent: that he in his guilt recognize himself as guilty, that he as a homosexual declare frankly— whether humbly or boastfully matters little—"I am a pederast." We ask here: Who is in bad faith? The homosexual or the champion of sincerity?

The homosexual recognizes his faults, but he struggles with all his strength against the crushing view that his misdeeds constitute for him a *destiny*. He does not wish to let himself be considered as a thing. He has an obscure but strong feeling that a homosexual is not a homosexual as this table is a table or as this red-haired man is red-haired. It seems to him that he has escaped from each misdeed as soon as he has posited it and recognized it; he even feels that the psychic duration by itself cleanses him from each sin, constitutes for him an undetermined future, enables him to be born anew. Is he wrong? Does he not recognize in himself the peculiar, irreducible character of human reality? His attitude includes then an undeniable comprehension of truth. But at the same time he needs this perpetual rebirth, this constant escape in order to live; he must constantly put himself beyond reach in order to avoid the terrible judgment of the social group. Thus he plays on the word *being*. He would be right actually if he understood the phrase, "I am not a pederast" in the sense of "I am not what I am." That is, if he declared to himself, "To the extent that a pattern of behavior is defined as the behavior of a pederast and to the extent that I have adopted this conduct, I am a pederast. But to the extent that human reality cannot be finally defined by patterns of behavior, I am not one." But instead he slides surreptitiously toward a different connotation of the word "being." He understands "not being" in the sense of "not-being-in-itself." He lays claim to "not being a pederast" in the sense in which this table is *not* an inkwell. He is in bad faith.

But the champion of sincerity is not ignorant of the transcendence of human reality, and he knows how when necessary to appeal to it for his own advantage. He makes use of transcendence even in making his present demand. Does he not wish, first in the name of sincerity, then of freedom, that the homosexual reflect on himself and acknowledge himself as a homosexual? Does he not let the other understand that such a confession will win indulgence for him? What does this mean if not that the man who will acknowledge himself as a homosexual will no longer be *the same* as the homosexual whom he acknowledges being and that he will escape into the region of freedom and of good will? The critic asks the man then to be what he is in order no longer to be what he is. It is the profound meaning of the saying, "A sin confessed is half condoned." The critic demands of the guilty one that he constitute himself as a thing, precisely in order no longer to treat him as a thing. And this contradiction is constitutive of the demand of sincerity. Who cannot see how offensive to the Other and how reassuring for me is a statement such as, "He's just a pederast," which erases a disturbing freedom with one sweep and which aims at henceforth constituting all the acts of the Other as consequences following strictly from his essence. That is actually what the critic is demanding of his victim—that he constitute himself as a thing, that he should entrust his freedom to his friend as a fief, in order that the friend should return it to him subsequently—like a suzerain to his vassal. The champion of sincerity is in bad faith to the extent that in order to reassure himself, he pretends to judge, to the extent that he demands that freedom as freedom constitute itself as a thing. We have here only one episode in that battle to the death of consciousnesses which Hegel calls "the relation of the master and the slave." A person appeals to another and demands that in the name of his nature as consciousness he should radically destroy himself as consciousness, but while making this appeal he leads the other to hope for a rebirth beyond this destruction.

Very well, someone will say, but our man is abusing sincerity, playing one side against the other. We should not look for sincerity in the relation of the *Mit-sein* but rather where it is pure —in the relations of a person with himself. But who cannot see that objective sincerity is constituted in the same way? Who cannot see that the sincere man constitutes himself as a thing in order to escape the condition of a thing by the same act of sincerity? The man who confesses that he is evil has exchanged his disturbing "freedom-for-evil" for an inanimate character of evil; he *is* evil, he clings to himself, he is what he is. But at the same time, he escapes from that *thing*, since it is he who contemplates it, since it depends on him to maintain it under his look or to let it collapse in an infinite number of particular acts. He derives a *merit* from his sincerity, and the deserving man is not the evil man as he is evil but as he is beyond his evilness. At the same time the evil is disarmed since it is nothing, save on the plane of determinism, and since in confessing it, I posit my freedom in respect to it; my future is virgin; everything is allowed to me.

Thus the essential structure of sincerity does not differ from that of bad faith since the sincere man constitutes himself as what he is *in order not to be it*. This explains the truth recognized by all that one can fall into bad faith through being sincere. As Valéry pointed out, this is the case with Stendhal. Total,

CONSCIOUSNESS AND BEING

constant sincerity as a constant effort to adhere to oneself is by
nature a constant effort to dissociate oneself from oneself. A
person frees himself from himself by the very act by which he
makes himself an object for himself. To draw up a perpetual inventory of what one is means constantly to repudiate oneself
and to take refuge in a sphere where one is no longer anything
but a pure, free look. The goal of bad faith, as we said, is to put
oneself out of reach; it is an escape. Now we see that we must use
the same terms to define sincerity. What does this mean?

In the final analysis the goal of sincerity and the goal of bad
faith are not so different. To be sure, there is a sincerity which
bears on the past and which does not concern us here; I am sincere if I confess *having had* this pleasure or that intention. We
shall see that if this sincerity is possible, it is because in his fall
into the past, the being of man is constituted as a being-in-itself.
But here our concern is only with the sincerity which aims
at itself in present immanence. What is its goal? To bring me to
confess to myself what I am in order that I may finally coincide
with my being; in a word, to make myself to be, in the mode of
the in-itself, what I am in the mode of "not being what I am." Its
assumption is that fundamentally I am already, in the mode of
the in-itself, what I have to be. Thus we find at the base of sincerity a continual game of mirror and reflection, a perpetual
transition from the being which is what it is, to the being which
is not what it is, and inversely from the being which is not what
it is to the being which is what it is. And what is the goal of bad
faith? To make me be what I am, in the mode of "not being what
one is," or not to be what I am in the mode of "being what one is."
We find here the same game of mirrors. In fact in order for me
to have an intention of sincerity, I must at the outset simultaneously be and not be what I am. Sincerity does not assign to
me a mode of being or a particular quality, but in relation to that
quality it aims at making me pass from one mode of being to another mode of being. This second mode of being, the ideal of sincerity, I am prevented by nature from attaining; and at the very
moment when I struggle to attain it, I have a vague prejudicative
comprehension that I shall not attain it. But all the same, in order for me to be able to conceive an intention in bad faith, I must
have such a nature that within my being I escape from my being. If I were sad or cowardly in the way in which this inkwell is
an inkwell, the possibility of bad faith could not even be con-

ceived. Not only should I be unable to escape from my being; I could not even imagine that I could escape from it. But if bad faith is possible as a simple project, it is because so far as my being is concerned, there is no difference between being and non-being if I am cut off from my project.

Bad faith is possible only because sincerity is conscious of missing its goal inevitably, due to its very nature. I can try to apprehend myself as *"not being cowardly,"* when I *am* so, only on condition that the "being cowardly" is itself "in question" at the very moment when it is, on condition that it is itself a question, and that at the very moment when I wish to apprehend it, it escapes me on all sides and is annihilated. The condition under which I can attempt an effort in bad faith is that in one sense, I *am not* this coward which I do not wish to be. But if I were not cowardly in the simple mode of not-being-what-one-is-not, I would be "in good faith" by declaring that I am not cowardly. Thus this inapprehensible coward is evanescent; in order for me not to be cowardly, I must in some way also be cowardly. That does not mean that I must be "a little" cowardly, in the sense that "a little" signifies "to a certain degree cowardly—and not cowardly to a certain degree." No. I must at once both be and not be totally and in all respects a coward. Thus in this case bad faith requires that I should not be what I am; that is, that there be an imponderable difference separating being from not-being in the mode of being of human reality.

But bad faith is not restricted to denying the qualities which I possess, to not seeing the being which I am. It attempts also to constitute myself as being what I am not. It apprehends me positively as courageous when I am not so. And that is possible, once again, only if I am what I am not; that is, if not-being in me does not have being even as not-being. Of course it is necessary that I not be courageous; otherwise bad faith would not be *bad*. But in addition my effort in bad faith must include the ontological comprehension that even in my usual being what I *am*, I am not really it and that there is very great difference between the being of "being-sad," for example—which I *am* in the mode of not being what I am—and the "not-being" of not-being-courageous which I wish to hide from myself. Moreover it is particularly requisite that the very negation of being should be itself the object of a perpetual nihilation, that the very meaning of "not-being" be perpetually in question in human reality. If I *were not* courageous in the way in which this inkwell is not a table; that is, if I were isolated in my cowardice, propped firmly against it, incapable of putting it in relation to its opposite, if I were not capable of *determining* myself as cowardly—that is, of denying courage to myself and thereby of escaping my cowardice in the very moment that I posit it—if it were not on principle impossible for me to coincide with my *not-being-courageous* as well as with my being-courageous—then any project of bad faith would be prohibited me. Thus in order for bad faith to be possible, sincerity itself must be in bad faith. The condition of the possibility for bad faith is that human reality, in its most immediate being, in the intrastructure of the pre-reflective *cogito,* must be what it is not and not be what it is.

## 5 THE "FAITH" OF BAD FAITH

We have indicated for the moment only those conditions which render bad faith conceivable, the structures of being which permit us to form concepts of bad faith. We cannot limit ourselves to these considerations: we have not yet distinguished bad faith from falsehood. The equivocal concepts which we have described would without a doubt be utilized by a liar to discountenance his questioner, although their equivocal quality, being based on the being of man and not on some empirical circumstance, can and ought to be obvious to all. The true problem of bad faith stems obviously from the fact that bad faith is *faith.* It cannot be either a cynical lie or certainty—if certainty is the intuitive possession of the object. But if we take belief as meaning the adherence of being to its object when the object is not given or is given indistinctly, then bad faith is belief; and the essential problem of bad faith is a problem of belief.

How can we believe by bad faith in the concepts which we forge expressly to persuade ourselves? We must note in fact that the project of bad faith must be itself in bad faith. I am not only in bad faith at the end of my attempt when I have constructed my equivocal concepts and when I have persuaded myself. In truth, I have not persuaded myself; to the extent that I could be so persuaded, I have always been so. And at the very moment when I was disposed to put myself in bad faith, I of necessity was in bad faith with respect to this same disposition. For me to have represented it to myself as bad faith would have been cynicism; to believe it sincerely innocent would have been in good faith. The decision to be in bad faith does not dare to speak its name; it believes itself and does not believe itself in bad faith; it believes itself and does not believe itself in good faith. It is this which from the emergence of bad faith, determines the later attitude and, as it were, the *Weltanschauung* of bad faith.

Bad faith does not hold the norms and criteria of truth as they are accepted by the critical thought of good faith. What it decides first, in fact, is the nature of truth. With bad faith a truth appears, a method of thinking, a type of being which is like that of objects; the ontological characteristic of the world of bad faith with which the subject suddenly surrounds himself is this: that here being is what it is not, and is not what it is. Consequently a peculiar type of evidence appears; *non-persuasive* evidence. Bad faith apprehends evidence but it is resigned in advance to not being fulfilled by this evidence, to not being persuaded and transformed into good faith. It makes itself humble and modest; it is not ignorant, it says, that faith is decision and that after each intuition, it must decide and *will what it is.* Thus bad faith in its primitive project and in its coming into the world decides on the exact nature of its requirements. It takes shape in the firm resolution *not to demand too much*, to count itself satisfied when it is barely persuaded, to force itself in decisions to adhere to uncertain truths. This original project of bad faith is a decision in bad faith on the nature of faith. Let us understand clearly that there is no question of a reflective, voluntary decision, but of a spontaneous determination of our being. One *puts oneself* in bad faith as one goes to sleep and one is in bad faith as one dreams. Once this mode of being has been realized, it is as difficult to get out of it as to wake oneself up; bad faith is a type of being-in-the-world, like waking or dreaming, which by itself tends to perpetuate itself, although its structure is of the *metastable* type. But bad faith is conscious of its structure, and it has taken precautions by deciding that the metastable structure is the structure of being and that non-persuasion is the structure of all convictions. It follows that if bad faith is faith and if it includes in its original project its own negation (it determines itself to be not quite convinced in order to convince itself that I am what I am not), then to start with, a faith which wishes itself to be not quite convinced must be possible. What are the conditions for the possibility of such a faith?

I believe that my friend Peter feels friendship for me. I believe it in *good faith*. I believe it but I do not have any self-evident intuition, for the nature of the object does not lend itself to intuition. I *believe* it; that is, I allow myself to give in to all impulses to trust it; I decide to believe in it, and to maintain myself in this decision; I conduct myself, finally, as if I were certain of it—and all this in the synthetic unity of one and the same attitude. This which I define as good faith is what Hegel would call the *immediate*. It is simple faith. Hegel would demonstrate at once that the immediate calls for mediation and that belief by becoming *belief for itself*, passes to the state of non-belief. If I *believe* that my friend Peter likes me, this means that his friendship appears to me as the meaning of all his acts. Belief is a particular consciousness of *the meaning* of Peter's acts. But if I know that I believe, the belief appears to me as pure subjective determination without external correlative. This is what makes the very word "to believe" a term utilized indifferently to indicate the unwavering firmness of belief ("My God, I believe in you") and its character as defenseless and strictly subjective. ("Is Peter my friend? I do not know; I believe so.") But the nature of consciousness is such that in it the mediate and the immediate are one and the same being. To believe is to know that one believes, and to know that one believes is no longer to believe. Thus to believe is not to believe any longer because that is only to believe—this in the unity of one and the same non-thetic self-consciousness. To be sure, we have here forced the description of the phenomenon by designating it with the word *to know;* non-thetic consciousness is not to *know*. But it is in its very translucency at the origin of all knowing. Thus the non-thetic consciousness (of) believing is destructive of belief. But at the same time the very law of the pre-reflective *cogito* implies that the being of believing ought to be the consciousness of believing.

Thus belief is a being which questions its own being, which can realize itself only in its destruction, which can manifest itself to itself only by denying itself. It is a being for which to be is to appear and to appear is to deny itself. To believe is not-to-believe. We see the reason for it; the being of consciousness is to exist by itself, then to make itself be and thereby to pass beyond itself. In this sense consciousness is perpetually escaping itself, belief becomes non-belief, the immediate becomes mediation, the absolute becomes relative, and the relative becomes absolute. The ideal of good faith (to believe what one believes) is, like that of sincerity (to be what one is), an ideal of being-in-it-self. Every belief is a belief that falls short; one never wholly believes what one believes. Consequently the primitive project of bad faith is only the utilization of this self-destruction of the fact of consciousness. If every belief in good faith is an impossible belief, then there is a place for every impossible belief. My inability to *believe* that I am courageous will not discourage me since every belief involves not quite believing. I shall define this impossible belief as *my* belief. To be sure, I shall not be able to hide from myself that I believe in order not to believe and that I do not believe *in order to* believe. But the subtle, total annihilation of bad faith by itself cannot surprise me; it exists as the basis of all faith. What is it then? At the moment when I wish to believe myself courageous I *know* that I am a coward. And this certainly would come to destroy my belief. But *first,* I *am* not any more courageous than cowardly, if we are to understand this in the mode of being of the in-itself. In the second place, I do not *know* that I am courageous; such a view of myself can be accompanied only by *belief,* for it surpasses pure reflective certitude. In the third place, it is very true that bad faith does not succeed in believing what it wishes to believe. But it is precisely as the acceptance of not believing what it believes that it is bad faith. Good faith wishes to flee the "not-believing-what-one-believes" by finding refuge in being. Bad faith flees being by taking refuge in "not-believing-what-one-believes." It has disarmed all beliefs in advance—those which it would like to take hold of and, at the same time, the others, those which it wishes to flee. In *willing* this self-destruction of belief, from which science escapes by searching for evidence, it ruins the beliefs which are opposed to it, which reveal themselves as *being only* belief. Thus we can better understand the original phenomenon of bad faith.

In bad faith there is no cynical lie nor knowing preparation for deceitful concepts. But the first act of bad faith is to flee what it cannot flee, to flee what it is. The very project of flight reveals to bad faith an inner disintegration in the heart of being, and it is this disintegration which bad faith wishes to be. In truth the two immediate attitudes which we can take in the face of our being are conditioned by the very nature of this being and its immediate relation with the in-itself. Good faith seeks to flee the inner disintegration of my being in the direction of the in-itself which it should be and is not. Bad faith seeks to flee the in-itself by means of the inner disintegration of my being. But it denies this very disintegration as it denies that it is itself bad faith. Bad faith seeks by means of "not-being-what-one-is" to escape from the in-itself which I am not in the mode of being-what-one-is-not. It denies itself as bad faith and aims at the in-itself which I am not in the mode of "not-being-what-one-is-not."* If bad faith is possible, it is because it is an immediate, permanent threat to every project of the human being; it is because consciousness conceals in its being a permanent risk of bad faith. The origin of this risk is the fact that the nature of consciousness simultaneously is to be what it is not and not to be what it is. In the light of these remarks we can now approach the ontological study of consciousness, not as the totality of the human being, but as the instantaneous nucleus of this being. . . .

*Being and Nothingness*, 47–70.

* If it is indifferent whether one is in good or in bad faith, because bad faith reapprehends good faith and slides to the very origin of the project of good faith, that does not mean that we cannot radically escape bad faith. But this supposes a recovery of being which was corrupted by itself. This recovery we shall call authenticity, the description of which has no place here.

# IV

———— • ————

## The Being of Consciousness

### 1 FACTICITY

The for-itself *is*. It *is*, we may say, even if it is a being which is
not what it is and which is what it is not. It *is* since whatever
reefs there may be to cause it to founder, still the project of sincerity is at least conceivable. The for-itself *is*, in the manner of an
event, in the sense in which I can say that Philip II *has been*, that
friend Peter is or exists. The for-itself *is*, insofar as it appears in
a condition which it has not chosen, as Peter is a French bourgeois in 1942, as Schmitt was a Berlin worker in 1870; it *is* insofar as it is thrown into a world and abandoned in a "situation";
it *is* as pure contingency inasmuch as for it as for things in the
world, as for this wall, this tree, this cup, the original question
can be posited: "Why is this being exactly such and not otherwise?" It *is* insofar as there is in it something of which it is not
the foundation—its *presence to the world*.

Being apprehends itself as not being its own foundation, and
this apprehension is at the basis of every *cogito*. In this connection it is to be noted that it reveals itself immediately to the *reflective cogito* of Descartes. When Descartes wants to profit from
this revelation, he apprehends himself as an imperfect being
"since he doubts." But in this imperfect being, he establishes the
presence of the idea of perfection. He apprehends then a cleavage
between the type of being which he can conceive and the being
which he is. It is this cleavage or lack of being which is at the
origin of the second proof of the existence of God. In fact if we
get rid of the scholastic terminology, what remains of this proof?
The very clear indication that the being which possesses in itself the idea of perfection cannot be its own foundation, for if it
were it would have produced itself in conformance with that
idea. In other words, a being which would be its own foundation

could not suffer the slightest discrepancy between what it is and what it conceives, for it would produce itself in conformance with its comprehension of being and could conceive only of what it is.

But this apprehension of being as a lack of being in the face of being is first a comprehension on the part of the *cogito* of its own contingency. I think, therefore I am. What am I? A being which is not its own foundation, which *qua* being, could be other than it is to the extent that it does not account for its being. This is that first intuition of our own contingency which Heidegger gives as the first motivation for the passage from the un-authentic to the authentic. There is restlessness, an appeal to the conscience (*Ruf des Gewissens*), a feeling of guilt. In truth Heidegger's description shows all too clearly his anxiety to es-tablish an ontological foundation for an Ethics with which he claims not to be concerned, as also to reconcile his humanism with the religious sense of the transcendent. The intuition of our contingency is not identical with a feeling of guilt. Nevertheless it is true that in our own apprehension of ourselves, we appear to ourselves as having the character of an unjustifiable fact. . . .

Earlier it was seen that we can be nothing without playing at being. "If I am a café waiter," it was said, "this can be only in the mode of *not being* one." And that is true. If I could *be* a café waiter, I should suddenly constitute myself as a contingent block of identity. And that I am not. This contingent being in-itself always escapes me. But in order that I may freely give a meaning to the obligations which my state involves, then in one sense at the heart of the for-itself, as a perpetually evanescent totality, being-in-itself must be given as the evanescent con-tingency of my *situation*. This is the result of the fact that while I must *play at being* a café waiter in order to be one, still it would be in vain for me to play at being a diplomat or a sailor, for I would not be one. This inapprehensible *fact* of my condition, this impalpable difference which distinguishes this drama of realization from drama pure and simple, is the reason that the for-itself, while choosing the *meaning* of its situation and while constituting itself as the foundation of itself in situation, does *not choose* its position. This is the reason I apprehend myself simul-taneously as totally responsible for my being—inasmuch as I am its foundation—and yet as totally unjustifiable. Without facticity consciousness could choose its attachments to the world in the same way as the souls in Plato's *Republic* choose their condition. I could determine myself to "be born a worker" or to "be born a bourgeois." But on the other hand facticity cannot constitute me as *being* a bourgeois or *being* a worker. It is not even strictly speaking a *resistance* of fact since it is only by recovering it in the substructure of the *pre-reflective cogito* that I confer on it its meaning and its resistance. Facticity is only one indication which I give myself of the being to which I must reunite myself in order to be what I am.

It is impossible to grasp facticity in its brute nudity, since all that we will find of it is already recovered and freely constructed. The simple *fact* of "being there," at that table, in that chair, is already the pure object of a limiting concept and as such cannot be grasped. Yet it is contained in my "consciousness of being-there," as its full contingency, as the nihilated in-itself on the basis of which the for-itself produces itself as consciousness of being there. The for-itself looking deep into itself as the consciousness of being there will never discover anything in itself but *motivations;* that is, it will be perpetually referred to itself and to its constant freedom. (I am there in order to . . . etc.) But the contingency which paralyzes these motivations to the same degree as they totally found themselves is the facticity of the for-itself. The relation of the for-itself, which is its own foundation *qua* for-itself, to facticity can be correctly termed a factual necessity. It is indeed this factual necessity which Descartes and Husserl seized upon as constituting the evidence of the *cogito*. The for-itself is necessary insofar as it provides its own foundation. And this is why it is the object reflected by an apodictic intuition. I cannot doubt that I am. But insofar as this for-itself as such could also not be, it has all the contingency of fact. Just as my nihilating freedom is apprehended in anguish, so the for-itself is conscious of its facticity. It has the feeling of its complete gratuity; it apprehends itself as being there *for nothing*, as being *de trop*.

We must not confuse facticity with that Cartesian substance whose attribute is thought. To be sure, thinking substance exists only as it thinks; and since it is a created thing, it participates in the contingency of the *ens creatum*. But it *is*. It preserves the character of being-in-itself in its integrity, although the for-itself is its attribute. This is what is called Descartes' substantialist illusion. For us, on the other hand, the appearance of the for-itself or absolute event refers indeed to the effort of an in-itself to found itself; it corresponds to an attempt on the part of being to remove contingency from its being. But this attempt results in the nihilation of the in-itself, because the in-itself cannot found *itself* without introducing the *self* or a reflective, nihilating reference into the absolute identity of its being and consequently degenerating into *for-itself*. The for-itself corresponds then to an expanding de-structuring of the in-itself, and the in-itself is nihilated and absorbed in its attempt to found itself. Facticity is not then a substance of which the for-itself would be the attribute and which would produce thought without exhausting itself in that very production. It simply resides in the for-itself as a memory of being, as its unjustifiable *presence in the world*. Being-in-itself can found its nothingness but not its being. In its decompression it nihilates itself in a for-itself which becomes *qua* for-itself its own foundation; but the contingency which the for-itself has derived from the in-itself remains out of reach. It is what *remains* of the in-itself in the for-itself as facticity and what makes the for-itself have only a factual necessity; that is, it is the foundation of its *consciousness-of-being* or *existence*, but on no account can it found its *presence*. Thus consciousness can in no case keep itself from being and yet it is totally responsible for its being. . . .

## 2  TRANSCENDENCE

By nature the *cogito* refers to the lacking and to the lacked, for the *cogito* is haunted by being, as Descartes well realized. Such is the origin of transcendence. Human reality is its own transcending toward what it lacks; it transcends itself toward the particular being which it would be if it were what it is. Human reality is not something which exists first in order afterwards to lack this or that; it exists first as lack [*manque*] and in immediate, synthetic connection with what it lacks. Thus the pure event by which human reality emerges as a presence in the world is apprehended by itself as *its* own *lack*. In its coming into existence human reality grasps itself as an incomplete being. It apprehends itself as being insofar as it is not, in the presence of the particular totality which it lacks and which it is in the form of not being it and which is what it is. Human reality is a perpetual transcending toward a coincidence with itself which is never given. If the *cogito reaches* toward being, it is because by its very thrust it transcends itself toward being by qualifying itself in its being as the being to which coincidence with self is lacking in order for it to be what it is. The *cogito* is indissolubly linked to being-in-itself, not as a thought to its object —which would make the in-itself relative—but as a lack to that which defines its lack. In this sense the second Cartesian proof is valid. Imperfect being transcends itself toward perfect being; the being which is the foundation only of its nothingness transcends itself toward the being which is the foundation of its being. But the being toward which human reality transcends itself is not a transcendent God; it is at the heart of human reality; it is only human reality itself as totality.

This totality is not the pure and simple contingent in-itself of the transcendent. If what consciousness apprehends as the being toward which it transcends itself were the pure in-itself, it would coincide with the annihilation of consciousness. But consciousness does not transcend itself toward its annihilation; it does not want to lose itself in the in-itself of identity at the limit of its transcending. It is for the for-itself as such that the for-itself lays claim to being-in-itself.

Thus this perpetually absent being which haunts the for-itself is itself fixed in the in-itself. It is the impossible synthesis of the for-itself and the in-itself; it would be its own foundation not as nothingness but as being and would preserve within it the necessary translucency of consciousness along with the coincidence with itself of being-in-itself. It would preserve in it that turning back upon the self which conditions every necessity and every foundation. But this return to the self would be without distance; it would not be presence to itself, but identity with itself. In short, this being would be exactly the *self* which we have shown can exist only as a perpetually evanescent relation, but it would be this self as substantial being. Thus human reality emerges as such in the presence of its own totality or self as a lack of that totality. And this totality cannot be given by nature, since it combines in itself the incompatible characteristics of the in-itself and the for-itself.

Let no one reproach us with capriciously inventing a being of this kind; when by a further movement of thought the being and absolute absence of this totality are hypostasized as transcendence beyond the world, it takes on the name of God. Is not God a being who is what he is—in that he is all positivity and the foundation of the world—and at the same time a being who is not what he is and who is what he is not—in that he is self-consciousness and the necessary foundation of himself? The being of human reality is suffering because it emerges in being as perpetually haunted by a totality which it is without being able to be it, precisely because it could not attain the in-itself without losing itself as for-itself. Human reality therefore is by nature an unhappy consciousness with no possibility of transcending its unhappy state.

But what exactly is the nature of this being toward which unhappy consciousness transcends itself? Shall we say that it does not exist? Those contradictions which we discovered in it prove only that it cannot be *realized*. Nothing can hold out against this self-evident truth: consciousness can exist only as involved in this being which surrounds it on all sides and which paralyzes it with its phantom presence. Shall we say that it is a being *relative* to consciousness? This would be to confuse it with the object of a *thesis*. This being is not posited through and before consciousness; there is no consciousness *of* this being since it haunts non-thetic self-consciousness. It points to consciousness as the meaning of its being and yet consciousness is no more conscious *of* it than *of* itself. Still it cannot escape from consciousness; but inasmuch as consciousness enjoys being a consciousness (of) being, *this* being is there. Consciousness does not confer meaning on this being as it does on this inkwell or this pencil; but without this being, which it is in the form of not being it, consciousness would not be consciousness—*i.e.*, lack. On the contrary, consciousness derives for itself its meaning as consciousness from this being. This being emerges in the world along with consciousness, at once in its heart and outside it; it is absolute transcendence in absolute immanence. It has no priority over consciousness, and consciousness has no priority over it. They *form a dyad*. Of course this being could not exist without the for-itself, but neither could the for-itself exist without it. Consciousness in relation to this being stands in the mode of *being* this being, for this being is consciousness, but as a being which consciousness cannot be. It is consciousness itself, in the heart of consciousness, and yet out of reach, as an absence, an unrealizable. Its nature is to inclose its own contradiction within itself; its relation to the for-itself is a total immanence which is completed in total transcendence.

Furthermore this being need not be conceived as present to consciousness with only the abstract characteristics which our investigation has established. The concrete consciousness emerges in situation, and it is a unique, individualized consciousness *of* this situation and (of) itself in situation. It is to this concrete consciousness that the self is present, and all the concrete characteristics of consciousness have their correlates in the totality of the self. The self is individual; it is the individual completion of the self which haunts the for-itself.

A feeling, for example, is a feeling in the presence of a norm; that is, a feeling of the same type but one which would be what it is. This norm or totality of the effective self is directly present as a lack *suffered* in the very heart of suffering. One suffers and one suffers from not suffering enough. The suffering of which we *speak* is never exactly that which we feel. What we call "noble" or "good" or "true" suffering and what moves us is the suffering which we read on the faces of others, or rather in portraits, in the face of a statue, in a tragic mask. It is a suffering which has *being*. It is presented to us as a compact, objective whole which did not await our coming in order to be and which overflows the consciousness which we have of it; it is there in the midst of the world, impenetrable and dense, like this tree or this stone; it endures; finally it is what it is. We can speak of it—that suffering there which is expressed by that set of the mouth, by that frown. It is supported and expressed by the physiognomy but not created by it. Suffering is posited upon the physiognomy; it is beyond passivity as beyond activity, beyond negation as beyond affirmation—it is. However it can be only as consciousness of self. We know well that this mask does not express the unconscious grimace of a sleeper or the rictus of a dead man. It refers to possibilities, to a situation in the world. The suffering is the conscious relation to these possibilities, to this situation, but it is solidified, cast in the bronze of being. And it is as such that it fascinates us; it stands as a degraded approximation of that suffering-in-itself which haunts our own suffering. The suffering which I experience, in contrast, is never adequate suffering, due to the fact that it nihilates itself as in itself by the very act by which it founds itself. It escapes as suffering toward the consciousness of suffering. I can never be *surprised* by it, for it *is* only to the exact degree that I experience it. Its translucency removes from it all depth. I cannot observe it as I observe the suffering of the statue, since I make my own suffering and since I know it. If I must suffer, I should prefer that my suffering would seize me and flow over me like a storm, but instead I must raise it into existence in my free spontaneity. I should like simultaneously to be it and to conquer it, but this enormous, opaque suffering, which should transport me out of myself, continues instead to touch me lightly with its wing, and I cannot seize it. I find only *myself*, myself who moans, myself who wails, myself who, in order to realize this suffering which I am, must play without respite the drama of suffering. I wring my hands, I cry in order that beings, their sounds, their gestures may run through the world, ridden by the suffering-in-itself which I cannot be. Each groan, each facial expression of the man who suffers aims at sculpturing a statue-in-itself of suffering. But this statue will never exist save through others and for others. My suffering suffers from being what it is not and from not being what it is. At the point of being made one with itself, it escapes, separated from itself by nothing, but that nothingness of which it is itself the foundation. It is loquacious because it is not adequate, but its ideal is silence—the silence of the statue, of the overwhelmed man who lowers his head and veils his face without speaking. But with this man too—it is *for me* that he does not speak. In himself he chatters incessantly, for the words of the inner language are like adumbrations of the "self" of suffering. It is for my eyes that he is "crushed" by suffering; in himself he feels himself responsible for that grief which he wills even while not wishing it and which he does not wish even while willing it, that grief which is haunted by a perpetual absence—the absence of the motionless, mute suffering which is the *self*, the concrete out-of-reach totality of the for-itself which suffers, the *for* of human reality in suffering. We can see that my suffering never posits this suffering-in-itself which visits it. My real suffering is not an *effort* to reach the self. But it can *be* suffering only as consciousness (of) *not being enough* suffering in the presence of that full and absent suffering.

### 3 VALUE

Now we can ascertain more exactly what is the being of the self: it is value. Value is affected with the double character, which

moralists have very inadequately explained, of both being unconditionally and not being. Qua value indeed, value has being, but
this normative existent has no being as reality. Its being is to be
value; that is, not-to-be being. Thus the being of value *qua*
value is the being of what does not have being. Value then appears inapprehensible. To take it as being is to risk totally
misunderstanding its unreality [*irréalité*] and to make of it, as
sociologists do, an actual requirement among other actual facts.
In this case the contingency of being destroys value. But conversely if one looks only at the ideality of values, one is going to
extract being from them, and then for lack of being, they dissolve. Of course, as Scheler has shown, I can achieve an intuition
of values in terms of concrete exemplifications; I can grasp nobility in a noble act. But value thus apprehended is not given as
existing on the same level of being as the act on which it confers
value—in the way, for example, that the essence "red" is in
relation to a particular red. Value is given as a beyond of the acts
confronted, as the limit, for example, of the infinite progression
of noble acts. Value is beyond being. Yet if we are not to be
taken in by fine words, we must recognize that this being which
is beyond being possesses being in some way at least.

These considerations suffice to make us admit that human
reality is that by which value arrives in the world. But the meaning of being for value is that it is that toward which a being
transcends its being; every value-oriented act is a wrenching
away from its own being toward —. Since value is always and
everywhere the beyond of all transcendings, it can be considered
as the unconditioned unity of all transcendings of being. Thereby
it makes a dyad with the reality which originally transcends its
being and by which transcending comes into being—*i.e.*, with
human reality. We see also that since value is the unconditioned
beyond of all of transcendings, it must be originally the beyond of
the very being which transcends, for that is the only way in
which value can be the original beyond of all possible transcendings. If every transcending must be able to be transcended, it is
necessary that the being which transcends should be *a priori insofar* as it is the very source of transcendings. Thus value taken
in its origin, or the supreme value, is the beyond and the *for* of
transcendence. It is the beyond which transcends and which
provides the foundation for all my transcendings but toward
which I can never transcend myself, precisely because my
transcendings presuppose it.

In all cases of lack value is "the lacked;" it is not "the lacking." Value is the self insofar as the self haunts the heart of the for-itself as that for which the for-itself *is*. The supreme value toward which consciousness at every instant transcends itself by its very being is the absolute being of the self with its characteristics of identity, of purity, of permanence, etc., and as its own foundation. This is what enables us to conceive why value can simultaneously be and not be. It *is* as the meaning and the beyond of all transcending; it *is* as the absent in-itself which haunts being-for-itself. But as soon as we consider value, we see that it is itself a transcending of this being-in-itself, since value *gives being to itself*. It is beyond its own being for its own being is of the type of being that coincides with itself, and it therefore at once transcends this being, its permanence, its purity, its consistency, its identity, its silence, by claiming these qualities by virtue of its presence to itself. And conversely if we start by considering it as presence to itself, this presence immediately is solidified, congealed in the in-itself. Moreover it is in its being the missing [*manquant*] totality toward which a being makes itself be. It emerges for a being, not as this being is what it is in full contingency, but as it is the foundation of its own nihilation. In this sense value haunts being as being founds itself but not as being *is*. Value haunts *freedom*. This means that the relation of value to the for-itself is a peculiar relationship: it is the being which has to be insofar as it is the foundation of its nothingness of being. Yet while it has to be this being, this is not because it is under the pressure of an external constraint, nor because value, like the Unmoved Mover of Aristotle, exercises over it an actual attraction, nor is it because its being has been received; but it is because in its being it makes itself be as having to be this being. In a word the *self*, the for-itself, and their inter-relation stand within the limits of an unconditioned freedom—in the sense that *nothing* makes value exist—unless it is that freedom which by the same token makes me myself exist—and also within the limits of concrete facticity—since as the foundation of its nothingness, the for-itself cannot be the foundation of its being. There is then a total contingency of being-for-value (which will overtake morality and paralyze and relativize it) and at the same time a free and absolute necessity.*

* One will perhaps be tempted to translate the trinity under consideration into Hegelian terms and to make of the in-itself, the thesis, of the for-itself the antithesis, and of the in-itself-for-itself or value the synthesis. But it must be noted

Value in its original emergence is not *posited* by the for-itself; it is consubstantial with it—to such a degree that there is no consciousness which is not haunted by *its* value and that human reality in the broad sense includes both the for-itself and value. If value haunts the for-itself without being posited by it, this is because value is not the object of a thesis; in effect the for-itself would have to be a posited object to itself since value and the for-itself can arise only in the consubstantial unity of a dyad. Thus the for-itself as a non-thetic self-consciousness does not exist *in the face of* value in the sense that for Leibniz the monad exists "alone in the face of God." Value therefore is not *known* at this stage since knowledge posits the object in the face of consciousness. Value is merely given with the non-thetic translucency of the for-itself, which makes itself be as the consciousness of being. Value is everywhere and nowhere; at the heart of the nihilating relation "reflection-reflecting," it is present and out of reach, and it is simply lived as the concrete meaning of that lack which makes my present being. In order for value to become the object of a thesis, the for-itself which it haunts must also appear before the look of reflection. Reflective consciousness in fact accomplishes two things by the same act; the *Erlebnis* reflected-on is posited in its nature as lack and value is disengaged as the out-of-reach meaning of what is lacked. Thus reflective consciousness can be properly called a moral consciousness since it cannot emerge without at the same moment disclosing values. It is obvious that I remain free in my reflective consciousness to direct my attention on these values or to neglect them—exactly as it depends on me to look more closely at this table, my pen, or my package of tobacco. But whether they are the object of a detailed attention or not, in any case they *are*.

It is not necessary to conclude, however, that the reflective

---

here that while the for-itself *lacks* the in-itself, the in-itself does not *lack* the for-itself. There is then no reciprocity in the opposition. In short, the for-itself remains non-essential and contingent in relation to the in-itself, and it is this non-essentiality which we earlier called its facticity. In addition, the synthesis or value would indeed be a return to the thesis, thus a return upon itself; but as this is an unrealizable totality, the for-itself is not a moment which can be surpassed. As such its nature approaches nearer to the "ambiguous" realities of Kierkegaard. Furthermore we find here a double play of unilateral oppositions: the for-itself in one sense lacks the in-itself, which does not lack the for-itself; but in another sense the in-itself lacks its own possibility (or the lacking for-itself), which in this case does not lack the in-itself.

look is the only one which can make value appear, nor should we by analogy project the values of our for-itself into the world of transcendence. If the object of intuition is a phenomenon of human reality but transcendent, it is released immediately with its value, for the for-itself of the Other is not a hidden phenomenon which would be given only as the conclusion of a reasoning by analogy. It manifests itself originally to my for-itself; as we shall see, the presence of the for-itself as for-others is even the necessary condition for the constitution of the for-itself as such. In this emergence of the for-others, value is given as in the emergence of the for-itself, although in a different mode of being. But we cannot treat here the objective encounter with values in the world since we have not yet elucidated the nature of the for-others. . . .

## 4 THE CIRCUIT OF SELFNESS

We shall use the expression *Circuit of selfness* [*Circuit de ipséité*] for the relation of the for-itself with the possible which it is, and "world" for the totality of being insofar as it is traversed by the circuit of selfness.

We are now in a position to elucidate the mode of being of the possible. The possible is *the something* which the for-itself lacks *in order to* be itself. Consequently it is not appropriate to say that it *is qua* possible—unless by being we are to understand the being of an existent which "is made-to-be" insofar as it is made-not-to-be, or if you prefer, the appearance at a distance of what I am. The possible does not exist as a pure representation, not even as a denied one, but as a real lack of being which, *qua* lack, is beyond being. It has the being of a lack and as lack, it lacks being. The possible is not, the possible is possibilized to the exact degree that the for-itself makes itself be; the possible determines in schematic outline a location in the nothingness which the for-itself is beyond itself. Naturally it is not at first thematically posited; it is delineated beyond the world and gives my present perception its meaning as this is apprehended in the world in the circuit of selfness. But neither is the possible ignored or unconscious; it delineates the limits of the non-thetic self-consciousness as a non-thetic consciousness. The non-reflective consciousness (of) thirst is apprehended *by means of* the glass of water as desirable, without putting the self in the centripetal position as the end of the desire. But the possible repletion appears as a non-positional correlate of the non-thetic self-consciousness on the horizon of the glass-in-the-midst-of-the-world.

In *The Transcendence of the Ego* I attempted to show that the ego does not belong to the domain of the for-itself. I shall not repeat myself here. Let us note only the reason for the transcendence of the ego: as a unifying pole of *Erlebnisse* the ego is in-itself, not for-itself. If it did *belong to consciousness*, in fact, it would be to itself its own foundation in the translucency of the immediate. But then we would have to say that it is what it is not and that it is not what it is, and this is by no means the mode of being of the I. In fact the consciousness which I have of the I never exhausts it, and consciousness is not what causes it to come into existence; the I is always given as *having been there before* consciousness—and at the same time as possessing depths which have to be revealed gradually. Thus the ego appears to consciousness as a transcendent in-itself, as an existent in the human world, not as *belonging to* consciousness.

Yet we need not conclude that the for-itself is a pure and simple "impersonal" contemplation. But the ego is far from being the personalizing pole of a consciousness which without it would remain in the impersonal stage; on the contrary, it is consciousness in its fundamental selfness which under certain conditions allows the appearance of the ego as the transcendent phenomenon of that selfness. As we have seen, it is actually impossible to say of the in-itself that it is *itself*. It simply *is*. In this sense, some will say that the I, which they wrongly hold to be the inhabitant of consciousness, is the Me of consciousness but not its own *self*. Thus through hypostatizing the being of the for-itself which is reflected-on and making it into an in-itself, these writers fix and destroy the movement of reflection upon the self; consciousness then would be a pure return to the ego as to its *self*, but the ego no longer refers to anything. The reflexive relation has been transformed into a simple centripetal relation, the center, moreover, being a nucleus of opacity. We, on the contrary, have shown that the *self* on principle cannot inhabit consciousness. It is, if you like, *the reason* for the infinite movement by which the reflection refers to the reflecting and this again to the reflection; by definition it is an ideal, a limit. What makes it emerge as a limit is the nihilating reality of the presence of being to being within the unity of being as a type of being.

Thus from its first emerging, consciousness by the pure nihilating movement of reflection makes itself *personal;* for what confers personal existence on a being is not the possession of an ego—which is only the *sign* of the personality—but it is the fact that the being exists for itself as a presence to itself.

Now this first reflective movement involves in addition a second or selfness. In selfness my possible is reflected on my consciousness and determines it as what it is. Selfness represents a degree of nihilation carried further than the pure presence to itself of the pre-reflective *cogito*—in the sense that the possible which I am is not pure presence to the for-itself as reflection to reflecting, but that it is *absent-presence.* Due to this fact the existence of *reference* as a structure of being in the for-itself is still more clearly marked. The for-itself is itself over there, beyond its grasp, in the far reaches of its possibilities. This free necessity of being—over there—what one is in the form of lack constitutes selfness or the second aspect of the person. In fact how can the person be defined if not as a free relation to himself?

As for the world—*i.e.,* the totality of beings as they exist within the compass of the circuit of selfness—this can be only what human reality transcends toward itself. To borrow Heidegger's definition, the world is "that in terms of which human reality makes known to itself what it is." The possible which is *my* possible is a possible for-itself and as such a presence to the in-itself as consciousness *of* the in-itself. What I seek in the face of the world is the coincidence with a for-itself which I am and which is consciousness *of* the world. But this possible which is *non-thetically* an absent-present to present consciousness is not present as an object of a positional consciousness, for in that case it would be reflected-on. The satisfied thirst which haunts my actual thirst is not consciousness (of) thirst as a satisfied thirst; it is a thetic consciousness of *itself-drinking-from-a-glass* and a non-positional self-consciousness. It then makes itself transcend itself toward the glass *of which it* is conscious; and as a correlate of this possible non-thetic consciousness, the glass-drunk-from haunts the full glass as its possible and constitutes it as a glass to be drunk from. Thus the world by nature is *mine* insofar as it is the correlative in-itself of nothingness; that is, of the necessary obstacle beyond which I find myself as that which I am in the form of "having to be it." Without the world there is no selfness, no person; without selfness, without the person, there is no world. But the world's belonging to the *person* is never posited on the level of the pre-reflective *cogito*. It would be absurd to say that the world as it is known is known as mine. Yet this quality of "my-ness" in the world is a fugitive structure, always present, a structure which I *live*. The world (*is*) mine because it is haunted by possibles, and the consciousness of each of these is a possible self-consciousness which *I am;* it is these possibles as such which give the world its unity and its meaning as the world. . . .

*Being and Nothingness, 79–80, 83–84, 89–95, 102–104.*

# CONSCIOUSNESS
# AND THE OTHER

# I

———•———

## Hell Is Other People

INEZ   Wait! You'll see how simple it is. Childishly simple. There isn't any physical torture. And yet we're in Hell. And no one else will come here. We'll stay in this room together, the three of us, for ever and ever. In short there's someone missing here, the official torturer.

GARCIN (*Sotto voce*)   I'd noticed that.

INEZ   It's obvious they're economizing on manpower. The same idea as in a cafeteria, where the customers serve themselves.

ESTELLE   What are you getting at?

INEZ   I mean that each of us will act as a torturer for the other two. . . .

> (ESTELLE *is powdering her face. She looks around for a mirror, fumbles in her bag, then turns toward* GARCIN)

ESTELLE   Pardon, sir, have you a mirror? (GARCIN *does not answer*) Any sort of glass, a pocket mirror will do. (GARCIN *remains silent*) Even if you won't speak to me, you might lend me a mirror.
> (*His head buried in his hands,* GARCIN *remains silent*)

INEZ (*Eagerly*)   Don't worry. I've a mirror in my bag. (*She opens her bag, looks annoyed*) It's gone! They must have taken it at the entrance.

ESTELLE   How tiresome!
> (ESTELLE *shuts her eyes and sways, as if about to faint.* INEZ *runs forward and holds her up*)

INEZ   What's the matter?

ESTELLE (*Opens her eyes and smiles*) I feel so queer. (*She pats herself*) Don't you ever feel that way too? When I can't see myself I begin to wonder if I really exist. I pat myself just to make sure, but it doesn't help.

INEZ You're well off. I, I always feel conscious of myself. It's a feeling in my mind.

ESTELLE Yes, in one's mind. But everything that goes on in one's head is so vague. It puts me to sleep. (*She is silent for a moment*) I've six huge looking-glasses in my bedroom. I can see them, see them. But they don't see me. They reflect the couch, the carpet, the window—but how empty it is, a mirror where I am not. When I used to talk with people, I always made sure there was one nearby in which I could look at myself. I talked, I saw myself, talking, I saw myself as others saw me—that kept me awake. (*Despairingly*) My lipstick! I'm sure I've put it on crooked. I simply can't do without a looking-glass for all eternity.

INEZ Suppose I be your looking-glass? Come, join me. There's a place for you on my sofa. . . .

ESTELLE Are you sure it looks all right?

INEZ You're lovely, Estelle.

ESTELLE But how can I rely upon your taste? Is it *my* taste? Oh, how tormenting it is, enough to drive one crazy.

INEZ I do have your taste, because I like you so much. Look at me, carefully. Now give me a smile. I'm not so ugly either. Am I not better than your mirror?

ESTELLE I don't quite know. You scare me. My reflection in mirrors never did that. I was used to it, like something I had tamed. I knew it so well. I'm going to smile and my smile will sink down into your pupils, and heaven knows what will become of it.

INEZ And what keeps you from "taming" me? (*They look at each other,* ESTELLE *smiles, with a sort of fascination*) . . . Suppose the mirror started telling lies? Or suppose I shut my eyes, and refused to look at you, what could you do with all that loveliness of yours? Don't be afraid, I can't help looking

at you. I shan't look away. And I'll be nice to you, ever so nice. Only you must be friendly, too.
(*A pause*)

ESTELLE   Do I really—attract you?

INEZ   A lot.
(*Another pause*)

ESTELLE (*Indicating* GARCIN *with a slight gesture of her head*) But I'd like him to look at me, too.

INEZ   Of course! Because he's a Man! (*To* GARCIN) You've won. . . .

GARCIN   You're crazy, both of you. Don't you see where this will end up? Now shut up. (*Pause*) Let's all of us sit down again quietly, close our eyes. Each of us must try to forget the presence of the others.
(*A pause.* GARCIN *sits down. The women are returning hesitantly to their places. Suddenly* INEZ *swings round*)

INEZ   Forget? How silly can you get! I feel you even in my bones. Your silence shrieks in my ears. You can nail up your mouth, cut your tongue out, but how can that keep you from being there? Can you stop thinking? I hear it, ticking away like an alarm clock, and I know you hear me thinking. It's all very well slouching on your sofa, but you are everywhere, and every sound comes to me soiled, because you've intercepted it on its way. Why, you've stolen even my face from me; you know it, and I don't! And what about Estelle? You've stolen her from me, too; if she and I were alone, do you think she'd dare to treat me as she does?

*No Exit,* 22–23, 24–25, 27–29.

# II

The Encounter with the Other

## 1 THE LOOK

We have described human reality from the standpoint of negative behavior and from the standpoint of the *cogito*. Following
this lead we have discovered that human reality is-for-itself. Is
this *all* that it is? Without going outside our attitude of reflective
description, we can encounter modes of consciousness which
seem, even while themselves remaining strictly in for-itself, to
point to a radically different type of ontological structure. This
ontological structure is *mine*; . . . I am concerned about myself, and yet this concern for-myself reveals to me a being
which is *my* being without being-for-me.

Consider, for example, shame. Here we are dealing with a
mode of consciousness which has a structure identical with all
those which we have previously described. It is a non-positional
self-consciousness, conscious (of) itself as shame; as such, it
is an example of what the Germans call *Erlebnis*, and it is accessible to reflection. In addition its structure is intentional; it is a
shameful apprehension *of* something and this something is *me*.
I am ashamed of what I *am*. Shame therefore realizes an intimate
relation of myself to myself. Through shame I have discovered
an aspect of *my* being. Yet although certain complex forms derived from shame can appear on the reflective plane, shame is
not originally a phenomenon of reflection. In fact no matter
what results one can obtain in solitude by the religious *practice* of shame, it is in its primary structure shame *before somebody*. I have just made an awkward or vulgar gesture. This gesture clings to me; I neither judge it nor blame it. I simply live it.
I realize it in the mode of for-itself. But now suddenly I raise my
head. Somebody was there and has seen me. Suddenly I realize
the vulgarity of my gesture, and I am ashamed. It is certain

that my shame is not reflective, for the presence of another in my consciousness, even as a catalyst, is incompatible with the reflective attitude; in the field of my reflection I can never meet with anything but the consciousness which is mine. But the Other is the indispensable mediator between myself and me. I am ashamed of myself *as I appear* to the Other.

By the mere appearance of the Other, I am put in the position of passing judgment on myself as on an object, for it is as an object that I appear to the Other. Yet this object which has appeared to the Other is not an empty image in the mind of another. Such an image, in fact, would be imputable wholly to the Other and so could not "touch" me. I could feel irritation, or anger before it as before a bad portrait of myself which gives to my expression an ugliness or baseness which I do not have, but I could not be touched to the quick. Shame is by nature *recognition*. I recognize that I *am* as the Other sees me. There is however no question of a comparison between what I am for myself and what I am for the Other as if I found in myself, in the mode of being of the for-itself, an equivalent of what I am for the Other. In the first place this comparison is not encountered in us as the result of a concrete psychic operation. Shame is an immediate shudder which runs through me from head to foot without any discursive preparation. In addition the comparison is impossible; I am unable to bring about any relation between what I am in the intimacy of the for-itself, without distance, without withdrawal [*recul*], without perspective, and this unjustifiable being-in-itself which I am for the Other. There is no standard here, no table of correlation. Moreover the very notion of *vulgarity* implies an inter-monadic relation. Nobody can be vulgar all by himself!

Thus the Other has not only revealed to me what I was; he has established me in a new type of being which can support new qualifications. This being was not in me potentially before the appearance of the Other, for it could not have found any place in the for-itself. Even if some power had been pleased to endow me with a body wholly constituted before it should be for-others, still my vulgarity and my awkwardness could not lodge there potentially; for they are meanings and as such they transcend the body and at the same time refer to a witness capable of understanding them and to the totality of my human reality. But this new being which appears *for* the other does not reside *in* the Other; I am responsible for it as is shown very well by the educational procedure of making children ashamed of what they are.

Thus shame is shame *of oneself before the Other;* these two structures are inseparable. But at the same time I need the Other in order to realize fully all the structures of my being. The for-itself refers to the for-others. Therefore if we wish to grasp in its totality the relation of man's being to being-in-itself, we cannot be satisfied with the descriptions outlined in the earlier chapters of this work. We must answer two far more formidable questions: first that of the existence of the Other, then the question of my ontological relation to the being of the Other. . . .

I am in a public park. Not far away there is a lawn and along the edge of that lawn there are benches. A man passes by those benches. I see this man; I apprehend him as an object and at the same time as a man. What does this mean? What do I imply when I assert that this object *is a man*?

If I were to think of him as being only a puppet, I should apply to him the categories which I ordinarily use to group temporal-spatial "things." That is, I should apprehend him as being "beside" the benches, two yards and twenty inches from the lawn, as exercising a certain pressure on the ground, etc. His relation with other objects would be of the purely additive type; this means that I could have him disappear without the relations of the other objects around him being perceptibly *changed.* In short, no new relation would appear *through him* between those things in my universe: grouped and synthesized *from my point of view* into instrumental complexes, they would *from his point of view* disintegrate into a plurality of indifferent relations. Perceiving him as a *man,* on the other hand, is not to apprehend an additive relation between the chair and him; it is to register an organization *without distance* of the things in my universe around that privileged object. To be sure, the lawn remains two yards and twenty inches away from him, but it is also *as a lawn* linked with him in a relation which at once both transcends distance and contains it. Instead of the two terms of the distance being indifferent, interchangeable, and in a reciprocal relation, the distance *is unfolded starting from* the man whom I see and *extending up to* the lawn as the synthetic emergence of a unilateral relation. We are dealing with a relation which is without *parts*, given immediately, inside of which there unfolds a spatiality which is not *my* spatiality; for instead of a grouping *toward me* of the objects, there is now an orientation *which flees from me.*

Of course this relation without distance and without parts is in no way that original relation of the Other to me which I am seeking. In the first place, it concerns only the man and the things in the world. In addition it is still an object of knowledge; I would express it, for example, by saying that this man sees the lawn, or that in spite of the prohibiting sign he is preparing to walk on the grass, etc. Finally it still retains a merely probable character: First, it is *probable* that this object is a man. Second, even granted that he is a man, it remains only probable that he *sees* the lawn at the moment that I perceive him; it is possible that he is dreaming of some project without exactly being aware of what is around him, or that he is blind, etc., etc. Nevertheless this new relation of the object-man to the object-lawn has a particular character; it is simultaneously given to me as a whole, since it is there in the world as an object which I can know (it is, in fact, an objective relation which I express by saying: Peter has glanced at this watch, John has looked out the window, etc.), and at the same time it entirely escapes me. To the extent that the man-as-object is the fundamental term of this relation, to the extent that the relation goes *toward him,* it escapes me. I cannot put myself at the center of it. The distance which unfolds between the lawn and the man across the synthetic emergence of this primary relation is a negation of the distance which I establish—as a pure type of external negation —between these two objects. The distance appears as a pure *disintegration* of the relations which I apprehend between the objects of my universe. It is not I who realize this disintegration; it appears to me as a relation which I aim at emptily across the distances which I originally established between things. It stands as a background of things, a background which on principle escapes me and which is conferred on them from without. Thus the appearance among the objects of *my* universe of an element of disintegration in that universe is what I mean by the appearance of a man in my universe.

The Other is first the permanent flight of things toward a limit which I apprehend as an object at a certain distance from me but which escapes me inasmuch as it unfolds about itself its own distances. Moreover this process of disintegration gains momentum; if there exists between the lawn and the Other a relation which is without distance and which creates distance, then there exists necessarily a relation between the Other and the statue which stands on a pedestal *in the middle of* the lawn, and a relation between the Other and the big chestnut trees which border the walk; there is a total space which is grouped around the Other, and this space is made *with my space;* there is a regrouping in which I participate but which escapes me, a regrouping of all the objects which people my universe. This regrouping does not stop there. The grass is something qualified; it is *this* green grass which exists for the Other; in this sense the very quality of the object, its deep, raw green is in direct relation to this man. This green turns toward the Other an aspect which escapes me. I apprehend the relation of the green to the Other as an objective relation, but I cannot apprehend the green *as* it appears to the Other. Thus suddenly an object has appeared which has stolen the world from me. Everything is in place; everything still exists for me; but everything is traversed by an invisible flight and congealed in the direction of a new object. The appearance of the Other in the world corresponds therefore to a congealed sliding of the whole universe, to a decentralization of the world which undermines the centralization which I am simultaneously effecting.

But *the Other* is still an object *for me.* He belongs to *my distances;* the man is there, twenty paces from me, he is turning his back on me. As such he is again two yards, twenty inches from the lawn, six yards from the statue; hence the disintegration of my universe is contained within the limits of this same universe; we are not dealing here with a flight of the world toward nothingness or outside itself. Rather it appears that the world has a kind of drain hole in the middle of its being and that it is perpetually flowing off through this hole. The universe, the flow, and the drain hole are all once again recovered, reapprehended, and congealed into an object. All this is there *for me* as a partial structure of the world, even though the total disintegration of the universe is involved. Moreover these disintegrations may often be contained within more narrow limits. There, for example, is a man who is reading while he walks. The disintegration of the universe which he represents is purely virtual; he has ears which do not hear, eyes which see nothing except his book. Between his book and him I apprehend an undeniable re-

lation without distance of the same type as that which earlier
connected the walker with the grass. But this time the form has
closed in on itself. There is a full object for me to grasp. In the
midst of the world I can say "man-reading" as I could say "cold
stone," "fine rain." I apprehend a closed "Gestalt" in which the
*reading* forms the essential quality; for the rest, it remains blind
and mute, lets itself be known and perceived as a pure and simple temporal-spatial thing, and seems to be related to the rest
of the world by a purely indifferent externality. The quality
"man-reading" as the relation of the man to the book is simply a
little particular crack in my universe. At the heart of this solid,
visible form he makes himself a particular emptying. The
form is massive only in appearance; its peculiar meaning is to
be—in the midst of my universe, at ten paces from me, at the
heart of that massivity—a closely consolidated and localized
flight.

None of this enables us to leave the level on which the Other
is an *object*. At most we are dealing with a particular type of
objectivity akin to that which Husserl designated by the term
*absence* without, however, his noting that the Other is defined
not as the absence of a consciousness in relation to the body
which I see but by the absence of the world which I perceive, an
absence discovered at the very heart of my perception of this
world. On this level the Other is an object in the world, an object which can be defined by the world. But this relation of flight
and of absence on the part of the world in relation to me is only
probable. If it is this which defines the objectivity of the Other,
then to what original presence of the Other does it refer? Now
we can give this answer: if the Other-as-object is defined in connection with the world as the object which *sees* what I see,
then my fundamental connection with the Other-as-subject
must be able to be referred back to my permanent possibility
of *being seen* by the Other. It is in and through the revelation of
my being-as-object for the Other that I must be able to apprehend the presence of his being-as-subject. For just as the Other
is a probable object for me-as-subject, so I can discover myself
in the process of becoming a probable object for only a certain
subject. This revelation cannot derive from the fact that *my
universe is an object for the Other-as-object,* as if the Other's
look after having wandered over the lawn and the surrounding
objects came following a definite path to place itself on me. I

have observed that I cannot be an object for an object. A radical conversion of the Other is necessary if he is to escape objectivity. Therefore I cannot consider the look which the Other directs on me as one of the possible manifestations of his objective being; the Other cannot look at *me* as he looks at the grass. Furthermore my objectivity cannot itself derive *for me* from the objectivity of the world since I am precisely the one by whom *there is* a world; that is, the one who on principle cannot be an object for himself.

Thus this relation which I call "being-seen-by-another," far from being merely one of the relations signified by the word *man,* represents an irreducible fact which cannot be deduced either from the essence of the Other-as-object, or from my being-as-subject. On the contrary, if the concept of the Other-as-object is to have any meaning, this can be only as the result of the conversion and the degradation of that original relation. In a word, my apprehension of the Other in the world as *probably being* a man refers to my permanent possibility of *being-seen-by-him;* that is, to the permanent possibility that a subject who sees me may be substituted for the object seen by me. "Being-seen-by-the-Other" is the *truth* of "seeing-the-Other." Thus the notion of the Other cannot under any circumstances aim at a solitary, extra-mundane consciousness which I cannot even think. The man is defined by his relation to the world and by his relation to myself. He is that object in the world which determines an internal flow of the universe, an internal hemorrhage. He is the subject who is revealed to me in that flight of myself toward objectivation. But the original relation of myself to the Other is not only an absent truth aimed at across the concrete presence of an object in my universe; it is also a concrete, daily relation which at each instant I experience. At each instant the Other *is looking at me.* It is easy therefore for us to attempt with concrete examples to describe this fundamental relationship which must form the basis of any theory concerning the Other. If the Other is on principle the *one who looks at me,* then we must be able to explain the meaning of the Other's look.

Every look directed toward me is manifested in connection with the appearance of a sensible form in our perceptive field, but contrary to what might be expected, it is not connected with any specific form. Of course what *most often* manifests a look is the convergence of two ocular globes in my direction. But the look will be given just as well on occasion when there is a rustling of branches, or the sound of a footstep followed by silence, or the slight opening of a shutter, or a light movement of a curtain. During an attack, men who are crawling through the brush apprehend as a *look to be avoided,* not two eyes, but a white farmhouse which is outlined against the sky at the top of a little hill. It is obvious that the object thus constituted still manifests the look as being probable. It is only probable that behind the bush which has just moved there is someone hiding who is watching me. But this probability need not detain us for the moment; we shall return to this point later. What is important first is to define the look in itself. Now the bush, the farmhouse are not the look; they only represent the *eye,* for the eye is not at first apprehended as a sensible organ of vision but as the support for the look. They never refer therefore to the actual eye of the watcher hidden behind the curtain, behind a window in the farmhouse. In themselves they are already eyes. On the other hand neither is the look one quality among others of the object which functions as an eye, nor is it the total form of that object, nor a "worldly" relation which is established between that object and me. On the contrary, far from perceiving the look *on* the objects which manifest it, my apprehension of a look turned toward me appears on the ground of the destruction of the eyes which "look at me." If I apprehend the look, I cease to perceive the eyes; they are there, they remain in the field of my perception as pure *presentations,* but I do not make any use of them; they are neutralized, put out of play; they are no longer the object of a thesis but remain in that state of "disconnection" in which the world is put by a consciousness practicing the phenomenological reduction prescribed by Husserl. It is never when eyes are looking at you that you can find them beautiful or ugly, that you can notice their color. The Other's look disguises his eyes; he seems to go *in front of them.* This illusion stems from the fact that eyes as objects of my perception remain at a precise distance which unfolds from me to them (in a word, I am present to the eyes without distance, but they are distant from the place where I "find myself"), whereas the look is upon me without distance while at the same time it holds me at a distance—that is, its immediate presence to me unfolds a distance which removes me from it. I cannot there-fore direct my attention on the look without at the same time having my perception decompose and pass into the background. There is produced here something analogous to what I attempted to show elsewhere in connection with the subject of the imagination. We cannot, I said then, perceive and imagine simultaneously; it must be either one or the other. I would add here: we cannot perceive the world and at the same time apprehend a look fastened upon us; it must be either one or the other. This is because to perceive is to *look at,* and to apprehend a look is not to apprehend a look-as-object in the world (unless the look is not directed upon us); it is to be conscious of *being looked at.* The look which the eyes manifest, no matter what kind of eyes they are, is a pure reference to myself. What I apprehend immediately when I hear the branches crackling behind me is not that *there is someone there;* it is that I am vulnerable, that I have a body which can be hurt, that I occupy a place and that I cannot in any case escape from the space in which I am without defense—in short, that I *am seen.* Thus the look is first an intermediary which refers from me to myself. What is the nature of this intermediary? What does *being seen* mean for me?

## 2 SHAME

Let us imagine that moved by jealousy, curiosity, or vice I have just glued my ear to the door and looked through a keyhole. I am alone and on the level of a non-thetic self-consciousness. This means first of all that there is no self to inhabit my consciousness, nothing therefore to which I can refer my acts in order to qualify them. They are in no way *known;* I *am my* acts and hence they carry in themselves their whole justification. I am a pure consciousness *of* things, and things, caught up in the circuit of my selfness, offer to me their potentialities as the replica of my non-thetic consciousness (of) my own possibilities. This means that behind that door a spectacle is presented as "to be seen," a conversation as "to be heard." The door, the keyhole are at once both instruments and obstacles; they are presented as "to be handled with care"; the keyhole is given as "to be looked through close by and a little to one side," etc. Hence from this moment "I do what I have to do." No transcending view comes to confer upon my acts the character of a *given* on which a judgment can be brought to bear. My consciousness clings to my acts, it *is* my acts; and my acts are commanded only by the ends to be attained and by the instruments to be employed. My attitude, for example, has no "outside"; it is a pure process of relating the instrument (the keyhole) to the end to be attained (the spectacle to be seen), a pure mode of losing myself in the world, of making myself absorbed by things as ink is by a blotter in order that an instrumental complex oriented toward an end may be synthetically detached on the ground of the world. The order is the reverse of causal order. It is the end to be attained which organizes all the moments which precede it. The end justifies the means; the means do not exist for themselves and outside the end.

Moreover the ensemble exists only in relation to a free project of my possibilities. Jealousy, as the possibility which I *am*, organizes this instrumental complex by transcending the complex toward itself. But I *am* this jealousy; I do not *know* it. If I contemplated it instead of making it, then only the worldly complex of instrumentality could teach it to me. This complex with its double and inverted determination (there is a spectacle to be seen behind the door only because I am jealous, but my jealousy is nothing except the simple objective fact that *there is* a sight to *be seen* behind the door)—this we shall call *situation*. This situation reflects to me at once both my facticity and my freedom; on the occasion of a certain objective structure of the world which surrounds me, it refers my freedom to me in the form of tasks to be freely done. There is no constraint here since my freedom gnaws away at my possibles and since correlatively the potentialities of the world indicate and offer only themselves. Moreover I cannot truly define myself as *being* in a situation: first because I am not a positional consciousness of myself; second because I am my own nothingness. In this sense— and since I am what I am not and since I am not what I am—I cannot even define myself as truly *being* in the process of listening at doors. I escape this temporary definition of myself by means of all my transcendence. There as we have seen is the origin of bad faith. Thus not only am I unable to *know* myself, but my very being escapes—although I *am* that very escape from my being—and I am absolutely nothing. There is nothing *there* but a pure nothingness encircling a certain objective complex and throwing it into relief upon the world, but this complex is a real system, a disposition of means in view of an end.

But suddenly I hear footsteps in the hall. Someone is looking at me! What does this mean? It means that I am suddenly affected in my being and that essential modifications appear in my structure—modifications which I can apprehend and fix conceptually by means of the reflective *cogito*.

First of all, I now exist as *myself* for my unreflective consciousness. This irruption of the self has often been described: I see *myself* because *somebody* sees me—as it is usually expressed. This way of putting it is not wholly accurate. Let us look more carefully. So long as we considered the for-itself in its isolation, we were able to maintain that the unreflective consciousness cannot be inhabited by a self; the self was given in the form of an object and only for the reflective consciousness. But here the self comes to haunt the unreflective consciousness. Now the unreflective consciousness is a consciousness *of* the world. Therefore for the unreflective consciousness the self exists on the level of objects-in-the-world; this role which devolved only on the reflective consciousness—the making-present of the self—belongs now to the unreflective consciousness. Only the reflective consciousness has the self directly for an object. The unreflective consciousness does not apprehend the *person* directly or as *its* object; the person is presented to consciousness *insofar as the person is an object for the Other*. This means that all of a sudden I am conscious of myself as escaping myself, not in that I am the foundation of my own nothingness but in that I have my foundation outside myself. I am for myself only as I am a pure reference to the Other.

Nevertheless we must not conclude here that the object is the Other and that the *ego* present to my consciousness is a secondary structure or a meaning of the Other-as-object; the Other is not an object here and cannot be an object, as we have shown, unless at the same time *my* self ceases to be an object-for-the-Other and vanishes. Thus I do not aim at the Other as an object nor at my *ego* as an object for myself; I do not even direct an empty intention toward the *ego* as toward an object presently out of my reach. In fact it is separated from me by a nothingness which I cannot fill since I apprehend it *as not being for me* and since on principle it exists for the *Other*. Therefore I do not aim at it as if it could someday be given me but on the contrary insofar as it on principle flees from me and will never belong to me.

Nevertheless I *am that ego;* I do not repudiate it as an alien image, but it is present to me as a self which I *am* without *knowing* it; for I discover it in shame and, in other instances, in pride. It is shame or pride which reveals to me the Other's look and myself at the terminus of that look. It is the shame or pride which makes me *live*, not *know* the situation of being looked at.

Now, shame, as we noted at the beginning of this chapter, is shame of *self;* it is the *recognition* of the fact that I *am* indeed that object which the Other is looking at and judging. I can be ashamed only as my freedom escapes me in order to become a *given* object. Thus originally the relation between my unreflective consciousness and my *ego*, which is being looked at, is a relation not of knowing but of being. Beyond any knowledge which I can have, I am this self which another knows. And this self which I am—this I am in a world which the Other has made alien to me, for the Other's look embraces my being and correlatively the walls, the door, the keyhole. All these instrumental things in the midst of which I am, now turn toward the Other an aspect which on principle escapes me. Thus I am my *ego* for the Other in the midst of a world which flows toward the Other. Earlier we were able to describe as an internal hemorrhage the flow of *my* world toward the Other-as-object. For in effect the flow of blood was trapped and localized by the very fact that I congealed into an object in my world that Other toward which this world was bleeding. Thus not a drop of blood was lost; all was recovered, surrounded, localized although in a being which I could not penetrate. Here in contrast the flow is without limit; it is lost externally; the world flows out of the world and I flow outside myself. The Other's look makes me be beyond my being in this world and puts me in the midst of the world which is at once *this world* and beyond this world. What sort of relations can I enter into with this being which I am and which shame reveals to me?

In the first place there is a relation of being. I *am* this being. I do not for an instant think of denying it; my shame is a confession. I shall be able later to use bad faith so as to hide it from myself, but bad faith is also a confession since it is an effort to flee the being which I am. But I am this being, neither in the mode of "having to be" nor in that of "was"; I do not found it in its being; I cannot produce it directly. But neither is it the indirect, strict effect of my acts as when my shadow on the ground or my reflection in the mirror is moved in correlation with the gestures which I make. This being which I am preserves a certain indeterminacy, a certain unpredictability. And these new characteristics do not come only from the fact that I cannot *know* the Other; they stem also and especially from the fact that the Other is free. Or to be exact and to reverse the terms, the Other's freedom is revealed to me across the uneasy indeterminacy of the being which I am for him. Thus this being is not my possible; it is not always in question at the heart of my freedom. On the contrary, it is the other side of my freedom. It is given to me as a burden which I carry without ever being able to turn back to know it, without even being able to realize its weight. If it is comparable to my shadow, it is like a shadow which is projected on a moving and unpredictable material such that no table of reference can be provided for calculating the distortions resulting from these movements. Yet we still have to do with *my* being and not with an image of my being. We are dealing with my being as it is inscribed in and by the Other's freedom. Everything takes place as if I had a dimension of being from which I was separated by a radical nothingness; and this nothingness is the Other's freedom. The Other has to make my being-for-him *be* insofar as he has to be his being. Thus each of my free acts involves me in a new setting where the very material of my being is the unpredictable freedom of another. Yet by my very shame I claim as mine that freedom of another. I affirm a profound unity of consciousnesses, not that harmony of monads which has sometimes been taken as a guarantee of objectivity but a unity of being; for I accept and wish that others should confer upon me a being which I recognize.

Shame reveals to me that I *am* this being, not in the mode of "was" or of "having to be"" but *in-itself*. When I am alone, I cannot realize my "being-seated"; at most it can be said that I simultaneously both am it and am not it. But in order for me to be what I am, it suffices merely that the Other look at me. It is not for myself, to be sure; I myself shall never succeed at realizing this being-seated which I grasp in the Other's look. I shall remain forever a consciousness. But it is for the Other. Once more the nihilating escape of the for-itself is congealed, once more the in-itself closes in upon the for-itself. But once more this metamorphosis is effected at a *distance*. For the Other I *am seated* as this inkwell *is* on the table; for the Other, I *am bending over* the keyhole as this tree *is bent* by the wind. Thus for the Other I have stripped myself of my transcendence. This is because my transcendence becomes for whoever makes himself a witness of it (*i.e.*, determines himself as *not being* my transcendence) a purely observed transcendence, a given transcendence; that is, it acquires a nature by the sole fact that the *Other* confers on it an outside. This is achieved, not by any distortion or by a refraction which the Other would impose on my transcendence through his categories, but by his very being. If there is an Other, whatever or whoever he may be, whatever may be his relations with me, and without his acting upon me in any way except by the pure emergence of his being—then I have an outside, I have a *nature*. My original fall is the existence of the Other. Shame—like pride—is the apprehension of myself as a nature although that very nature escapes me and is unknowable as such. Strictly speaking, it is not that I perceive myself losing my freedom in order to become a *thing*, but my nature is—over there, outside my lived freedom—as a given attribute of this being which I am for the Other.

I grasp the Other's look at the very center of my *act* as the solidification and alienation of my own possibilities. In fear or in anxious or prudent anticipation, I perceive that these possibilities which I *am* and which are the condition of my transcendence are given also to another, given as about to be transcended in turn by his own possibilities. The Other as a look is only that —my transcendence transcended. Of course I still *am* my possibilities in the mode of non-thetic consciousness (of) these possibilities. But at the same time the look alienates them from me. Hitherto I grasped these possibilities thetically on the world and in the world in the form of the potentialities of instruments: the dark corner in the hallway referred to me the possibility of hiding—as a simple potential quality of its shadow, as the invitation of its darkness. This quality or instrumentality of the object belonged to it alone and was given as an objective, ideal property marking its real belonging to that complex which we have called *situation*. But with the Other's look a new organization of complexes comes to superimpose itself on the first. To apprehend myself as seen is, in fact, to apprehend myself as seen *in the world* and from the standpoint of the world. The look does not carve me out in the universe; it comes to search for me at the heart of my situation and grasps me only in irresolvable relations with instruments. If I am seen as seated, I must be seen as "seated-on-a chair," if I am grasped as bent over, it is as "bent-over-the-keyhole," etc. But suddenly the alienation of myself, which is the act of being-looked-at, involves the alienation of the world which I organize. I am seen as seated on this chair with the result that I do not see it at all, that it is impossible for me to see it, that it escapes me so as to organize itself into a new and differently oriented complex—with other relations and other distances in the midst of other objects which similarly have for me a secret aspect.

Thus I who, insofar as I am my possibles, am what I am not and am not what I am—behold now I *am* somebody! And the one who I am—and who on principle escapes me—I am he *in the midst of the world* insofar as he escapes me. Due to this fact my relation to an object or the potentiality of an object decomposes under the Other's look and appears to me in the world as my possibility of utilizing the object, but only as this possibility on principle escapes me; that is, insofar as it is transcended by the Other toward his own possibilities. For example, the potentiality of the dark corner becomes a given possibility of hiding in the corner by the sole fact that the Other can transcend it toward his possibility of illuminating the corner with his flashlight. This possibility is there, and I apprehend it but as absent, as *in the Other;* I apprehend it through my anguish and through my decision to give up that hiding place which is *"too risky."* Thus my possibilities are present to my unreflective consciousness insofar as the Other *is watching for me.* If I see him ready for anything, his hand in his pocket where he has a weapon, his finger placed on the electric bell and ready "at the slightest movement on my part" to call the police, I apprehend my possibilities from outside and through him at the same time that I *am* my possibilities, somewhat as we objectively apprehend our thought through language at the same time that we think it *in order to* express it in language. This inclination to run away, which dominates me and carries me along and which I *am*—this I read in the Other's watchful look and in that other look—the gun pointed at me. The Other apprehends this inclination in me insofar as he has anticipated it and is already prepared for it. He apprehends it in me insofar as he surpasses it and disarms it. But I do not grasp the actual transcending; I grasp simply the death of my possibility. A subtle death: for my possibility of hiding still remains *my* possibility; inasmuch as I *am* it, it still lives; and the dark corner does not cease to indicate to me its potentiality to me. But if instrumentality is defined as the fact of "being able to be transcended toward ———," then my very possibility becomes an instrumentality. My possibility of hiding in the corner becomes the fact that the Other can transcend it toward his possibility of pulling me out of concealment, of identifying me, of arresting me. *For the Other* my possibility is at once an obstacle and a means as all instruments are. It is an obstacle, for it will compel him to certain new acts (to advance toward me, to turn on his flashlight). It is a means, for once I am discovered in this cul-de-sac, I "am caught." In other words every act performed against the Other can on principle be for the Other an instrument which will serve him against me. And I grasp the Other not in the clear vision of what he can make out of my act but in a fear which *lives* all my possibilities as ambivalent. The Other is the hidden death of my possibilities insofar as I live that death as hidden in the midst of the world. The connection between my possibility and the instrument is no more than between two instruments which are adjusted externally to each other to achieve an end which eludes me. *Both* the obscurity of the dark corner and my possibility of hiding there are transcended by the Other when, before I have been able to make a move to take refuge there, he throws the light on the corner. Thus in the jolt I feel when I apprehend the Other's look, suddenly I experience a subtle alienation of all my possibilities, which are now associated with objects of the world, far from me in the midst of the world. . . .

With the Other's look the "situation" escapes me. To use an everyday expression which better expresses our thought, I *am no longer master of the situation.* Or more exactly, I remain master of it, but it has one real dimension by which it escapes me, by which unforeseen reversals cause it *to be* otherwise than it appears for me. To be sure it can happen that in strict solitude I perform an act whose consequences are completely opposed to my anticipations and to my desires; for example I gently draw toward me a small platform holding this fragile vase, but this movement results in tipping over a bronze statuette which breaks the vase into a thousand pieces. Here, however, there is nothing which I could not have foreseen if I had been more careful, if I had observed the arrangement of the objects, etc.—*nothing which on principle escapes me*. The appearance of the Other, on the contrary, causes the appearance in the situation of an aspect which I did not wish, of which I am not master, and which on principle escapes me since it is *for the Other*. This is what Gide has appropriately called "the devil's part." It is the unpredictable but still real *reverse side*.

It is this unpredictability which Kafka's art attempts to describe in *The Trial* and *The Castle*. In one sense everything which K. and the Surveyor are doing belongs strictly to them in their own right, and insofar as they act upon the world the results conform strictly to anticipations; they are successful acts. But at the same time the *truth* of these acts constantly escapes them; the acts have on principle a meaning which is their *true meaning* and which neither K. nor the Surveyor will ever know. Without doubt Kafka is trying here to express the transcendence of the divine; it is for the divine that the human act is constituted in truth. But God here is only the concept of the Other pushed to the limit. We shall return to this point. That gloomy, evanescent atmosphere of *The Trial,* that ignorance which, however, is lived as ignorance, that total opacity which can only be felt as a presentiment across a total translucency—this is nothing but the description of our being-in-the-midst-of-the-world-for-others. . . .

### 3 FEAR AND PRIDE

Fear implies that I appear to myself as threatened by virtue of my being a presence in the world, not in my capacity as a for-itself which makes a world exist. It is the object which *I* am which is in danger in the world and which as such, because of its indissoluble unity of being with the being which I have to be, can involve in its own ruin the ruin of the for-itself which I have to be. Fear is therefore the discovery of my being-as-object on the occasion of the appearance of another object in my perceptive field. It reflects the origin of all fear, which is the fearful discovery of my pure and simple object-state insofar as it is transcended by possibles which are not my possibles. It is by thrusting myself toward my possibles that I shall escape fear to the extent that I shall consider my objectivity as non-essential. This can happen only if I apprehend myself as being responsible for the Other's being. The Other becomes then *that which I make myself not-be,* and his possibilities are possibilities which I refuse and which I can simply contemplate—hence dead-possibilities. Therefore I transcend my present possibilities insofar as I consider them as always able to be transcended by the Other's possibilities, but I also transcend the Other's possibilities by considering them from the point of view of the only quality which he has which is not his own possibility—his very character as Other inasmuch as I make there to be an Other. I transcend the Other's possibilities by considering them as possibilities of transcending me which I can always transcend toward new possibilities. Thus at one and the same time I have regained my being-for-itself through my consciousness (of) myself as a perpetual center of infinite possibilities, and I have transformed the Other's possibilities into dead-possibilities by affecting them all with the character of *"not-lived-by-me"*—that is as *simply given*.

Similarly shame is only the original feeling of having my being *outside,* engaged in another being and as such without any defense, illuminated by the absolute light which emanates from a pure subject. Shame is the consciousness of being irremediably what I always was: "in suspense"—that is, in the mode of the "not-yet" or of the "already-no-longer." Pure shame is not a feeling of being this or that guilty object but in general of being *an* object; that is, of *recognizing myself* in this degraded, fixed, and dependent being which I am for the Other. Shame is the feeling of an *original fall,* not because of the fact that I may have committed this or that particular fault but simply that I have "fallen" into the world in the midst of things and that I need the mediation of the Other in order to be what I am.

Modesty and in particular the fear of being surprised in a state of nakedness are only a symbolic specification of original shame; the body symbolizes here our defenseless state as objects. To put on clothes is to hide one's object-state; it is to claim the right of seeing without being seen; that is, to be pure subject. That is why the Biblical symbol of the fall after the original sin is the fact that Adam and Eve "know that they are naked."

The reaction to shame will consist in apprehending as an object the one who apprehended *my* own object-state. In fact from the moment that the Other appears to me as an object, his subjectivity becomes a simple *property* of the object considered. It is degraded and is defined as "a set of *objective* properties which on principle elude me." The-Other-as-object "has" a subjectivity as this hollow box has "an inside." In this way I *recover* myself, for I cannot be *an object for an object*. I certainly do not deny that the Other remains connected with me "inside him," but the consciousness which he has of me, since it is consciousness-as-an-object, appears to me as pure interiority without efficacy. It is just one property among others of that "inside," something comparable to a sensitized plate in the closed compartment of a camera. Insofar as I make there be an Other, I apprehend myself as the free source of the knowledge which the Other has of me, and the Other appears to me as *affected* in his being by that knowledge which he has of my being inasmuch as I have *affected* him with the character of Other. This knowledge takes on then a *subjective* character in the new sense of "relative"; that is, it remains in the subject-as-object as a quality *relative* to the being-other with which I have affected him. It no longer *touches* me; it is an image of *me in him*. Thus subjectivity is degraded into interiority, free consciousness into a pure absence of principles, possibilities into properties, and the knowledge by which the Other touches me in my being, into a pure *image* of me in the Other's "consciousness." Shame motivates the reaction which transcends and overcomes the shame inasmuch as the reaction encloses within it an implicit and non-thematized comprehension of being-able-to-be-an-object on the part of the subject for whom I am an object. This implicit comprehension is nothing other than the consciousness (of) my "being-myself"; that is, of my selfness reinforced. In fact in the structure which expresses the experience "I am ashamed of myself," shame supposes a me-as-object for the Other but also a selfness which is ashamed and which is imperfectly expressed by the I of the formula. Thus shame is a unitary apprehension with three dimensions: *"I* am ashamed of *myself* before the *Other."*

If any one of these dimensions disappears, the shame disappears as well. If, however, I conceive of the "they" as a subject before whom I am ashamed, then it cannot become an object without being scattered into a plurality of Others; and if I posit it as the absolute unity of the subject which can in no way become an object, I thereby posit the eternity of my being-as-object and so perpetuate my shame. This is shame before God; that is, the recognition of my being-an-object before a subject which can never become an object. At the same time I *realize* my object-state in the absolute and hypostatize it. The positing of God is accompanied by a reification of my object-ness. Or better yet, I posit my being-an-object-for-God as more real than my for-itself; I exist alienated and I have to learn from outside what I must be. This is the origin of fear before God. Black Masses, desecration of the Host, demonic associations, etc., are so many attempts to confer the character of object on the absolute Subject. In desiring Evil for Evil's sake I attempt to contemplate the divine transcendence—for which Good is the peculiar possibility—as a purely given transcendence and one which I transcend toward Evil. Then I "make God suffer," I "irritate him," etc. These attempts, which imply the absolute *recognition* of God as a subject who cannot be an object, carry their own contradiction within them and are always failures.

Pride does not exclude original shame. In fact it is on the ground of fundamental shame or shame of being an object that pride is built. It is an ambiguous feeling. In pride I recognize the Other as the subject through whom my being gets its object-state, but I recognize as well that I myself am also responsible for my objectivity. I emphasize my responsibility and I assume it. In one sense therefore pride is at first resignation; in order to be proud of *being that,* I must of necessity first resign myself to *being only that.* We are therefore dealing with a primary reaction to shame, and it is already a reaction of flight and of bad faith; for without ceasing to hold the Other as a subject, I try to apprehend myself as *affecting* the Other by my object-state. In short there are two authentic attitudes: that by which I recognize the Other as the subject through whom I get my objectivity—this is shame; and that by which I apprehend myself as the free object by which the Other gets his being-other —this is arrogance or the affirmation of my freedom confronting the Other-as-object. But pride—or vanity—is a feeling without equilibrium, and it is in bad faith. In vanity I attempt in my capacity as object to act upon the Other. I take this beauty or this strength or this intelligence which he confers on me—insofar as he constitutes me as an object—and I attempt to make use of the recoil so as to affect him passively with a feeling of admiration or of love. But at the same time I demand that this feeling as the sanction of my being-as-object should be entertained by the Other in his capacity as subject—*i.e.,* as a freedom. This is, in fact, the only way of conferring an absolute objectivity on my strength or on my beauty. Thus the feeling which I demand from the other carries within itself its own contradiction since I must affect the Other with it insofar as he is free. The feeling is entertained in the mode of bad faith, and its internal development leads it to disintegration. In fact as I play my assumed role of my being-as-object, I attempt to recover it *as an object*. Since the Other is the key to it, I attempt to lay hold of the Other so that he may release to me the secret of my being. Thus vanity impels me to get hold of the Other and to constitute him as an object in order to burrow into the heart of this object to discover there my own object-state. But this is to kill the hen that lays the golden eggs. By constituting the Other as object, I constitute myself as an image at the heart of the Other-as-object; hence the disillusion of vanity. In that image which I wanted to grasp in order to recover it and merge it with my own being, I no longer recognize myself. I must willy-nilly impute the image to the Other as one of his own subjective properties. Freed in spite of myself from my object-state, I remain alone confronting the Other-as-object in my unqualifiable selfness which I have to be forever without reprieve.

Shame, fear, and pride are my original reactions; they are only various ways by which I recognize the Other as a subject beyond reach, and they include within them a comprehension of my selfness which can and must serve as my motivation for constituting the Other as an object. . . .

*Being and Nothingness, 221–223, 254–265, 288–291.*

# III

---

## The Body

### 1 DESIRE

Everything which holds for me in my relations with the Other holds for him as well. While I attempt to free myself from the hold of the Other, the Other is trying to free himself from mine; while I seek to enslave the Other, the Other seeks to enslave me. We are by no means dealing with unilateral relations with an object-in-itself, but with reciprocal and moving relations. The following descriptions of concrete behavior must therefore be envisaged within the perspective of *conflict*. Conflict is the original meaning of being-for-others.

If we start with the first revelation of the Other as a *look*, we must recognize that we experience our inapprehensible being-for-others in the form of a *possession*. I am possessed by the Other; the Other's look shapes my body in its nakedness, makes it emerge, sculptures it, produces it as it *is*, sees it as I shall never see it. The Other holds a secret—the secret of what I am. He makes me be and thereby he possesses me, and this possession is nothing other than the consciousness of possessing me. In recognizing my objectivity, I experience the fact that he has this consciousness. As consciousness the Other is for me simultaneously the one who has stolen my being from me and the one who makes "there to be" a being which is my being. Thus I have a comprehension of this ontological structure: I am responsible for my being-for-others, but I am not the foundation of it. It appears to me therefore in the form of a contingent given for which I am nevertheless responsible; the Other founds my being insofar as this being is in the form of the "there is." But he is not responsible for my being although he founds it in complete freedom—in and by means of his free transcendence. Thus to the extent that I am revealed to myself as responsible for my being, I *lay claim to* this being which I am; that is, I wish to recover it, or, more exactly, I am the project of the recovery of my being. I want to stretch out my hand and grab hold of this being which is presented to me as *my being* but at a distance—like the dinner of Tantalus; I want to found it by my very freedom. For if in one sense my being-as-object is an unbearable contingency and the pure "possession" of myself by another, still in another sense this being stands as the indication of what I should be obliged to recover and found in order to be the foundation of myself. But this is conceivable only if I assimilate the Other's freedom. Thus my project of recovering myself is fundamentally a project of absorbing the Other. . . .

My original attempt to get hold of the Other's free subjectivity through his objectivity-for-me is *sexual desire*. Perhaps it will come as a surprise to see a phenomenon which is usually classified among "psycho-physiological reactions" now mentioned on the level of primary attitudes which manifest our original mode of realizing being-for-others. For the majority of psychologists indeed, desire, as a fact of consciousness, is in strict correlation with the nature of our sexual organs, and it is only in connection with an elaborate study of these that sexual desire can be understood. But since the differentiated structure of the body (mammalian, viviparous, etc.) and consequently the particular sexual structure (uterus, Fallopian tubes, ovaries, etc.) are in the domain of absolute contingency and in no way derive from the ontology of "consciousness" or of the *"Dasein,"* it seems that the same must be true for sexual desire. Just as the sex organs are a contingent and particular formation of our body, so the desire which corresponds to them would be a contingent modality of our psychic life; that is, it would be described only on the level of an empirical psychology based on biology. This is indicated sufficiently by the term *sex instinct,* which is reserved for desire and all the psychic structures which refer to it. The term "instinct" always in fact qualifies contingent formations of psychic life which have the double character of being co-extensive with all the duration of this life—or in any case of not deriving from our "history"—and of nevertheless not being such that they cannot be deduced as belonging to the very essence of the psychic. This is why existential philosophies have not believed it necessary to concern themselves with sexuality. Heidegger, in particular, does not make the slightest allusion to it in his existential analytic with the result that his "*Dasein*" appears to us as asexual. Of course one may consider that it is contingent for "human reality" to be specified as "masculine" or "feminine"; of course one may say that the problem of sexual differentiation has nothing to do with that of *Existence* (*Existenz*) since man and woman equally exist.

These reasons are not wholly convincing. That sexual differentiation lies within the domain of facticity we accept without reservation. But does this mean that the for-itself is sexual "accidentally," by the pure contingency of having this particular body? Can we admit that this tremendous matter of the sexual life comes as a kind of addition to the human condition? Yet it appears at first glance that desire and its opposite, sexual repulsion, are fundamental structures of being-for-others. It is evident that if sexuality derives its origin from sex as a physiological and contingent determination of man, it cannot be indispensable to the being of the for-Others. . . . Man, it is said, is a sexual being because he possesses a sex organ. And if the reverse were true? If a sex organ were only the instrument and, so to speak, the *image* of a fundamental sexuality? If man possessed a sex organ only because he is originally and fundamentally a sexual being as a being who exists in the world in relation with other men? Infantile sexuality precedes the physiological maturation of the sex organs. Men who have become eunuchs do not thereby cease to feel desire. Nor do many old men. The fact of being able to *make use of* a sex organ fit to fertilize and to procure enjoyment represents only one phase and one aspect of our sexual life. There is one mode of sexuality "with the possibility of satisfaction," and the developed sex organ represents and makes concrete this possibility. But there are other modes of sexuality of the type which cannot get satisfaction, and if we take these modes into account we are forced to recognize that sexuality appears with birth and disappears only with death. Moreover neither the tumescence of the penis nor any other physiological phenomenon can ever explain or provoke sexual desire—no more than the vasoconstriction or the dilation of the pupils (or the simple consciousness of these physiological modifications) will be able to explain or to provoke fear. In one case as in the other although the body plays an important role, we must—in order to understand it—refer to being-in-the-world and to being-for-others. I desire a human being, not an insect or a mollusk, and I desire him (or her) as he is and as I am in situation in the world and as he is an Other for me and as I am an Other for him.

The fundamental problem of sexuality can therefore be formulated thus: is sexuality a contingent accident linked with our physiological nature, or is it a necessary structure of being-for-itself-for-others? From the sole fact that the question can be put in these terms, we see that we must go back to ontology to settle it. Moreover ontology can settle this question only by determining the meaning of sexual existence for-the-Other. To be sexual means—in accordance with the description of the body which we attempted in the preceding chapter—to exist sexually for an Other who exists sexually for me. And it must be well understood that at first this Other is not necessarily *for me*—*nor* I for him—a *heterosexual* existent but only a sexual being. Considered from the point of view of the for-itself, this apprehension of the Other's sexuality could not be the pure disinterested contemplation of his primary or secondary sexual characteristics. *My first* apprehension of the Other as sexual does not come when I conclude from the distribution of his hair, from the coarseness of his hands, the sound of his voice, his strength that he is of the masculine sex. We are dealing there with derived conclusions which refer back to an original state. The first apprehension of the Other's sexuality insofar as it is lived and suffered can be only *desire;* it is by desiring the Other (or by discovering myself as incapable of desiring him) or by apprehending his desire for me that I discover his being-sexual. Desire reveals to me simultaneously *my* being-sexual and *his* being-sexual, *my* body as sexual and *his* body. Here therefore in order to settle the nature and ontological location of sex we are referred to the study of desire. What then is desire? . . .

The man who desires *exists* his body in a particular mode and thereby places himself on a particular level of existence. In fact everyone will agree that desire is not only *longing,* a clear and translucent *longing* which directs itself through our body toward a certain object. Desire is defined as *troubled*—as stirred up and disturbing. This notion can help us better to determine the nature of desire. We contrast troubled water with transparent water, a troubled look with a clear look. Troubled water remains water; it preserves the fluidity and the essential characteristics

The Body

of water; but its translucency is "troubled" by an inapprehensible presence which is indiscernibly with it, which is everywhere and nowhere, and which appears as an incorporated obscuring of the water by itself. To be sure, we can explain the troubled quality by the presence of fine solid particles suspended in the liquid, but this explanation is that of the *scientist*. Our original apprehension of the troubled water presents it as changed by the presence of an invisible *something* which is not itself distinguished and which is manifested as a pure factual resistance. If the desiring consciousness is *troubled*, it is because it is analogous to the troubled water.

To make this analogy precise, we should compare sexual desire with another form of desire—for example, with hunger. Hunger, like sexual desire, supposes a certain state of the body, defined here as the impoverishment of the blood, abundant salivary secretion, contractions of the tunica, etc. These various phenomena are described and classified from the point of view of the Other. For the for-itself they are manifested as pure facticity. But this facticity *does not compromise* the nature of the for-itself, for the for-itself immediately flees it toward its possibles; that is, toward a certain state of satisfied-hunger which, . . . is the in-itself-for-itself of hunger. Thus hunger is a pure transcending of corporal facticity; and to the extent that the for-itself becomes conscious of this facticity in a non-thetic form, the for-itself becomes conscious of it as a surpassed facticity. The body here is indeed the *past, the passed-beyond*. In sexual desire, to be sure, we can find that structure common to all appetites—a state of the body. The Other can note various physiological modifications (the erection of the penis, the turgescence of the nipples of the breasts, changes in the circulatory system, rise in temperature, etc.) The desiring consciousness exists this facticity; it is *in terms of this facticity*—we could even say *through* it—that the desired body appears as desirable. Nevertheless if we limited ourselves to this description, sexual desire would appear as a *distinct and clear desire*, comparable to the desire of eating and drinking. It would be a pure flight from facticity toward other possibles. Now everyone is aware that there is a great abyss between sexual desire and other appetites. We all know the famous saying, "Make love to a pretty woman when you want her just as you would drink a glass of cold water when you are thirsty." We know also how unsatisfactory and even shocking this statement is to the mind. This is because when we do desire a woman, we do not keep ourselves wholly outside the desire; the desire *compromises* me; I am the accomplice of my desire. Or rather the desire has fallen wholly into complicity with the body. Let any one consult his own experience; he knows how consciousness becomes clogged and sticky [*empâté*] with sexual desire; it seems that one is invaded by facticity, that one ceases to flee it and that one slides toward a *passive* consent to the desire. At other moments it seems that facticity invades consciousness in its very flight and renders consciousness opaque to itself. It is like a sticky tumescence of *fact*.

The expressions which we use to designate desire sufficiently show its specific character. We say that it *takes hold of you*, that it *overwhelms you*, that it *paralyzes you*. Can one imagine employing the same words to designate hunger? Can one think of a hunger which "would overwhelm" one? Strictly speaking, this would be meaningful only when applied to impressions of emptiness. But, on the contrary, even the feeblest desire is already overwhelming. One cannot hold it at a distance as one can with hunger and "think of something else" while keeping the desire as an undifferentiated tonality of non-thetic consciousness which would serve as a sign of the body in the background. But *desire is consent to desire*. The heavy, fainting consciousness slides toward a languor comparable to sleep. Everyone has been able to observe the appearance of desire in another. Suddenly the man who desires becomes a heavy tranquillity which is frightening; his eyes are fixed and appear half-closed, his movements are stamped with a heavy and sticky, gentle, sweetness; many seem to be falling asleep. And when one "struggles against desire," it is precisely this languor which one resists. If one succeeds in resisting it, the desire before disappearing will become wholly distinct and clear, like hunger. And then there will be "an awakening." One will feel that one is lucid but with heavy head and beating heart. Naturally all these descriptions are inexact; they show rather the way in which we interpret desire. However they indicate the primary fact of desire: in desire consciousness chooses to exist its facticity on another plane. It no longer flees it; it attempts to subordinate itself to its own contingency—as it apprehends another body—*i.e.*, another contingency—as desirable. In this sense desire is not only the revelation of the Other's body but the revelation of my own body. And this, not insofar as this body *is an instrument* or a *point of view*, but insofar as it is pure facticity; that is, a simple contingent form of the necessity of my contingency. I *feel* my skin and my muscles and my breath, and I feel them not in order to transcend them *toward* something as in emotion or appetite but as a living and inert datum, not simply as the pliable and discrete instrument of my action upon the world but as a *passion* by which I am engaged in the world and in danger in the world. The for-itself *is not* this contingency; it continues to exist but it experiences the vertigo of its own body. Or, if you prefer, this vertigo is precisely its way of existing its body. The nonthetic consciousness allows itself to go over to the body, *wishes to be* the body and to be only body. In desire the body instead of being only the contingency which the for-itself flees toward possibles which are peculiar to it, becomes at the same time the most immediate possible of the for-itself. Desire is not only the desire of the Other's body; it is—within the unity of a single act—the non-thetically lived project of being swallowed up in the body. Thus the final state of sexual desire can be swooning as the final stage of consent to the body. It is in this sense that desire can be called the desire of one body for another body. It is in fact an appetite directed *toward* the Other's body, and it is lived as the vertigo of the for-itself before its own body. The being which desires is consciousness *making itself body*.

## 2 THE CARESS

But granted that desire is a consciousness which makes itself body in order to appropriate the Other's body apprehended as an organic totality in situation with consciousness at the horizon—what then is the meaning of desire? That is, why does consciousness make itself body—or vainly attempt to do so—and what does it expect from the object of its desire? The answer is easy if we realize that in desire I make myself flesh *in the presence of the Other in order to appropriate* the Other's flesh. This means that it is not merely a question of my grasping the Other's shoulders or thighs or of my drawing a body over against me: it is necessary as well for me to apprehend them with this particular instrument which is the body as it produces a clogging of consciousness. In this sense when I grasp these shoulders, it can be said not only that my body is a means for touching the shoulders but that the Other's shoulders are a means for my discovering my body as the fascinating revelation of facticity—that is, as flesh. Thus desire is the desire to appropriate a body as this appropriation reveals to me my body as flesh. But this body which I wish to appropriate, I wish to appropriate as *flesh*. Now at first the Other's body is not flesh for me; it appears as a synthetic form in action. . . . The Other's body is originally a body in situation; flesh on the contrary, appears as the *pure contingency of presence*. Ordinarily it is hidden by cosmetics, clothing, etc.; in particular it is disguised by *movements*. Nothing is less "in the flesh" than a dancer even though she is nude. Desire is an attempt to strip the body of its movements as of its clothing and to make it exist as pure flesh; it is an attempt to *incarnate* the Other's body.

It is in this sense that the caress is an appropriation of the Other's body. It is obvious that if caresses were only a stroking or light touching of the surface, there could be no relation between them and the powerful desire which they claim to fulfill; they would remain on the surface like looks and could not *appropriate* the Other for me. We know well how delusive seems that famous expression, "The contact of two epidermises." The caress does not want mere *contact;* it seems that man alone can reduce the caress to a contact, and then he loses its unique meaning. This is because the caress is not a simple stroking; it is a *shaping.* In caressing the Other I make her* flesh to emerge beneath my caress, under my fingers. The caress is the set of those rituals which *incarnate* the Other. But, someone will object, was the Other not already incarnated? To be precise, *no.* The Other's flesh did not exist explicitly for me since I grasped the Other's body in situation; neither did it exist for her since she transcended it toward her possibilities and toward the object. The caress makes the Other emerge as flesh for me and for herself. And by flesh we do not mean a *part* of the body such as the dermis, the connective tissues or, specifically, epidermis; neither need we assume that the body will be "at rest" or relaxed although often it is thus that its flesh is best revealed. But the caress reveals the flesh by stripping the body of its action, by cutting it off from the possibilities which surround it; the caress is designed

---

* The pronouns in French are masculine because they refer to *autrui* (the Other) which may stand for either man or woman but which, grammatically, is masculine. The feminine sounds more natural in English.—Trans.

to uncover the fabric of inertia beneath the action—*i.e.*, the pure "being-there"—which sustains it. For example, by *clasping* the Other's hand and *caressing* it, I discover underneath the act of *clasping,* which this hand is *at first,* an extension of flesh and bone which can be grasped; and similarly my look caresses when it discovers underneath this leaping which is at first the dancer's legs, the curved extension of the thighs. Thus the caress is in no way distinct from the desire: to caress with the eyes and to desire are one and the same. *Desire is expressed by the caress as thought is by language.* The caress reveals the Other's flesh as flesh to myself *and to the Other.* But it reveals this flesh in a very special way. To take hold of the Other reveals to her her inertia and her passivity as a transcendence-transcended; but this is not to caress her. In the caress it is not my body as a synthetic form in action which caresses the Other; it is my body as flesh which makes the Other's flesh emerge. The caress is designed to make the Other's body emerge, through pleasure, for the Other—and for myself—as a *touched* passivity in such a way that my body is made flesh in order to touch the Other's body with its own passivity; that is, by caressing itself with the Other's body rather than by caressing her. This is why amorous gestures have a languor which could almost be said to be deliberate; it is not a question so much of taking hold of a part of the Other's body as of placing one's own body against the Other's body. Not so much to push or to touch in the active sense but to place against. It seems that I lift my own arm as an inanimate object and that I *place* it against the flank of the desired woman, that my fingers which I run over her arm are inert at the end of my hand. Thus the revelation of the Other's flesh is made through my own flesh; in desire and in the caress which expresses desire, I incarnate myself in order to realize the incarnation of the Other. The caress by *realizing* the Other's incarnation reveals to me my own incarnation; that is, I make myself flesh in order to impel the Other to realize *for-herself* and *for me* her own flesh, and my caresses make my flesh emerge for me insofar as it is for the Other *flesh* making *her* emerge as *flesh.* I make her enjoy my flesh through her flesh in order to compel her to feel herself flesh. And so possession truly appears as a *double reciprocal incarnation.* Thus in desire there is an attempt at the incarnation of consciousness (this is what we called earlier the clogging of consciousness, a troubled consciousness, etc.) in order to realize the incarnation of the Other.

The being of existents is ordinarily veiled by their function. The same is true for the being of the Other. If the Other appears to me as a servant, as an employee, as a civil servant, or simply as the passer-by whom I must avoid or as this voice which is speaking in the next room and which I try to *understand* (or on the other hand, which I want to forget because it "keeps me from sleeping"), it is not only the Other's extra-mundane transcendence which escapes me but also his "being-there" as a pure contingent existence in the midst of the world. This is because it is exactly insofar as I treat him as a servant, or as an office clerk, that I transcend his potentialities (transcendence-transcended, dead-possibilities) by the very project by which I transcend and nihilate my own facticity. If I want to return to his simple presence and taste it *as presence*, it is necessary for me to reduce myself to my own presence. Every transcending of my being-there is in fact a transcending of the Other's being-there. And if the world is around me as the situation which I transcend toward myself, then I apprehend the Other in terms of *his situation;* that is, already as a center of reference.

Of course the desired Other must also be apprehended in situation: I desire a woman *in the world,* standing *near a table,* lying naked *on a bed,* or seated *at my side*. But if the desire flows back from the situation upon the being who is in situation, it is in order to dissolve the situation and to corrode the Other's relations in the world. The movement of desire which goes from the surrounding "environment" to the desired person is an isolating movement which destroys the environment and cuts off the person in question in order to effect the emergence of his pure facticity. But this is possible only if each object which refers me to the person is congealed in its pure contingency at the same time that it indicates him to me; consequently this return movement to the Other's being is a movement of return to myself as pure being-there. I destroy my possibilities in order to destroy those of the world and to constitute the world as a "world of desire"; that is, as a destructured world which has lost its meaning, a world in which things jut out like fragments of pure matter, like brute qualities. Since the for-itself is a choice, this is possible only if I project myself toward a new possibility: that of being "absorbed by my body as ink is by a blotter," that of being reduced to my pure being-there. This project, inasmuch as it is not simply conceived and thematically posited but rather lived—that is, inasmuch as its realization is not distinct from its conception—is "disturbing." Indeed we must not understand the preceding descriptions as meaning that I deliberately stir myself up with the purpose of rediscovering the Other's pure "being-there." Desire is a lived project which does not suppose any preliminary deliberation but which includes within itself its meaning and its interpretation. As soon as I throw myself toward the Other's facticity, as soon as I wish to push aside his acts and his functions so as to touch him in his flesh, I incarnate myself, for I can neither wish nor even conceive of the incarnation of the Other except in and by means of my own incarnation. Even the delineation of a desire (as when one absent-mindedly "undresses a woman with one's look") is a delineation of my disturbance, for I desire only with my stirred consciousness, and I disrobe the Other only by disrobing myself; I adumbrate and delineate the Other's flesh only by delineating my own flesh.

But my *incarnation* is not only the preliminary condition of the appearance of the Other as flesh to *my eyes*. My goal is to make him incarnated as flesh in *his own eyes*. It is necessary that I drag him onto the level of pure facticity; he must be reduced for himself to being only flesh. Thus I shall be reassured as to the permanent possibilities of a transcendence which can at any moment transcend me on all sides. This transcendence *will be no more than this;* it will remain enclosed within the limits of an object; in addition and because of this very fact, I shall be able to touch it, feel it, possess it. Thus the other meaning of my incarnation—that is, of my troubled disturbance—is that it is a magical language which casts a spell. I make myself flesh so as to fascinate the Other by my nakedness and to provoke in her the desire for my flesh—exactly because this desire will be nothing else in the Other but an incarnation similar to mine. Thus desire is an invitation to desire. It is my flesh alone which knows how to find the route to the Other's flesh, and I lay my flesh next to her flesh so as to awaken her to the meaning of flesh. In the caress when I slowly lay my inert hand against the Other's flank, I am making that flank feel my flesh, and this can be achieved only if it renders itself inert. The shiver of pleasure which it feels is precisely the awakening of its consciousness as flesh. If I extend my hand, remove it, or clasp it, then it becomes again body in action; but at the same time I make my hand disappear as flesh. To let it flow indifferently over the length of her body, to reduce my hand to a soft stroking almost stripped of meaning, to a pure existence, to a pure matter, slightly silky, slightly satiny, slightly rough—this is to give up for oneself being the one who establishes reference points and unfolds distances; it is to be made pure membrane. At this moment the communion of desire is realized; each consciousness by incarnating itself has realized the incarnation of the other; each one's disturbance has disturbed the Other and is thereby so much enriched. By each caress I experience my own flesh and the Other's flesh through my flesh, and I am conscious that this flesh which I feel and appropriate through my flesh is flesh-realized-by-the-Other. It is not by chance that desire while aiming at the body as a whole attains it especially through masses of flesh which are very little differentiated, largely nerveless, hardly capable of spontaneous movement, through breasts, buttocks, thighs, stomach: these form a sort of image of pure facticity. This is why also the true caress is the contact of two bodies in their mostly fleshy parts, the contact of stomachs and breasts; the caressing hand is too delicate, too much like a perfected instrument. But the full pressing together of the flesh of two people against one another is the true goal of desire.

Nevertheless desire is itself doomed to failure. As we have seen, coitus, which ordinarily terminates desire, is not its essential goal. To be sure, several elements of our sexual structure are the necessary expression of the nature of desire, in particular the erection of the penis and the clitoris. This is nothing else in fact but the affirmation of the flesh by the flesh. Therefore it is absolutely necessary that it should not be accomplished *voluntarily;* that is, that we cannot use it as an instrument but that we are dealing with a biological and autonomous phenomenon whose autonomous and involuntary expression accompanies and signifies the submerging of consciousness in the body. It must be clearly understood that no fine, prehensible organ provided with striated muscles can be a sex organ. If sex were to appear as an organ, it could be only one manifestation of the vegetative life. But contingency reappears if we consider that there *are two particular* sexes. Consider especially the penetration of the female by the male. This does, to be sure, conform to that radical incarnation which desire wishes to be. (We may in fact observe the organic passivity of sex organs in coitus. It is the whole body which advances and withdraws, which *carries* the sex organ forward or withdraws it. Hands help to introduce the penis; the penis itself appears as an instrument which one manages, which one makes penetrate, which one withdraws, which one utilizes. And similarly the opening and the lubrication of the vagina cannot be obtained voluntarily.) Yet coitus remains a perfectly contingent modality of our sexual life. It is as much a pure contingency as sexual pleasure proper. In truth the ensnarement of consciousness in the body normally has its own peculiar result—that is, a sort of particular ecstasy in which consciousness is no more than consciousness (of) the body and consequently a reflective consciousness *of* corporeality. Pleasure in fact—like too keen a pain—motivates the appearance of reflective consciousness which is *"attention to pleasure."*

But pleasure is the death and the failure of desire. It is the death of desire because it is not only its fulfillment but its limit and its end. This, moreover, is only an organic contingency: it *happens that* the incarnation is manifested by erection and that the erection ceases with ejaculation. But in addition pleasure closes the sluice to desire because it motivates the appearance of a reflective consciousness *of* pleasure, whose object becomes a reflective enjoyment; that is, it is *attention to the incarnation of the for-itself which is reflected-on* and by the same token it is forgetful of the Other's incarnation. Here we are no longer within the province of contingency. Of course it remains contingent that the passage to the fascinated reflection should be effected on the occasion of that particular mode of incarnation which is pleasure (although there are numerous cases of passage to the reflective without the intervention of pleasure), but there is a permanent danger for desire insofar as it is an attempt at incarnation. This is because consciousness by incarnating itself loses sight of the Other's incarnation, and its own incarnation absorbs it to the point of becoming the ultimate goal. In this case the pleasure of caressing is transformed into the pleasure of being caressed; what the for-itself demands is to feel within it its own body expanding to the point of nausea. Immediately there is a rupture of contact and desire misses its goal. It happens very often that this failure of desire motivates a transition to masochism; that is, consciousness apprehending itself in its facticity demands to be apprehended and transcended as body-for-the-Other by means of the Other's consciousness. In this case the Other-as-object collapses, the Other-as-look appears, and my consciousness is a consciousness swooning in its flesh beneath the Other's look.

Yet conversely desire stands at the origin of its own failure inasmuch as it is a desire of *taking* and of *appropriating*. It is not enough merely that the disturbance should effect the Other's incarnation; desire is the desire to appropriate this incarnated consciousness. Therefore desire is naturally continued not by *caresses* but by acts of taking and of penetration. The caress has for its goal only to impregnate the Other's body with consciousness and freedom. Now it is necessary to take this saturated body, to seize it, to enter into it. But by the very fact that I now attempt to seize the Other's body, to pull it toward me, to grab hold of it, to bite it, my own body ceases to be flesh and becomes again the synthetic instrument *which I am.* And by the same token the *Other* ceases to be an incarnation; she becomes once more an instrument in the midst of the world which I apprehend in terms of its situation. Her consciousness, which played on the surface of her flesh and which I tried to *taste* with my flesh,* disappears under my sight; she remains no more than an *object* with object-images inside her. At the sàme time my disturbance disappears. This does not mean that I cease to desire but that desire has lost its matter; it has become *abstract;* it is a desire to handle and to take. I insist on taking the Other's body but my very insistence makes my incarnation disappear. Now I transcend my body anew toward my own possibilities (here the possibility of taking), and similarly the Other's body which is transcended toward its potentialities falls from the level of *flesh* to the level of pure object. This situation brings about the rupture of that reciprocity of incarnation which was precisely the unique goal of desire. The Other may remain disturbed; she may remain flesh *for herself,* and I can understand it. But it is a flesh which I no longer apprehend through my flesh, a flesh which is no longer anything but the property of an Other-as-object and not the incarnation of an Other-as-consciousness. Thus I *am* body (a synthetic totality in situation) confronting a *flesh.* I find myself in almost the same situation as that from which I tried to escape by means of desire; that is, I want the Other

* Doña Prouhèze (*Soulier de Satin,* 2e *journée*): *"Il ne connaîtra pas le goût que j'ai."* (He will not know the taste which I have.)

to count as a transcendence by my attempt to utilize her as an object, and precisely because she is *all* object she escapes me with *all* her transcendence. Once again I have even lost the precise comprehension of what I am searching for and yet I am involved in the search. I take and discover myself in the process of taking, but what I take in my hands is *something else* than what I wanted to take. I feel this and I suffer from it but without being capable of saying what I wanted to take; for along with my disturbance, the very comprehension of my desire escapes me. I am like a sleepwalker who wakens to find himself in the process of gripping the edge of the bed while he cannot recall the nightmare which provoked his gesture. It is this situation which is at the origin of *sadism*.

### 3 THE OBSCENE

As for the type of incarnation which sadism would like to realize, this is precisely what is called the Obscene. The obscene is a species of being-for-Others which belongs to the genus of the ungraceful. But not everything which is ungraceful is obscene. In *grace* the body appears as something psychical which is in situation. It reveals above all its transcendence as a transcendence-transcended; it is in act and is understood in terms of the situation and of the end pursued. Each movement therefore is apprehended in a perceptive process which moves from the future to the present. For this reason the graceful act has on the one hand the precision of a finely perfected machine and on the other hand the perfect unpredictability of the psychic since, as we have seen, the psychic is for others the *unpredictable object*. Therefore the graceful act is at each instant perfectly understandable insofar as one considers that in it which has *elapsed*. Better yet, that part of the act which has elapsed is implied by a sort of esthetic necessity which stems from its perfect adaptation. At the same time the goal to come illuminates the act in its totality. But all the future part of the act remains unpredictable although one has the feeling, from the body which is engaged in the act, that the future part of the act will appear as necessary and adapted once it too has elapsed. It is this moving image of necessity and of freedom (as the property of the Other-as-object) which, strictly speaking, constitutes grace. Bergson has given a good description of it. In grace the body is the instrument which manifests freedom. The graceful act insofar as it reveals the body as a precision instrument, furnishes it at each instant with its justification for existing; the hand *is* in order to grasp and manifests above all its being-in-order-to-grasp. Insofar as it is apprehended in terms of a situation which requires grasping, the hand appears as itself *required* in its being, as summoned. And insofar as it manifests its freedom through the unpredictability of its gesture, it appears at the origin of its being. It seems that the hand is itself produced as the result of a justifying appeal from the situation. Grace therefore forms an objective image of a being which would be the *foundation of itself in order to* ———. Facticity then is clothed and disguised by grace; the nudity of the flesh is wholly present, but it cannot be seen. Therefore the supreme coquetry and the supreme challenge of grace is to exhibit the body unveiled with no clothing, with no veil except grace itself. The most graceful body is the naked body whose acts enclose it with an invisible garment while entirely disrobing its flesh, while the flesh is totally present to the eyes of the spectators.

The ungraceful, on the contrary, appears when one of the elements of grace is thwarted in its realization. A movement may become *mechanical*. In this case the body always forms part of a whole which justifies it but in the capacity of a pure instrument; its transcendence-transcended disappears, and along with it the *situation* disappears as the lateral over-determination of the instrumental-objects of *my* universe. It can happen also that the actions are abrupt and violent; in this case it is the adaptation of the situation which collapses; the situation remains but a hiatus slips in like an emptiness between it and the *Other* in situation. In this case the Other remains free, but this freedom is apprehended only as pure unpredictability; it resembles the *clinamen* of Epicurean atoms, in short an indeterminism. At the same time the end remains posited, and it is always in terms of the future that we perceive the Other's gesture. But the fall from adaptation involves this consequence, that the perceptual interpretation by reference to the future is always too broad or too narrow; it is an approximate interpretation. Consequently the justification of the gesture and the being of the Other is imperfectly realized. In the final analysis the awkward is the unjustifiable; all its facticity, which was engaged in the situation, is absorbed by it, flows back upon it. The awkward one frees his facticity at the wrong moment and suddenly exposes it to our sight; hence where we expected to seize a key to the situation, spontaneously emanating from the very situation, we suddenly encounter the unjustifiable contingency of an unadapted presence; we are faced with the existence of an existent.

Nevertheless if the body is wholly within the act, the facticity is not yet flesh. The *obscene* appears when the body adopts postures which entirely strip it of its acts and which reveal the inertia of its flesh. The sight of a naked body from behind is not obscene. But certain involuntary waddlings of the rump are obscene. This is because then it is only the legs which are acting for the walker, and the rump is like an isolated cushion which is carried by the legs and the balancing of which is a pure obedience to the laws of gravity. It cannot be justified by the situation; on the contrary, it is entirely destructive of any situation since it has the passivity of a thing and since it is made to rest like a thing upon the legs. Suddenly it is revealed as an unjustifiable facticity; it is superfluous [*de trop*] like every contingent. It is isolated from the rest of the body for which the present meaning is walking; it is naked even if something veils it, for it no longer shares in the transcendence-transcended of the body in action. Its movement of balancing instead of being interpreted in terms of what is to come is interpreted and known as a physical fact in terms of the past. These remarks naturally can apply to cases in which it is the whole body which is made flesh, either by some sort of flabbiness in its movements, which cannot be interpreted by the situation, or by a deformity in its structure (for example the proliferation of the fat cells) which exhibits a superabundant facticity in relation to the effective presence which the situation demands. This revealed flesh is specifically obscene when it is revealed to someone who is not in a state of desire and *without exciting his desire*. A particular lack of adaptation which destroys the situation at the very moment when I apprehend it and which presents to me the inert expanding of flesh as an abrupt appearance beneath the thin veil of the movements which cover it (when I am not in a state of desire for this flesh): this is what I shall call the obscene.

Now we can see the meaning of the sadist's demand: grace reveals freedom as a property of the Other-as-object and refers obscurely—just as do the contradictions in the sensible world in the case of Platonic recollection—to a transcendent Beyond of which we preserve only a confused memory and which we can reach only by a radical modification of our being; that is, by resolutely assuming our being-for-others. Grace both unveils and veils the Other's flesh, or if you prefer, it unveils the flesh in order immediately to veil it; in grace flesh is the inaccessible Other. The sadist aims at destroying grace in order *actually* to constitute another synthesis of the Other. He wants to make the Other's flesh appear; and in its very appearance the flesh will destroy grace, and facticity will reabsorb the Other's freedom-as-object. This reabsorption is not annihilation; for the sadist it is the Other-as-free who is manifested as flesh. The identity of the Other-as-object is not destroyed through these avatars, but the relations between flesh and freedom are reversed. In grace freedom subsumed and veiled facticity; in the new synthesis to be effected it is facticity which subsumes and hides freedom. The sadist aims therefore at making the flesh appear abruptly and by compulsion; that is, by the aid not of his own flesh but of his body as instrument. He aims at making the Other assume attitudes and positions such that his body appears under the aspect of the *obscene;* thus the sadist himself remains on the level of instrumental appropriation since he makes flesh emerge by exerting force upon the Other, and the Other becomes an instrument in his hands. The sadist manipulates the Other's body, leans on the Other's shoulders so as to bend him toward the earth and to make his haunches stick up, etc. On the other hand, the goal of this instrumental utilization is immanent in the very utilization; the sadist treats the Other as an instrument in order to make the Other's flesh appear. The sadist is the being who apprehends the Other as the instrument whose function is his own incarnation. The ideal of the sadist will therefore be to achieve the moment when the Other will be already flesh without ceasing to be an instrument, flesh to make flesh emerge, the moment at which the thighs, for example, already offer themselves in an obscene expanding passivity, and yet are instruments which are managed, which are pushed aside, which are bent so as to make the buttocks stick out in order in turn to incarnate them. But let us not be deceived here. What the sadist thus so tenaciously seeks, what he wants to knead with his hands and bend under his wrists is the Other's freedom. The freedom is there in that flesh; it is freedom which is this flesh since there is a facticity of the Other. It is therefore this freedom which the sadist tries to appropriate.

Thus the sadist's effort is to ensnare [*engluer*] the Other in his flesh by means of violence and pain, by appropriating the Other's body in such a way that he treats it as flesh so as to make flesh emerge. But this appropriation transcends the body which it appropriates, for its purpose is to possess the body only insofar as the Other's freedom has been ensnared within it. This is why the sadist will want manifest proofs of this enslavement of the Other's freedom through the flesh. He will aim at making the Other ask for pardon, he will use torture and threats to force the Other to humiliate himself, to abjure what he holds most dear. It is often said that this is done through the will to dominate or thirst for power. But this explanation is either vague or absurd. It is the will to dominate which should be explained first. This cannot be prior to sadism as its foundation, for in the same way and on the same plane as sadism, it is born from anxiety in the face of the Other. . . .

In fact no matter what pressure is exerted on the victim, the abjuration remains *free;* it is a spontaneous production, a response to a situation; it manifests human-reality. No matter what resistance the victim has offered, no matter how long he has waited before begging for mercy, he would have been able despite all to wait ten minutes, one minute, one second longer. He has decided the moment at which the pain became unbearable. The proof of this is the fact that he will later live out his abjuration in remorse and shame. Thus he is entirely responsible for it. On the other hand the sadist for his part considers himself entirely the cause of it. If the victim resists and refuses to beg for mercy, the game is only that much more pleasing. One more turn of the screw, one extra twist and the resistance will finally give in. The sadist presents himself as "having all the time in the world." He is calm, he does not hurry. He uses his instruments like a technician; he tries them one after another as the locksmith tries various keys in a keyhole. He enjoys this ambiguous and contradictory situation. On the one hand indeed he is the one who patiently at the heart of universal determinism employs means in view of an end which will be *automatically* attained—just as the lock will automatically open when the locksmith finds the "right" key; on the other hand, this determined end can be realized only with the Other's free and complete co-operation. Therefore until the last the end remains both predictable and unpredictable. For the sadist the object realized is ambiguous, contradictory, without equilibrium since it is both the strict consequence of a technical utilization of determinism and the manifestation of an unconditioned freedom. The spectacle which is offered to the sadist is that of a freedom which struggles against the expanding of the flesh and which finally freely chooses to be submerged in the flesh. At the moment of the abjuration the result sought is attained: the body is wholly flesh, panting and obscene; it holds the position which the torturers have given to it, not that which it would have assumed by itself; the cords which bind it hold it as an inert thing, and thereby it has ceased to be the object which moves spontaneously. In the abjuration a freedom chooses to be wholly identified with this body; this distorted and heaving body is the very image of a broken and enslaved freedom.

These few remarks do not aim at exhausting the problem of sadism. We wanted only to show that it is as a seed in desire itself, as the failure of desire; in fact as soon as I seek to *take* the Other's body, which through my incarnation I have induced to incarnate itself, I break the reciprocity of incarnation, I transcend my body toward its own possibilities, and I orient myself in the direction of sadism. Thus sadism and masochism are the two reefs on which desire may founder—whether I transcend my troubled disturbance toward an appropriation of the Other's flesh or, intoxicated with my own disturbance, pay attention only to my flesh and ask nothing of the Other except that he should be the look which aids me in realizing my flesh. It is because of this inconstancy on the part of desire and its perpetual oscillation between these two perils that "normal" sexuality is commonly designated as "sadomasochistic."

Nevertheless sadism too—like . . . desire—bears within itself the principle of its own failure. In the first place there is a profound incompatibility between the apprehension of the body as flesh and its instrumental utilization. If I make an instrument out of flesh, it refers me to other instruments and to potentialities, in short to a future; it is partially justified in its *being-there* by the situation which I create around myself, just as the presence of nails and of a picture to be nailed on the wall justifies the existence of the hammer. Suddenly the body's character as flesh —that is, its unutilizable facticity—gives way to that of an instrumental thing. The complex "flesh-as-instrument" which the sadist has attempted to create disintegrates. This profound disintegration can be hidden so long as the flesh is the instrument to reveal flesh, for in this way I constitute an instrument with an immanent end. But when the incarnation is achieved, when I have indeed before me a panting body, then I no longer know how to *utilize* this flesh. No goal can be assigned to it, precisely because I have effected the appearance of its absolute contingency. It *is there*, and it is there *for nothing*. As such I cannot get hold of it as flesh; I cannot integrate it in a complex system of instrumentality without its materiality as flesh, its "fleshliness" immediately escaping me. I can only remain disconcerted before it in a state of contemplative astonishment or else incarnate myself in turn and allow myself again to be disturbed, so as to place myself once more at least on the level where flesh is revealed to flesh in its entire "fleshliness." Thus sadism at the very moment when its goal is going to be attained gives way to desire. Sadism is the failure of desire, and desire is the failure of sadism. One can get out of the circle only by means of satiation and so-called "physical possession." In this a new synthesis of sadism and of desire is given. The tumescence of sex manifests incarnation, the fact of "entering into" or of "being penetrated" symbolically realizes the sadistic and masochistic attempt to appropriate. But if pleasure enables us to get out of the circle, this is because it kills both the desire and the sadistic passion without satisfying them.

At the same time and on a totally different level sadism harbors a new motive for failure. What the sadist seeks to appropriate is in actuality the transcendent freedom of the victim. But this freedom remains in principle out of reach. And the more the sadist persists in treating the other as an instrument, the more this freedom escapes him. He can act upon this freedom only as an objective property of the Other-as-object; that is, on freedom in the midst of the world with its dead-possibilities. But since the sadist's goal is to recover his being-for-others, he misses it in principle, for the only Other with whom he has to do is the Other in the world who has only "images in his head" of the sadist assaulting him.

The sadist discovers his error when his victim *looks* at him; that is, when the sadist experiences the absolute alienation of his being in the Other's freedom; he realizes then not only that he has not recovered his *being-outside* but also that the activity by which he seeks to recover it is itself transcended and congealed in "sadism" as a *habitus* and a property with its cortege of dead-possibilities and that this transformation takes place through and for the Other whom he wishes to enslave. He discovers then that he cannot act on the Other's freedom even by forcing the Other to humiliate himself and to beg for mercy, for it is precisely in and through the Other's absolute freedom that there exists a world in which there are sadism and instruments of torture and a hundred pretexts for being humiliated and for abjuring oneself. Nobody has better portrayed the power of the victim's look at his torturers than Faulkner has done in the final pages of *Light in August*. The "decent citizens" have just hunted down the Negro, Christmas, and have castrated him. Christmas is at the point of death:

> But the man on the floor had not moved. He just lay there, with his eyes open and empty of everything save consciousness, and with something, a shadow, about his mouth. For a long moment he looked up at them with peaceful and unfathomable and unbearable eyes. Then his face, body, all, seemed to collapse, to fall in upon itself and from out the slashed garments about his hips and loins the pent black blood seemed to rush like a released breath. It seemed to rush out of his pale body like the rush of sparks from a rising rocket; upon that black blast the man seemed to rise soaring into their memories forever and ever. They are not to lose it, in whatever peaceful valleys, beside whatever placid and reassuring streams of old age, in the mirroring faces of whatever children they will contemplate old disasters and newer hopes. *It will be there, musing, quiet, steadfast, not fading and not particularly threatful, but of itself alone serene, of itself alone triumphant.* Again from the town, deadened a little by the walls, the scream of the siren mounted toward its unbelievable crescendo, passing out of the realm of hearing. [Italics added.]

Thus this explosion of the Other's look in the world of the sadist makes the meaning and goal of sadism collapse. The sadist discovers that it was *that freedom* which he wished to enslave, and at the same time he realizes the futility of his efforts. Here once more we are referred from the being-in-the-act-of-looking to the being-looked-at; we have not got out of the circle. . . .

*Being and Nothingness, 364, 382–384, 387–391, 394–406.*

# CONSCIOUSNESS
# AND ACTION

# I

## The Resistance

We were never more free than under the German Occupation.
We had lost all our rights, above all the right to speak; we were
insulted daily and had to remain silent, we were deported, because we were workers, because we were Jews, because we were
political prisoners. All around us on the walls, in the newspapers, on the screen, we met that foul and insipid image that
our oppressors wanted us to accept as ourselves. Because of all
this we were free. Since the Nazi poison was seeping into our
thinking, each accurate thought was a victory; since an all-
powerful police was trying to force silence upon us, each word
became precious as a declaration of principle; since we were
hunted, each gesture had the weight of a commitment. The often frightful circumstances of our struggle enabled us finally to
live, undisguised and unconcealed, that anxious, unbearable
situation which is called the human predicament. Exile, captiv-
ity, death, which in happier times are skillfully hidden, were our
perpetual concern, and we learned that they are not avoidable
accidents nor an external menace; in them we had to recognize
our lot, our destiny, the deep source of our reality as men. At
each moment we were living to the full the meaning of that
banal little phrase: "All men are mortal." The choice that each
of us made of himself was authentic, because it was made in
the presence of death, since it could always be expressed in the
form, "Rather death than —."

I am not speaking here of that elite who were actual Resist-
ants, but of all those Frenchmen who by day and by night, for
four years, said "No." The cruelty of our enemy drove us to the
limits of our condition, forcing us to ask those questions which
can be avoided in peace. All those who were aware—and what
Frenchman was not, at one time or another—of some informa-

tion about the Resistance, asked himself anxiously, "If they torture me, can I hold out?" Thus the question of freedom was posed, and we were brought to the edge of the deepest knowledge a man can have of himself. For the secret of a man is not his Oedipus complex or his inferiority complex, it is the limit of his freedom, his ability to resist torture and death.

For those involved in underground activity, the circumstances of their struggle were a new experience: they were not fighting in the open as soldiers; hunted alone, arrested alone, they resisted torture in the most complete abandonment; alone and naked before torturers who were clean-shaven, well-fed, well-dressed, who regarded this wretched flesh with contempt— torturers whose smug consciences and enormous social power gave every appearance of their being right. Nevertheless, at the depth of this solitude, others were present, all the comrades of the Resistance they were defending; a single word was enough to trigger ten, a hundred arrests. This total responsibility in total solitude, is it not the revelation of our freedom? . . .

*Situations III, 11–13.*

# II

## The Deed

**JUPITER**  My lad, on your way! What are you looking for here? Do you want to assert your rights? Yes, you're strong and spirited. You'd make a good captain of fighting men. You have better things to do than reigning over a town more dead than alive—a carrion town plagued by flies. The people here are great sinners, but they have taken the path of redemption. Leave them alone, lad. Respect their sorrowful endeavor, and slip away. You cannot share in their repentance, since you did not share their crime; your insolent innocence is a gulf between you and them. On your way, if you have any feeling for them. On your way, or you will be their doom. If you hinder them, if even for a moment you turn them aside from their remorse, all their sins will harden on them like cold fat. They have guilty consciences, they're afraid—and fear and guilty consciences have a delightful savor in the nostrils of the Gods. Yes, the Gods take pleasure in these poor souls. Would you oust them from the favor of the Gods? What then could you offer them in return? Good digestions, the peaceful monotony of provincial life, and boredom—ah, the day-after-day boredom of happiness. Go your way, my lad. Social stability and the stability of men's souls are precarious. Tamper, and everything will collapse. (*Looking him in the eyes*) A frightful catastrophe, which will involve you too. . . .

**ORESTES**  (*Takes some steps toward the palace*)  That is *my* palace. There my father was born. There a whore and her pimp slew him. I, myself, I was born there, too. I was nearly three when the mercenaries of Aegisthus took me away. We must have gone out by that door, one of them carrying me in his arms. I must have opened my eyes wide; no doubt I was

235

crying. And yet now I have no memories. I see a huge building, solemn, pretentious, provincial. I see it for the first time.

THE TUTOR   No memories, master? What ingratitude, after I've spent ten years of my life providing you with memories! What about all our trips together? All the towns we visited? And the course in archaeology I presented just for you. No memories? Palaces, shrines, and temples—with so many of them is your memory stocked that you could write a guidebook to Greece.

ORESTES   Palaces! True enough. Palaces, pillars, statues! With all those stones in my head, why am I not heavier? . . . You've left me as free as the threads torn by the wind from spider's webs that one sees floating way above the ground. I weigh no more, I'm as light as air. I know this is my good fortune, and I know what it's worth. (*A pause*) Some men are born with their path laid out in front of them; they did not choose it, it was assigned to them, and at its end there is something for them to do. *Their* deed awaits them. They go their way, their bare feet press down on the ground, are bruised against the rocks. I suppose that strikes you as commonplace —the joy of going somewhere. And there are other men, those of few words, who feel in the depths of their hearts, the burden of their imaginings, troubled and earthy; their lives had been changed because, one day in childhood, when they were five, or seven—sure, I admit they're not great men. As for me, when I was seven, I already knew that I was an exile. The scents and sounds, the noise of the rain on the roof, the rippling of the light, I let them all slide past my body and drop down around me. I knew they belonged to others, I could never make *my* memories out of them. For memories are a heavy, rich diet which nourish those who own houses, cattle, servants, and fields. Whereas for me—! I'm free as the breeze, thank God. My soul is a glorious absence. (*He goes nearer the palace*) There I would have lived. I'd not have read any of your books, perhaps I'd not have learned to read. Usually a prince doesn't. But by that door I'd have come in and gone out ten thousand times. As a child, I'd have played with its wings. I'd have pushed against them, they would have creaked without yielding, and my arms would have learned their resistance. Later on I'd have pushed them open stealthily by night and gone out after girls. Later still, on the day I came of age, slaves would have flung the doors wide open and I would have crossed the threshold on horseback. My old wooden door! With my eyes shut I'd have been able to locate your lock. And that scratch down there, I might have made it in my clumsiness, the first time they let me hold a spear. (*He steps back*) Dorian provincial the style, I'd say. And what do you think of the gold inlay? I've seen the same motif at Dodona. Superb workmanship. And now something you will be glad to hear: this isn't *my* palace, and it isn't *my* door. There's nothing for us to do here. . . .

———

ELECTRA   At last you have come, Orestes, and you've made your decision. And here I am with you—just as in my dreams —on the brink of a deed beyond redemption. And I'm frightened; that too was in my dreams. This day, so long I've waited for it, dreaded it. From now on, all the moments will mesh together, like the cogs in a machine, and we shall never rest until both of them are lying on their backs, with faces like crushed mulberries. Blood all over! To think that it's you who are going to spill it, you with your gentle eyes. I'm sorry I'll never see that gentleness again. . . .

———

JUPITER   All crimes do not displease me equally, Aegisthus. As one king to another, I speak to you frankly. The first crime was mine: I made man mortal. Once I had done that, what was left for you to do, the other murderers? To kill your victims? Come now, they were already mortal; all you could do was to hurry things up. Do you know what would have happened to Agamemnon if you had not slain him? Three months later he'd have died of a heart attack in the arms of a pretty slave-girl. But still your crime suited me.

AEGISTHUS   Suited you? For fifteen years I've been atoning for it—and you say it suited you? What a business!

JUPITER   Why not? It's because you are atoning for it that it suited me. I like crimes there's something to show for. I liked yours because it was a clumsy, boorish crime, that did not know what it was up to, an old-fashioned crime, more like a cataclysm than a human undertaking. Not for a moment did you defy me. You struck out in a frenzy of rage and fear. And then, when you cooled off, you looked upon your deed with loathing and disowned it. Yet look at what I got out of it! For one dead man, twenty thousand others wallowing in repentance; that's a good bargain.

AEGISTHUS   I see what lies behind your words. Orestes will have no remorse.

JUPITER   Not a shadow of remorse. At this moment he is working out his plan, coolly, methodically, unpretentiously. What good to me is a murder without remorse, a calm, carefree murder, that lies light as a breath of air on the murderer's conscience? No, I'll not allow it. How I loathe the crimes of this younger generation: thankless and fruitless as a thistle! He'll kill you like a chicken, that gentle lad will, and he'll go his way, with red hands and a clean conscience. . . .

––––––––––––

JUPITER   You talk big, my lad. You butchered a defenseless man and an old woman who begged for mercy. But to hear you talk, one would think you'd fought outnumbered, and were the savior of your native town.

ORESTES   Perhaps I am.

JUPITER   You a savior? Do you know what's behind that door? The men of Argos, all of them. They are waiting for their savior with stones, sticks, and pitchforks, to show their gratitude. You're as lonely as a leper.

ORESTES   So.

JUPITER   Come now, not so proud. The solitude into which they have rejected you is the solitude of scorn and loathing, you, the most cowardly of murderers.

ORESTES   The most cowardly of murderers is he who feels remorse.

JUPITER   Orestes, I created you and I created all things. Open your eyes. (*The walls of the temple draw apart, revealing the firmament, spangled with the stars in their courses. Jupiter is standing in the background. His voice [amplified by loudspeakers] becomes overwhelming, but he becomes shadowy*) Behold these planets never swerving, never colliding. It is I who have ordained their courses, according to justice. Listen to the music of the spheres, this vast, mineral hymn of praise, resounding throughout the heavens. (*Sounds of music*) By my command the species increase and multiply, man shall always beget man, and dog give birth to dog. By my command the gentle tongue of the tides laps the sand and draws back at the appointed hour. I make the plants grow, and my breath guides round the earth the yellow clouds of pollen. This is not your own home, intruder; you are in the world as the splinter is in the flesh, as the poacher is in the forest of his lord. For the world is good; I created it according to my will, and I am the Good. But you, you have sinned, and things accuse you with their petrified voices. The Good is everywhere, it is the pith of the elder tree, the coolness of the spring, the grain of the flint, the heaviness of the stone. You will find it even in the nature of fire and of light; even your own body betrays you, for your body obeys my laws. The Good is in you, and around you: it cuts into you like a scythe, it crushes you like a mountain, buoys you up like the sea, and sweeps you on. The Good is that which allowed your evil plan to succeed, for it was the brightness of the candles, the hardness of your sword, the strength of your arm. And this Evil of which you are so proud, which you claim as your doing, what is it but a reflection of being, a phantom, a deceitful mimicry maintained in existence by the Good. Return to yourself, Orestes. The universe proclaims you wrong, and you are but a mite in the universe. Return to nature, unnatural son. Recognize your sin, abhor it, pull it up by the roots, as if it were a rotten stinking tooth. . . .

ORESTES Yesterday, when I was with Electra, I was one with this nature of yours. It hymned your Good, the siren, and lavished advice on me. To lull me into gentleness, the fierce light of day became as gentle and tender as a veiled look; to preach the remission of sin, the heaven became as bland as forgiveness. Obedient to your commands, my youth rose up, and pleaded with me like a girl afraid that her lover will leave her. That was the last time I saw my youth. Suddenly freedom pounced upon me, nature leapt out of the way, my youth was left behind, and I felt myself alone, in the middle of this well-meaning little universe of yours. I was like someone who has lost his shadow. And there was nothing left in heaven, no Good, nor Evil, no one to command me.

JUPITER  So what? Should I admire the mangy sheep that has to be kept away from the herd, or the leper quarantined? Think back, Orestes, you were once of my flock, you fed in my pastures among my sheep. Your freedom is a mange that makes you itchy, it is exile.

ORESTES  Yes, exile.

JUPITER  But the disease can be caught in time, it was only contracted yesterday. Come back to the fold. See how alone you are; even your sister is forsaking you. You're pale, your eyes are swollen with anguish. Don't you want to live? Gnawing at you is a disease which is not human; alien to me, alien to yourself. Come back. I am forgetfulness, I am peace.

ORESTES  Alien to myself, I know it. Outside nature, against nature, without excuse, without recourse save myself. But I shall not return under your law; I'm condemned to have no other law but my own. Nor shall I return to nature, where a thousand paths are marked out, all leading up to you. I can only follow my own path. For I'm a man, Jupiter, and each man must find his own way.

———

ELECTRA  Thief! I had so little, so very little that I could call my own—a little peace and a few dreams. You took everything, stealing from a beggar-girl. You were my brother, the head of our house, and it was your duty to protect me. But no, you must drag me into the carnage, I'm as red as a flayed ox; those hungry flies are swarming after me, and my heart is a horrible hive.

ORESTES  True, my love, I've taken everything from you, and I have nothing to offer you in return—only my crime. But what a vast gift. Can't you believe that it weighs on my soul like lead? We were too light, Electra; now our feet sink into the ground like chariot wheels in a rut. So come, we'll go heavily on our way, bent beneath our precious load. You will give me your hand, and we will go—

ELECTRA  Where?

ORESTES  I don't know. Toward ourselves. Beyond the rivers and the mountains are an Orestes and an Electra waiting for us. Patiently we must look for them.

*The Flies, 75–76, 79–80, 123, 132–133, 154–156, 158–159, 161.*

# III

———————•———————

*Being and Doing*

## 1 INTENTION AND MOTIVE

Ever since the reaction against the doctrine of substance has won out in modern philosophy, the majority of thinkers have tried to do in the area of human behavior what their predecessors had done in physics—to replace substance by simple motion. For a long time the aim of ethics was to provide man with a way of *being*. This was the meaning of Stoic morality or of Spinoza's Ethics. But if the being of man is to be reabsorbed in the succession of his acts, then the purpose of ethics will no longer be to raise man to a higher ontological status. In this sense the Kantian morality is the first great ethical system which substitutes doing [*le faire*] for being as the supreme value of action. The heroes of *L'Espoir* are for the most part on the level of *doing*, and Malraux shows us the conflict between the old Spanish democrats who still try to *be* and the Communists, whose morality resolves into a series of definite obligations, determined by circumstances, each of these obligations having reference to a particular action. Who is right? Is the supreme value of human activity a *doing* or a *being*? And whichever solution we adopt, what is to become of *having*? Ontology should be able to inform us concerning this problem; moreover it is one of ontology's essential tasks if the for-itself is the being which is defined by *action*. . . .

It is strange that philosophers have been able to argue endlessly about determinism and free-will, to cite examples in favor of one or the other thesis without ever attempting first to make explicit the structures contained in the very idea of *action*. The concept of an act contains, in fact, numerous subordinate notions which we shall have to organize and arrange in a hierarchy: to act is to modify the *shape* of the world; it is to arrange means in view of an end; it is to produce an organized instrumental complex such that by a series of concatenations and connections the modification effected on one of the links modifies modifications throughout the whole series and finally produces an anticipated result. But this is not important for us yet. We should observe first that an action is on principle *intentional*. The careless smoker who has through negligence caused the explosion of a powder magazine has not *acted*. On the other hand the worker who is charged with dynamiting a quarry and who obeys the given orders has acted when he has produced the expected explosion; he knew what he was doing or, if you prefer, he intentionally realized a conscious project.

This does not mean, of course, that one must foresee all the consequences of his act. The emperor Constantine when he established himself at Byzantium, did not foresee that he would create a center of Greek culture and language, the appearance of which would ultimately provoke a schism in the Christian Church and which would contribute to weakening the Roman Empire. Yet he performed an act just insofar as he realized his project of creating a new residence for emperors in the Orient. The result conforms sufficiently with his intention for us to be able to speak of action. But if this is the case, we observe that the action necessarily implies as its condition the recognition of a "desideratum"; that is, of an objective lack or again of a negation. *The intention* of providing a rival for Rome can come to Constantine only through the apprehension of an objective lack: Rome lacks a counterweight; to this still profoundly pagan city ought to be opposed a Christian city which at the moment *is lacking*. Creating Constantinople is understood as an *act* only if first the conception of a new city has preceded the action itself or at least if this conception serves as an organizing theme for all later steps. But this conception cannot be the pure representation of the city as *possible*. It apprehends the city in its essential characteristic, which is to be a *desirable* and not yet realized possible.

This means that from the moment of the first conception of the act, consciousness has been able to withdraw itself from the full world of which it is consciousness and to leave the level of being in order to approach directly that of non-being. Consciousness insofar as it is considered exclusively in its being, is perpetually referred from being to being and cannot find in being any motive for revealing non-being. The imperial system with Rome as its capital functions positively and in a certain real way which can be easily discovered. Will someone say that the taxes are collected badly, that Rome is not secure from invasions, that it does not have the geographical location which is suitable for the capital of a Mediterranean empire which is threatened by barbarians, that its corrupt morals make the spread of the Christian religion difficult? How can anyone fail to see that all these considerations are *negative;* that is, that they aim at what is not, not at what is. To say that sixty per cent of the anticipated taxes have been collected can pass, if need be, for a positive appreciation of the situation *such as it is.* To say that they are *badly* collected is to consider the situation in terms of a situation which is posited as an absolute end but which precisely *is not.* To say that the corrupt morals at Rome hinder the spread of Christianity is not to consider this diffusion for what it is; that is, for a propagation at a rate which the reports of the clergy can enable us to determine. It is to posit the diffusion in itself as insufficient; that is, as suffering from a secret nothingness. But it appears as such only if it is transcended toward a limiting-situation posited *a priori* as a value (for example, toward a certain rate of religious conversions, toward a certain morality of the population). This limiting-situation cannot be conceived in terms of the mere consideration of the real state of affairs; for the most beautiful girl in the world can offer only what she *has,* and in the same way the most miserable situation can by itself be designated only as it *is* without any reference to an ideal nothingness.

Insofar as man is immersed in the historical situation, he does not even succeed in conceiving of the failures and lacks in a political organization or specific economy; this is not, as is stupidly said, because he "is accustomed to it," but because he apprehends it in its plentitude of being and because he cannot even imagine that it can be otherwise. For it is necessary here to invert ordinary opinion and on the basis of what is not, to recognize the harshness or the sufferings which it imposes, which are motives for conceiving of another state of affairs in which things would be better for everybody. It is on the day that we can conceive of a different state of affairs that a new light falls on our troubles and our suffering and that we *decide* that these are unbearable. A worker in 1830 is capable of revolting if his salary is

lowered, for he easily conceives of a situation in which his
wretched standard of living would not be as low as the one which
is about to be imposed on him. But he does not represent his sufferings to himself as unbearable; he adapts himself to them not
through resignation but because he lacks the education and reflection necessary for him to conceive of a social state in which
these sufferings would not exist. Consequently *he does not act*.
Masters of Lyon following a riot, the workers at Croix-Rousse
do not know what to do with their victory; they return home be-
wildered, and the regular army has no trouble in overcoming
them. Their misfortunes do not appear to them "habitual" but
rather *natural;* they *are*, that is all, and they constitute the worker's condition. They are not detached; they are not seen in a
clear light, and consequently they are integrated by the worker
with his being. He suffers without considering his suffering and
without conferring value upon it. To suffer and to *be* are one and
the same for him. His suffering is the pure affective tenor of his
non-positional consciousness, but he does not *contemplate* it.
Therefore this suffering cannot be in itself a *motive* for his acts.
Quite the contrary, it is after he has formed the project of changing the situation that it will appear intolerable to him. This
means that he will have had to give himself room, to withdraw in
relation to it, and will have to have effected a double nihilation:
on the one hand, he must posit an ideal state of affairs as a pure
*present* nothingness; on the other hand, he must posit the actual
situation as nothingness in relation to this state of affairs. He
will have to conceive of a happiness attached to his class as a
pure possible—that is, presently as a certain nothingness—and
on the other hand, he will turn back to the present situation in
order to illuminate it in the light of his nothingness and in order
to nihilate it in turn by declaring: "I *am not* happy."

Two important consequences result. (1) No factual state of
affairs whatever it may be (the political and economic structure
of society, the psychological "state," etc.) is capable by itself of
motivating any act whatsoever. For an act is a projection of the
for-itself toward what is not, and what is can in no way determine by itself what is not. (2) No factual state of affairs can determine consciousness to apprehend it as a negation or as a
lack. Or rather, no factual state can determine consciousness to
define it and to circumscribe it since, as we have seen, Spinoza's
statement, *"Omnis determinatio est negatio,"* remains profoundly

true. Now every action has for its express condition not only the discovery of a state of affairs as "lacking in ——," *i.e.*, as a negation—but also, and before all else, the constitution of the state of affairs under consideration into an isolated system. There *is* a factual state—satisfying or not—only by means of the nihilating power of the for-itself. But this power of nihilation cannot be limited to realizing a simple *withdrawal* in relation to the world. In fact insofar as consciousness is "invested" by being, insofar as it simply suffers what is, it must be included in being. It is the organized form—worker-finding-his-suffering-natural—which must be surmounted and denied in order for it to be able to form the object of a revealing contemplation. This means evidently that it is by a pure wrenching away from himself and the world that the worker can posit his suffering as unbearable suffering and consequently can *make of it the motive* for his revolutionary action. This implies for consciousness the permanent possibility of effecting a rupture with its own past, of wrenching itself away from its past so as to be able to consider it in the light of a non-being and so as to be able to confer on it the meaning which *it has* in terms of the project of a meaning which it *does not have*. Under no circumstances can the past in any way by itself produce *an act;* that is, the positing of an end which turns back upon itself so as to illuminate it. This is what Hegel caught sight of when he wrote that "the spirit is the negative," although he seems not to have remembered this when he came to presenting his own theory of action and of freedom. In fact as soon as one attributes to consciousness this negative power with respect to the world and itself, as soon as the nihilation forms an integral part of the *positing* of an end, we must recognize that the indispensable and fundamental condition of all action is the freedom of the acting being.

Thus at the outset we can see what is wrong with those tedious discussions between determinists and the proponents of free-will. The latter are concerned to find cases of decision for which there exists no prior reason, or deliberations concerning two opposed acts which are equally possible and possess reasons (and motives)* of exactly the same weight. To which the determinists may easily reply that there is no action without a reason and that

---

* I am translating Sartre's *motif* as "reason" or "reason for"; his *mobile*, as "motive." But he is drawing a sharper distinction than these English terms (or even the French) suggest.—Ed.

the most insignificant gesture (raising the right hand rather than the left hand, etc.) refers to reasons and motives which confer its meaning upon it. Indeed the case could not be otherwise since every action must be *intentional;* each action must, in fact, have an end, and the end in turn refers to a reason. Such indeed is the unity of the three temporal *ekstases;* the end or temporalization of my future implies a reason (or motive); that is, it points toward my past, and the present is the emergence of the act. To speak of an act without a reason is to speak of an act which would lack the intentional structure of every act; and the proponents of free-will by searching for it on the level of the act which is in the process of being performed can only end up by rendering the act absurd. But the determinists in turn are weighting the scale by stopping their investigation of the reason and motive. The essential question in fact lies beyond the complex organization "reason-intention-act-end"; indeed we ought to ask how a reason (or motive) can be constituted as such.

Now we have just seen that if there is no act without a reason, this is not in the sense that we can say that there is no phenomenon without a reason. In order to be a *reason,* the *reason* must be *experienced* as such. Of course this does not mean that it is to be thematically conceived and made explicit as in the case of deliberation. But at the very least it means that the for-itself must confer on it its value as reason or motive. And, as we have seen, this constitution of the reason as such cannot refer to another real and positive existence; that is, to a prior reason. For otherwise the very nature of the act as engaged intentionally in nonbeing would disappear. The motive is understood only by the end; that is, by the non-existent. It is therefore in itself a negation. If I accept a niggardly salary it is doubtless because of fear; and fear is a motive. But it is *fear of dying from starvation;* that is, this fear has meaning only outside itself in an end ideally posited, which is the preservation of a life which I apprehend as "in danger." And this fear is understood in turn only in relation to the *value which I* implicitly give to this life; that is, it is referred to that hierarchal system of ideal objects which are values. Thus the motive makes itself understood as what it is by means of the complex of beings which "are not," by ideal existences, and by the future. Just as the future turns back upon the present and the past in order to elucidate them, so it is the complex of my projects which turns back in order to confer upon the *motive* its structure as a motive. It is only because I escape the in-itself by nihilating myself toward my possibilities that this in-itself can take on value as reason or motive. Reasons and motives have meaning only inside a projected complex which is precisely a complex of non-existents. And this complex is ultimately myself as transcendence; it is Me insofar as I have to be myself outside of myself.

If we recall the principle which we established earlier—namely that it is the apprehension of a revolution as possible which gives to the workman's suffering its value as a motive—we must thereby conclude that it is by fleeing a situation toward our possibility of changing it that we organize this situation into complexes of reasons and motives. The nihilation by which we achieve a withdrawal in relation to the situation is the same as the *ekstasis* by which we project ourselves toward a modification of this situation. The result is that it is in fact impossible to find an act without a motive but that this does not mean that we must conclude that the motive causes the act; the motive is an integral part of the act. For as the resolute project toward a change is not distinct from the act, the motive, the act, and the end are all constituted in a single emergence. Each of these three structures claims the two others as its meaning. But the organized totality of the three is no longer explained by any particular structure, and its emergence as the pure temporalizing nihilation of the in-itself is one with freedom. It is the act which decides its ends and its motives, and the act is the expression of freedom. . . .

## 2 MOTIVE AND REASON

Generally by "reason" we mean the reason for the act; that is, the complex of rational considerations which justify it. If the government decides on a conversion of government bonds, it will give the reasons for its act: the lessening of the national debt, the rehabilitation of the treasury. Similarly it is by *reasons* that historians are accustomed to explain the acts of ministers or monarchs; they will seek the *reasons* for a declaration of war: the occasion is propitious, the attacked country is disorganized because of internal troubles; it is time to put an end to an economic conflict which is in danger of lasting interminably. If Clovis is converted to Catholicism, then inasmuch as so many barbarian

kings are Arians, it is because Clovis sees an opportunity of getting into the good graces of the episcopate which is all-powerful
in Gaul. And so on. One will note here that the reason is characterized as an objective evaluation of the situation. The cause
of Clovis' conversion is the political and religious state of Gaul;
it is the relative strengths of the episcopate, the great landown-
ers, and the common people. The reason for the conversion of
the bonds is the state of the national debt. Nevertheless this objective evaluation can be made only in the light of a presupposed
end and within the limits of a project of the for-itself toward this
end. In order for the power of the episcopate to be revealed to
Clovis as the reason for his conversion (that is, in order for him
to be able to envisage the objective consequences which this
conversion could have), it is necessary first for him to posit as
an end the conquest of Gaul. If we suppose that Clovis has other
ends, he can find in the situation of the Church reasons for his
becoming Arian or for remaining pagan. It is even possible that
in the consideration of the Church he can even find no reason
for acting in any way at all; he will then discover nothing in relation to this subject; he will leave the situation of the episcopate
in the state of "unrevealed," in a total obscurity. We shall therefore use the term *reason* for the objective apprehension of a specific situation as this situation is revealed in the light of a certain end as being able to serve as the means for attaining this
end.

The motive, on the contrary, is generally considered as a subjective fact. It is the complex of desires, emotions, and passions
which impel me to accomplish a certain act. The historian looks
for motives and takes them into account only as a last resort
when the reasons are not sufficient to explain the act under consideration. Ferdinand Lot, for example, after having shown that
the reasons which are ordinarily given for the conversion of Constantine are insufficient or erroneous, writes: "Since it is established that Constantine had everything to lose and apparently
nothing to gain by embracing Christianity, there is only one conclusion possible—that he yielded to a sudden impulse, pathological or divine as you prefer."* Lot is here abandoning the explanation by reasons, which seems to him unenlightening, and prefers
to it an explanation by motives. The explanation must then be

* Ferdinand Lot: *La fin du monde antique et le début du moyen âge*, Renais-
sance du Livre, 1927, p. 35.

sought in the psychic state—even in the "mental" state—of the historical agent. It follows naturally that the event becomes wholly contingent since another individual with other passions and other desires would have acted differently. In contrast to the historian the psychologist will by preference look for motives, usually he supposes, in fact, that they are "contained in" the state of consciousness which has provoked the action. The ideal rational act would therefore be the one for which the motives would be practically nil and which would be uniquely inspired by an objective evaluation of the situation. The irrational or passionate act will be characterized by the reverse proportion.

It remains for us to explain the relation between reasons and motives in the everyday case in which they exist side by side. For example, I can join the Socialist Party because I judge that this party serves the interests of justice and of humanity or because I believe that it will become the principal historical force in the years which will follow my joining: these are reasons. And at the same time I can have motives: a feeling of pity or charity for certain classes of the oppressed, a feeling of shame at being on the "right side of the barricade," as Gide says, or again an inferiority complex, a desire to shock my relatives, etc. What can be meant by the statement that I have joined the Socialist Party for these reasons *and* these motives? Evidently we are dealing with two radically distinct layers of meaning. How are we to compare them? How are we to determine the part played by each of them in the decision under consideration? This difficulty, which certainly is the greatest of those raised by the current distinction between reasons and motives, has never been resolved; few people indeed have so much as caught a glimpse of it. Actually under a different name it amounts to positing the existence of a conflict between the will and the passions. But if the classic theory is discovered to be incapable of assigning to reason and motive their proper influence in the simple instance when they join together to produce a single decision, it will be wholly impossible for it to explain or even to conceive of a conflict between reasons and motives, a conflict in which each set would urge its individual decision. Therefore we must start over again from the beginning.

To be sure, the reason is objective; it is the state of contemporary things as it is revealed to a consciousness. It is *objective* that the Roman plebs and aristocracy were corrupted by the time of Constantine or that the Catholic Church is ready to favor a monarch who at the time of Clovis will help it triumph over Arianism. Nevertheless this state of affairs can be revealed only to a for-itself since in general the for-itself is the being by which "there is" a world. Better yet, it can be revealed only to a for-itself which chooses itself in this or that particular way—that is, to a for-itself which has made its own individuality. The for-itself must have projected itself in this or that way in order to discover the instrumental implications of instrumental-things. Objectively the knife is an instrument made of a blade and a handle. I can grasp it objectively as an instrument to slice with, to cut with. But lacking a hammer, I can just as well grasp the knife as an instrument to hammer with. I can make use of its handle to pound in a nail, and this apprehension is no less *objective*. When Clovis evaluates the aid which the Church can furnish him, it is not certain that a group of prelates or even one particular priest has made any overtures to him, nor even that any member of the clergy has clearly thought of an alliance with a Catholic monarch. The only strictly objective facts, those which any for-itself whatsoever can establish, are the great power of the Church over the people of Gaul and the anxiety of the Church with regard to Arian heresy. In order for these observed facts to be organized into a reason for conversion, it is necessary to isolate them from the complex—and for this purpose to nihilate them—and it is necessary to transcend them toward a particular potentiality: the Church's potentiality objectively apprehended by Clovis will be to give its support to a converted king. But this potentiality can be revealed only if the situation is transcended toward a state of things which does not yet exist—in short, toward a nothingness. In a word the world gives advice only if one questions it, and one can question it only for a specified end.

Therefore the reason, far from determining the action, appears only in and through the project of an action. It is in and through the project of imposing his rule on all of Gaul that the state of the Western Church appears objectively to Clovis as a reason for his conversion. In other words the consciousness which carves out the reason in the complex of the world has already its own structure; it has given its own ends to itself, it has projected itself toward its possibles, and it has its own manner of suspending itself from its possibilities: this peculiar manner of holding to its possibles is here affectivity. This internal organization which consciousness has given to itself in the form of non-positional self-consciousness is strictly correlative with the carving out of reasons in the world. Now if one reflects on the matter, one must recognize that the internal structure of the for-itself by which it effects in the world the emergence of reasons for acting is an "irrational" fact in the historical sense of the term. Indeed we can easily understand rationally the technical usefulness of the conversion of Clovis under the hypothesis by which he would have projected the conquest of Gaul. But we cannot do the same with regard to his project of conquest. It is not "self-explanatory." Ought it to be interpreted as a result of Clovis' *ambition*? But precisely what is the ambition if not the purpose of conquering? How could Clovis' ambition be distinguished from the precise project of conquering Gaul? Therefore it would be useless to conceive of this original project of conquest as "impelled" by a pre-existing motive which would be ambition. It is indeed true that the ambition is a motive since it is wholly subjectivity. But as it is not distinct from the project of conquering, we shall say that this first project of his possibilities in the light of which Clovis discovers a reason for being converted is precisely the *motive*. Then all is made clear and we can conceive of the relations of these three terms: reasons, motives, ends. We are dealing here with a particular case of being-in-the-world: just as it is the emergence of the for-itself which makes there be a world, so here it is the very being of the for-itself—insofar as this being is a pure project toward an end—which causes there to be a certain objective structure of the world, one which deserves the name of reason in the light of this end. The for-itself is therefore the consciousness of this reason. But this positional consciousness *of* the reason is on principle a non-thetic consciousness of itself as a project toward an end. In this sense it is a motive; that is, it experiences itself non-thetically as a project, more or less keen, more or less passionate, toward an end at the very moment at which it is constituted as a revealing consciousness of the organization of the world into reasons.

Thus reason and motive are correlative, exactly as the non-thetic self-consciousness is the ontological correlate of the thetic consciousness *of* the object. Just as the consciousness *of* something is self-consciousness, so the motive is nothing other than the apprehension of the reason insofar as this apprehension is self-consciousness. But it follows obviously that the reason, the motive, and the end are the three indissoluble terms of the thrust of a free and living consciousness which projects itself toward its possibilities and makes itself defined by these possibilities.

How does it happen then that the motive appears to the psychologist as the affective content of a fact of consciousness as this content determines another fact of consciousness or a decision? It is because the motive, which is nothing other than a non-thetic self-consciousness, slips into the past with this same consciousness and along with it ceases to be living. As soon as a consciousness is made-past, it is what I have to be in the form of the "was." Consequently when I turn back toward my consciousness of yesterday, it preserves its intentional significance and its meaning as subjectivity, but, as we have seen, it is congealed; it is outside like a thing, since the past is in-itself. The motive becomes then that *of which* there is consciousness. It can appear to me in the form of "knowledge"; as we saw earlier, the dead past haunts the present in the aspect of a *knowing*. It can also happen that I turn back toward it so as to make it explicit and formulate it while guiding myself by the knowledge which it is for me in the present. In this case it is an object of consciousness; it is this very consciousness *of which I am conscious*. It appears therefore—like my memories in general—simultaneously as *mine* and as transcendent. Ordinarily we are surrounded by these motives into which we "no longer enter," for we not only have to decide concretely to accomplish this or that act but also to accomplish actions which we decided upon the day before or to pursue enterprises in which we are engaged. In a general way consciousness at whatever moment it is grasped is apprehended as involved and this very apprehension implies a knowledge of the motives of the involvement or even a thematic and positional explanation of these reasons. It is obvious that the apprehension of the motive refers at once to the reason, its correlate, since the motive, even when made-past and congealed in in-itself, at least maintains as its meaning the fact that it has been a consciousness of a reason; *i.e.*, the discovery of an objective structure of the world. But as the motive is *in-itself* and as the reason is objective, they are presented as a dyad without ontological distinction; we have seen, indeed, that our past is lost in the midst of the world. That is why we put them on the same level and why we are able to speak of the reasons *and* of the motives of an action as if they could enter into conflict or both concur in a specific proportion in a decision.

Yet if the motive is transcendent, if it is only the irremediable being which we have to be in the mode of the "was," if like all our past it is separated from us by a breadth of nothingness, then it can act only if it is *recovered;* in itself it is without force. It is therefore by the very thrust of the involved consciousness that a value and a weight will be conferred on motives and on prior reasons. What they have been does not depend on consciousness, but consciousness has the duty of maintaining them in their existence in the past. I have willed this or that: here is what remains irremediable and which even constitutes my essence, since my essence is what I have been. But the meaning held for me by this desire, this fear, these objective considerations of the world when presently I project myself toward my futures— this must be decided by me alone. I decide them precisely and only by the very act by which I project myself toward my ends. The recovery of former motives—or the rejection or new appreciation of them—is not distinct from the project by which I assign new ends to myself and by which in the light of these ends I apprehend myself as discovering a supporting reason in the world. Past motives, past reasons, present motives and reasons, future ends, all are organized in an indissoluble unity by the very upsurge of a freedom which is beyond reasons, motives, and ends.

The result is that a voluntary deliberation is always doctored. How can I evaluate reasons and motives on which I myself confer their value before all deliberation and by the very choice which I make of myself? The illusion here stems from the fact that we endeavor to take reasons and motives for entirely transcendent things which I balance in my hands like weights and which possess a weight as a permanent property. Yet on the other hand we try to view them as contents of consciousness, and this is self-contradictory. Actually reasons and motives have only the weight which my project—*i.e.*, the free production of the end and of the known act to be realized—confers upon them. When I deliberate, the chips are down. And if I am brought to the point of deliberating, this is simply because it is a part of my original project to realize motives by means of *deliberation* rather than by some other form of discovery (by passion, for example, or simply by action, which reveals to me the organized complex of causes and of ends as my language informs me of my thought). There is therefore a choice of deliberation as a procedure which will make known to me what I project and consequently what I am. And *the choice* of deliberation is organized with the complex motives-causes and ended by free spontaneity. When the will intervenes, the decision is taken, and it has no other value than that of making the announcement. . . .

### 3 CHOICE

Common opinion does not hold that to be free means only to choose oneself. A choice is said to be free if it is such that it could have been other than what it is. I start out on a hike with friends. At the end of several hours of walking my fatigue increases and finally becomes very painful. At first I resist and then suddenly I let myself go, I give up, I throw my knapsack down on the side of the road and let myself fall down beside it. Someone will reproach me for my act and will mean thereby that I was free—that is, not only was my act not determined by anything or person, but also I could have succeeded in resisting my fatigue longer, I could have done as my companions did and reached the resting place before relaxing. I shall defend myself by saying that I was *too tired*. Who is right? Or rather does the debate not assume incorrect premises? There is no doubt that I could have done otherwise, but that is not the problem. It ought to be formulated rather like this: could I have done otherwise without perceptibly modifying the organic totality of the projects which I am; or is the fact of resisting my fatigue such that instead of remaining a purely local and accidental modification of my behavior, it could be effected only by means of a radical transformation of my being-in-the-world—a transformation, moreover, which is *possible*? In other words: I could have done otherwise. Agreed. But *at what price*?

We are going to reply to this question by first presenting a *theoretical* description which will enable us to grasp the principle of our thesis. We shall see subsequently whether the concrete reality is not shown to be more complex and whether without contradicting the results of our theoretical inquiry, it will not lead us to enrich them and make them more flexible.

Let us note first that the fatigue by itself could not provoke my decision. . . . Fatigue is only the way in which I exist my body. It is not at first the object of a positional consciousness, but it is the very facticity of my consciousness. If then I hike across the country, what is revealed to me is the surrounding world; this is the object of my consciousness, and this is what I transcend toward possibilities which are my own—those, for example, of arriving this evening at the place which I have set for myself in advance. Yet to the extent that I apprehend this countryside with my eyes which unfold distances, with my legs which climb the hills and consequently make new sights and new obstacles appear and disappear, with my back which carries the knapsack—to this extent I have a non-positional consciousness (of) this body which regulates my relations with the world and which signifies my engagement in the world, in the form of fatigue. Objectively and in correlation with this non-thetic consciousness the roads are revealed as interminable, the slopes as *steeper*, the sun as more burning, etc. But I do not yet *think* of my fatigue; I apprehend it as the quasi-object of my reflection. Nevertheless there comes a moment when I do seek to consider my fatigue and to recover it. We really ought to provide an interpretation for this same intention; however, let us take it for what it is. It is not at all a contemplative apprehension of my fatigue; rather, . . . I *suffer* my fatigue. That is, a reflective consciousness is directed upon my fatigue in order to live it and to confer on it a value and a practical relation to myself. It is only on this plane that the fatigue will appear to me as bearable or intolerable. It will never be anything in itself, but it is the reflective for-itself which emerging suffers the fatigue as intolerable.

Here is posed the essential question: my companions are in good health—like me; they have had practically the same training as I so that although it is not possible to *compare* psychic events which occur in different subjectivities, I usually conclude—and witnesses after an objective consideration of our bodies-for-others conclude—that they are for all practical purposes "as fatigued as I am." How does it happen therefore that they suffer their fatigue differently? Someone will say that the difference stems from the fact that I am a "sissy" and that the others are not. But although this evaluation undeniably has a practical bearing on the case and although one could take this into account when there arose a question of deciding whether or not it would be a good idea to take me on another expedition, such an evaluation cannot satisfy us here. We have seen that to be ambitious is to project conquering a throne or honors; it is not a *given* which would incite one to conquest; it is this conquest itself. Similarly to be a "sissy" cannot be a factual given and is only a name given to the way in which I suffer my fatigue. If therefore I wish to understand under what conditions I can suffer a fatigue as unbearable, it will not help to address oneself to so-called factual givens, which are revealed as being only a choice; it is necessary to attempt to examine this choice itself and to see whether it is not explained within the perspective of a larger choice in which it would be integrated as a secondary structure. If I question one of my companions, he will explain to me that he is fatigued, of course, but that he *enjoys* his fatigue; he gives himself up to it as to a bath; it appears to him in some way as the privileged instrument for discovering the world which surrounds him, for adapting himself to the rocky roughness of the paths, for discovering the "mountainous" quality of the slopes. In the same way it is this light sunburn on the back of his neck and this slight ringing in his ears which will enable him to realize a direct contact with the sun. Finally the feeling of effort is for him that of fatigue overcome. But as his fatigue is nothing but the passion which he endures so that the dust of the highways, the burning of the sun, the roughness of the roads may exist to the fullest, his effort (*i.e.*, this sweet familiarity with a fatigue which he enjoys, to which he abandons himself and which nevertheless he himself directs) is given as a way of appropriating the mountain, of suffering it to the end and being victor over it. We shall see in the next chapter what is the meaning of the word *having* and to what extent *doing* is a method of *appropriating*. Thus my companion's fatigue is lived in a vaster project of a trusting abandon to nature, of a passion consented to in order that it may exist at full strength, and at the same time the project of sweet mastery and appropriation. It is only in and through this project that the fatigue will be able to be understood and that it will have meaning for him.

But this meaning and this vaster, more profound project are still by themselves *unselbständig*. They are not sufficient. For they precisely presuppose a particular relation of my companion to his body, on the one hand, and to things, on the other. It is easy to see, indeed, that there are as many ways of existing one's body as there are for-itselfs, although naturally certain original structures are invariable and in each for-itself constitute human-reality. We shall be concerned elsewhere with what is incorrectly called the relation of the individual to species and to the conditions of a universal truth. For the moment we can conceive in connection with thousands of meaningful events that there is, for example, a certain type of flight before facticity, a flight which consists precisely in abandoning oneself to this facticity; that is, in short, in trustingly reassuming it and enjoying it in order to try to recover it. This original project of recovery is therefore a certain choice which the for-itself makes of itself in the presence of the problem of being. Its project remains a nihilation, but this nihilation turns back upon the in-itself which it nihilates and expresses itself by a particular valorization of facticity. This is expressed especially by the thousands of behavior patterns called *abandon*. To abandon oneself to fatigue, to warmth, to hunger, to thirst, to let oneself fall back upon a chair or a bed with sensual pleasure, to relax, to attempt to let oneself be drunk in by one's own body, not now beneath the eyes of others as in masochism but in the original solitude of the for-itself—none of these types of behavior can ever be limited to itself. We perceive this clearly since in another person they irritate or attract. Their condition is an initial project of the recovery of the body; that is, an attempt at a solution of the problem of the absolute (of the in-itself-for-itself).

This initial form can itself be limited to a profound acceptance of facticity; the project of "making oneself body" will mean then a happy abandon to a thousand little passing gluttonies, to a thousand little desires, a thousand little weaknesses. One may recall from Joyce's *Ulysses,* Mr. Bloom satisfying his natural needs and inhaling with complacency "the intimate odor rising from beneath him." But it is also possible (and this is the case with my companion) that by means of the body and by compliance with the body, the for-itself seeks to recover the totality of the non-conscious—that is, the whole universe as the ensemble of material *things.* In this case the desired synthesis of the in-itself with the for-itself will be the quasi-pantheistic synthesis of the totality of the in-itself with the for-itself which recovers it. Here the body is the instrument of the synthesis; it loses itself in fatigue, for example, in order that this in-itself may exist to the fullest. And since it is the body which the for-itself exists as its own, this passion of the body coincides for the for-itself with the project of "making the in-itself exist." The complex this attitude involves—which is that of one of my companions—can be expressed by the vague feeling of a kind of mission: he is going on this expedition because the mountain which he is going to climb and the forest which he is going to cross *exist;* his mission is to be the one by whom their meaning will be made manifest. Therefore he attempts to be the one who founds them in their very existence.

We shall return later to this appropriative relation between the for-itself and the world, but we do not yet have at hand the elements necessary to elucidate it fully. In any case it is obvious following our analysis that the way in which my companion *suffers* his fatigue necessarily demands—if we are to understand it—that we undertake a regressive analysis which will lead us back to an initial project. Is this project we have delineated finally *selbständig*? Certainly—and it can be easily proved to be so. In fact by going further and further back we have reached the original relation which for-itself chooses with its facticity and with the world. But this original relation is nothing other than the for-itself's being-in-the-world inasmuch as this being-in-the-world is a choice—that is, we have reached the original type of nihilation by which the for-itself has to be its own nothingness. No interpretation of this can be attempted, for it would implicitly suppose the being-in-the-world of the for-itself just as all the demonstrations attempted by Euclid's Postulate implicitly suppose the adoption of this postulate.

Therefore if I apply this same method to interpret the way in which I suffer my fatigue, I shall first apprehend in myself a distrust of my body—for example, a way of wishing not "to have anything to do with it," wanting not to take it into account, which is simply one of numerous possible modes in which I can *exist my body*. I shall easily discover an analogous distrust with respect to the in-itself and, for example, an original project for recovering the in-itself which I nihilate *through the intermediacy of others*, which project in turn refers me to one of the initial projects which we enumerated in our preceding discussion. Hence my fatigue instead of being suffered "flexibly" will be grasped "stiffly" as an importunate phenomenon which I want to get rid of—and this simply because it incarnates my body and my brute contingency in the midst of the world at a time when my project is to preserve my body and my presence in the world by means of the looks of others. I am referred to myself as well as to my original project; that is, to my being-in-the-world insofar as this being is a choice. . . .

## 4 CONVERSION

The world by means of its very articulation refers to us exactly the image of what we are. Not, as we have seen so many times, that we can decipher this image—*i.e.*, break it down and subject it to analysis—but because the world necessarily appears to us as we are. In fact, it is by transcending the world toward ourselves that we make it appear such as it is. We choose the world, not in its contexture as in-itself, but in its meaning, by choosing ourselves. Through the internal negation by denying that we are the world, we make the world appear as world, and this internal negation can exist only if it is at the same time a projection toward a possible. It is the very way in which I entrust myself to the inanimate, in which I abandon myself to my body (or, on the other hand, the way in which I resist either one of these) which causes the appearance of both my body and the inanimate world with their respective value. Consequently there also I enjoy a full consciousness of myself and of my fundamental projects, and this time the consciousness is positional. Nevertheless, precisely because it is positional, what it presents to me is the transcendent image of what I am. The value of things, their instrumental role, their proximity and real distance (which have no relation to their spatial proximity and distance) do nothing more than to delineate my image—that is, my choice. My clothing (a uniform or a lounge suit, a soft or a starched shirt) whether neglected or cared for, carefully chosen or ordinary, my furniture, the street on which I live, the city in which I reside, the books with which I surround myself, the recreation which I enjoy, everything which is mine (that is, finally, the world of which I am perpetually conscious, at least by way of a meaning implied by the object which I look at or use): all this informs me of my choice—that is, my being. But such is the structure of the positional consciousness that I can trace this knowledge back to a subjective apprehension of myself, and it refers me to other objects which I produce or which I dispose of in connection with the order of the preceding without being able to perceive that I am thus more and more sculpturing my figure in the world. Thus we are fully conscious of the choice which we are. And if someone objects that in accordance with these observations it would be necessary to be conscious not of our *being-chosen* but of *choosing* ourselves, we shall reply that this consciousness is expressed by the twofold "feeling" of anguish and of responsibility. Anguish, abandonment, responsibility, whether muted or full strength, constitute the *quality* of our consciousness insofar as this is pure and simple freedom.

Earlier we posed a question: I have yielded to fatigue, we said, and doubtless I *could have* done otherwise but *at what price?* At present we are in a position to answer this. Our analysis, in fact, has just shown us that this act was not *gratuitous*. To be sure, it was not explained by a motive or a reason conceived as the content of a prior state of consciousness, but it had to be interpreted in terms of an original project of which it formed an integral part. Hence it becomes evident that we cannot suppose that the act could have been modified without at the same time supposing a fundamental modification of my original choice of myself. This way of yielding to fatigue and of letting myself fall down at the side of the road expresses a certain initial stiffening against my body and the inanimate in-itself. It is placed within the compass of a certain view of the world in which difficulties can appear "not worth the trouble of being borne"; or, to be exact, since the motive is a pure non-thetic consciousness and consequently an initial project of itself toward an absolute end (a certain aspect of the in-itself-for-itself), it is an apprehension of the world (warmth, distance from the city, uselessness of effort, etc.) as the reason for my ceasing to walk. Thus this *possible*—to stop—*theoretically* takes on its meaning only in and through the hierarchy of the possibles which I am in terms of the ultimate and initial possible. This does not imply that I *must necessarily* stop but merely that I can refuse to stop only by a radical conversion of my being-in-the-world; that is, by an abrupt metamorphosis of my initial project—*i.e.*, by another choice of myself and of my ends. Moreover this modification is always possible.

The anguish which, when this possibility is revealed, manifests our freedom to our consciousness is witness of this perpetual modifiability of our initial project. In anguish we do not simply apprehend the fact that the possibles which we project are perpetually gnawed away by our freedom-to-come; in addition we apprehend our choice—*i.e.*, ourselves—as *unjustifiable*. This means that we apprehend our choice as not deriving from any prior reality but rather as being about to serve as foundation for the complex of significations which constitute reality. Unjustifiability is not only the subjective recognition of the absolute contingency of our being but also that of the interiorization and recovery of this contingency on our own account. For the choice—as we shall see—issues from the contingency of the in-itself which it nihilates and transports it to the level of the gratuitous determination of the for-itself-by-itself. Thus we are perpetually engaged in our choice and perpetually conscious of the fact that we ourselves can abruptly invert this choice and "reverse steam"; for we project the future by our very being, but our existential freedom perpetually gnaws it away as we make known to ourselves what we are by means of the future but without getting a grip on this future which remains always possible without ever passing to the rank of the *real*. Thus we are perpetually *threatened* by the nihilation of our actual choice and perpetually threatened with choosing ourselves—and consequently with becoming—other than we are. By the sole fact that our choice is absolute, it is *fragile;* that is, by positing our freedom by means of it, we posit by the same stroke the perpetual possibility that the choice may become a "here and now" which has been made-past in the interests of a "beyond" which I shall be. . . .

At each moment I apprehend my initial choice as contingent and unjustifiable; at each moment therefore I am in a position suddenly to consider it objectively and consequently to transcend it and to make-it-past by making the liberating *moment* emerge. Hence my anguish, the fear which I have of being suddenly exorcised (*i.e.*, of becoming radically other); but hence also the frequent emergence of "conversions" which make me metamorphose totally my original project. These conversions which have not been studied by philosophers, have often inspired novelists. One may recall the *moment* at which Gide's Philoctetes casts off his hate, his fundamental project, his reason for being, and his being. One may recall the *moment* when Raskolnikov decides to give himself up. These extraordinary and

marvelous moments when the prior project collapses into the
past in the light of a new project which emerges from its ruins
and which as yet exists only in outline, in which humiliation,
anguish, joy, hope are delicately blended, in which we let go in
order to grasp and grasp in order to let go—these have often appeared to furnish the clearest and most moving image of our
freedom. But they are only one among others of its many manifestations.

Thus presented, the "paradox" of the inefficacy of voluntary
decisions will appear less offensive. It amounts to saying that
by means of the will, we can *construct* ourselves entirely, but
that the will which presides over this construction finds its meaning in the original project which it can appear to deny, that consequently this construction has a function wholly different from
that which it advertises, and that finally it can reach only details
of structures and will never modify the original project from
which it has issued any more than the consequences of a
theorem can turn back against it and change it.

## 5 FREEDOM

At the end of this long discussion, it seems that we have succeeded
in making a little more precise our ontological understanding of
freedom. It will be well at present to gather together and summarize the various results obtained.

1. A first glance at human reality informs us that for it being
is reduced to doing. The psychologists of the nineteenth century
who pointed out the "motor" structures of drives, of the attention,
of perception, etc. were right. But motion itself is an act. Thus
we find no *given* in human-reality in the sense that temperament,
character, passions, principles of reason would be acquired or
innate *data* existing in the manner of things. The empirical
consideration of the human being shows him as an organized
unity of behavior patterns. To be ambitious, cowardly, or ir-
ritable is simply to behave in this or that manner in this or that
circumstance. The Behaviorists were right in considering that
the sole positive psychological study ought to be of behavior
in strictly defined situations. Just as the work of Janet and the
Gestalt school have put us in a position to discover types of emotional behavior, so we ought to speak of types of perceptive behavior since perception is inconceivable except as an attitude

with respect to the world. Even the disinterested attitude of the
scientist, as Heidegger has shown, is the adoption of a disinterested position with respect to the object and consequently
one mode of behavior among others. Thus human reality does
not exist first in order to act later; but for human reality, to be is
to act, and to cease to act is to cease to be.

2. But if human reality is action, this means obviously that its
determination to action is itself action. If we reject this principle,
and if we admit that human reality can be determined to action
by a prior state of the world or of itself, this amounts to putting
a *given* at the beginning of the series. Then these *acts* disappear
as acts in order to give place to a series of *movements*. Thus the
notion of behavior is itself destroyed as with Janet and with the
Behaviorists. The existence of the act implies its autonomy.

3. Furthermore, if the act is not pure motion, it must be defined by an *intention*. No matter how this intention is considered,
it can be only a transcending of the given toward a result to be attained. This given, in fact, since it is pure presence, cannot
leave itself behind. Precisely because it is, it is fully and solely
what it is. Therefore it cannot provide the reason for a phenomenon which derives all its meaning from a result to be attained; that is, from a non-existent. When the psychologists,
for example, view the drive as a factual state, they do not see that
they are removing from it all its character as an *appetite* (*ad-
petitio*). Indeed, if the sexual drive can be differentiated from the
desire to sleep, for example, this can be only by means of its end,
and this end does not exist. Psychologists ought to have asked
what could be the ontological structure of a phenomenon such
that it makes known to itself what it is by means of something
which does not yet exist. The intention, which is the fundamental structure of human-reality, can in no case be explained
by a given, not even if it is presented as an emanation from a
given. But if one wishes to interpret the intention by its end,
care must be taken not to confer on this end an existence as a
*given*. In fact if we could admit that the end is given prior to
the result to be attained, it would then be necessary to concede
to this end a sort of being-in-itself at the heart of its nothingness
and an attractive virtue of a truly magical type. Moreover we
should not succeed any better in understanding the connection
between a given human reality and a given end than in understanding the connection between consciousness-substance and

reality-substance in the realists' arguments. If the drive or the act is to be interpreted by its end, this is because the intention has for its structure *positing* its end outside itself. Thus the intention makes itself be by choosing the end which makes it known.

4. Since the intention is a choice of the end and since the world reveals itself through our behavior, it is the intentional choice of the end which reveals the world, and the world is revealed as this or that (in this or that order) according to the end chosen. The end, illuminating the world, is a state of the world to be attained and not yet existing. The intention is a thetic consciousness of the end. But it can be so only by making itself a non-thetic consciousness of its own possibility. Thus my *end* can be a good meal if I am hungry. But this meal which beyond the dusty road on which I am traveling is projected as the *meaning* of this road (it goes *toward* a hotel where the table is set, where the dishes are prepared, where I am expected, etc.) can be apprehended only correlatively with my non-thetic project toward my own possibility of eating this meal. Thus by a double but unitary emergence the intention illuminates the world in terms of an end not yet existing and is itself defined by the choice of its possible. My end is a certain objective state of the world, my possible is a certain structure of my subjectivity; the one is revealed to the thetic consciousness, the other flows back over the non-thetic consciousness in order to characterize it.

5. If the given cannot explain the intention, it is necessary that the intention by its very emergence realize a rupture with the given, whatever this may be. Such must be the case, for otherwise we should have a present plenitude succeeding in continuity a present plenitude, and we could not prefigure the future. Moreover, this rupture is necessary for the *evaluation* of the given. The given, in fact, could never be a *reason* for an action if it were not evaluated. But this evaluation can be realized only by a withdrawal in relation to the given, a putting of the given into brackets, which supposes a break in continuity. In addition, the evaluation, if it is not to be gratuitous, must be effected in the light of something. And this something which serves to evaluate the given can be only the end. Thus the intention by a single unitary emergence posits the end, chooses itself, and evaluates the given in terms of the end. Under these conditions the

given is evaluated in terms of something which does not yet exist; it is in the light of non-being that being-in-itself is illuminated. There results a double nihilating coloration of the given; on the one hand, it is nihilated in that the rupture makes it lose all efficacy over the intention; on the other hand, it undergoes a new nihilation due to the fact that efficacy is returned to it in terms of a nothingness. Since human reality is act, it can be conceived only as being at its core a rupture with the given. It is the being which causes *there to be* a given by breaking with it and illuminating it in the light of the not-yet-existing.

6. The necessity on the part of the given to appear only within the compass of a nihilation which reveals it is actually the same as the *internal negation* which we described before. It would be in vain to imagine that consciousness can exist without a given; in that case it would be consciousness (of) itself as consciousness of nothing—that is, absolute nothingness. But if consciousness exists in terms of the given, this does not mean that the given conditions consciousness; consciousness is a pure and simple negation of the given, and it exists as the disengagement from a certain existing given and as an engagement toward a certain not yet existing end. But in addition this internal negation can be only the fact of a being which is in perpetual withdrawal in relation to itself. If this being were not its own negation, it would be what it is—*i.e.*, a pure and simple given. Due to this fact it would have no connection with any other *datum* since the given is by nature only what it is. Thus any possibility of the appearance of a world would be excluded. In order not *to be* a given, the for-itself must perpetually constitute itself as in withdrawal in relation to itself; that is, it must leave itself behind it as a *datum* which it already no longer is. This characteristic of the for-itself implies that it is the being which finds *no help, no support* in what it *was*. But on the other hand, the for-itself is free and can make there be a world because the for-itself is *the being which has to be what it was in the light of what it will be*. Therefore the freedom of the for-itself appears as its *being*. But since this freedom is neither a given nor a property, it can be only by choosing itself. The freedom of the for-itself is always *involved;* there is no question here of a freedom which could be undetermined and which would pre-exist its choice. We shall never apprehend ourselves except as a choice in the making. But freedom is simply the fact that this choice is always unconditioned.

7. Such a choice made without support and dictating its own reasons to itself, can very well appear *absurd,* and in fact it is absurd. This is because freedom is a *choice* of its being but not the *foundation* of its being. We shall return to this relation between freedom and facticity later. For the moment it will suffice us to say that human-reality can choose itself as it intends but is not able not to choose itself. It cannot even refuse to be; suicide, in fact, is a choice and affirmation—of being. By this being which is *given* to it, human-reality participates in the universal contingency of being and thereby in what we may call absurdity. This choice is absurd, not because it is without reason but because there has never been any possibility of not choosing oneself. Whatever the choice may be, it is founded and caught up with by being, for it is choice which *is.* But what must be noted here is that this choice is not absurd in the sense in which in a rational universe a phenomenon might emerge which would not be linked with other phenomena by any *reasons.* It is absurd in this sense—that the choice is that by which all foundations and all reasons come into being, that by which the very notion of the absurd receives a meaning. It is absurd as being beyond all reasons. Thus freedom is not pure and simple contingency insofar as it turns back toward its being in order to illuminate its being in the light of its end. It is the perpetual escape from contingency; it is the interiorization, the nihilation, and the subjectivizing of contingency, which thus modified passes wholly into the gratuitousness of the choice.

8. The free project is fundamental, for it is my being. Neither ambition nor the passion to be loved nor the inferiority complex can be considered as fundamental projects. On the contrary, they of necessity must be understood in terms of a primary project which is recognized as the project which can no longer be interpreted in terms of any other and which is total. A special phenomenological method will be necessary in order to make this initial project explicit. This is what we shall call existential psychoanalysis. . . . For the present we can say that the fundamental project which I am is a project concerning not my relations with this or that particular object in the world, but my total being-in-the-world; since the world itself is revealed only in the light of an end, this project posits for its end a certain type of relation to being which the for-itself wills to adopt. This project is not instantaneous, for it cannot be "in" time. Neither is it non-temporal in order to "give time to itself" afterwards.

That is why we reject Kant's "choice of intelligible character." The structure of the choice necessarily implies that it be a choice in the world. A choice which would be a choice *in terms of nothing,* a choice *against nothing* would be a choice of nothing and would be annihilated as choice. There is only phenomenal choice, provided that we understand that the phenomenon is here the absolute. . . .

## 6 THE GIVEN

By its very projection toward an end, freedom constitutes as a being in the midst of the world a particular *datum* which it has to be. Freedom does not choose it, for this would be to choose its own existence; but by the choice which it makes of its end, freedom makes the *datum* be revealed in this or that way, in this or that light in connection with the revelation of the world itself. Thus the very contingency of freedom and the world which surrounds this contingency with its own contingency will appear to freedom only in the light of the end which it has chosen; that is, not as brute existents but in the unity of the illumination of a single nihilation. And freedom would never be able to reapprehend this complex as a pure *datum,* for in that case it would be necessary that this freedom be outside of all choice and therefore that it should cease to be freedom. We shall use the term *situation* for the contingency of freedom in the *plenum* of being of the world inasmuch as this *datum,* which is there only *in order not to constrain* freedom, is revealed to this freedom only as *already illuminated* by the end which freedom chooses. Thus the *datum* never appears to the for-itself as a brute existent in-itself; it is discovered always *as a reason* since it is revealed only in the light of an end which illuminates it. Situation and motivation are really one. The for-itself discovers itself as engaged in being, hemmed in by being, threatened by being; it discovers the state of affairs which surrounds it as the reason for a reaction of defense or attack. But it can make this discovery only because it freely posits the end in relation to which the state of things is threatening or favorable.

These observations should show us that the *situation,* the common product of the contingency of the in-itself and of freedom, is an ambiguous phenomenon in which it is impossible for the for-itself to distinguish the contribution of freedom from that of the brute existent. In fact, just as freedom is the escape from a contingency which it has to be in order to escape it, so the situation is the free co-ordination and the free qualification of a brute given which does not allow itself to be qualified in any way at all. Here I am at the foot of this cliff which appears to me as "not climbable." This means that the rock appears to me in the light of a projected climbing—a secondary project which finds its meaning in terms of an initial project which is my being-in-the-world. Thus the rock is carved out on the ground of the world by the effect of the initial choice of my freedom. But on the other hand, what my freedom cannot determine is whether the rock "to be climbed" will or will not lend itself to climbing. This is part of the brute being of the rock. Nevertheless the rock can show its resistance to the climbing only if the rock is integrated by freedom in a "situation" of which the general theme is climbing. For the simple traveler who passes over this road and whose free project is a pure esthetic ordering of the landscape, the cliff is not revealed either as climbable or as not climbable; it is manifested only as beautiful or ugly.

Thus it is impossible to determine in each particular case what is attributable to freedom and what to the brute being of the for-itself. The given in-itself as *resisting* or as *co-operating* is revealed only in the light of the projecting freedom. But the projecting freedom organizes an illumination such that the in-itself is revealed by it *as it is* (*i.e.*, resisting or favorable); but we must clearly understand that the resistance of the given is not directly admissible as an in-itself quality of the given but only as an indication—across a free illumination and a free refraction—of something inapprehensible. Therefore it is only in and through the free emergence of a freedom that the world develops and reveals the resistance which can render the projected end unrealizable. Man encounters an obstacle only within the field of his freedom. Or rather, it is impossible to decree *a priori* what is attributable to the brute existent and what to freedom in the character of this or that particular existent functioning as an obstacle. What is an obstacle for me may not be so for another. There is no obstacle in an absolute sense, but the obstacle reveals its coefficient of adversity across freely invented and freely acquired techniques. The obstacle reveals this coefficient also in terms of the value of the end posited by freedom. The rock will not be an obstacle if I wish at any cost to arrive at the top of the mountain. On the other hand, it will discourage me if I have freely decided limits to my desire of making the projected climb. Thus the world by coefficients of adversity reveals to me the way in which I stand in relation to the ends which I assign myself, so that I can never know if it is giving me information about myself or about it. Furthermore the coefficient of adversity of the given is never a simple relation to my freedom as a pure nihilating upsurge. It is a relation, illuminated by freedom, between the *datum* which is the cliff and the *datum* which my freedom has to be; that is, between the contingent which it is not and its pure facticity. If the desire to climb it is equal, the cliff will be easy for one athletic climber but difficult for another, a novice, who is not well trained and who has a weak body. But the body in turn is revealed as well or poorly trained only in relation to a free choice. It is because I am there and because I have made of myself what I am that the cliff develops in relation to my body a coefficient of adversity. For the lawyer who has remained in the city and who is pleading a case, whose body is hidden under his lawyer's robe, the cliff is neither hard nor easy to climb; it is dissolved in the totality "world" without in any way emerging from it. And in one sense it is I who choose my body as weak by making it face the difficulties which I make emerge (mountain climbing, cycling, sport). If I have not chosen to take part in sports, if I live in the city, and if I concern myself exclusively with business or intellectual work, then from this point of view my body will have no quality whatsoever.

Thus we begin to catch a glimpse of the paradox of freedom: there is freedom only in a *situation*, and there is a situation only through freedom. Human-reality everywhere encounters resistance and obstacles which it has not created, but these resistances and obstacles have meaning only in and through the free choice which human-reality is. . . .

## 7 MY PAST

The meaning of the past is strictly dependent on my present project. This certainly does not mean that I can make the meaning of my previous acts vary in any way I please; quite the contrary, it means that the fundamental project which I am decides absolutely the meaning which the past which I have to be can have for me and for others. I alone in fact can decide at each moment the significance of the past. I do not decide it by discussion, by deliberation, and in each instance evaluating the importance of this or that prior event; but by projecting myself toward my ends, I preserve the past with me, and by action I *decide* its meaning. Who shall decide whether that mystical crisis in my fifteenth year "was" a pure accident of puberty or, on the contrary, the first sign of a future conversion? I myself, according to whether I shall decide—at twenty years of age, at thirty years —to be converted. The project of conversion at one and the same time confers on an adolescent crisis the value of a premonition which I had not taken seriously. Who shall decide whether the period which I spent in prison after a theft was fruitful or deplorable? I—according to whether I·give up stealing or become hardened. Who can decide the educational value of a trip, the sincerity of a profession of love, the purity of a past intention, etc.? It is I, always I, according to the ends by which I illuminate these past events.

Thus all my past is there pressing, urgent, imperious, but its meanings and the orders which it gives me I choose by the very project of my end. Of course the engagements which I have undertaken weigh upon me. Of course the marriage I made earlier, the house I bought and furnished last year limit my possibilities and dictate my conduct; but precisely because my projects are such I reassume the marriage relationship. In other words, precisely because I do not make of it a "marriage relationship which is past, transcended, dead" and because, on the contrary, my projects imply fidelity to the engagements undertaken or the decision to have an "honorable life" as a husband and a father, etc., these projects necessarily come to illuminate the past marriage vow and to confer on it its always actual value. Thus the urgency of the past comes from the future.

Suppose that in the manner of Schlumberger's hero* I radically modify my fundamental project, that I seek, for example, to free myself from a continued state of happiness, and my earlier engagements will lose all their urgency. They will no longer be here except as the towers and ramparts of the Middle Ages are here, structures which one cannot deny but which have no other meaning than that of recalling a stage previously traversed, a civilization and a period of political and economic existence which today are transcended and perfectly dead. It is the future

* Jean Schlumberger: *Un homme heureux*, N.R.F.

which decides whether the past is living or dead. The past, in fact, is originally a project, as the actual emergence of my being. And to the same extent that it is a project, it is an anticipation; its meaning comes to it from the future which it adumbrates. When the past slips wholly into the past, its absolute value depends on the validation or invalidation of the anticipations which it was. But it depends on my actual freedom to confirm the meaning of these anticipations by again accepting responsibility for them—*i.e.*, by anticipating the future which they anticipated—or to invalidate them by simply anticipating another future. In this case the past falls back as a disarmed and duped expectation; it is "without force." This is because the only force of the past comes to it from the future; no matter how I live or evaluate my past, I can do so only in the light of a project of myself toward the future.

Thus the order of my choices of the future is going to determine an order of my past, and this order will contain nothing of the chronological. There will be first the *always living past* which is always confirmed: my promise of love, certain business contracts, a certain picture of myself to which I am faithful. Then there is the ambiguous past which has ceased to please me and to which I still hold indirectly: for example, this suit which I am wearing, and which I bought at a certain period when I had the desire to be fashionable, displeases me extremely at present; hence the past in which I "chose" the suit is truly dead. But on the other hand, my actual project of economy is such that I must continue to wear this suit rather than get another. Hence it belongs to a past which is both dead and living like those social institutions which having been created for a determined end, have now outlived the regime which established them and have been made to serve altogether different ends, sometimes even opposed ends. A living past, a half-dead past, survivals, ambiguities, discrepancies: these strata of pastness are organized by the unity of my project. It is by means of this project that there is installed the complex system of references which makes any fragment of my past enter into a hierarchical, polyvalent [*i.e.*, having many values or facets] organization in which, as in a work of art, each partial structure indicates, in different ways, various other partial structures and the total structure.

Furthermore this decision with respect to the value, the order, and the nature of our past is simply the *historical choice* in general. If human societies are historical, this does not stem simply from the fact that they have a past but from the fact that they reassume the past by making it a *memorial*. When American capitalism decides to enter the European war of 1914-1918 because it sees there the opportunity for profitable transactions, it is not *historical;* it is only utilitarian. But when in the light of its utilitarian projects, it recovers the previous relations of the United States with France and gives to them the *meaning* of paying of a debt of honor by Americans to France, then it becomes historical. In particular it makes itself historical by the famous sentence: "Lafayette, we are here!" . . .

### 8 MY SITUATION

It is now possible for us to define more precisely this "being-in-situation," which characterizes the for-itself insofar as it is responsible for its manner of being without being the foundation of its being.

1. I am an existent *in the midst of* other existents. But I cannot "realize" this existence in the midst of others; I cannot apprehend as *objects* the existents which surround me nor apprehend myself as a *surrounded* existence nor even give a meaning to this notion of "in the midst of" except by choosing myself—not in my being but in my manner of being. The choice of this end is the choice of what is *not-yet-existing*. My position in the midst of the world is defined by the relation between the instrumental utility or adversity in the realities which surround me and my own facticity; that is, the discovery of the dangers which I risk in the world, of the obstacles which I can encounter there, the aid which can be offered me, all in the light of a radical nihilation of myself and of a radical, internal negation of the in-itself and all effected from the point of view of a freely posited end. This is what we mean by the *situation*.

2. The situation exists only in correlation with the transcending of the given toward an end. It is the way in which the given which I am and the given which I am not are revealed to the for-itself which I am in the mode of not-being it. When we speak of *situation*, therefore, we are speaking of a "position apprehended by the for-itself which is in situation." It is impossible to consider a situation from the outside; it is congealed into a *form in itself*. Consequently the situation cannot be called either ob-

jective or subjective although the partial structures of this situation (the cup which I use, the table on which I lean, etc.) can and must be strictly objective.

The situation cannot be *subjective,* for it is neither the sum nor the unity of the *impressions* which things make on us. It is *the things themselves* and myself among things; for my emergence into the world as the pure nihilation of being has no other result but to make there be things, and it adds *nothing.* In this aspect the situation betrays my *facticity;* that is, the fact that things simply *are there* as they are without the necessity or the possibility of being otherwise a. that I *am there* among them.

But neither can the situation be *objective* in the sense that it would be a pure given which the subject would establish without being in any way involved in the system thus constituted. In fact the situation by the very meaning of the given (a meaning without which there *would not even be* any given) reflects to the for-itself its freedom. If the situation is neither subjective nor objective, this is because it does not constitute a *knowledge* or even an affective comprehension of the state of the world by a subject. The situation is a *relation of being* between a for-itself and the in-itself which the for-itself nihilates. The situation is the whole subject (he is *nothing but* his situation) and it is also the whole "thing" (*there is* never anything more than things). The situation is the subject illuminating things by his very transcending, if you like; it is things reflecting to the subject his own image. It is the total facticity, the absolute contingency of the world, of my birth, of my place, of my past, of my environment, of the fact of my fellow man—and it is my freedom without limits as that which makes there be for me a facticity. It is this dusty, ascending road, this burning thirst which I have, the refusal of these people to give me anything to drink because I do not have any money or because I am not of their country or of their race; it is my abandonment in the midst of these hostile populations along with this fatigue in my body which will perhaps prevent me from reaching the goal which I had set for myself. But also it is precisely this *goal,* not insofar as I clearly and explicitly formulate it but insofar as it is there everywhere around me as that which unifies and explains all these facts, that which organizes them in a totality capable of description instead of making of them a disordered nightmare.

3. If the for-itself is nothing other than its situation, then it follows that being-in-situation defines human reality by accounting both for its *being-there* and for its *being-beyond*. Human reality is indeed the *being which is always beyond its being-there*. And the situation is the organized totality of the being-there, interpreted and lived in and through being-beyond. Therefore there is no privileged situation. We mean by this that there is no situation in which the *given* would crush beneath its weight the freedom which constitutes it as such—and that conversely there is no situation in which the for-itself would be *more free* than in others. This must not be understood in the sense of that "inward freedom" of Bergson's which Politzer ridiculed in *La fin d'une parade philosophique* [*The End of a Philosophical Parade*] and which simply amounted to recognizing in the slave the independence of the inner life and of the heart in chains. When we declare that the slave in chains is as free as his master, we do not mean to speak of a freedom which would remain indeterminate. The slave in chains is free *to break them;* this means that the very meaning of his chains will appear to him in the light of the end which he will have chosen: to remain a slave or to risk the worst in order to get rid of his slavery. Of course the slave will not be able to obtain the wealth and the standard of living of his master; but these are not the objects of his *projects;* he can only dream of the possession of these treasures. The slave's *facticity* is such that the world appears to him with another countenance and that he has to posit and to resolve different problems; in particular it is necessary fundamentally to choose himself on the ground of *slavery* and thereby to give a meaning to this obscure constraint. For example, if he chooses revolt, then slavery, far from being *at the start* an obstacle to this revolt, takes on its meaning and its coefficient of adversity only through the revolt. To be exact, just because the life of the slave who revolts and dies in the course of this revolt is a free life, just because the situation illuminated by a free project is full and concrete, just because the urgent and principal problem of this life is "Shall I attain my goal?"—just because of all this, the situation of the slave *cannot be compared* with that of the master. Each of them in fact takes on its meaning only for the for-itself in situation and in terms of the free choice of its ends. A comparison could be made only by a third person and consequently it could take place only between two objective

forms in the midst of the world; moreover it could be established only in the light of a project freely chosen by this third person. There is no absolute point of view which one can adopt so as to compare different situations, each person realizes only one situation—*his own*.

4. Since the situation is illumined by ends which are themselves projected only in terms of the *being-there*, which they illuminate, it is presented as eminently *concrete*. Of course it contains and sustains abstract and universal structures, but it must be understood as the *single countenance* which the world turns toward us as our unique and personal chance. We may recall here a fable of Kafka's: A merchant comes to plead his case at the castle where a terrifying guard bars the entrance. The merchant does not dare to go further; he waits and dies still waiting. At the hour of death he asks the guardian, "How does it happen that I was the only one waiting?" And the guardian replies, "This gate was made only for you." Such is precisely the case with the for-itself if we may add in addition that *each man makes for himself his own gate.* The concreteness of the situation is expressed particularly by the fact that the for-itself never aims at ends which are fundamentally abstract and universal. . . .

5. Just as the situation is neither objective nor subjective, so it can be considered neither as the free result of a freedom nor as the set of constraints to which I am subject; it stems from the illumination of constraint by freedom which gives to it its meaning as constraint. Between brute existents there can be no relationship; it is freedom which founds the relations by grouping the existents into instrumental-complexes; and it is freedom which projects the *reason* for the *relations*—that is, its end. But precisely because I project myself toward an end across a world of *relations*, I now meet with sequences, with linked series, with complexes, and I must determine to act according to laws. These laws and the way I make use of them decide the failure or the success of my attempts. But it is through freedom that lawful relations come into the world. Thus freedom enchains itself in the world as a free project toward ends.

6. The for-itself is a temporalization. This means that it *is* not but that it "makes itself." It is the *situation* which must account for that *substantial permanence* which we readily recognize in people ("He has not changed." "He is always the same.") and

which the person experiences in most cases as being his own. The free perseverance in a single project does not imply any permanence; quite the contrary, it is a perpetual renewal of my engagement—as we have seen. On the other hand, the realities enveloped and illuminated by a project which develops and confirms itself present the permanence of the in-itself; and to the extent that they reflect our image to us, they support us with their endurance; in fact it frequently happens that we take their permanence for our own. In particular the permanence of place and environment, of the judgments passed on us by our fellow men, of our past—all *shape* a degraded image of our *perseverance*. While I am temporalizing myself, I am *always* French, a civil servant or a proletarian *for others*. . . .

Alain has perceived correctly that character is a *vow*. When a man says, "I am not easy to please," he is entering into a free engagement with his ill-temper, and by the same token his words are a free interpretation of certain ambiguous details in his past. In this sense there is no character; there is only a project of oneself. But we must not, however, misunderstand the *given* aspect of the character. It is true that for the Other who apprehends me as the Other-as-object, I *am* ill-tempered, hypocritical or frank, cowardly or courageous. This aspect is referred to me by the Other's look; by the experience of the look, this character, which was a free project lived and self-conscious, becomes an . . . invariable to be assumed. It depends then not only on the Other but on the position which I have taken with respect to the Other and on my perseverance in maintaining this position. So long as I let myself be fascinated by the Other's look, my character will figure in my own eyes as an . . . invariable, the substantial permanence of my being—the kind of thing expressed in such ordinary everyday remarks as, "I am forty-five years old, and I'm not going to start changing myself today." The character often is what the for-itself tries to recover in order to become the in-itself-for-itself which it projects being. . . .

#### 9 MY RESPONSIBILITY

Man being condemned to be free carries the weight of the whole world on his shoulders; he is responsible for the world and for himself as a way of being. We are taking the word "responsibility" in its ordinary sense as "consciousness (of) being the incontestable author of an event or of an object." In this sense the responsibility of the for-itself is overwhelming since he is the one by whom it happens that *there is* a world; since he is also the one who makes himself be, then whatever may be the situation in which he finds himself, the for-itself must wholly assume this situation with its peculiar coefficient of adversity, even though it be insupportable. He must assume the situation with the proud consciousness of being the author of it, for the very worst disadvantages or the worst threats which can endanger my person have meaning only in and through my project; and it is on the ground of the engagement which I am that they appear. It is therefore senseless to think of complaining since nothing alien has decided what we feel, what we live, or what we are.

Furthermore this absolute responsibility is not resignation; it is simply the logical requirement of the consequences of our freedom. What happens to me happens through me, and I can neither affect myself with it nor revolt against it nor resign myself to it. Moreover everything which happens to me is *mine*. By this we must understand first of all that I am always equal to what happens to me *qua* man, for what happens to a man through other men and through himself can be only human. The most terrible situations of war, the worst tortures do not create a non-human state of things; there is no non-human situation. It is only through fear, flight, and recourse to magical types of behavior that I shall decide on the non-human, but this decision is human, and I shall carry the entire responsibility for it. But in addition the situation is *mine* because it is the image of my free choice of myself, and everything which it presents to me is *mine* in that this represents me and symbolizes me. Is it not I who decide the coefficient of adversity in things and even their unpredictability by deciding for myself?

Thus there are no *accidents* in a life; a community event which suddenly bursts forth and involves me in it does not come from the outside. If I am mobilized in a war, this war is *my* war; it is in my image and I deserve it. I deserve it first because I could always get out of it by suicide or by desertion; these ultimate possibles are those which must always be present for us when there is a question of envisaging a situation. For lack of getting out of it, I have *chosen* it. This can be due to inertia, to cowardice in the face of public opinion, or because I prefer certain other values to the value of the refusal to join in the war

(the good opinion of my relatives, the honor of my family, etc.).
Any way you look at it, it is a matter of a choice. This choice will
be repeated later on again and again without a break until the
end of the war. Therefore we must agree with the statement by
J. Romains, "In war there are no innocent victims." * If therefore I have preferred war to death or to dishonor, everything
takes place as if I bore the entire responsibility for this war. Of
course others have declared it, and one might be tempted perhaps to consider me as a simple accomplice. But this notion of
complicity has only a juridical sense, and it does not hold here.
For it depended on me that for me and by me this war should
not exist, and I have decided that it does exist. There was no
compulsion here, for the compulsion could have got no hold on a
freedom. I did not have any excuse; for as we have said repeat-
edly in this book, the peculiar character of human-reality is that
it is without excuse. Therefore it remains for me only to lay
claim to this war.

But in addition the war is *mine* because, by the sole fact that
it arises in a situation which I make be and that I can discover it
there only by engaging myself for or against it, I can no longer
distinguish at present the choice which I make of myself from
the choice which I make of the war. To live this war is to choose
myself through it and to choose it through my choice of myself.
There can be no question of considering it as "four years of va-
cation" or as a "reprieve," as a "recess," the essential part of
my responsibilities being elsewhere in my married, family, or
professional life. In this war which I have chosen I choose myself from day to day, and I make it mine by making myself. If it
is going to be four empty years, then it is I who bear the responsibility for this.

Finally, as we pointed out earlier, each person is an absolute
choice of self from the standpoint of a world of knowledges
and of techniques which this choice both assumes and illumines;
each person is an absolute emergence at an absolute date and is
perfectly unthinkable at another date. It is therefore a waste of
time to ask what I should have been if this war had not broken
out, for I have chosen myself as one of the possible meanings of the epoch which imperceptibly led to war. I am not distinct from this same epoch; I could not be transported to another epoch without contradiction. Thus *I am* this war which

* Jules Romains: *Les hommes de bonne volonté* and *Prélude à Verdun.*

restricts and limits and makes comprehensible the period which preceded it. In this sense we may define more precisely the responsibility of the for-itself if to the earlier quoted statement, "There are no innocent victims," we add the words, "We have the war we deserve." Thus, totally free, indistinguishable from the period for which I have chosen to be the meaning, as profoundly responsible for the war as if I had myself declared it, unable to live without integrating it in *my* situation, engaging myself in it wholly and stamping it with my seal, I must be without remorse or regrets as I am without excuse; for from the instant of my emergence in being, I carry the weight of the world by myself alone without anything or anyone being able to lighten it.

Yet this responsibility is of a very particular type. Someone will say, "I did not ask to be born." This is a naïve way of throwing greater emphasis on our facticity. I am responsible for everything, in fact, except for my very responsibility, for I am not the foundation of my being. Therefore everything takes place as if I were compelled to be responsible. I am *abandoned* in the world, not in the sense that I might remain abandoned and passive in a hostile universe like a board floating on the water, but rather in the sense that I find myself suddenly alone and without help, involved in a world for which I bear the whole responsibility without being able, whatever I do, to tear myself away from this responsibility for an instant. For I am responsible for my very desire of fleeing responsibilities. To make myself passive in the world, to refuse to act upon things and upon Others is still to choose myself, and suicide is one mode among others of being-in-the-world. Yet I find an absolute responsibility for the fact that my facticity (here the fact of my birth) is directly inapprehensible and even inconceivable, for this fact of my birth never appears as a brute fact but always across a projective reconstruction of my for-itself. I am ashamed of being born or I am astonished at it or I rejoice over it, or in attempting to get rid of my life I affirm that I live and I assume this life as bad. Thus in a certain sense I *choose* being born. This choice itself is integrally affected with facticity since I am not able not to choose, but this facticity in turn will appear only insofar as I transcend it toward my ends. Thus facticity is everywhere but inapprehensible; I never encounter anything except my responsibility. That is why I cannot ask, "*Why* was I born?" or curse the day of my birth or declare that I did not ask to be born, for these various attitudes toward my birth—*i.e.*, toward the *fact* that I realize a presence in the world—are absolutely nothing else but ways of assuming this birth in full responsibility and of making it *mine*. Here again I encounter only myself and my projects so that finally my abandonment—*i.e.*, my facticity— consists simply in the fact that I am condemned to be wholly responsible for myself. I am the being which *is* in such a way that in its being its being is in question. And this "is" of my being *is* as present and inapprehensible.

Under these conditions since every event in the world can be revealed to me only as an *occasion* (an occasion made use of, missed, neglected, etc.), or rather since everything which happens to us can be considered as an *opportunity* (*i.e.*, can appear to us only as a way of realizing this being which is in question in our being) and since others as transcendences-transcended are themselves only *occasions* and *opportunities*, the responsibility of the for-itself extends to the entire world as a peopled-world. It is precisely thus that the for-itself apprehends itself in anguish; that is, as a being which is neither the foundation of its own being nor of the Other's being nor of the in-itselfs which form the world, but a being which is compelled to decide the meaning of being—within it and everywhere outside of it. The one who realizes in anguish his condition as *being* thrown into a responsibility which extends to his very abandonment has no longer either remorse or regret or excuse; he is no longer anything but a freedom which perfectly reveals itself and whose being resides in this very revelation. But as we pointed out earlier, most of the time we flee anguish in bad faith.

> *Being and Nothingness*, *431–438*, *445–451*, *453–457*, *463–465*, *475–480*, *487–489*, *498–500*, *548–552*, *553–556*.

# IV

---•---

## Doing and Having

If it is true that human reality—as we have attempted to establish—declares and defines itself by the ends which it pursues, then an investigation and classification of these ends becomes indispensable. In the preceding chapter we have considered the for-itself only from the point of view of its free project, which is the impulse by which it thrusts itself toward its end. We should now question this end itself, for it *is a feature* of absolute subjectivity, serving as its transcendent, objective limit. This is what empirical psychology has suspected by defining man in terms of his desires. Here, however, we must be on our guard against two errors. First, the empirical psychologist, when he defines man in terms of desires, remains the victim of the illusion of substance. He views desire as being *in* man as a "content" of his consciousness, and he believes that the meaning of the desire is inherent in the desire itself. Thus he avoids everything which could evoke the idea of transcendence. But if I desire a house or a glass of water or a woman's body, how could this body, this glass, this piece of property reside in my desire, and how can my desire be anything but the consciousness of these objects as desirable? Let us beware then of considering these desires as little psychic entities dwelling in consciousness; they are consciousness itself in its original projective, transcendent structure, for consciousness is on principle consciousness *of* something.

The other error, which fundamentally is closely connected with the first, consists in considering psychological investigation as terminated as soon as the investigator has reached the concrete set of empirical desires. Thus a man would be defined by the bundle of drives or tendencies which empirical obser-

282

vation could establish. Naturally the psychologist will not always limit himself to adding up the *sum* of these tendencies; he will want to bring to light their relationships, their agreements and harmonies; he will try to present the set of desires as a synthetic organization in which each desire acts on the others and influences them. A critic, for example, wishing to explain the "psychology" of Flaubert, will write that he "appeared in his early youth to know as his normal state, a continual exaltation resulting from the twofold feeling of his grandiose ambition and his invincible power. . . . The effervescence of his young blood therefore turned into literary passion, as happens about the eighteenth year in precocious souls who find in the energy of style or the intensities of fiction some way of appeasing the need of violent action or of intense feeling, which torments them." *

In this passage there is an effort to reduce the complex personality of an adolescent to a few basic desires, as the chemist reduces compound bodies to merely a combination of simple bodies. The primitive givens will be grandiose ambition, the need of violent action and of intense feeling; these elements when they enter into combination, produce a permanent exaltation. Then—as Bourget remarks in a few words which we have not quoted—this exaltation nourished by numerous well-chosen readings, is going to seek to appease itself by self-expression in fictions which will satisfy it symbolically and channel it. There in outline is the genesis of a literary "temperament."

Now in the first place such a psychological *analysis* proceeds from the postulate that an individual fact is produced by the intersection of abstract, universal laws. The fact to be explained —which is here the literary disposition of the young Flaubert —is resolved into a combination of *typical*, abstract desires such as we meet in "the average adolescent." What is concrete here is only their combination; in themselves they are only schematic. The abstract then is by hypothesis prior to the concrete, and the concrete is only an organization of abstract qualities; the individual is only the intersection of universal schemata. But— aside from the logical absurdity of such a postulate—we see clearly in the example chosen, that it simply fails to explain what constitutes the individuality of the project under consideration. The fact that "the need to feel intensely," a universal

* Paul Bourget: "Essais de Psychologie contemporaine: G. Flaubert."

pattern, is disguised and channeled into becoming the need to write—this is not the *explanation* of the "vocation" of Flaubert; on the contrary, it is what must be explained. Doubtless one could invoke a thousand circumstances, known to us and unknown, which have shaped this need to feel into the need to act. But this is to give up any attempt at an explanation.* In addition this method rejects the pure individual who has been banished from the subjectivity of Flaubert into the external circumstances of his life. Finally, Flaubert's correspondence proves that long before the "crisis of adolescence," from his earliest childhood, he was tormented by the need to write.

At each stage in the description just quoted, we meet with a hiatus. Why did ambition and the feeling of his power produce in Flaubert *exaltation* rather than tranquil waiting or gloomy impatience? Why did this exaltation express itself specifically in the need to act violently and feel intensely? Or rather why does this need make a sudden appearance by spontaneous generation at the end of the paragraph? And why does this need instead of seeking to appease itself in acts of violence, by amorous adventures, or in debauch, choose precisely to satisfy itself symbolically? And why does Flaubert turn to writing rather than to painting or music for this symbolic satisfaction; he could just as well not resort to the artistic field at all (there is also mysticism, for example). "I could have been a great actor," wrote Flaubert somewhere. Why did he not try to be one? In a word, we have understood nothing; we have seen a succession of accidental happenings, of desires springing forth fully armed, one from the other, without our being able to grasp their genesis. The *transitions*, the becomings, the transformations, have been carefully veiled from us, and we have been limited to putting order into the succession by invoking empirically observed but literally unintelligible sequences (the need to act preceding in the adolescent the need to write).

Yet this is called psychology! Open any biography at random, and this is the kind of description which you will find more or less interspersed with accounts of external events and allusions to the great explanatory idols of our epoch—heredity, education, environment, physiological constitution. Occasionally,

---

* Since Flaubert's adolescence, so far as we can know it, offers us nothing specific in this connection, we must suppose the action of imponderable facts which on principle escape the critic.

in the better works the connection established between antecedent and consequent or between two concomitant desires and their reciprocal action is not conceived merely as a type of regular sequence; sometimes it is "comprehensible" in the sense which Jaspers understands in his general treatise on psychopathology. But this comprehension remains a grasp of general connections. For example we will realize the link between chastity and mysticism, between fainting and hypocrisy. But we are ignorant always of the concrete relation between *this* chastity (this abstinence in relation to a particular woman, *this* struggle against a definite temptation) and the individual content of the mysticism; in the same way psychiatry is too quickly satisfied when it throws light on the general structures of delusions and does not seek to comprehend the individual, concrete content of the psychoses (why this man believes himself to be that particular historical personality rather than some other; why his compensatory delusion is satisfied with specifically these ideas of grandeur instead of others, etc.).

But most important of all, these "psychological" explanations resort ultimately to inexplicable original givens. These are the simple bodies of psychology. We are told, for example, that Flaubert had a "grandiose ambition" and all of the previously quoted description depends on this original ambition. So far so good. But this ambition is an irreducible fact which by no means satisfies the mind. The irreducibility here has no justification other than refusal to push the analysis further. There where the psychologist stops, the fact confronted is given as primary. This is why we experience a troubled feeling of mingled resignation and dissatisfaction when we read these psychological treatises. "See," we say to ourselves, "Flaubert was ambitious. He was that kind of man." It would be as futile to ask why he was such as to seek to know why he was tall and blond. Of course we have to stop somewhere; it is the very contingency of all real existence. This rock is covered with moss, the rock next to it is not. Gustave Flaubert had literary ambition, and his brother Achille lacked it. That's the way it is. In the same way we want to know the properties of phosphorus, and we attempt to reduce them to the structure of the chemical molecules which compose it. But why are there molecules of this type? That's the way it is, that's all. The explanation of Flaubert's psychology will consist, if it is possible, in reducing the complexity of his behavior patterns, his feelings, and his tastes to certain *properties,* comparable to those of chemical bodies, beyond which it would be foolish to attempt to proceed. Yet we feel obscurely that Flaubert had not been "handed" his ambition. It is meaningful; therefore it is free. Neither heredity nor bourgeois background nor education can account for it, still less those physiological considerations regarding the "nervous temperament," which have been the vogue for some time now. The nerve is not *meaningful;* it is a colloidal substance which can be described in itself and which does not have the quality of transcendence; that is, it does not transcend itself in order to make known to itself by means of other realities what it is. Under no circumstances could the nerve provide a meaning. In one sense Flaubert's ambition is a fact with all a fact's contingency—and it is true that it is impossible to advance beyond that fact—but in another sense *it makes itself,* and our satisfaction is a guarantee to us that we may be able to grasp beyond this ambition something more, something like a radical decision which, without ceasing to be contingent, would be the genuine psychic irreducible.

What we are demanding then—and what nobody ever attempts to give us—is a *genuine* irreducible; that is, an irreducible of which the irreducibility would be self-evident, which would not be presented as the postulate of the psychologist and the result of his refusal or his inability to go further, but which when established would produce in us an accompanying feeling of satisfaction. This demand on our part does not come from that ceaseless pursuit of a cause, that infinite regress which has often been described as constitutive of rational research and which consequently—far from being exclusively associated with psychological investigation—may be found in all disciplines and in all problems. This is not the childish quest of a "because," which allows no further "why?" It is on the contrary a demand based on a pre-ontological comprehension of human reality and on the related refusal to consider man as capable of being analyzed and reduced to original givens, to determined desires (or "drives"), supported by the subject as properties by an object. Even if we were to consider him as such, it would be necessary to choose: either *Flaubert,* the man, whom we can love or detest, blame or praise, who represents for us *the Other,* who directly attacks our being by the very fact that he has existed, would be originally a substratum unqualified by these desires;

that is, a sort of indeterminate clay which would have to receive them passively or he would be reduced to the simple bundle of these irreducible drives or tendencies. In either case the *man* disappears; we can no longer find "the individual" to *whom* this or that experience has *happened;* either in looking for the *person,* we encounter a useless, contradictory metaphysical substance—or else the being whom we seek disintegrates into phenomena bound together by external connections. But what each one of us requires in his very effort to comprehend another is that he should never have to resort to this idea of substance which is inhuman because it is well this side of the human. Finally the fact is that the being considered does not crumble into fragments, and one can discover in him that unity—of which substance was only a caricature—which must be a unity of responsibility, a unity agreeable or hateful, blamable and praiseworthy, in short *personal.* This unity, which is the being of the man under consideration, is a *free unification,* and this unification cannot come *after* a diversity which it unifies.

But *to be,* for Flaubert, as for every subject of "biography," means to be unified in the world. The irreducible unification which we ought to find, which is Flaubert, and which we require biographers to reveal to us—this is the unification of an *original project,* a unification which should reveal itself to us as a *nonsubstantial absolute.* Therefore we should renounce these so-called irreducible elements, and, taking the evident as a criterion, not halt in our investigation before it is evident that we neither can nor should go any further. In particular we must avoid trying to reconstruct a person by means of his inclinations, just as Spinoza warns us not to attempt to reconstruct a substance or its attributes by the summation of its modes. Every desire if presented as an irreducible is an absurd contingency and involves in its absurdity human reality taken as a whole. For example, if I declare of one of my friends that he "likes to go rowing," I deliberately intend to stop my investigation there. But on the other hand, I thus establish a contingent *fact,* which nothing can explain and which, though it has the gratuity of free decision, by no means has its autonomy. I cannot in fact consider this fondness for rowing as the fundamental project of Peter; it contains something secondary and derived. Those who portray a character in this way by successive strokes come close to holding that each of these strokes—each one of the desires confronted—is bound to the others by connections which are purely contingent and simply external. Those who, on the other hand, try to explain this liking will adopt the view which Comte called *materialism;* that is, of explaining the higher by the lower. Someone will say, for example, that the subject considered is a sportsman who likes violent exercise and is in addition a man of the outdoors who especially likes open-air sports. By more general and less differentiated tendencies he will try to explain *this* desire, which stands in exactly the same relation to them as the zoölogical species does to the genus. Thus the psychological explanation, when it does not suddenly decide to halt, is sometimes the mere putting into relief relations of pure concomitance or of constant succession, and it is at other times a simple classification. To explain Peter's fondness for rowing is to make it a member of the family of fondness for open-air sports and to attach this family to that of fondness for sport in general. Moreover we will be able to find still more general and barren rubrics if we classify the taste for sports as one aspect of the love of chance, which will itself be given as a specific instance of the fundamental fondness for play. It is obvious that this so-called explanatory classification has no more value or interest than the classifications in ancient botany; like the latter it amounts to assuming the priority of the abstract over the concrete—as if the fondness for play existed first in general to be subsequently made specific by the action of certain circumstances in the love of sport, the latter in the fondness for rowing, and finally the rowing in the desire to row on a particular stream, under certain circumstances in a particular season—and like the ancient classifications it fails to explain the concrete enrichment which at each stage is undergone by the abstract inclination considered.

Furthermore how are we to believe that a desire to row is *only* a desire to row? Can we truthfully admit that it can be reduced so simply to what it is? The most discerning moralists have shown how a desire reaches beyond itself. Pascal believed that he could discover in hunting, for example, or tennis, or in a hundred other occupations, the need of being diverted. He pointed out that in an activity which would be absurd if reduced to itself, there was a meaning which transcended it; that is, a reference to the reality of man in general and to his condition. Similarly Stendhal in spite of his connection with the *idéologues,* and

Proust in spite of his intellectualistic and analytical tendencies, have shown that love and jealousy cannot be reduced to the strict desire of possessing a *particular* woman, but that these emotions aim at laying hold of the world as a whole through the woman. This is the meaning of Stendhal's crystallization, and it is precisely for this reason that love as Stendhal describes it appears as a mode of being in the world. Love is a fundamental relation of the for-itself to the world and to itself (selfness) through a particular woman; the woman represents only a conducting body which is placed in the circuit. These analyses may be inaccurate or only partially true; nevertheless they suggest a method other than pure analytical description. In the same way Catholic novelists immediately see in carnal love its transcendence toward God—in Don Juan, "the eternally unsatisfied," in sin, "the place empty of God." There is no question here of finding again an abstract behind the concrete; the impulse toward God is no *less concrete* than the impulse toward a particular woman. On the contrary, it is a matter of rediscovering under the partial and incomplete aspects of the subject the veritable concreteness which can be only the totality of his impulse toward being, his original relation to himself, to the world, and to the Other, in the unity of internal relations and of a fundamental project. This impulse can be only purely individual and unique. Far from estranging us from the person, as Bourget's analysis, for example, does in constituting the individual by means of a summation of general maxims, this impulse will not lead us to find in the need of writing—and of writing particular books—the need of activity in general. On the contrary, rejecting equally the theory of malleable clay and that of the bundle of drives, we will discover the individual person in the initial project which constitutes him. It is for this reason that the irreducibility of the result attained will be revealed as self-evident, not because it is the poorest and the most abstract but because it is the richest. The intuition here will be accompanied by an individual fullness.

The problem poses itself in roughly these terms: If we admit that the person is a totality, we cannot hope to reconstruct him by an addition or by an organization of the diverse tendencies which we have empirically discovered in him. On the contrary, in each inclination, in each tendency the person expresses himself completely, although from a different angle, a little as Spinoza's substance expresses itself completely in each of its attributes. But if this is so, we should discover in each tendency, in each attitude of the subject, a meaning which transcends it. A jealousy of a particular date in which a subject historicizes himself in relation to a certain woman, implies, for the one who knows how to interpret it, the total relation to the world by which the subject constitutes himself as a self. In other words this *empirical* attitude is by itself the expression of the "choice of an intelligible character." There is no mystery about this. We no longer have to do with an intelligible pattern which can be present in our thought only, while we apprehend and conceptualize the unique pattern of the subject's empirical existence. If the empirical attitude implies the choice of the intelligible character, it is because it is itself this choice. Indeed the distinguishing characteristic of the intelligible choice, as we shall see later, is that it can exist only as the transcendent meaning of each concrete, empirical choice. It is by no means first effected in some unconscious or on the noumenal level to be *subsequently* expressed in a particular observable attitude; there is not even an *ontological* pre-eminence over the empirical choice, but it is on principle that which must always detach itself from the empirical choice as its *beyond* and the infinity of its transcendence. Thus if I am rowing on the river, I am nothing—either here or in any other world—save this concrete project of rowing. But this project itself inasmuch as it is the totality of my being, expresses my original choice in particular circumstances; it is nothing other than the choice of myself as a totality in these circumstances. That is why a special method must aim at detaching the fundamental meaning which the project entails and which can be only the individual secret of the subject's being-in-the-world. It is then rather by a *comparison* of the various empirical drives of a subject that we try to discover and disengage the fundamental project which is common to them all—and not by a simple addition or reconstruction of these tendencies; each drive or tendency is the person as a whole.

There is naturally an infinite number of possible projects as there is an infinite number of possible human beings. Nevertheless, if we are to recognize certain common characteristics among them and if we are going to attempt to classify them in larger categories, it is best first to undertake individual investigations in the cases which we can study more easily. In our research, we will be guided by this principle: to halt only in the presence of evident irreducibility; that is, never to believe that we have reached the initial project until the projected end appears as *the very being* of the subject under consideration. This is why we cannot stop at those classifications of "authentic project" and "inauthentic project of the self" which Heidegger wishes to establish. In addition to the fact that such a classification, in spite of its author's intent, is tainted with an ethical concern shown by its very terminology, it is based on the attitude of the subject toward his own death. Now if death causes anguish, and if consequently we can either flee the anguish or throw ourselves resolutely into it, it is a truism to say that this is because we wish to hold on to life. Consequently anguish before death and resolute decision or flight into inauthenticity cannot be considered as fundamental projects of our being. On the contrary, they can be understood only on the foundation of an original project of *living;* that is, on an original choice of our being. It is right then in each case to pass beyond the results of Heidegger's interpretation toward a still more fundamental project.

This fundamental project must not of course refer to any other and should be conceived by itself. It can be concerned neither with death nor life nor any particular characteristic of the human condition; the original project of a for-itself *can aim only at its being.* The project of being or desire of being or tendency toward being does not originate in a physiological differentiation or in an empirical contingency; in fact it is not distinguished from the being of the for-itself. The for-itself is a being such that in its being, its being is in question in the form of a project of being. To the for-itself *being* means to make known to oneself what one is by means of a possibility appearing as a value. Possibility and value belong to the being of the for-itself. The for-itself is defined ontologically as a *lack of being,* and possibility belongs to the for-itself as that which it lacks, in the same way that value haunts the for-itself as the totality of being which is lacking. What we have expressed . . . in terms of lack can be just as well expressed in terms of *freedom.* The for-itself chooses because it is lack; freedom is really synonymous with lack. Freedom is the concrete mode of being of the lack of being. Ontologically then it amounts to the same thing to say that value and possibility exist as internal limits of a lack of being which can exist only as a lack of being—or that the emergence of freedom determines its possibility and thereby circumscribes *its* value.

## 2 THE DESIRE TO BE

Thus we can advance no further but have encountered the self-evident irreducible when we have reached the *project of being;* for obviously it is impossible to advance further than *being,* and there is no difference between the project of being, possibility, value, on the one hand, and *being,* on the other. Fundamentally man is *the desire to be,* and the existence of this desire is not to be established by an empirical induction; it is the result of an *a priori* description of the being of the for-itself, since desire is a lack and since the for-itself is the being which is to itself its own lack of being. The original project which is expressed in each of our empirically observable tendencies is then the *project of being;* or rather, each empirical tendency is related to the original project of being, as its expression and symbolic satisfaction just as conscious drives, with Freud, are related to the complexes and to the original libido. Moreover the desire to be by no means exists *first* in order to find itself expressed subsequently by desires *a posteriori.* There is nothing outside of the symbolic expression which it finds in concrete desires. There is not first a single desire of being, then a thousand particular feelings, but the desire to be exists and manifests itself only in and through jealousy, greed, love of art, cowardice, courage, and a thousand contingent, empirical expressions whereby human reality appears to us only as *manifested* by *a particular man,* by a specific person.

As for the being which is the object of this desire, we know *a priori* what this is. The for-itself is the being which is to itself its own lack of being. The being which the for-itself lacks is the in-itself. The for-itself emerges as the nihilation of the in-itself and this nihilation is defined as the project toward the in-itself. Between the nihilated in-itself and the projected in-itself the for-itself is nothingness. Thus the end and the goal of the nihilation which I am is the in-itself. Thus human reality is the desire of being-in-itself. But the in-itself which it desires cannot be pure contingent, absurd in-itself, comparable in every respect to that which it encounters and which it nihilates. The nihilation, as we have seen, is in fact like a revolt of the in-itself, which nihilates itself against its contingency. To say that the for-itself exists its facticity, as we have seen in the chapter concerning the body, amounts to saying that the nihilation is the vain effort of a being to found its own being and that it is the withdrawal to found being which provokes the slight displacement by which nothingness enters into being. The being which forms the object of the desire of the for-itself is then an in-itself which would be to itself its own foundation; that is, which would be to its facticity in the same relation as the for-itself is to its motivations. In addition the for-itself, being the negation of the in-itself, could not desire the pure and simple return to the in-itself. Here, as with Hegel, the negation of the negation cannot bring us back to our point of departure. Quite the contrary, what the for-itself demands of the in-itself is precisely the totality detotalized—"in-itself nihilated in for-itself." In other words the for-itself projects *being as for-itself,* a being which is what it is. It is as being which is what it is not, and which is not what it is, that the for-itself projects being what it is. It is as consciousness that it wishes to have the impermeability and infinite density of the in-itself. It is as the nihilation of the in-itself and a perpetual evasion of contingency and of facticity that it wishes to be its own foundation. This is why the possible is projected in general as what the for-itself lacks in order to become in-itself-for-itself. The fundamental value which presides over this project is exactly the in-itself-for-itself; that is, the ideal of a consciousness which would be the foundation of its own being-in-itself by virtue of the pure consciousness which it would have of itself. It is this ideal which can be called God. Thus the best way to conceive of the fundamental project of human reality is to say that man is the being whose project is to be God. Whatever may be the myths and rites of any particular religion, man is first aware of God in his heart as the one who identifies and defines him in his ultimate and fundamental project. If man possesses a pre-ontological comprehension of the being of God, it is not the great wonders of nature nor the power of society which have conferred it upon him. God, value and supreme end of transcendence, represents the permanent limit in terms of which man makes known to himself what he is. To be man means to reach toward being God. Or if you prefer, man fundamentally is the desire to be God.

It may be asked, if man's emergence is his being borne toward God as toward his limit, if he can choose only to be God, what becomes of freedom? For freedom is nothing other than a choice which creates for itself its own possibilities, but it now seems that the initial project of being God, which "defines" man, comes close to being the same as a human "nature" or an "essence." The answer is that while the *meaning* of the desire is ultimately the project of being God, the desire is never *constituted* by this meaning; on the contrary, it always represents a *particular discovery* of its ends. These ends in fact are pursued in terms of a particular empirical situation, and it is this very pursuit which constitutes the environment *a situation*. The desire of being is always realized as the desire of a mode of being. And this desire of a mode of being expresses itself in turn as the meaning of the thousands of concrete desires which constitute the web of our conscious life. Thus we find ourselves before very complex symbolic structures which have *at least* three levels. In empirical desire I can discern a symbolization of a fundamental concrete desire which is the *person* and which represents the mode in which he has decided that being would be in question in his being. This fundamental desire in turn expresses concretely in the world the particular situation enveloping the individual, an abstract meaningful structure which is the desire of being in general and which must be considered as human reality in the person. This constitutes his community with others, justifying the claim that there is a truth about man and not about individuals who cannot be compared. Absolute concreteness, completion, existence as a totality belong then to the free and fundamental desire or person. Empirical desire is only a symbolization of this; it refers back to this and derives its meaning from it while remaining partial and reducible, for the empirical desire cannot be conceived by itself. On the other hand, the desire of being in its abstract purity is the *truth* of the concrete fundamental desire, but it does not exist as a reality. Thus the fundamental project, the person, the free realization of human truth is present in all desires (except for those . . . which are a matter of indifference). It is never apprehended except through desires—as we can apprehend space only through bodies which occupy it, though space is a particular reality and not a concept. Alternatively, it is like the *object* in Husserl, which reveals itself only by *Abschattungen*, and which nevertheless does not allow itself to be absorbed by any one *Abschattung*.

These comments make clear that the abstract, ontological "desire to be" is unable to represent the fundamental *human* structure of the individual; it cannot be an obstacle to his freedom. Freedom in fact, as we have shown in the preceding chapter, is strictly identical with nihilation. The only being which can be called free is the being which nihilates its being. Moreover we know that nihilation is *lack of being* and cannot be otherwise. Freedom is precisely the being which makes itself a lack of being. But since desire, as we have established, is identical with lack of being, freedom can emerge only as being which makes itself a desire of being; that is, as the project-for-itself of being in-itself-for-itself. Here we have arrived at an abstract structure which can by no means be regarded as the nature or essence of freedom. Freedom is existence, and in it existence precedes essence. The emergence of freedom is immediate and concrete and is not to be distinguished from its choice; that is, from the person himself. But the structure under consideration can be called the *truth* of freedom; that is, it is the human meaning of freedom.

It should be possible to ascertain the human truth of the person, as we have attempted to do by an ontological phenomenology. The cataloguing of empirical desires should be the object of strictly psychological investigations; observation and induction and, when necessary, experimentation can be employed in drawing up this list. They will indicate to the philosopher the comprehensible relations which can unite to each other various desires and various patterns of behavior, and will bring to light certain concrete connections between the subject of experience and "situations" experimentally defined (which at bottom originate only from restrictions applied in the name of positive science to the fundamental situation of the subject in the world). But in observing and classifying fundamental desires or *persons* neither of these methods is appropriate. Actually there can be no question of determining *a priori* and ontologically what appears with all the unpredictability of a free act. This is why we shall restrict ourselves here to indicating very broadly the possibilities of such an investigation and its perspectives. The fact that any man whatever can be the subject of such an investigation is a characteristic human reality in general. It can be established by an ontology. But the investigation itself and its results are on principle entirely outside the possibilities of an ontology.

On the other hand, pure, simple, empirical description can only catalogue and put us in the presence of pseudo-irreducibles (the desire to write, to swim, a taste for adventure, jealousy, etc.). It is not enough in fact to draw up a list of behavior patterns, of drives and inclinations, it is necessary also to *decipher* them; that is, it is necessary to know how to *question* them. This investigation can be conducted only according to the rules of a particular method. It is this method which we call existential psychoanalysis.

## 3 EXISTENTIAL PSYCHOANALYSIS

The *principle* of this psychoanalysis is that man is a totality and not a collection. Consequently he expresses himself as a whole in even his most insignificant and his most superficial behavior. In other words there is not a taste, a mannerism, or a human act which is not *revealing.*

The *goal* of psychoanalysis is to *decipher* the observable behavior patterns of man; that is, to elucidate the revelations each of them involves and to define them conceptually.

Its *point of departure* is *experience;* its basis is the fundamental, pre-ontological comprehension which man has of the human person. Although most people may neglect the implications in a gesture, a word, a sign, and can mistake the revelation which they carry, each human person nevertheless possesses *a priori* the *meaning* of the revelatory value of these manifestations and is capable of deciphering them, at least if he is aided and guided. Here as elsewhere, truth is not encountered by chance; it does not belong to a domain where one must seek it without ever having any presentiment of its location, as one can go look for the source of the Nile or of the Niger. It belongs *a priori* to human comprehension and the essential task is a hermeneutic;* that is, a deciphering, and a conceptualization.

Its *method* is comparative. Since each example of human conduct symbolizes in its own way the fundamental choice which must be brought to light, and since at the same time each one disguises this choice under accidental features and its historical occasion, only the comparison of these modes of behavior can bring out the unique revelation which they all express in a different way. The first outline of this method has been fur-

* *Cf. Being and Time,* 37f.—Ed.

nished for us by the psychoanalysis of Freud and his disciples. For this reason it will be worth-while here to indicate more specifically where existential psychoanalysis will be inspired by empirical psychoanalysis and where it will radically differ from it.

Both kinds of psychoanalysis treat all objectively discernible manifestations of "psychic life" as symbolizing the fundamental, total structures which constitute the person. Both assume that there are no such primary givens as hereditary dispositions, character, etc. Existential psychoanalysis recognizes nothing *before* the original emergence of human freedom; empirical psychoanalysis holds that the original affectivity of the individual is unformed wax *before* its history. The libido, as compared with its concrete fixations, is nothing more than the permanent possibility of fixation upon anything whatever in any way whatever. Both consider the human being as a perpetual historialization. Rather than static, constant givens, both search for the meaning, orientation, and adventures of this history. Therefore, both consider man in the world and do not suppose that one can question the being of a man without taking into account his *situation* as a whole. Psychoanalytical investigations aim at reconstructing the life of the subject from birth to the moment of the "cure"; they utilize all the objective documentation which they can find; letters, witnesses, intimate diaries, "social" facts of every kind. What they aim at restoring is less a pure psychic event than a structure, which is the conjunction of the crucial event of infancy and the psychic crystallization around this event. Here again we have to do with a *situation*. Each "historical" fact from this point of view will be considered at once as a *factor* in the psychic evolution and as a *symbol* of that evolution. For it is nothing in itself. Its influence depends entirely on the way in which the individual takes it, and his way of taking it translates symbolically the internal disposition of the individual.

Empirical psychoanalysis and existential psychoanalysis both explore an existing situation for a fundamental attitude which cannot be expressed by simple, logical definitions because it is prior to all logic, and which requires reconstruction according to the laws of specific syntheses. Empirical psychoanalysis seeks to determine the *complex,* the very name of which indicates the polyvalence of all the meanings which are related to it.

Existential psychoanalysis seeks to determine the *original choice*. This original choice confronts the world, and since a choice of position in the world is total like the complex, it is prior to logic like the complex. It is this choice which decides the attitude of the person when confronted with logic and principles; therefore there can be no possibility of questioning it in conformity with the requirements of logic. It brings together in a pre-logical synthesis the totality of the existent, and as such it is the center of reference for an infinity of polyvalent meanings.

Both our psychoanalyses refuse to admit that the subject is in a privileged position to undertake the investigation of himself. Both insist on a strictly objective method, using as documentary evidence the data of reflection as well as the testimony of others. Of course the subject *can* undertake a psychoanalytic investigation of himself. But in this case he must renounce at the outset any advantage stemming from his peculiar position and must question himself exactly as if he were someone else. Empirical psychoanalysis in fact is based on the hypothesis of the existence of an unconscious psyche, which on principle escapes the intuition of the subject. Existential psychoanalysis rejects the hypothesis of the unconscious; it makes the psychic act coextensive with consciousness. But if the fundamental project is fully experienced by the subject and hence wholly conscious, that certainly does not mean that it must be *known* by him; quite the contrary. The reader will perhaps recall the care we took . . . to distinguish between consciousness and knowledge.* To be sure, as we have seen earlier, reflection can be considered as a quasi-knowledge. But what it grasps at each moment is not the pure project of the for-itself as it is symbolically expressed—often in several ways at once—by the concrete behavior which it apprehends. It grasps the concrete behavior itself; that is, the specific dated desire in all its characteristic network. It grasps at once symbol and symbolization. This apprehension, to be sure, is entirely constituted by a pre-ontological comprehension of the fundamental project; or rather, insofar as reflection is also a non-thetic consciousness of itself as reflection, it *is* this same project, as well as the non-reflective consciousness. But it does not follow that it has at its disposal the instruments and techniques necessary to isolate

* *Cf.* above, p. 102.—Ed.

the choice symbolized, to define it by concepts, and to bring it forth into the full light of day. It is pervaded by a great light without being able to express what this light is illuminating. We are not dealing with an unsolved riddle, as the Freudians believe; everything is there, luminous; everything is experienced and apprehended by reflection. But this "mystery in broad daylight" is due to the fact that this experience is deprived of the means which would ordinarily permit *analysis* and *conceptualization*. Reflection grasps everything, all at once, without shading, without relief, without differences of scale—not that these shadows, these values, these reliefs exist somewhere and are hidden from it, but rather because they can only be ascertained by another human attitude and because they can exist only *by means of* and *for* knowledge. Reflection, unable to serve as the basis for existential psychoanalysis, will then simply furnish us with the raw materials toward which the psychoanalyst must take an objective attitude. Only in this way will he be able to *know* what he *already understands*. The result is that complexes uprooted from the depths of the unconscious, like projects revealed by existential psychoanalysis, will be apprehended *from the point of view of the Other*. The *object* thus brought into the light will be articulated according to the structures ·of the transcended-transcendence; that is, its being will be the being-for-others even if the psychoanalyst and the subject of the psychoanalysis are actually the same person. Thus the project which is brought to light by either kind of psychoanalysis can be only the totality of the individual human being, the irreducible factor of the transcendence with the structure of *being-for-others*. What always eludes these methods of investigation is the project as it is for itself, the complex in its own being. This project-for-itself can only be *experienced;* there is an incompatibility between existence for-itself and objective existence. But the object of the two psychoanalyses has nonetheless the *reality of a being;* the subject's knowledge of it can in addition contribute to the *clarification* of the reflection, and that reflection can then become an experience which will be quasi-knowledge.

At this point the similarity between the two kinds of psychoanalysis ceases. They differ fundamentally in that empirical psychoanalysis has decided upon its own irreducible, instead of allowing this to make itself known in a self-evident intuition. The libido or the will to power in actuality constitutes a psychobiological residue which is not clear in itself and which does not appear to us as *being* in advance of the investigation as being its irreducible limit. Finally it is experience which establishes that the foundation of complexes is this libido or this will to power; and these results of empirical inquiry are perfectly contingent, they are not compelling. Nothing prevents our conceiving *a priori* of a "human reality" which would not be expressed by the will to power, for which the libido would not constitute the original, undifferentiated project.

On the other hand, the choice to which existential psychoanalysis will lead us back, precisely because it is a choice, accounts for its original contingency, for the contingency of the choice is the reverse side of its freedom. Furthermore, inasmuch as it is established on the *lack of being*, conceived as a fundamental characteristic of being, it receives its legitimacy *as a choice*, and we know that we do not have to push further. Each result then will be at once fully contingent and legitimately irreducible. Moreover it will always remain *particular*; that is, we will not achieve as the ultimate goal of our investigation and the foundation of all behavior an abstract, general term, libido for example, which would be differentiated and made concrete first in complexes and then in detailed acts of conduct, due to the action of external facts and the history of the subject. On the contrary, it will be a choice which remains unique and which is from the start absolute concreteness. Details of behavior can express or *particularize* this choice, but they cannot make it more concrete than it already is. That is because the choice is nothing other than the being of each human reality; this amounts to saying that a particular partial behavior *is* or expresses the original choice of this human reality, since for human reality there is no difference between existing and choosing oneself. From this fact we understand that existential psychoanalysis does not have to proceed from the fundamental "complex," which is exactly the choice of being, to an abstraction like the libido which would explain it. The complex is the ultimate choice, it is the choice of being and *makes itself such*. Bringing it into the light will reveal it each time as evidently irreducible. It follows necessarily that the libido and the will to power will appear to existential psychoanalysis neither as general characteristics common to all mankind nor as irreducibles. At most it will be possible after the investigation to establish that they express by virtue of particular ensembles in certain subjects a fundamental choice which cannot be reduced to either one of them. We have seen in fact that desire and sexuality in general express an original effort of the for-itself to recover its being which has become alienated by the Other. The will to power also originally supposes being-for-others, the comprehension of the Other, and the choice of winning its own salvation by means of the Other. The foundation of this attitude must be an original choice which would make us understand the radical assimilation of being-in-itself-for-itself with being-for-others.

The fact that the ultimate term of this existential inquiry must be a *choice,* distinguishes even better the psychoanalysis for which we have outlined the method and principal features. It thereby abandons the supposition that the environment acts mechanically on the subject under consideration. The environment can act on the subject only to the exact extent that he comprehends it; that is, transforms it into a situation. Hence no objective description of this environment could be of any use to us. From the start the environment conceived as a situation refers to the for-itself which is choosing, just as the for-itself refers to the environment by the very fact that the for-itself is in the world. By renouncing all mechanical causation, we renounce at the same time all *general* interpretation of the symbolization confronted. Our goal could not be to establish empirical laws of succession, nor could we constitute a universal symbolism. Rather the psychoanalyst will have to rediscover at each step a symbol functioning in the particular case which he is considering. If each being is a totality, it is not conceivable that there can exist elementary symbolic relationships (*e.g.,* the feces = gold, or a pincushion = the breast) which preserve a constant meaning in all cases; that is, which remain unaltered when they pass from one meaningful complex to another. Furthermore the psychoanalyst will never lose sight of the fact that the choice is living and consequently can be *revoked* by the subject who is being studied. We have shown . . . the importance of the moment, which involves abrupt changes in orientation and the assuming of a new position in the face of an unalterable past.* From this moment on, we must always be ready to consider that symbols change meaning and to abandon the symbolism used hitherto. Thus existential psychoanalysis will have

* *Cf.* above, p. 262.—Ed.

to be completely flexible and adapt itself to the slightest observable changes in the subject. Our concern here is to understand what is *individual* and often even momentary. The method which has served for one subject will not necessarily be suitable to use for another subject or for the same subject at a later period.

Precisely because the goal of the inquiry must be to discover a *choice* and not a *state*, the investigator must recall on every occasion that his object is not a datum buried in the darkness of the unconscious but a free, conscious decision—which is not even resident in consciousness, but which is one with this consciousness itself. Empirical psychoanalysis, to the extent that its method is better than its principles, is often in sight of an existential discovery, but it always halts too soon. When it approaches the fundamental choice, the resistance of the subject collapses suddenly and he *recognizes* the image of himself which is presented to him as if he were seeing himself in a mirror. This involuntary testimony of the subject is valuable to the psychoanalyst; he sees there the sign that he has reached his goal; he can pass on from the investigation proper to the "cure." But nothing in his principles or in his initial postulates permits him to understand or to utilize this testimony. Where could he get any such right? If the complex is really unconscious—that is, if there is a barrier separating the sign from the thing signified—how could the subject *recognize* it? Does the unconscious complex recognize itself? But haven't we been told that it lacks *understanding*? And if of necessity we granted to it the faculty of understanding the signs, would this not be to make of it thereby a conscious unconscious? What is understanding if it does not involve consciousness of having understood? Or shall we say instead that it is the subject as conscious who recognizes the image presented? But how could he compare it with his true feeling, since that is out of reach and since he has never had any knowledge of it? At most he will be able to judge that the psychoanalytic explanation of his case is a *probable* hypothesis, which derives its probability from the number of behavior patterns which it explains. His relation to this interpretation is that of a third party, that of the psychoanalyst himself; he has no privileged position. And if he *believes* in the probability of the psychoanalytic hypothesis, is this simple belief, which remains within the limits of his consciousness, able to effect the breakdown of the barriers which dam up the unconscious tendencies? The psychoanalyst doubtless has some obscure picture of an abrupt coincidence of conscious and unconscious. But he has discarded any positive way of conceiving this coincidence.

Still, the enlightenment of the subject is a fact. There is an intuition here which is accompanied by evidence. The subject guided by the psychoanalyst does more than give his agreement to a hypothesis; he touches it, he sees what it is. This is really understandable only if the subject has never ceased being conscious of his deep tendencies; or rather, only if these tendencies are not distinguished from his consciousness itself. In this case as we have seen, the traditional psychoanalytic interpretation does not have him attain *consciousness* of what he is; it has him attain *knowledge* of what he is. It is existential psychoanalysis then which claims the final intuition of the subject as decisive.

This comparison allows us to understand better what an existential psychoanalysis must be if it can exist. It is a method destined to bring to light, in a strictly objective form, the subjective choice by which each living person makes himself a person; that is, makes known to himself what he is. Since what the method seeks is a *choice of being* at the same time as a *being*, it must reduce particular behavior patterns to fundamental relations—not of sexuality or of the will to power, but *of being*—which are expressed in this behavior. It is then guided from the start toward an understanding of being and must not assign itself any other goal than to discover being and the mode of being of the being confronting this being. It is forbidden to halt before attaining this goal. It will utilize the understanding of being which characterizes the investigator inasmuch as he is himself a human reality; and as it seeks to disengage being from its symbolic expressions, it will have to rediscover each time on the basis of a comparative study of acts and attitudes, a symbol destined to decipher them. Its criterion of success will be the number of facts which its hypothesis permits it to explain and to unify as well as the self-evident intuition of the irreducibility of the end attained. To this criterion will be added in all cases where it is possible, the testimony of the subject's own decisions. The results thus achieved—that is, the ultimate ends of the individual—can then become the object of a classification, and it is by the comparison of these results that we will be able to establish general considerations about human reality as an empirical choice of its own ends. The behavior studied by this psychoanalysis will include not only dreams, frustrated actions, obsessions, and neuroses, but also and especially the thoughts of waking life, successfully adjusted acts, style, etc. This psychoanalysis has not yet found its Freud. At most we can find the foreshadowing of it in certain particularly successful biographies. We hope to be able to attempt elsewhere two examples in relation to Flaubert and Dostoevsky. But it matters little to us whether it now exists; the important thing is that it is possible.

## 4 THE DESIRE TO MAKE

The information which ontology can furnish concerning behavior patterns and desire must serve as the principles of existential psychoanalysis. This does not mean that there are abstract desires which are common to all men and which exist prior to any specification; it means that concrete desires have structures which emerge during the study of ontology because each desire—the desire of eating or of sleeping as well as the desire of creating a work of art—expresses human reality as a whole. The knowledge of man must be a totality; empirical, partial pieces of knowledge on this level lack all significance. We shall complete our task if we utilize the knowledge achieved up to this point, for laying down the bases of existential psychoanalysis. Indeed this is the point where ontology must halt; its final discoveries are the first principles of psychoanalysis. Henceforth we must have another method since the object is different. What then does ontology teach us about desire, since desire is the being of human reality?

Desire is a lack of being. As such it is immediately *directed toward* the being of which it is a lack. This being, as we have said, is the in-itself-for-itself, consciousness become substance, substance become the cause of itself, the Man-God. Thus the being of human reality is originally not a substance but a lived relationship. The terms of this relationship are first the original in-itself, concealed in its contingency and its facticity, its essential characteristic being that it is, that it exists; and second the in-itself-for-itself or value, which exists as the ideal of the contingent in-itself and which is characterized as beyond all contingency and all existence. Man is neither the one nor the other of these beings, for strictly speaking, we should never say of him that he *is* at all. He is what he is not and he is not what he is; he is the nihilation of the contingent in-itself insofar as the self of this nihilation is its flight forward toward the in-itself as self-cause. Human reality is the pure endeavor to become God without there being any given substratum for that endeavor, without there being *anything* which undertakes the endeavor. Desire expresses this endeavor.

Nevertheless desire is not defined solely in relation to the in-itself-as-self-cause. It is also relative to a brute, concrete existent which we commonly call the object of the desire. This object may be now a slice of bread, now an automobile, now a woman, now an object not yet realized and yet defined—as when the artist desires to create a work of art. Thus by its very structure desire expresses a man's relation to one or several objects in the world; it is one of the aspects of being-in-the-world. From this point of view we see first that this type of relation is not unique. It is only by a sort of abbreviation that we speak of "the desire of something." Actually a thousand empirical examples show that we desire to *possess* this object or to *do* that thing or to *be* someone. If I desire this picture, it means that I desire to buy it, to appropriate it, for myself. If I desire to write a book, to go for a walk, it means that I desire to "do" this book, to "make" this walk [*faire ce livre, faire cette promenade*]. If I dress up, it is because I desire to be handsome. I train myself in order to *be* a scientist, etc. Thus, from the outset, the three large categories of concrete human existence appear to us in their original relation: making, having, being.

It is easy to see, however, that the desire to make is not irreducible. One makes an object in order to enter into a certain relation with it. This new relation can be immediately reducible to *having*. For example, I cut a cane from a branch of a tree (I make a cane out of a branch) in order to *have* this cane. The "making" is reduced to a mode of having. This is the most common example. But it can also happen that my activity does not immediately appear reducible. It can appear gratuitous as in the case of scientific research, or sport, or esthetic creation. Yet in these various examples doing is still not irreducible. If I create a picture, a drama, a melody, it is in order that I may be at the origin of a concrete existence. This existence interests me only to the degree that the bond of creation which I establish between it and me gives to me a particular right of property over it. It is not enough that a certain picture which I have in mind should exist; it is necessary as well that it exist *through* me. Evidently in one sense the ideal would be that I should sustain the picture in being by a sort of continuous creation and that consequently it should be *mine* as though by a perpetually renewed emanation. But in another sense it must be radically distinct from myself—in order that it may be *mine* but not *me*. Here, as in the Cartesian theory of substances, there is danger that the being of the created object may be reabsorbed in my being because of lack of independence and objectivity; hence it must of necessity exist also *in itself*, must perpetually renew its existence *by itself*.

Consequently my work appears to me as a continuous creation but congealed in the in-itself; it carries indefinitely my "mark"; that is, it is for an indefinite period "my" thought. Every work of art is a thought, an "idea"; its characteristics are plainly ideal to the extent that it is nothing but a meaning. But on the other hand, this meaning, this thought which is in one sense perpetually active as if I were perpetually forming it, as if a mind were conceiving it without respite—a mind which would be *my* mind —this thought sustains itself alone in being; it by no means ceases to be active when I am not actually thinking it. I stand to it then in the double relation of the consciousness which conceives it and the consciousness which encounters it. It is precisely this double relation which I express by saying that it is *mine*. We shall see the significance of it when we have defined precisely the meaning of the category "to have." It is in order to enter into this double relation in the synthesis of appropriation that I *create* my work. In fact it is this synthesis of self and not-self (the intimacy and translucency of thought on the one hand and the opacity and indifference of the in-itself on the other) that I am aiming at and which will establish my ownership of the work. In this sense it is not only strictly artistic works which I appropriate in this manner. This cane which I have cut from the branch will also be my property in two senses: first as an object for everyday use, which is at my disposal and which I possess as I possess my clothes or my books, and second as my own work. Thus people who like to surround themselves with everyday objects which they themselves have made, are enjoying subtleties of appropriation. They unite in a single object and in one syncretism the appropriation by enjoyment and the appropriation by creation. We find this same uniting into a single project everywhere from artistic creation to the cigarette which "is better when I roll it myself." Later we shall meet this project in connection with a special type of property, which is, as it were, the degradation of property—luxury—for we shall see that luxury is distinguished not as a quality of the object possessed but as a quality of possession.

*Knowing* also . . . is a form of appropriation. That is why scientific research is nothing other than an effort to appropriate. The truth discovered, like the work of art, is *my* knowledge; it is the *noema* of a thought which is discovered only when I form the thought and which consequently appears in a certain way as maintained in existence by me. It is through me that a facet of the world is revealed; it is to me that it reveals itself. In this sense I am creator and possessor, not that I consider the aspect of being which I discover, as a pure representation, but on the contrary, because this aspect, which is revealed only by me, profoundly and really is. I can say only that I *manifest* it in the sense that Gide tells us that "we ought always to manifest." But I find again an independence analogous to that of the work of art in the character of the *truth* of my thought; that is, in its objectivity. This thought which I form and which derives its existence from me pursues at the same time its own independent existence to the extent that it is everyone's thought. It is doubly myself; it is the world revealed to myself and it is myself present to others, myself forming my thought with the mind of the other. At the same time it is doubly closed against me: it is the being which I am not (inasmuch as it reveals itself to me), and since it is everyone's thought from the moment of its appearance, it is a thought devoted to anonymity. This synthesis of self and not-self can be expressed here by the term "mine."

In addition the idea of discovery, of revelation, includes an idea of appropriative enjoyment. What is seen is possessed; to see is to *deflower*. If we examine the comparisons ordinarily used to express the relation between the knower and the known, we see that many of them are represented as being a kind of *violation by sight*. The unknown object is given as immaculate, as virgin, comparable to a *whiteness*. It has not yet "surrendered" its secret; man has not yet "wrested" its secret away from it. All these images insist that the object is ignorant

of the investigation and the instruments aimed at it; it is unconscious of being known; it goes about its business without
noticing the glance which spies on it, like a woman whom a
passer-by catches unaware at her bath. Figures of speech, sometimes vague and sometimes more precise, like that of the "un-
violated depths" of nature, suggest the idea of sexual intercourse
more plainly. We speak of snatching away her veils from nature,
of unveiling her (cf. Schiller's *Veiled Image of Saïs*). Every investigation implies the idea of a nakedness which one exposes
by pushing aside the obstacles which conceal it, just as Actaeon
pushes aside the branches so that he can have a better view of
Diana at her bath. More than this, knowledge is a hunt. Bacon
called it the hunt of Pan. The scientist is the hunter who takes a
white nakedness by surprise and violates it by looking at it. Thus
the constellation of these images reveals something which we
shall call the *Actaeon complex*.

By taking this idea of the hunt as a guiding thread, we shall
discover another symbol of appropriation, perhaps still more
primitive: a person hunts for the sake of eating. Curiosity in an
animal is always either sexual or alimentary. To know is to devour with the eyes.* In fact we can note here, so far as knowledge through the senses is concerned, a process the reverse of
that which was discovered in connection with the work of art.
We remarked that the work of art is like a congealed emanation of the mind. The mind is continually creating it and yet it
stands alone and indifferent in relation to that creation. This
same relation exists in the act of knowing, but its opposite is
not excluded. In knowing, consciousness draws the object to itself and incorporates it in itself. Knowledge is assimilation.
The writings of French epistemology swarm with alimentary
metaphors (absorption, digestion, assimilation). There is a
movement of dissolution which passes from the object to the
knowing subject. The known is transformed into *me*; it becomes
my thought and thereby consents to receive its existence from
me alone. But this movement of dissolution is congealed in that
the known remains in the same place, indefinitely absorbed, de-
voured, and yet indefinitely intact, wholly digested and yet
wholly outside, as indigestible as a stone. For naïve imaginations the symbol of the "digested indigestible" is very important;

---

* For the child, knowing involves actually eating: he wants to taste what he
sees.

for example, the stone in the stomach of the ostrich or Jonah in the stomach of the whale. The symbol represents the dream of a non-destructive assimilation. The misfortune is—as Hegel noted—that desire destroys its object. In this sense, he said, desire is the desire of devouring. In reaction against this dialectical necessity, the for-itself dreams of an object which may be entirely assimilated by me, which would be *me*, without dissolving into me but still keeping the structure of the *in-itself;* for what I desire exactly is *this* object; and if I eat it, I do not have it any more, I do not encounter anything beside myself.

This impossible synthesis of assimilation and an assimilated which maintains its integrity, has deep-rooted connections with basic sexual drives. "Carnal possession" offers us the provoking and seductive image of a body perpetually possessed and perpetually new, on which possession leaves no trace. This is deeply symbolized in the quality of "smooth" or "polished." What is smooth can be taken and felt but remains nonetheless impenetrable, and flows away under the appropriate caress —like water. This is the reason why erotic descriptions insist on the smooth whiteness of a woman's body. The "smooth" [*lisse*] it what re-forms itself under the caress, as water re-forms itself over the path of the stone which has pierced it. At the same time, as we have seen earlier, the lover's dream is to identify the beloved object with himself and still preserve for it its own individuality; let the Other become me without ceasing to be the Other. It is this which we meet in scientific research: the known object, like the stone in the stomach of the ostrich, is entirely within me, assimilated, transformed into myself, and it is entirely *me;* but at the same time it is impenetrable, untransformable, entirely smooth, with the indifferent nakedness of a body which is loved and caressed in vain. It remains outside; to know it is to devour it yet without consuming it. We see here how the sexual and alimentary themes melt into each other and interpenetrate in order to constitute the Actaeon complex and the Jonah complex; we can see the digestive and sensual sources which come together to give birth to the desire of knowing. Knowledge is at one and the same time *penetration* and the caressing of a surface, a digestion and the contemplation from a distance of an object which cannot be transformed, the production of a thought by a continuous creation and the recognition of the total objective independence of that thought. The known object is *my thought as a thing*. This is precisely what I profoundly desire when I undertake my research—to apprehend my thought as a thing and the thing as my thought. The syncretic relation which provides the basis for the ensemble of such diverse tendencies can be only a relation of *appropriation*. That is why the desire to know, no matter how disinterested it may appear, is a relation of appropriation. Knowing is one of the forms which can be assumed by having.

## 5 PLAY

One type of activity is left which obviously seems entirely gratuitous: the activity of *play* and the "drives" which relate to it. Can we discover an appropriative drive in sport? To be sure, it must be noted first that play as contrasted with the spirit of seriousness appears to be the least possessive attitude; it strips the real of its reality. Seriousness involves taking the world as one's starting point and attributing more reality to the world than to oneself; or reality to oneself only to the extent one belongs to the world. It is not by chance that materialism is serious; it is not by chance that it is found at all times and places as the preferred doctrine of the revolutionary. This is because revolutionaries are serious. They come to know themselves first in terms of the world, which oppresses them and which they wish to change. In this one respect they are in agreement with their traditional adversaries, the possessors, who also come to know and value themselves in terms of their position in the world. Thus all serious thought is thickened by the world; it coagulates; it is a resignation of human reality in favor of the world. The serious man is of the world and has no resource in himself. He does not even imagine any longer the possibility of *getting out of* the world, for he has given himself the type of existence of the rock, the consistency, the inertia, the opacity of being-in-the-midst-of-the-world. It is obvious that the serious man at bottom is hiding from himself the consciousness of his freedom; he is in *bad faith* and his bad faith aims at presenting himself to his own eyes as a consequence; everything is a consequence for him, and there is never any beginning. That is why he is so concerned with the consequences of his acts. Marx stated the original dogma of the serious when he asserted the priority of object over subject. Man is serious when he takes himself for an object.

## Doing and Having

Play, like Kierkegaard's irony, releases subjectivity. What indeed is play if not an activity of which man is the first origin, for which man himself sets the rules, and which has no consequences except according to the rules he has set? As soon as a man apprehends himself as free and wishes to use his freedom, whatever may be his anguish, then his activity is play. The first principle of play is man himself; through it he escapes his natural nature; he himself sets the value and rules for his acts and consents to play only according to the rules which he himself has established and defined. As a result, there is in a sense "little reality" to the world. It might appear then that when a man is playing, bent on discovering himself as free in his very action, he certainly could not be concerned with *possessing* a being in the world. His goal, which he aims at through sports or mimicry or games, is to attain himself as a certain being, namely, that being which is in question in his being.

The point of these remarks, however, is not to show us that in play the desire to *do* is irreducible. On the contrary we must conclude that the desire to do is here reduced to a certain desire to be. The act is not its own goal for itself; neither does its explicit end represent its goal and its profound meaning; but the function of the act is to make manifest and to present to *itself* the absolute freedom which is the very being of the person. This particular type of project, which has freedom for its foundation and its goal, deserves a special investigation. It is radically different from all others in that it aims at a radically different type of being. It would be necessary to explain in full detail its relations with the project of being-God, which has appeared to us as the deep-seated structure of human reality. But such an investigation cannot be made here; it belongs rather to an *Ethics* and it supposes that there has been a preliminary definition of nature and the role of purifying reflection (our descriptions have hitherto aimed only at *accessory* reflection); it supposes in addition taking a position which can be *moral* only in the face of values which haunt the for-itself. Nevertheless the fact remains that the desire to play is fundamentally the desire to be.

Thus the three categories "being," "doing," and "having" are reduced here as everywhere to two; "doing" is purely transitional. Ultimately a desire can be only the desire *to be* or the desire *to have*. But play usually involves some appropriative tendency. I am passing over the desire of achieving a good performance or of beating a record which can act as a stimulant for the sportsman; I am not even speaking of the desire "to have" a handsome body and harmonious muscles, which springs from the desire of appropriating objectively to myself my own being-for-others. These desires do not always enter in and anyway they are not fundamental. But there is always in sport an appropriative component. In reality sport is a free transformation of the worldly environment into the supporting element of the action. Sport thereby is creative like art. The environment may be a field of snow, an Alpine slope. To see it is already to possess it. In itself it is already apprehended by sight as a symbol of being. It represents pure exteriority, radical spatiality; its undifferentiation, its monotony, and its whiteness manifest the absolute nakedness of substance; it is the in-itself which is only in-itself, the being of the phenomenon, which being is manifested suddenly outside all phenomena. At the same time its *solid* immobility expresses the permanence and the objective resistance of the in-itself, its opacity and its impenetrability. Yet this first intuitive enjoyment cannot suffice. That pure in-itself, comparable to the absolute, intelligible plenum of Cartesian extension, fascinates me as the pure appearance of the not-me; what I wish precisely is that this in-itself might be a sort of emanation of myself while still remaining in itself. This is the meaning even of the snowmen and snowballs which children make; the goal is to "do something with the snow"; that is, to impose on it a form which adheres so deeply to the matter that the matter appears to exist for the sake of the form. But if I approach, if I want to establish an appropriative contact with the field of snow, everything is changed. Its scale of being is modified; it exists bit by bit instead of existing in vast spaces; markings and crevices come to individualize each square inch. At the same time its solidity melts into water. I sink into the snow up to my knees; if I pick some up with my hands, it turns to liquid in my fingers; it flows away; there is nothing left. The in-itself is transformed into nothingness. My dream of appropriating the snow vanishes at the same moment. Moreover I *do not know what to do* with this snow which I have just come to see close at hand. I cannot grasp the field; I cannot even reconstitute it as that substantial totality which offered itself to my look and which has, abruptly, doubly collapsed.

The significance of *skiing* is not only that it enables me to make swift movements [*déplacements*] and to acquire a techni-

cal skill, nor is it merely playing by increasing according to my
whim the speed or difficulties of the course; it also enables me
to possess this field of snow. At present I am making something
of it. That means that by my very activity as a skier, I am changing the matter and meaning of the snow. From the fact that now
in my course it appears to me as a slope to go down, it finds again
a continuity and a unity which it had lost. It is connective tissue.
It is included between two limiting terms; it unites the point
of departure with the point of arrival. Since in the descent I do
not consider it in itself, bit by bit, but am always fixing on a
point to be reached beyond the position which I now occupy, it
does not collapse into an infinity of individual fragments but is
*traversed toward* the point which I assign myself. This trav-
ersal is not only an activity of movement; it is also and especially
a synthetic activity of organization and connection; I extend the
skiing field before me in the same way that the geometrician,
according to Kant, can apprehend a straight line only by drawing one. Furthermore this organization is marginal and not focal;
it is not for itself and in itself that the field of snow is unified; the goal, posited and clearly grasped, the object of my attention is the point at the edge of the field where I shall arrive.
The snowy space is massed underneath implicitly; its cohesion
is that of the blank space presupposed within a circumference,
for example, when I look at the black line of the circle without
paying explicit attention to the interior space. And precisely
because I keep the space marginal, implicit, and presupposed, it
adapts itself to me, I have it in hand, under control; I transcend
it toward its end just as a man hanging a tapestry transcends
the hammer which he uses, toward its end, which is to nail a
tapestry on the wall.*

No appropriation can be more complete than this instrumental appropriation; the synthetic activity of appropriation is here
a technical activity of utilization. The snow appears as the matter of my act in the same way that the hammer appears as the
fulfillment of the hammering. At the same time I have
chosen a certain point of view in order to apprehend this snowy
slope: this point of view is a specific *speed,* which emanates
from me, which I can increase or diminish as I like; through it
the field traversed is constituted as a definite object, entirely
distinct from what it would be at another speed. The speed or-

* Cf. *Being and Time,* p. 69.—Ed.

ganizes the materials at will; a specific object does or does not
form a part of a particular synthesis depending on the speed I
am traveling. (Think, for example, of Provence seen "on foot,"
"by car," "by train," "by bicycle." It offers as many different aspects depending on whether or not Béziers is one hour, a
morning's trip, or two days distant from Narbonne: that is, depending on whether Narbonne is isolated and posited for itself
with its environs or whether it constitutes a coherent grouping
with Béziers and Sète, for example. In this last case Narbonne's
*relation to the sea* is directly accessible to intuition; in the other
it is denied; it can form the object only of a pure concept.) It is
I myself then who give form to the field of snow by the free
speed which I give myself. But at the same time I am acting
upon *my matter*. The speed is not limited to imposing a form
on a matter given from the outside; it *creates* its matter. The
snow, which sank under my weight when I walked, which
melted into water when I tried to pick it up, solidifies suddenly
under the action of my speed; it supports me. It is not that I
have lost sight of its lightness, its non-substantiality, its perpetual evanescence. Quite the contrary. It is precisely that lightness, that evanescence, that secret liquidity which bear me up;
that is, which condense and melt in order to support me. This is
because I hold a special relation of appropriation with the snow:
*sliding* [*glissement*]. This relation we shall study later in detail, but we can already grasp its essential meaning. We think of
sliding as remaining on the surface. This is not accurate; to be
sure, I only skim the surface, and this skimming [*effleurement*]
is worth a whole investigation itself. Nevertheless I realize a
synthesis which has depth. I realize that the bed of snow organizes itself in its depths in order to bear me up; the sliding is
action *at a distance;* it assures my mastery over the material
without my needing to sink into that material and become stuck
in it in order to overcome it. Sliding is the opposite of taking
root. The root is already half assimilated to the soil which
nourishes it; it is a living concretion of the earth; it can utilize
the earth only by making itself earth; that is, by submitting itself, in a sense, to the matter which it wishes to utilize. Sliding,
on the contrary, realizes a material unity in depth without pene-
trating farther than the surface; it is like the dreaded master
who does not need to insist nor to raise his voice in order to be
obeyed. An admirable picture of power. Hence the famous piece

of advice: "Slide, mortals, don't bear down! [*Glissez, mortels, n'appuyez pas!*]." This does not mean, "Remain superficial, don't go deeply into things," but on the contrary, "Realize syntheses in depth without compromising yourself."

Sliding is appropriation precisely because the synthesis of support realized by the speed is effective only for the slider and during the actual time when he is sliding. The solidity of the snow is effective only for me, is felt only by me; it is a secret which the snow releases to me alone and which is already no longer true *behind my back*. Sliding realizes a strictly individual relation with matter, an historical relation; the matter collects itself and solidifies in order to bear me up, and it falls back exhausted and scattered behind me. Thus by my passage I have realized that which is unique *for me*. The ideal for sliding then is a sliding which does not leave any trace. It is sliding on water with a rowboat or motorboat or especially with water skis, which, though recently invented, represent from this point of view the ideal limit of aquatic sports. Sliding on snow is already less perfect; there is a trace behind me by which I am compromised, however slightly. Sliding on ice, which scratches the ice and finds a matter already organized, is very inferior, and if people continue to skate despite this, it is for other reasons. Hence that slight disappointment which always seizes us when we see behind us the imprints which our skis have left on the snow. How much better it would be if the snow re-formed itself as we passed over it! Besides when we slide down the slope, we entertain the illusion of not making any mark; we ask the snow to behave like that water which secretly it is. Thus the sliding appears assimilable to a continuous creation. The speed is comparable to consciousness and here symbolizes consciousness. It produces in the material the deep quality which lasts only so long as the speed lasts, a sort of collecting which conquers its indifferent exteriority and which falls back in a spray behind the moving slider. The informing unification and synthetic condensation of the field of snow, which collects into an instrumental organization which is *utilized*, like the hammer or the anvil, and which docilely adapts itself to an action which presupposes it and fulfills it; a continued and creative action on the very matter of the snow; the solidification of the *snowy mass* by the sliding; the assimilation of the snow to the water which gives support, docile and without memory, or to the naked body of the woman, which the caress leaves intact and disturbed to her depths—such is the action of the skier on the real. But at the same time the snow remains impenetrable and out of reach; in one sense the action of the skier only develops its *potentialities*. *The skier makes it yield* what it can yield; the homogeneous, solid matter surrenders to him a solidity and homogeneity only through the act of skiing, but this solidity and this homogeneity dwell as properties potential in the matter. This synthesis of self and not-self which the sportsman's action here realizes is expressed, as in the case of speculative knowledge and the work of art, by the affirmation of the right of the skier over the snow. It is *my* field of snow; I have traversed it a hundred times, a hundred times I have through my speed produced this force of condensation and support; it is *mine*.

To this aspect of appropriation through sport, there must be added another—a difficulty overcome. It is more generally understood, and we shall scarcely insist on it here. Before descending this snowy slope, I must climb up it. And this ascent has offered to me another aspect of the snow—resistance. I have realized this resistance through my fatigue, and I have been able to measure at each moment the progress of my victory. Here the snow is assimilated to *the Other*, and the common expressions "to overcome," "to conquer," "to master," etc., indicate sufficiently that it is a matter of establishing between me and the snow the relation of master to slave. This aspect of appropriation which we find in the ascent, exists also in swimming, in an obstacle course, etc. The peak on which a flag is planted is a peak which has been *appropriated*. Thus a principal aspect of sport—and in particular of open-air sports—is the conquest of these enormous masses of water, of earth, and of air, which seem *a priori* indomitable and unutilizable; and in each case it is a question of possessing not the element for itself, but the type of existence in-itself which is expressed by means of this element; it is the homogeneity of substance which we wish to possess in the form of snow; it is the impenetrability of the in-itself and its non-temporal permanence which we wish to appropriate in the form of the earth or of the rock, etc. Art, science, play are activities of appropriation, either wholly or in part, and what they want to appropriate beyond the concrete object of their quest is being itself, the absolute being of the in-itself.

## 6 THE DESIRE TO HAVE

Thus ontology teaches us that desire is originally a desire *of being* and that it is characterized as the free lack of being. But it teaches us also that desire is a relation with a concrete existent in the midst of the world and that this existent is conceived as a type of in-itself; it teaches us that the relation of the for-itself to this desired in-itself is appropriation. We are, then, in the presence of a double determination of desire: on the one hand, desire is determined as a desire to be a certain being, which is the *in-itself-for-itself* and whose existence is ideal; on the other hand, desire is determined in the vast majority of cases as a relation with a contingent and concrete in-itself which it has the project of appropriating.* Is there over-determination? Are the two characteristics compatible? Existential psychoanalysis can be assured of its principles only if ontology has given a preliminary definition of the relation of these two beings—the concrete and contingent in-itself or object of the desire, and the in-itself-for-itself or ideal of the desire—and if it has made explicit the relation which unites appropriation as a type of relation to the in-itself, to being, as a type of relation to the in-itself-for-itself. This is what we must attempt now.

What is meant by "appropriating"? Or if you prefer, what do we understand by possessing an object? We have seen the reducibility of the category "making," which allows us to see in it at one time "being" and at another "having." Is it the same with the category "having"?

It is obvious that in a great number of cases, to possess an object is to be able to *use it.* However, I am not satisfied with this definition. In this café I use this plate and this glass, yet they are not mine. I cannot "use" that picture which hangs on my wall, and yet it *belongs to me.* The right which I have in certain cases to destroy what I possess is no more decisive. It would be purely abstract to define ownership by this right, and furthermore in a society with a "planned economy" an owner can possess his factory without having the right to close it; in imperial Rome the master possessed his slave but did not have the right to put him to death. Besides what is meant here by the *right* to destroy, the

* Except where there is simply a *desire to be*—the desire to be happy, to be strong, etc.

317

right to use? I can see that this right refers me to the social sphere and that ownership [*propriété*] seems to be defined within the context of life in society. But I see also that the right is purely negative and is limited to preventing another from destroying or using what belongs to me. Of course we could try to define ownership as a social function. But first of all, although society confers in fact the *right* to possess according to certain rules, it does not follow that it creates the relation of appropriation. At the very most it makes it legal. If ownership is to be elevated to the rank of the *sacred,* it must first of all exist as a relation spontaneously established between the for-itself and the concrete in-itself. If we can imagine the future existence of a more just collective organization, where individual possession will cease to be protected and sanctified at least within certain limits—this does not mean that the appropriative tie will cease to exist; it can remain as at least a *private* relation of men to things. Thus in primitive societies where the matrimonial bond is not yet a legal one and where hereditary descent is still matrilineal, the sexual tie exists at most as a kind of concubinage. It is necessary then to distinguish between possession and the right to possess. For the same reason I must reject any definition of the type which Proudhon gives—such as "property is theft"—for it begs the question. It is possible of course for private property to be the *product* of theft and for the holding of this property to have *for its result* the robbing of another. But whatever may be its origin and its results, ownership remains no less capable of description and definition in itself. The thief considers himself the owner of the money which he has stolen. Our problem then includes describing the precise relation of the thief to the stolen goods as well as the relation of the lawful owner to property "honestly acquired."

If I consider the object which I possess, I see that the quality of *being possessed* does not indicate a purely external denomination marking the object's external relation to me; on the contrary, this quality defines it fundamentally; it appears to me and it appears to others as making a part of the object's being. This is why primitive societies say of certain individuals that they are "possessed"; the "possessed" are thought of as *belonging to.* . . . This is also the significance of primitive funeral ceremonies where the dead are buried with the objects which belong to them. The rational explanation, "so that they can use the objects," is obviously a rationalization. It is more probable that at the period when this kind of custom appeared spontaneously, no explanation seemed to be required. The objects had the specific quality *belonging to the deceased*. They formed a whole with him; there was no more question of burying the dead man without his usual objects than of burying him without one of his legs. The corpse, the cup from which the dead man drank, the knife which he used *make a single dead person*. The custom of burning widows in Malabar can very well be included under this principle; the woman has been possessed; the dead man takes her along with him in his death. By right she is dead; it is only necessary to help her pass from this death by right to death in fact. Objects which cannot be put in the grave are haunted. A ghost is only the concrete materialization of the idea that the house and furnishings "are possessed." To say that a house is haunted means that neither money nor effort will efface the metaphysical, absolute fact of *its possession* by a former occupant. It is true that the ghosts which haunt ancestral castles are degraded Lares. But what are these Lares if not layers of possession which have been deposited one by one on the walls and furnishings of the house? The very expression which designates the relation of the object to its owner indicates sufficiently the deep penetration of the appropriation; to be possessed means *to be for someone* [*être à . . .*]. This means that the possessed object is reached *in its being*. We have seen moreover that the destruction of the possessor involves the destruction of the right of the possessed and inversely the survival of the possessed involves the survival of the right of the possessor. The bond of possession is an internal bond of *being*. I meet the possessor in and through the object which he possesses. This is evidently the explanation of the importance of *relics;* and we mean by this not only religious relics, but also and especially the whole of the property of a famous man in which we try to rediscover him, the souvenirs of the beloved dead which seem to "perpetuate" his memory. (Consider, for example, the Victor Hugo Museum, or the "objects which belonged" to Balzac, to Flaubert.)

This internal, ontological bond between the possessed and the possessor (which customs like branding have often attempted to materialize) cannot be explained by a "realistic" theory of appropriation. If we are right in defining realism as a doctrine which makes subject and object two independent substances, each possessing existence for itself and by itself, then a realistic theory can no more account for appropriation than it can for knowledge, which is one of the forms of appropriation; both remain external relations uniting temporarily subject and object. But we have seen that substantial existence must be attributed to the object known. It is the same with ownership in general: the possessed object exists in itself, is defined by permanence, nontemporality, a sufficiency of being, in a word by substantiality. Therefore we must put *Unselbständigkeit* on the side of the possessing subject. A substance cannot appropriate another substance, and if we apprehend in things a certain quality of "being possessed," it is because originally the internal relation of the for-itself to the in-itself, which is ownership, derives its origin from the insufficiency of being in the for-itself. It is obvious that the object possessed is not *really* affected by the act of appropriation, any more than the object known is affected by knowledge. It remains untouched (except in cases where the possessed is a human being, like a slave or a prostitute). But this quality of being possessed nonetheless affects its meaning ideally; in a word, its meaning is to reflect this possession to the for-itself.

If the possessor and the possessed are united by an internal relation based on the insufficiency of being in the for-itself, we must try to determine the nature and the meaning of the *couple* which they form. In fact the internal relation is synthetic and effects the unification of the possessor and the possessed. This means that the possessor and the possessed constitute ideally a single reality. To possess is to be united with the object possessed in the form of appropriation; to wish to possess is to wish to be united to an object in this relation. Thus the desire of a particular object is not the simple desire *of* this object; it is the desire to be united with the object in an internal relation, in the mode of constituting with it the unity "possessor-possessed." The desire *to have* is at bottom reducible to the desire to be related to a certain object in a certain *relation of being*.

In determining this relation, observations made earlier on the behavior of the scientist, the artist, and the sportsman will be very useful to us. We discovered in the behavior of each one a certain appropriative attitude, and the appropriation in each case was marked by the fact that the object appeared simultaneously to be a kind of subjective emanation of ourselves and yet to remain in an indifferently external relation with us. The "mine" appeared to us then as a relation of being intermediate between the absolute interiority of the *me* and the absolute exteriority of the *not-me*. This is within the same syncretism a self becoming not-self and a not-self becoming self. But we must describe this relation more carefully. In the project of possession we meet a for-itself which is *"unselbständig,"* separated by a nothingness from the possibility which it is. This possibility is the possibility of appropriating the *object*. We meet in addition a *value* which haunts the for-itself and which stands as the ideal indication of the total being which would be realized by the union in identity of the possible and the for-itself which is its possible; I mean here the being which would be realized if I were in the indissoluble unity of identity—myself and my property. Thus appropriation would be a relation of being between a for-itself and a concrete in-itself, and this relation would be haunted by the ideal indication of an identification between this for-itself and the in-itself which is possessed.

To possess means *to have for myself;* that is, to be the unique end of the existence of the object. If possession is entirely and concretely given, the possessor is the *raison d'être* of the possessed object. I possess this pen; that means this pen exists *for me,* has been made *for me.* Moreover originally it is I who make for myself the object which I want to possess. My bow and arrows—that means the objects which I have made for myself. Division of labor can dim this original relation but cannot make it disappear. *Luxury* is a degradation of it; in the primitive form of luxury I possess an object which I *have had made* for myself by people who are mine (slaves, servants born in the house). Luxury therefore is the form of ownership closest to primitive ownership; it is this which next to ownership itself throws the most light on the relation of creation which originally constitutes appropriation. This relation in a society where the division of labor is pushed to the limit, is hidden but not suppressed. The object which I possess is one which I have *bought.* Money represents my strength; it is less a possession in itself than an instrument for possessing. That is why except in most unusual cases of avarice, money is effaced before its possibility of purchasing; it is evanescent, its function is to unevil the object, the concrete thing; money has only a transitive being. But *to me* it appears as a creative force: to buy an object is a symbolic act which amounts to creating the object. That is why money is synonymous with power; not only because it is in fact capable of procuring for us what we desire, but especially because it represents the effectiveness of my desire as such. Precisely because it is transcended toward the thing, surpassed, and simply *implied,* it represents my magical bond with the object. Money suppresses the *technical* connection of subject and object and renders the desire immediately effective, like the magic wishes of fairy tales. Stop before a showcase with money in your pocket; the objects displayed are already more than half yours. Thus money establishes a bond of appropriation between the for-itself and the total collection of objects in the world. By means of money desire as such is already formative and creative.

Thus through a continuous degradation, the bond of creation is maintained between subject and object. To have is first to create. And the bond of ownership which is established then is a bond of continuous creation; the object possessed is inserted by me into the total form of *my* environment; its existence is determined by my situation and by its integration into this situation. *My* lamp is not only that electric bulb, that shade, that wrought-iron stand; it is a certain power of lighting *this* desk, *these* books, *this* table; it is a certain luminous nuance of my work at night, connected with my habits of reading or writing late; it is animated, colored, defined by the use which I make of it; it *is* that use and exists only through it. If isolated from my desk, from my work, and placed in a lot of objects on the floor of a salesroom, my lamp is radically extinguished; it is no longer *my* lamp; instead, merely a member of the class of lamps, it has returned to its original matter. Thus I am responsible for the existence of my possessions in the human sphere. Through ownership I raise them up to a certain type of functional being; and my simple life appears to me as creative exactly because by its continuity it perpetuates the quality of *being possessed* in each of the objects in my possession. I bring the collection of my surroundings into being along with myself. If they are severed from me, they die as my arm would die if it were severed from me.

But the original, fundamental relation of creation is a relation of emanation, and the difficulties encountered by the Cartesian theory of substance are there to help us discover this relation. What I create is still me—if by creating we mean to bring matter and form to existence. The tragedy of the absolute Creator, if he existed, would be the impossibility of getting out of himself, for whatever he created could be only himself. Where could my creation derive any objectivity and independence since its form and its matter are for me? Only a sort of inertia could close it off from my presence, but in order for this same inertia to function, I must sustain it in existence by a continuous creation. Thus to the extent that I appear to myself as *creating* objects by the sole relation of appropriation, these objects are *myself*. The pen and the pipe, the clothing, the desk, the house —are myself. The totality of my possessions reflects the totality of my being. I *am* what I have. It is I myself which I touch on this cup, on this trinket. This mountain which I climb is myself to the extent that I conquer it; and when I am at its summit, which I have "gained" at the cost of this effort, when I gain this magnificent view of the valley and the surrounding peaks, then I *am* the view; the panorama is myself dilated to the horizon, for it exists only through me, only for me.

But creation is an evanescent concept which can exist only through its movement. If we stop it, it disappears. At its limits, it is annihilated; either I find only my pure subjectivity or else I encounter a naked, indifferent materiality which no longer has any relation to me. *Creation* can be conceived and maintained only as a continued transition from one limit to the other. As the object emerges in my world, it must simultaneously be wholly me and wholly independent of me. This is what we believe that we are realizing in possession. The possessed object as possessed is a continuous creation; but still it remains there, it exists by itself; it is in-itself. If I turn away from it, it does not thereby cease to exist; if I go away, it *represents* me in my desk, in my room, in *this* place in the world. From the start it is impenetrable. This pen is entirely myself, at the very point at which I no longer even distinguish it from the act of writing, which is *my* act. And yet, on the other hand, it is intact; my ownership does not change it; there is only an ideal relation between it and me. In a sense I enjoy my ownership if I surpass it toward use, but if I wish to contemplate it, the bond of possession is effaced, I no longer understand what it means to possess. The pipe there on the table is independent, indifferent. I pick it up, I feel it, I contemplate it so as to realize this appropriation; but just because these gestures are meant to give me the *enjoyment* of this appropriation, they miss their mark. I have merely an inert, wooden stem between my fingers. It is only when I transcend *my* objects toward a goal, when I utilize them, that I can enjoy their possession.

Thus the relation of continuous creation encloses within it as its implicit contradiction the absolute, in-itself independence of the objects created. Possession is a magical relation; I *am* these objects which I possess, but outside, so to speak, facing myself; I create them as independent of me; what I possess is mine outside of me, outside all subjectivity, as an in-itself which escapes me at each moment and whose creation at each moment I perpetuate. But precisely because I am always somewhere outside of myself, as an incompleteness which makes its being known to itself by what it is not, now when I possess, I alienate myself in favor of the object possessed. In the relation of possession the dominant term is the object possessed; without it I am nothing save a nothingness which possesses, nothing other than pure and simple possession, an incompleteness, an insufficiency, whose sufficiency and completion are there in that object. In possession, I am my own foundation insofar as I exist in an in-itself. Insofar as possession is a continuous creation, I apprehend the possessed object as founded by me in its being. On the other hand, insofar as creation is emanation, this object is reabsorbed in me, it is only myself. Finally, insofar as it is originally in itself, it is not-me, it is myself facing myself, objective, in-itself, permanent, impenetrable, existing in relation to me in the relation of exteriority, of indifference. Thus I am the foundation for myself insofar as I exist as an indifferent in-itself in relation to myself. But this is precisely the project of the in-itself-for-itself. For this ideal being is defined as an in-itself which, for-itself, would be its own foundation, or as a for-itself whose original project would not be a mode of being, but a being precisely the being-in-itself which it is. We see that appropriation is nothing save the *symbol* of the ideal of the for-itself or value. The couple, for-itself possessing and in-itself possessed, is the same as that being which is in order to possess itself and whose possession is its own creation—God. Thus the possessor aims at enjoying his being-in-itself, his being-outside. Through possession I recover an object-being identical with my being-for-others. Consequently the Other cannot take me by surprise; the being which he wishes to bring up into the world, which is myself-for-the-Other—this being I already enjoy possessing. Thus possession is in addition a *defense against others*. What is mine is myself in a non-subjective form inasmuch as I am its free foundation.

We cannot insist too strongly on the fact that this relation is *symbolic* and *ideal*. My original desire of being my own foundation for myself is never satisfied through appropriation any more than Freud's patient satisfies his Oedipus complex when he dreams that a soldier kills the Czar (*i.e.*, his father). This is why ownership appears to the owner simultaneously as something given all at once in the eternal and as requiring an infinite time to be realized. No particular act of utilization really realizes the enjoyment of full possession; but it refers to other appropriative acts, each one of which has the value of an incantation. To possess a bicycle is to be able first to look at it, then to touch it. But touching is revealed as being insufficient; what is necessary is to be able to get on the bicycle and take a ride. But this *gratuitous* ride is likewise insufficient; it would be necessary to use the bicycle to go on some errands. And this refers us to uses longer and more complete, to long trips across France. But these trips themselves disintegrate into a thousand appropriative behavior patterns, each one of which refers to others. Finally as one could foresee, handing over a bank note is enough to make the bicycle belong to me, but my entire life is needed to realize this possession. In acquiring the object, I perceive that possession is an enterprise which death always renders still unfinished. Now we can understand why; it is because it is impossible to realize the relation symbolized by appropriation. In itself appropriation contains nothing concrete. It is not a real activity (such as eating, drinking, sleeping) which could serve in addition as a symbol for a particular desire. It exists, on the contrary, only as a symbol; it is its symbolism which gives it its meaning, its coherence, its existence. There can be found in it no positive enjoyment outside its symbolic value; it is only the indication of a supreme enjoyment of possession (that of the being which would *be its own foundation*), which is always beyond all the appropriative conduct meant to realize it.

This is precisely why the recognition that it is impossible to *possess* an object involves for the for-itself a violent urge to *destroy* it. To destroy is to reabsorb into myself; it is to enter along with the being-in-itself of the destroyed object into a relation as profound as that of creation. The flames which burn the farm which I myself have set on fire, gradually effect the fusion of the farm with myself. In annihilating it I am changing it into *myself*. Suddenly I rediscover the relation of being found in creation, but in reverse; I *am* the foundation of the barn which is burning; I *am* this barn since I am destroying its being. Destruction realizes appropriation perhaps more keenly than creation does, for the object destroyed is no longer there to show itself impenetrable. It has the impenetrability and the sufficiency of being of the in-itself which it *has been,* but at the same time it has the invisibility and translucency of the nothingness which I am, since it *no longer* exists. This glass which I have broken and which "was" on this table, is there still, but as an absolute transparency. I see all beings superimposed. This is what movie producers have attempted to render by overprinting the film. The destroyed object resembles a consciousness although it has the irreparability of the in-itself. At the same time it is positively mine because the mere fact that I have to be what I **was** keeps the destroyed object from being annihilated. I recreate it by recreating myself; thus to destroy is to recreate by taking upon oneself the sole responsibility for the being of what existed *for all.*

Destruction then is to be given a place among appropriative modes of behavior. Moreover many kinds of appropriative behavior have a destructive structure along with their other structures. To utilize is to use. In *making use* of my bicycle, I *use it up*—wear it out; that is, continuous appropriative creation is marked by a partial destruction. This wear can cause distress for strictly practical reasons, but in the majority of cases it brings a secret joy, almost like the joy of possession; this is because it is coming from us—we are consuming. It should be noted that the word "consume" holds the double meaning of an appropriative destruction and an alimentary enjoyment. To consume is to annihilate and it is to eat; it is to destroy by incorporating into oneself. If I ride on my bicycle, I can be annoyed at wearing out its tires because it is difficult to find others to replace them; but the image of enjoyment which my body invokes is that of a destructive appropriation, of a "creation-destruction." The bicycle gliding along, carrying me, by its very movement is created and made mine; but this creation is deeply imprinted on the object by the light, continued wear which is impressed on it and which is like the brand on the slave. The object is mine because it is I who have used it; the using up of what is *mine* is the reverse side of my life.*

These remarks will enable us to understand better the meaning of certain feelings or behavior ordinarily considered irreducible; for example, *generosity*. Actually the *gift* is a primitive form of destruction. We know for example that the potlatch involves the destruction of enormous quantities of merchandise. These destructions are taunts to the Other; the gifts enchain him. On this level it is indifferent whether the object is destroyed or given to another; in any case the potlatch is destruction and enchaining of the Other. I destroy the object by giving it away as well as by annihilating it; I suppress in it the quality of being *mine*, which constituted it to the depths of its being; I remove it from my sight; I constitute it—in relation to my table, to my room—as *absent;* I alone shall preserve for it the ghostly, transparent being of *past* objects, because I am the one through whom beings pursue an honorary existence after their annihilation. Thus generosity is above all a destructive function. The craze for giving which sometimes seizes certain people is first and foremost a craze to destroy; it is equivalent to a frantic attitude, a passion which accompanies the shattering of objects. But the craze to destroy which is at the bottom of generosity is nothing else than a craze to possess. All which I abandon, all which I give, I enjoy in a higher manner through the fact that I give it away; giving is a keen, brief enjoyment, almost sexual. To give is to enjoy possessively the object which one gives; it is a destructive-appropriative contact. But at the same time the gift casts a spell over the recipient; it obliges him to recreate, to maintain in being by a continuous creation this bit of myself which I no longer want, which I have just possessed up to its annihilation, and which finally remains only as an image. To give is to enslave. That aspect of the gift does not interest us here, for it concerns primarily our relations with others. What we wish to emphasize is that generosity is not irreducible; to give is to appropriate by destruction while utilizing this destruction to enslave another. Generosity then is a feeling structured by the existence of the Other and indicates a preference for *appropria-*

---

* Brummell carried his elegance to the extent of wearing only clothes which had been worn a little. He had a horror of anything new; what is new does not belong to anybody.

*tion by destruction.* In this way it leads us toward *nothingness* still more than toward the in-itself (we have here a nothingness of in-itself which is evidently itself in-itself, but which as nothingness can symbolize the being which is its own nothingness). If then existential psychoanalysis encounters evidence of *generosity* in a subject, it must search further for his original project and ask why the subject has chosen to appropriate by destruction rather than by creation. The answer to this question will reveal that original relation to being which constitutes the *person* who is being studied.

These observations aim only at bringing to light the *ideal* character of the appropriative relationship and the symbolic function of all appropriative behavior. It is necessary to add that the symbol is not deciphered by the subject himself. This is due, not to the symbol having been prepared by a process in the unconscious, but to the very structure of being-in-the-world. . . . Since the circuit of selfness is non-thetic, and consequently the identification of what I am remains non-thematic, this "being-in-itself" of myself which the world reflects as me is necessarily hidden from my *knowledge*. I can only adapt myself to it in and through the approximative action which makes it emerge. Consequently to possess does not mean to know that one's relation to the object possessed is identifiable as creation-destruction; rather to possess means *to be in this relation* or better yet to be this *relation*. The possessed object has for us an immediately apprehensible quality which transforms it entirely— the quality of being *mine*—but this quality is in itself strictly indecipherable; it reveals itself in and through action. It manifestly has a particular meaning, but from the moment that we want to withdraw a little in relation to the object and to contemplate it, the quality vanishes without revealing its deeper structure and its meaning. This withdrawal indeed is itself destructive of the appropriative connection. A moment earlier I was involved in an ideal totality, and precisely because I was involved in my being, I could not know it; a moment later the totality has been shattered and I cannot discover the meaning of it in the disconnected fragments which formerly composed it. This can be observed in that contemplative experience called depersonalization which certain patients have, in spite of efforts to resist it. We are forced then to have recourse to existential psychoanalysis to reveal in each particular case the meaning of the appropriative synthesis for which we have just determined the general abstract meaning by ontology.

It remains to determine in general the meaning of the object possessed. This investigation should complete our knowledge of the appropriative project. What then is it which we seek to appropriate?

It is easy to see abstractly that we originally aim at possessing not so much the mode of being of an object as the actual being of this particular object. In fact it is as a concrete representative of being-in-itself that I desire to appropriate it; that is, to apprehend that ideally I am the foundation of its being insofar as it is a part of myself and on the other hand to apprehend that empirically the appropriated object is never of value for itself alone nor for its individual use. No particular appropriation has any meaning outside its indefinite extensions; the pen which I possess is the same as all other pens; it is the class of pens which I possess in it. But in addition I possess in it the possibility of writing, of tracing with certain characteristic forms and color (for I combine the instrument itself and the ink which I use in it). These characteristic forms and color with their meaning are condensed in the pen as well as the paper, its special resistance, its odor, etc. With *all* possession there is made the crystallizing synthesis which Stendhal has described for the one case of love. Each object possessed emerges against the background of the world and manifests the entire world, just as a loved woman manifests the sky, the shore, the sea around her at the time she appeared. To appropriate this object is then to appropriate the world symbolically. Each one can recognize it by referring to his own experience: for myself, I shall cite a personal example, not to prove the point but to guide the reader in his inquiry.

Some years ago I brought myself to the decision not to smoke any more. The struggle was hard, and in truth I did not care so much for the *taste* of the tobacco which I was going to lose, as for the *meaning* of the act of smoking. A complete crystallization had been formed. I used to smoke at the theater, in the morning while working, in the evening after dinner, and it seemed to me that in giving up smoking I was going to deprive the theater of its interest, the evening meal of its savor, the morning work of its fresh animation. Whatever unexpected happening was going to meet my eye, it seemed to me that it was fundamentally impoverished from the moment that I could not welcome it while smoking. To-be-capable-of-being-encountered-by-me-smoking: such was the concrete quality which had been diffused over everything. It seemed to me that I was going to strip it away from everything and that in the midst of this universal impoverishment, life was scarcely worth the effort. But to smoke is an appropriative, destructive action. Tobacco is a symbol of "appropriated" being, since it is destroyed in the rhythm of my breathing, in a mode of "continuous destruction," since it passes into me and its change in myself is manifested symbolically by the transformation of the consumed solid into smoke. The connection between the landscape seen while I was smoking and this little crematory sacrifice was such that, as we have just seen, the tobacco symbolized the landscape. This means then that the act of destructively appropriating the tobacco was the symbolic equivalent of destructively appropriating the entire world. Across the tobacco which I was smoking was the world which was burning, which was going up in smoke, which was being reabsorbed in to vapor so as to re-enter into me. In order to maintain my decision not to smoke, I had to realize a sort of decrystallization; that is, without exactly paying attention to what I was doing, I reduced the tobacco to being nothing but itself—an herb which burns. I cut its symbolic ties with the world; I persuaded myself that I was not taking anything away from the play at the theater, from the landscape, from the book which I was reading, if I considered them without my pipe; that is, I rebuilt my possession of these objects in modes other than that sacrificial ceremony. As soon as I was persuaded of this, my regret was reduced to a very small matter; I deplored the thought of not perceiving the odor of the smoke, the warmth of the bowl between my fingers and so forth. But suddenly my regret was disarmed and quite bearable.

Thus what fundamentally we desire to appropriate in an object is its being and it is the world. These two ends of appropriation are in reality only one. I search behind the phenomenon to possess the being of the phenomenon. But this being, as we have seen, is very different from the phenomenon of being; it is being-in-itself, and not only the being of a particular thing. It is not because there is here a transition to the universal but rather the being considered in its concrete nakedness becomes suddenly the being of the totality. Thus the relation of possession appears to us clearly; to possess is to wish to possess the world across a particular object. And as possession is defined as the effort to apprehend ourselves as the foundation of a being insofar as it is ourselves ideally, every possessive project aims at constituting the for-itself as the foundation of the world or a concrete totality of the in-itself, and this totality is, as totality, the for-itself existing in the mode of the in-itself. To-be-in-the-world is to form the project of possessing the world; that is, to apprehend the total world as that which is lacking to the for-itself in order that it may become in-itself-for-itself. It is to be engaged in a totality which is precisely the ideal or value or totalized totality and which would be ideally constituted by the fusion of the for-itself as a detotalized totality which has to be what it is, with the world, as the totality of the in-itself which is what it is.

It must be understood of course that the project of the for-itself is not to establish a being of reason, that is a being which the for-itself would first conceive—form and matter—and then endow with existence. Such a being actually would be a pure abstraction, a universal; its conception could not be prior to being-in-the-world; on the contrary its conception would presuppose being-in-the-world as it supposes the pre-ontological comprehension of a being which is eminently concrete and present at the start, which is the "there" of the first being-there of the for-itself; that is the being of the world. The for-itself does not exist so as first to think the universal and determine itself in terms of concepts. It is its choice and its choice cannot be abstract without making the very being of the for-itself abstract. The being of the for-itself is an individual venture, and the choice must be an individual choice of a concrete being. This holds, as we have seen, of the *situation* in general. The choice of the for-itself is always a choice of a concrete situation in its incomparable uniqueness. But it holds as well for the ontological meaning of this choice. When we say that the for-itself is a project of *being,* we do not mean that the being-in-itself, which it projects being, is conceived by the for-itself as a structure common to all existents of a certain type; its project is in no way a conception, as we have seen. That which it projects being appears to it as an eminently concrete totality; it is *this* being. Of course we can foresee in this project the possibilities of a universalizing development; but it is in the same way as we say of a lover that he loves all women or woman as a whole in one woman. The for-itself projects being the foundation of this concrete being, which, as we have just seen, cannot be *conceived*—for the very reason that it is concrete; neither can it be imagined, for the imaginary is nothingness and this being is eminently being. It must *exist;* that is, it must be encountered, but this encounter is identical with the choice which the for-itself makes. The for-itself is an encountered-choice; that is, it is defined as a choice of founding the being which it encounters. This means that the for-itself as an individual enterprise is a choice of *this world,* as a totality of individual being; it does not transcend it toward a logical universal but toward a new concrete "state" of the same world, in which being would be an in-itself founded by the for-itself; that is, it transcends it toward a concrete-being-beyond-the-concrete-existing-being. Thus being-in-the-world is a project of possessing this world, and the value which haunts the for-itself is the concrete indication of an individual being constituted by the synthetic function of *this* for-itself and *this* world. Being, in fact, whatever it may be, wherever it may come from, and in whatever mode we may consider it, whether it is in-itself or for-itself or the impossible ideal of in-itself-for-itself, is in its original contingency an individual venture.

Now we can define the relations which unite the two categories, *to be* and *to have.* We have seen that desire can be originally either the desire to be or the desire to have. But the desire to have is not irreducible. While the desire *to be* bears directly on the for-itself and has the project of conferring on it without intermediary the dignity of in-itself-for-itself, the desire *to have* aims at the for-itself on, in, and through the world. It is by the appropriation of the world that the project *to have* aims at realizing the same value as the desire *to be.* That is why these desires, which can be distinguished by analysis, are in reality inseparable. It is impossible to find a desire to be which is not accompanied by a desire to have, and conversely. Fundamentally we have to do with two ways of looking toward a single goal, or if you prefer, with two interpretations of the same fundamental situation, the one tending to confer being on the for-itself without detour, the other establishing the circuit of selfness; that is, interposing the world between the for-itself and its being. As for the original situation, it is the lack of being which I am; that is, which I make myself be. But the being of which I make myself a lack is strictly individual and concrete; it is the being which *exists al-*

*ready* and in the midst of which I emerge as being *its* lack. Thus the very nothingness which I am is individual and concrete, as being *this* nihilation and not any other.

Every for-itself is a free choice; each of its acts—the most insignificant as well as the most weighty—expresses this choice and emanates from it. This is what we have called our freedom. We have now grasped the *meaning* of this choice; it is a choice of being, either directly or by the appropriation of the world, or rather by both at once. Thus my freedom is a choice of being God and all my acts, all my projects translate this choice and reflect it in a thousand and one ways, for there is an infinite number of ways of being and of ways of having. The goal of existential psychoanalysis is to rediscover through these empirical, concrete projects the original way in which each man has chosen his being. It remains to explain, someone will say, why I choose to possess the world through *this* particular object rather than another. We shall reply that here we see the peculiarity of freedom.

Yet the object itself is not irreducible. In it we aim at its *being* through its mode of being or quality. Quality—particularly a material quality like the fluidity of water or the density of a stone—is a mode of being and so can only present being in a certain way. What we choose is a certain way in which being reveals itself and lets itself be possessed. The yellow and red, the taste of a tomato or of split peas, the rough and the gentle are by no means irreducible givens according to our view. They translate symbolically a certain way which being has of giving itself, and we react by disgust or desire, according to how we see being burgeon in one way or another from their surface. Existential psychoanalysis must bring out the *ontological meaning* of qualities. It is only thus—and not by considerations of sexuality—that we can explain, for example, certain constants in poetic "imaginations" (Rimbaud's "geological," Poe's fluidity of water) or simply the *tastes* of each individual (those famous tastes which we are forbidden to dispute) without taking into account that they symbolize in their own way a whole *Weltanschauung,* a whole choice of being and that hence comes their *self-evidence* in the view of the individual who has made them his. We should next sketch in outline this particular task of existential psychoanalysis, for the sake of making suggestions for further research. For it is not on the level of a taste for sweetness or for bitterness and the like that the free choice is irreducible, but on the level of the choice of the aspect of being which is revealed through and by means of sweetness, bitterness, etc.

## 7 EXISTENTIAL SYMBOLISM

What must be attempted is a psychoanalysis of *things*. M. Gaston Bachelard has tried this and shown much talent in his last book, *Water and Dreams*. There is great promise in this work; in particular the author has made a real discovery in his "material imagination." Yet in truth this term *imagination* does not suit us and neither does that attempt to look behind things and their gelatinous, solid, or fluid matter, for the "images" which we project there. Perception, as I have shown elsewhere* has nothing in common with imagination; on the contrary each strictly excludes the other. To perceive does not mean to assemble images by means of sensations; this thesis, originating with the association theory in psychology, must be banished entirely. Consequently psychoanalysis will not look for images but rather will seek to explain the meaning which really belongs to things. Of course the "human" meaning of *sticky*, of *slimy*, etc. does not belong to the in-itself. But potentialities do not belong to it either, as we have seen, and yet it is these which constitute the world. Material meanings, the human significance of needles, snow, the clotted, the heaped, the greasy, etc., are as real as the world, neither more nor less, and to enter the world means to emerge in the midst of these meanings. But no doubt we have to do here with a simple difference in terminology. M. Bachelard appears bolder and seems to reveal what is fundamental to his thought when he speaks in his studies of psychoanalyzing plants or when he entitles one of his works *The Psychoanalysis of Fire*. Actually he is applying not *to the subject* but to things a method of objective decipherment which does not presuppose any prior reference to the subject. When for instance I wish to determine the objective meaning of snow, I see, for example, that it melts at certain temperatures and that this melting of the snow is its death. Here we merely have to do with objective observation. When I wish to determine the meaning of this melting, I must compare it to other objects located in other regions of existence

* See above, p. 78.

but equally objective, equally transcendent—ideas, friendship, persons—concerning which I can also say that they melt. Money *melts* in my hands. I am swimming and I *melt* in the water. Certain ideas—in the sense of socially objective meanings—"snowball" and others *melt* away.* We say, "How thin he has become! How he has melted away!" (*Comme il a fondu!*) Doubtless I shall thus obtain a certain relation linking certain forms of being to certain others.

The melting snow can be compared with certain other more mysterious examples of melting. Take for example the content of certain old myths. The tailor in Grimms' fairy tales takes a piece of cheese in his hands, pretends it is a stone, squeezes it so hard that the whey oozes out of it; those present believe that he has made a stone drip, that he is pressing the liquid from it. Such a comparison informs us of a secret liquid quality in solids, in the sense in which Audiberti by a happy inspiration spoke of the secret blackness of milk. This liquidity which ought to be compared to the juice of fruits and to human blood—which is to man something like his own secret and vital liquidity—this liquidity carries a reference to a certain permanent possibility which the "granulated compound (designating a certain quality of the being of the *pure in-itself*) possesses of changing itself into *homogenous, undifferentiated fluidity* (another quality of the being of the pure in-itself). We apprehend here in its origin and with all its ontological significance the polarity of the continuous and discontinuous, the feminine and masculine poles of the world, for which we shall subsequently see the dialectical development all the way to the quantum theory and wave mechanics. Thus we shall succeed in deciphering the secret meaning of the snow, which is an ontological meaning.

But in all this where is the relation to the subjective? To imagination? All we have done is to compare strictly objective structures and to formulate the hypothesis which can unify and group these structures. That is why psychoanalysis refers here to the things themselves, not to men. That is also why I should have less confidence than M. Bachelard in resorting at this level to the material imaginations of poets, whether Lautréamont, Rimbaud, or Poe. To be sure, it is fascinating to look for the "Bestiary of Lautréamont." But actually if in this research we have returned to the subjective, we shall attain results truly sig-

* We may recall also the "melting money" of Daladier.

nificant only if we consider Lautréamont as an original and pure
preference for animality and if we have first determined the objective meaning of animality.* In fact if Lautréamont *is what
he prefers,* it is necessary first to understand the nature of what
he prefers. To be sure, we know well that he is going "to put" into
animality something different and more than I put into it. But the
subjective enrichments which inform us about Lautréamont are
polarized by the objective structure of animality. This is why
the existential psychoanalysis of Lautréamont supposes first an
interpretation of the objective meaning of the *animal.* Similarly
I have thought for a long time of establishing a *lapidary* for
Rimbaud. But what meaning would it have unless we had previously established the significance of the geological in general?

It will be objected that a meaning presupposes man. We do
not deny this. But man, being transcendence, establishes the
meaningful by his very coming into the world, and the meaningful because of the very structure of transcendence is a reference to other transcendents which can be interpreted without recourse to the subjectivity which has established it. The potential
energy of a body is an objective quality of that body which can
be objectively calculated while taking into account exclusively objective circumstances. And yet this energy can come to dwell in
a body only in a world whose appearance is a correlate of that of
a for-itself. Similarly a rigorously objective psychoanalysis will
discover that deeply involved in the matter of things there are
other potentialities which remain entirely transcendent even
though they correspond to a still more fundamental choice of
human reality, a choice of *being.*

That brings us to the second point in which we differ with
M. Bachelard. Certainly any psychoanalysis must have its principles *a priori.* In particular it must know *what it is looking for,*
or how will it be able to find it? But since the goal of its research
cannot itself be established by the psychoanalysis, without falling into a vicious circle, such an end must be the object of a
postulate; either we seek it in experience, or we establish it by
means of some other discipline. The Freudian libido is obviously
a simple postulate; Adler's will to power seems to be an unme-
thodical generalization from empirical data—and in fact it is
this very lack of method which allows him to disregard the basic
principles of a psychoanalytic method. M. Bachelard seems to

* One aspect of this animality is exactly what Scheler calls *vital values.*

rely upon these predecessors; the postulate of sexuality seems to dominate his research; at other times we are referred to *Death*, to the trauma of birth, to the will to power. In short his psychoanalysis seems more sure of its method than of its principles and doubtless will count on its results to enlighten it concerning the precise goal of its research. But this is to put the cart before the horse; consequences will never allow us to establish the principle, any more than the summation of finite modes will permit us to grasp substance. It appears to us therefore that we must here abandon these empirical principles or these postulates which would make man *a priori* a sexuality or a will to power, and that we should establish the goal of psychoanalysis strictly from the standpoint of ontology. This is what we have just attempted. We have seen that human reality, far from being capable of being described as *libido* or will to power, is a *choice of being*, either directly or through appropriation of the world. And we have seen—when the choice is expressed through appropriation—that each *thing* is chosen in the last analysis, not for its sexual potential but for the mode in which it renders being, depending on the manner in which being burgeons from its surface. A psychoanalysis of *things* and of their *matter* ought above all to be concerned with ascertaining the way in which each thing is the *objective* symbol of being and of the relation of human reality to this being. We do not deny that we should discover afterwards a whole sexual symbolism in nature, but it is a secondary and reducible layer, which presupposes a psychoanalysis of pre-sexual structures. Thus M. Bachelard's investigation of water, which abounds in ingenious and profound insights, will be for us a set of suggestions, a precious collection of materials, which should now be utilized by a psychoanalysis which is aware of its own principles.

What ontology can teach psychoanalysis is first of all the *true* origin of the meanings of things and their *true* relation to human reality. Ontology alone in fact is located at the level of transcendence and from a single viewpoint can apprehend being-in-the-world with its two dimensions, because ontology alone is located originally in the perspective of the *cogito*. Once again the concepts of facticity and situation will enable us to understand the existential symbolism of things. We have seen that it is in theory possible but in practice impossible to distinguish facticity from the project which constitutes it a situation. This

337

observation can be of use to us here; . . . we must not regard the "this" as having any meaning whatever in the indifference and externality of its being and independently of the emergence of the for-itself. Actually its quality . . . is nothing other than its being. The yellow of the lemon is not a subjective mode of apprehending the lemon; it *is the lemon*. The whole lemon extends throughout its qualities and each one of the qualities extends through the others; that is what we have called "this." Every quality of being is all of being; it is the presence of its absolute contingency; it is its irreducibility of indifference. . . . Quality is the whole of being unveiling itself within the limitations of the *there is*. Thus the meaning of a quality cannot be attributed to being-in-itself, since the "there is" must already be; that is, the nihilating meditation of the for-itself must be there in order for qualities to be there. But it is easy to understand from this point of view that the meaning of quality in turn indicates something as a reinforcement of "there is," since we take it as our support in order to transcend the "there is" toward being as it is absolutely and in-itself.

In each apprehension of quality, there is in this sense a metaphysical effort to escape from our condition so as to pierce through the shell of nothingness encasing the "there is" and to penetrate to the pure in-itself. But obviously we can apprehend quality only as a symbol of a being which totally escapes us, even though it is totally there before us; in short, we can only make revealed being function as a symbol of being-in-itself. This means that a new structure of the "there is" is constituted which is the meaningful level although this level is revealed in the absolute unity of one and the same fundamental project. This structure we shall call the metaphysical import of all intuitive revelation of being; and this is precisely what we ought to achieve and disclose by psychoanalysis. What is the metaphysical import of yellow, of red, of polished, of rough? And *after* these elementary questions, what is the metaphysical coefficient of lemon, of water, of oil, etc.? Psychoanalysis must resolve all these problems if it wants to understand someday why Peter likes oranges and has a horror of water, why he gladly eats tomatoes and refuses to eat beans, why he vomits if he is forced to swallow oysters or raw eggs.

We have shown also, however, the error in believing that we "project" our affective dispositions *on* the thing, to illuminate it or color it. First, as we saw long ago, a feeling is not an inner disposition but an objectifying, transcending relation which learns from its object what it is. But this is not all. The explanation by projection, which is found in such trite sayings as, "A landscape is a spiritual state," always begs the question. Take for example that particular quality which we call "slimy" [*visqueux*]. Certainly for the European adult it signifies a host of *human* and *moral* characteristics which can easily be reduced to relations of being. A handshake, a smile, a thought, a feeling can be slimy. The common view is that, on the one hand, I have experienced certain behavior and certain moral attitudes which displease me and which I condemn, and that, on the other hand, I have a sensory intuition of the "slimy." Afterwards, according to this view, I establish a connection between these feelings and sliminess, and the slimy then functions as a symbol of a whole class of human feelings and attitudes. I would thereby have enriched the slimy by projecting upon it my knowledge with respect to this human category of behavior.

But how can we accept this explanation by projection? If we suppose that we have first grasped the feelings as pure psychic qualities, how will we be able to grasp their relation to the slimy? A feeling apprehended in its qualitative purity can reveal itself only as a certain purely unextended disposition, culpable because of its relation to certain values and certain consequences; in any case it will not "compose an image" unless the image has been given first. On the other hand if "slimy" is not originally charged with an affective meaning, if it is given only as a certain material quality, one does not see how it could ever be chosen as a symbolic representation of certain psychic unities. In a word, if we are to establish consciously and clearly a symbolic relation between sliminess and the sticky baseness [*bassesse*] of certain individuals, we must apprehend baseness already in sliminess and sliminess in certain forms of baseness. Consequently the explanation by projection explains nothing since it takes for granted what it ought to explain. Furthermore even if this objection on principle could be avoided, another objection would have to be faced, drawn from experience and no less serious; the explanation by projection implies actually that the projecting subject has arrived by experience and analysis at a certain knowledge of the structure and effects of the attitudes which he calls slimy. According to this concept the recourse to sliminess does not as *knowledge* enrich our experience of human baseness. At the most it serves as a thematic unity, as a picturesque rubric for pieces of knowledge already acquired. On the other hand, sliminess proper, considered in its isolated state, appears to us harmful in practice (because slimy substances stick to the hands and clothes, and because they stain), but sliminess then is not *repugnant*. In fact the disgust which it inspires can be explained only by the contamination of this physical quality by certain moral qualities. There would have to be a kind of apprenticeship for learning the symbolic value of "slimy." But observation teaches us that even very young children display repulsion in the presence of something slimy, as if it were already contaminated with the psychic. We know also that from the time they know how to talk, they *understand* the value of the words "soft," "low" [*bas*], etc., when applied to the description of feelings. All this transpires as if we emerged in a universe where feelings and acts are all charged with something material, have a substantial stuff, are *really* soft, dull, slimy, low, elevated, etc., and in which material substances have originally a psychic meaning which renders them repugnant, horrifying, attractive, etc. No explanation by projection or by analogy is acceptable here. To sum up, it is impossible to derive the meaning of the psychic symbol "slimy" from the brute quality of the *this* and equally impossible to project onto the *this* the meaning derived from a *knowledge* of psychic attitudes. How then are we to conceive of this immense and universal symbolism which finds expression in our repulsion, our hates, our sympathies, our attractions toward objects whose materiality must on principle remain non-meaningful? To make progress in this investigation it is necessary to abandon a certain number of postulates. In particular we must no longer postulate *a priori* that the attribution of sliminess to a particular feeling is only an image and not knowledge. We must also refuse to admit—until getting fuller information—that the psychic allows us to infuse the physical matter with symbolic meaning or that our experience with human baseness has any priority over the apprehension of the "slimy" as meaningful.

Let us return to the original project. It is a project of appropriation. It compels the *slimy* to reveal its being; since the emergence of the for-itself into being is appropriative, the slimy when perceived is "a slimy to be possessed"; that is, the original link between the slimy and myself is that I project being the establishment of its being, inasmuch as it is myself ideally. From the start then it appears as a possible "myself" to be established; from the start it has a psychic quality. This definitely does not mean that I endow it with a soul in the manner of primitive animism, nor with metaphysical faculties, but simply that even its materiality is revealed to me as having a psychic meaning— which is, moreover, identical with the symbolic value which the slimy has in relation to being-in-itself. This appropriative way of making the slimy express all its meanings can be considered as a formal *a priori*, although it is a free project and although it is identified with the being of the for-itself. In fact the appropriative mode does not depend originally on the mode of being of the slimy but only on its brute being-there, on its pure encountered existence; it is like any other encounter insofar as it is a simple project of appropriation, insofar as it is not distinguished in any way from the pure "there is" and is either pure freedom or pure nothingness, according to whether we consider it from one point of view or the other. But it is precisely within the context of this appropriative project that the slimy reveals itself and develops its sliminess. From the first appearance of the slimy, this sliminess is already a response to a demand, already a *bestowal of self;* the slimy appears as already the delineation of a fusion of the world with myself. What I learn from it about its characteristic suction, sucking me in, is already a reply to a concrete question; it responds with its very being, with its mode of being, with all its matter. The response which it gives is at the same time fully appropriate to the question and yet opaque and indecipherable, for it is rich with all its indescribable materiality. The reply is clear inasmuch as it is exactly appropriate; the slimy lets itself be apprehended as that which I lack; it lets itself be handled by an appropriative inquiry; it allows its sliminess to be revealed to this delineation of appropriation. Yet it is opaque because if the meaningful form is evoked in the slimy by the for-itself, all its sliminess comes to fulfill it. We are provided with a meaning which is full and dense, and this meaning presents us first with being-in-itself insofar as the slimy is now that which is manifesting the world, and second a *sketch of ourselves,* insofar as the appropriation delineates something like an act of establishment on the part of the slimy.

What comes back toward us then as an objective quality is a

new *nature* which is neither material (and physical) nor psychic, but which transcends the opposition of the psychic and the physical, by revealing itself to us as the ontological expression of the entire world; that is, which offers itself as a rubric for classifying all the "thises" in the world, whether material organizations or transcended transcendences. This means that the apprehension of the slimy as such has, at the same time, created for the in-itself of the world a particular mode of giving itself. In its own way this mode symbolizes being; that is, so long as the contact with the slimy endures, everything takes place for us as if sliminess were the meaning of the entire world—the unique mode of being of being-in-itself, in the same way as for the savages belonging to the clan of lizards all objects *are* lizards.

What mode of being is symbolized by the slimy? I see first that it is the homogeneity and the imitation of liquidity. A slimy substance like pitch is an aberrant fluid. At first, with the appearance of a fluid it manifests to us a being which is everywhere fleeing and yet everywhere similar to itself, which on all sides escapes yet on which one can float, a being without danger and without memory, which eternally changes into itself, on which one leaves no mark and which could not leave a mark on us, a being which slides and on which one can slide, which can be possessed by something sliding (by a rowboat, a motor boat, or water ski), and which never possesses because it rolls over us, a being which is eternity and infinite temporality because it is perpetual change without anything which changes, a being which best symbolizes in this synthesis of eternity and temporality, a possible fusion of the for-itself as pure temporality and the in-itself as pure eternity. But soon the slimy reveals itself as essentially equivocal [*louche*] because its fluidity exists in slow motion; there is a density to its liquidity; it represents in itself an emerging triumph of the solid over the liquid—that is, a tendency of the in-itself in its indifference which is represented by the pure solid, to congeal the liquidity, to absorb the for-itself which ought to dissolve it.

Slime is the agony of water. It presents itself as a phenomenon in process of becoming; it does not have the permanence within change that water has but on the contrary represents a phase in a change of state. This congealed instability of the slimy discourages possession. Water is more fleeing, but it can be possessed in its very flight as something fleeing. The slimy flees with a dense flight which resembles the flight of water as the heavy earthbound flight of the chicken resembles that of the hawk. Even this flight cannot be possessed because it denies itself as flight. It is already almost a solid permanence. Nothing testifies more clearly to its equivocal character as a "substance in between two states" than the slowness with which the slimy melts into itself. A drop of water touching the surface of a sheet of water is instantly transformed into the body of water; we do not see the operation as absorption by sucking, so to speak, of the drop of water by the sheet of water but rather as a spiritualizing and loss of individuality by a single being which is dissolved in the great whole from which it had come. The symbol of the sheet of water seems to play a very important role in the construction of pantheistic systems; it reveals a particular type of relation of being to being. But if we consider the slimy, we note that it presents a constant hysteresis in the phenomenon of being transmuted into itself.* The honey which flows off my spoon onto the honey contained in the jar first sculptures the surface by remaining detached from it in relief, and its fusion with the whole is presented as a gradual sinking, a collapse which appears at once as a *deflation* (think for example of the responsiveness of children to balloons which emit mournful sounds when deflating) and as a spreading—like the flattening out of the full breasts of a woman who is lying on her back.

In the slimy substance which dissolves into itself there is a visible resistance, like the refusal of an individual who does not want to be annihilated in the whole of being, and at the same time a softness pushed to its ultimate limit. For the *soft* [*mou*] is merely an annihilation which has halted halfway; the soft is what furnishes us with the best image of our own destructive power and its limitations. The slowness of the disappearance of the slimy drop in the bosom of the whole is interpreted first as *softness*, which is like a retarded annihilation and seems to be playing for time, but this softness lasts up to the end; the drop is sucked into the slimy substance. This phenomenon gives rise to several characteristics of the slimy. First it is *soft* to touch. Throw water on the ground; it *runs*. Throw a slimy substance; it

---

* But the slimy has mysteriously preserved *all* fluidity in slow motion; it must not be confused with *purées* where fluidity, roughly delineated, undergoes abrupt cascadings and stoppages and where the substance after a preliminary tendency to flow, tumbles abruptly head over heels.

stretches itself out, it spreads itself, it flattens itself out, it is *soft;* touch the slimy: it does not flee, it yields. There is in the very fact that we cannot grasp water a pitiless hardness which gives it a secret meaning of being *metal;* finally it is incompressible like steel. The slimy is compressible. It gives us at first the impression that it is a being which can be *possessed.* On the one hand, its sliminess, its adherence to itself prevent it from escaping; I can take it in my hands, separate a certain quantity of honey or of pitch from the rest in the jar, and with it *create* an individual object by a continuous creation; but on the other hand, the softness of this substance which is squashed in my hands gives me the impression that I am perpetually *destroying* it.

Actually we have here the image of destruction-creation. The slimy is *docile.* Only at the very moment when I believe that I possess it, behold, by a curious reversal, *it* possesses me. Here appears its essential character: its softness is sucking. If an object which I hold in my hands is solid, I can let go when I please; its inertia symbolizes for me my total power; I give it its foundation, but it does not furnish any foundation for me; the for-itself takes up the in-itself and raises it to the dignity of the in-itself without being compromised, but always remaining an assimilating and creative power. It is the for-itself which absorbs the in-itself. In other words, possession asserts the primacy of the for-itself in the synthetic being "in-itself-for-itself." Yet here is the slimy reversing the relationship; the for-itself is suddenly *compromised.* I start to remove my hands, I want to let go of the slimy and it sticks to me, it sucks at me. Its mode of being is neither the reassuring inertia of the solid nor a dynamism like that in water which is exhausted in fleeing from me. It is a soft, yielding action, a moist and feminine sucking, it lives obscurely under my fingers, and I feel it like a vertigo; it attracts me to it as the bottom of an abyss might attract me. There is something like a tactile fascination in the slimy. I am no longer the master in *halting* the process of appropriation. It continues. In one sense it is like the supreme docility of the possessed, the fidelity of a dog who *gives himself* even when one does not want him any longer, and in another sense there is underneath this docility a surreptitious appropriation of the possessor by the possessed.

Here we can see the symbol which abruptly discloses itself:

there is a sort of virulent possession; there is a possibility that
the in-itself might absorb the for-itself; that is, that a being
might be constituted in a manner just the reverse of the "in-itself-
for-itself," and that the in-itself would pull the for-itself into its
contingency, into its externality of indifference, into its foundationless existence. At this instant I suddenly grasp the snare of
the slimy: it is a fluidity which holds me and which compromises me; I cannot *slide* on this slime, all its suction holds me
back; it cannot slide over me, it clings to me like a leech. The
sliding however is not simply denied as in the case of the solid;
it is *degraded*. The slimy seems to lend itself, it invites me; for
the surface slime at rest is not noticeably distinct from a sheet of
very dense liquid. But it is a snare. The sliding is *sucked* in by
the slippery substance, and it leaves its traces upon me. The
slime is like a liquid seen in a nightmare, where all its properties
are animated by a sort of life and turn back against me. Slime
is the revenge of the in-itself. A gently-sweet [*douceâtre*] feminine revenge which will be symbolized on another level by the
quality "sweetish." This is why the sweetness to the taste—an
indelible sweetness, which remains indefinitely in the mouth
even after swallowing—perfectly completes the essence of the
slimy. A sweetish sliminess is the ideal of the slimy; it symbolizes the succulent death of the for-itself (like that of the wasp
which sinks into the jam and drowns in it).

But at the same time the slimy is *myself*, by the very fact that
I delineate an appropriation of the slimy substance. That sucking
of the slimy which I feel on my hands adumbrates a kind of
continuity of the slimy substance with myself. These long, soft
strands of substance which drip from me to the slimy surface
(when, for example, I plunge my hand into it and then pull it
out again) symbolize my sinking into the slime. And the hysteresis, which I observe in the fusion of these strands with the surface, symbolizes the resistance of my being to absorption into
the in-itself. If I dive into the water, if I plunge into it, I experience no discomfort, for I do not have any fear whatsoever that
I may dissolve in it; I remain a solid in its liquidity. If I sink in
the slimy, I feel that I am going to be lost in it; that is, that I may
dissolve in the slime precisely because the slimy is in process of
solidification. The doughy [*pâteux*] would present the same
aspect as the slimy from this point of view, but it does not fascinate, it does not compromise because it is inert. In the very ap-

prehension of the slimy there is a sticky substance, compromising and without equilibrium, like the haunting dread of a *metamorphosis*.

To touch the slimy is to risk being dissolved in sliminess. Now this dissolution by itself is frightening enough, because it is the absorption of the for-itself by the in-itself, as ink is absorbed by a blotter. But it is also frightening in that the metamorphosis is not just into a thing but into slime. Even if I could conceive of a liquefaction of myself (that is, a transformation of my being into water) I would not be inordinately affected because water is the symbol of consciousness—its movement, its fluidity, its continuity, its perpetual flight—everything in it recalls the for-itself; to such an extent that psychologists who first noted the characteristic of *duration* of consciousness (James, Bergson) have often compared it to a river. A river best evokes the image of the constant interpenetration of the parts by a whole and their perpetual dissociation and adaptability.

But the slimy offers a horrible image; it is horrible in itself for a consciousness to *become slimy*. This is because the being of the slimy is a soft clinging, there is a surreptitious complicity of its parts with each other, a vague, soft effort by each to individualize itself, followed by a falling back and flattening out that is emptied of the individual, sucked in on all sides by the substance. A consciousness which became slimy would be transformed by the sticking together of its ideas. From the time of our emergence into the world, we are haunted by the image of a consciousness which would launch forth into the future, toward a projection of self, and which, at the very moment when it was conscious of arriving there, would be surreptitiously and invisibly held back by the suction of the past and which would have to be present for its own slow dissolution in this past which it was fleeing, be present for the invasion of its project by a thousand parasites until its final complete loss of itself. The "flight of ideas" found in the psychosis of influence gives us the best image of this horrible condition. But what is it then which is expressed by this fear on the ontological level if not exactly the flight of the for-itself before the in-itself of facticity; that is, temporalization. The horror of the slimy is the horror that time might become slimy, that facticity might progress continually and insensibly and absorb the for-itself which *exists it*. It is the fear, not of death, not of the pure in-itself, not of nothingness,

but of a particular type of being, which does not actually exist
any more than the in-itself-for-itself and which is only *represented* by the slimy. It is an ideal being which I reject with all my
strength and which haunts me as *value* haunts my being, an
ideal being in which the foundationless in-itself has priority
over the for-itself. We shall call it an *Antivalue*.

Thus in the project of appropriating the slimy, the sliminess is
revealed suddenly as a symbol of an antivalue: it is a type of being not realized but threatening which perpetually haunts consciousness as the constant danger which it is fleeing, and hence
suddenly transforms the project of appropriation into a project
of flight. Something has appeared which is not the result of any
prior experience but only of the pre-ontological comprehension
of the in-itself and the for-itself, and this is the peculiar meaning of the slimy. In one sense it is an experience since sliminess
is an intuitive discovery; in another sense it is like the discovery of an adventure of being. Henceforth for the for-itself there
appears a new danger, a threatening mode of being which must
be avoided, a concrete category which it will discover everywhere. The slimy does not symbolize any psychic attitude *a priori;* it manifests a certain relation of being with itself and this
relation has originally a psychic quality because I have discovered it as an adumbration of appropriation and because the sliminess has reflected my image. Thus I am enriched from my first
contact with the slimy, by a valid ontological pattern beyond the
distinction between psychic and non-psychic, which will interpret the ontological meaning of all the existents of a certain category, this category emerging, moreover, like an empty skeletal
framework *before* the experience with different kinds of sliminess. I have projected it into the world by my original project
when faced with the slimy; it is an objective structure of the
world and at the same time an antivalue; that is, it determines
a region where slimy objects will find their place. Henceforth
each time that an object will manifest to me this relation of
being, whether it is a matter of a handshake, of a smile, or of a
thought, it will be apprehended by definition as slimy; that is,
beyond its phenomenal context, it will appear to me as constituting, along with pitch, glue, honey, etc., the great ontological
region of sliminess.

Conversely, to the extent that the *this* which I wish to appropriate, represents the entire world, the slimy, from my first

intuitive contact, appears to me rich with a host of obscure meanings and references which transcend it. The slimy is revealed in itself as "much more than the slimy." From the moment of its appearance it transcends all distinctions between psychic and physical, between the brute existent and the meanings of the world; it is a possible meaning of being. The first experience which the infant can have with the slimy enriches him psychologically and morally; he will not need to reach adulthood to discover the kind of adhesive baseness which we figuratively name "slimy"; it is there near him in the very sliminess of honey or of glue. What we say concerning the slimy holds for all the objects which surround the child. The simple revelation of their matter extends his horizon to the extreme limits of being and bestows upon him at the same time a set of clues for deciphering the being of all human facts. This certainly does not mean that he *knows* from the start the "ugliness," the "characteristics," or the "beauties" of existence. He is merely in possession of all the *meanings of being* of which ugliness and beauty, attitudes, psychic traits, sexual relations, etc. will never be more than particular exemplifications. The gluey, the sticky, the misty, etc., holes in the sand and in the earth, caves, the light, the night, etc.—all reveal to him modes of pre-psychic and pre-sexual being which he will spend the rest of his life explicating. There is no such thing as an "innocent" child. We will gladly recognize along with the Freudians the innumerable relations existing between sexuality and certain matter and forms in the child's environment. But we do not understand by this that a sexual instinct already constituted has charged them with a sexual significance. On the contrary it seems to us that this matter and these forms are apprehended in themselves, and they reveal to the child the for-itself's modes of being and relations to being which will illuminate and shape his sexuality.

To cite only one example—many psychoanalysts have been struck by the attraction which all kinds of holes exert on the child (whether holes in the sand or in the ground, crypts, caves, hollows, or whatever), and they have explained this attraction either by the anal character of infant sexuality, or by prenatal shock, or by a presentiment of the adult sexual act. But we cannot accept any of these explanations. The idea of "birth trauma" is highly fanciful. The comparison of the hole to the feminine sexual organ supposes in the child an experience which he cannot possibly have had or a presentiment which we cannot jus-

tify. As for the child's anal sexuality, we would not think of
denying it; but if it is going to clarify the holes which he encounters in the perceptual field and charge them with symbolism, then it is necessary that the child apprehend his anus as a
hole. To put it more clearly, the child would have to apprehend
the essence of the hole, of the orifice, as corresponding to the
sensation which he receives from his anus. But we have demonstrated sufficiently the subjective character of "my relation with
my body" so that we can understand the impossibility of saying
that the child apprehends a particular part of his body as an objective structure of the universe. It is only to another person
that the anus appears as an orifice. The child himself can never
have experienced it as such; even the intimate care which the
mother gives the child could not reveal the anus in this aspect,
since the anus as an erogenous or sensitive zone is not provided
with tactile nerve endings. On the contrary it is only through
another—through the words which the mother uses to designate
the child's body—that he learns that his anus is a *hole*. It is therefore the objective nature of the hole perceived in the world
which is going to clarify for him the objective structure and the
meaning of the anal zone and which will give a transcendent
meaning to the erogenous sensations which hitherto he has limited to merely "existing." In itself then the *hole* is the symbol of
a mode of being which existential psychoanalysis must elucidate.

We cannot make such a detailed investigation here. One can
see at once, however, that the hole is originally presented as a
nothingness "to be filled" with my own flesh; the child cannot re-
strain himself from putting his finger or his whole arm into the
hole. It presents itself to me as the empty image of myself. I
have only to shape myself to it in order to make myself exist in
the world which awaits me. The ideal of the hole is then an exca-
vation which can be carefully molded about my flesh in such a
manner that by squeezing myself into it and fitting myself
snugly inside it, I shall contribute to making a fullness of being
exist in the world. Thus to plug up a hole means originally to
make a sacrifice of my body in order that the plenitude of being
may exist; that is, to subject the passion of the for-itself so as to
shape, to perfect, and to preserve the totality of the in-itself.*

Here at its origin we grasp one of the most fundamental

* We should note as well the importance of the opposite tendency, to pierce
holes, which in itself demands an existential analysis.

tendencies of human reality—the tendency to fill. We shall meet
with this tendency again in the adolescent and in the adult. A
good part of our life is passed in plugging up holes, in filling
empty places, in realizing and symbolically establishing a plenitude. The child recognizes as the results of his first experiences
that he himself has holes. When he puts his fingers in his
mouth, he tries to wall up the holes in his face; he expects that
his finger will merge with his lips and the roof of his mouth and
block up the buccal orifice as one fills the crack in a wall with
cement; he seeks again the density, the uniform and spherical
plenitude of Parmenidean being; if he sucks his thumb, it is
precisely in order to dissolve it, to transform it into a sticky paste
which will seal the hole of his mouth. This tendency is certainly
one of the most fundamental among those which serve as the
basis for the act of eating; nourishment is the "cement" which
will seal the mouth; to eat is among other things to be filled up.

It is only from this standpoint that we can pass on to sexuality.
The obscenity of the feminine sex is that of everything which
"gapes open." It is *an appeal* to being as all holes are. In herself
woman appeals to a strange flesh which is to transform her into
a fullness of being by penetration and dissolution. Conversely
woman senses her condition as an appeal precisely because she
is "in the form of a hole." This is the true origin of Adler's complex. Beyond any doubt her sex is a mouth and a voracious
mouth which devours the penis—a fact which can easily lead
to the idea of castration. The amorous act is the castration of
the man; but this is above all because sex is a hole. We have to
do here with a *pre-sexual* stratum which will become one of the
components of sexuality as an empirical, complex, human attitude but which far from deriving its origin from the sexed being
has nothing in common with basic sexuality, the nature of
which we have explained already.* Nevertheless the experience
with the hole, when the infant sees the reality, includes the ontological presentiment of sexual experience in general; it is with
his flesh that the child stops up the hole and the hole, before all
sexual specification, is an obscene expectation, an appeal to the
flesh.

We can see the importance which the elucidation of these immediate and concrete existential categories will assume for existential psychoanalysis. In this way we can apprehend the very

* See above, p. 211.

general projects of human reality. But what chiefly interests the psychoanalyst is to determine the free project of the unique person in terms of the individual relation which unites him to these various symbols of being. I can love slimy contacts, have a horror of holes, etc. That does not mean that for me the slimy, the greasy, a hole, etc. have lost their general ontological meaning, but on the contrary that *because* of this meaning, I determine myself in this or that manner in relation to them. If the slimy is indeed the symbol of a being in which the for-itself is absorbed by the in-itself, what kind of a person am I if in encountering others, I love the slimy? To what fundamental project of myself am I referred if I want to explain this love of an in-itself which is equivocal and which swallows me up? In this way *tastes* do not remain irreducible givens; if one knows how to question them, they reveal to us the fundamental projects of the person. Down to even our alimentary preferences they all have a meaning. We can account for this fact if we will reflect that each taste is presented, not as an absurd *datum* which we must excuse but as an obvious value. If I like the taste of garlic, it seems irrational to me that other people cannot like it.

To eat is to appropriate by destruction; it is at the same time to be filled up with a certain being. And this being is given as a synthesis of temperature, density, and flavor proper. In a word this synthesis signifies *a certain being;* and when we eat, we do not limit ourselves to *knowing* certain qualities of this being through taste; by tasting them we appropriate them. Taste is assimilation; by the very act of biting the tooth reveals the density of a body which it is transforming into masticated food. Thus the synthetic intuition of food is in itself an assimilative destruction. It reveals to me the being which I am going to make my flesh. Henceforth, what I accept or what I reject with disgust is the very being of that existent, or if you prefer, the totality of the food proposes to me a certain mode of being of the being which I accept or refuse. This totality is organized as a form in which less intense qualities of density and of temperature are effaced behind the flavor proper which *expresses* them. The *sweetish,* for example, *expresses* the slimy when we eat a spoonful of honey or molasses, just as an analytical function expresses a geometric curve. This means that all qualities which are not strictly speaking the flavor but which are melted, buried in the flavor, represent the *matter* of the flavor. (The piece of chocolate which at first offers a resistance to my tooth, soon abruptly gives way and crumbles; its resistance first, then its crumbling *is* chocolate.) In addition they are united to certain temporal characteristics of flavor; that is, to its mode of temporalization. Certain tastes give themselves all at once, some are like delayed-action fuses, some release themselves by degrees, certain ones dwindle slowly until they disappear, and still others vanish at the very moment one thinks to possess them. These qualities are organized along with density and temperature; in addition on another level they express the visual aspect of the food. If I eat a pink cake, the taste of it is pink; the light sweetish perfume, the oiliness of the butter cream *are* the pink. Thus I eat the pink as I see the sweetish. We conclude that flavor, due to this fact, has a complex architecture and differentiated matter; it is this structured matter—which represents for us a particular type of being—that we can assimilate or reject with nausea, according to our original project. It is not a matter of indifference whether we like oysters or clams, snails or shrimp, if only we know how to unravel the existential significance of these foods.

Generally speaking there is no irreducible taste or inclination. They all represent a certain appropriative choice of being. It is up to existential psychoanalysis to compare and classify them. Ontology abandons us here; it has merely enabled us to determine the ultimate ends of human reality, its fundamental possibilities, and the value which haunts it. Each human reality is at the same time a direct project to metamorphose its own for-itself into an in-itself-for-itself and a project of the appropriation of the world as a totality of being-in-itself, in the form of a fundamental quality. Every human reality is a passion in that it projects losing itself so as to found being and at the same time to constitute the in-itself which escapes contingency by being its own foundation, the *ens causa sui*, which religions call God. Thus the passion of man is the reverse of that of Christ, for man loses himself as man in order that God may be born. But the idea of God is contradictory and we lose ourselves in vain. Man is a useless passion.

*Being and Nothingness*, 557–615.

# V

—————•—————

## Existential Metaphysics

We are finally able to reach conclusions. The for-itself is nothing but the pure nihilation of the in-itself; it is like a hole of being at the heart of Being. One may be reminded here of that convenient fiction by which certain popularizers are accustomed to illustrate the principle of the conservation of energy. If, they say, a single one of the atoms which constitute the universe were annihilated, there would result a catastrophe which would extend to the entire universe, and this would be, in particular, the end of the Earth and of the solar system. This metaphor can help us here. The for-itself is like a tiny nihilation which has its origin at the heart of Being; and this nihilation is sufficient to cause a total upheaval to *happen* to the in-itself. This upheaval is the world. The for-itself has no reality save that of being the nihilation of being. Its sole qualification comes to it from the fact that it is the nihilation of an individual and particular in-itself and not of a being in general. The for-itself is not nothingness in general but a particular privation; it constitutes itself as the privation of *this being*. Therefore we have no business asking about the way in which the for-itself can be united with the in-itself since the for-itself is in no way an autonomous substance. As a nihilation *it is made-to-be* by the in-itself; as an internal negation it must by means of the in-itself make known to itself what it is not and consequently what it has to be. If the *cogito* necessarily leads outside the self, if consciousness is a slippery slope on which one cannot take one's stand without immediately finding oneself tipped outside onto being-in-itself, this is because consciousness does not have by itself any sufficiency of being as an absolute subjectivity; from the start it refers to the thing.

For consciousness there is no being except for this precise obligation to be a revealing intuition of something. What does this

353

mean except that consciousness is the Platonic *Other*? We
may recall the fine description which the Stranger in the
*Sophist* gives of this "other,"* which can be apprehended only
"as in a dream," which has no being except its being-other (*i.e.*,
which enjoys only a borrowed being), which if considered by itself disappears and which takes on a marginal existence only
if one fixes his look on being, this other which is exhausted in being other than itself and other than being. It even seems that
Plato perceived the dynamic character which the otherness of
the other presented in relation to itself, for in certain passages
he sees in this the origin of motion. But he could have gone still
further; he would have seen then that the other, or relative non-
being, could have a semblance of existence only by virtue of
consciousness. To be other than being is to be self-consciousness
in the unity of the temporalizing *ekstasis*. Indeed what can the
otherness be if not that game of musical chairs played by the reflected and the reflecting which . . . [is] at the heart of the for-
itself? For the only way in which the other can exist as other
is to be consciousness (of) being other. Otherness is, in fact, an
internal negation, and only a consciousness can be constituted
as an internal negation. Every other conception of otherness
will amount to positing it as an in-itself—that is, establishing
between it and being an external relation which would necessitate the presence of a witness so as to establish that the other
is other than the in-itself. However the other cannot be other
without emanating from being; in this respect it is relative to the
in-itself. But neither can it be other without *making itself other;*
otherwise its otherness would become a given and therefore a
*being* capable of being considered in-itself. Insofar as it is relative to the in-itself, the other is affected with facticity; insofar
as it makes itself, it is an absolute. This is what we pointed out
when we said that the for-itself is not the foundation of its being-
as-nothingness-of-being but that it perpetually founds its noth-
ingness-of-being. Thus the for-itself is an absolute *Unselbständig*,
what we have called a non-substantial absolute. Its reality is
purely *interrogative*. If it can posit questions this is because it is
itself always *in question;* its being is never *given* but *interrogated*
since it is always separated from itself by the nothingness of
otherness. The for-itself is always in suspense because its being

* "The other" in this passage must of course not be confused with "The Other"
discussed in connection with the problem of human relationships.—Trans.

is a perpetual reprieve. If it could ever join with its being, then the otherness would at the same time disappear and along with it possibles, knowledge, the world. Thus the *ontological* problem of knowledge is resolved by the affirmation of the ontological primacy of the in-itself over the for-itself.

But this immediately gives rise to a *metaphysical* interrogation. The emergence of the for-itself from the in-itself is in no way comparable to the *dialectical* genesis of the Platonic Other from being. "Being" and "other" are, for Plato, *genera*. But we, on the contrary, have seen that being is an individual venture. Similarly the appearance of the for-itself is the absolute event which comes to being. There is therefore room here for a *metaphysical problem which could be formulated thus:* Why does the for-itself emerge from being? We, indeed, apply the term "metaphysical" to the study of individual processes which have given birth to *this* world as a concrete and particular totality. In this sense metaphysics is to ontology as history is to sociology. We have seen that it would be absurd to ask why being is other, that the question can have meaning only within the limits of a for-itself and that it even supposes the ontological priority of nothingness over being. It can be posited only if combined with another question which is externally analogous and yet very different: Why is it that *there is* being? But we know now that we must carefully distinguish between these two questions. The first is devoid of meaning: all the "Whys" in fact are subsequent to being and presuppose it. Being is without reason, without cause, and without necessity; the very definition of being presents to us its original contingency. To the second question we have already replied, for it is not posited on the metaphysical level but on that of ontology: "There is" being because the for-itself is such that there is being. The character of a *phenomenon* comes to being through the for-itself.

But while questions on the origin of being or on the origin of the world are either devoid of meaning or receive a reply within the actual province of ontology, the case is not the same for the origin of the for-itself. The for-itself is such that it has the right to turn back on itself toward its own origin. The being by which the "Why" comes into being has the right to posit its own "Why" since it is itself an interrogation, a "Why." To this question ontology cannot reply, for the problem here is to explain an event, not to describe the structures of a being. At most it can

355

point out that the nothingness which *is made-to-be* by the in-itself is not a simple emptiness devoid of meaning. The meaning of the nothingness of the nihilation is to-be-made-to-be in order to found being. Ontology furnishes us two pieces of information which serve as the basis for metaphysics: first that every process of a foundation of the self is a rupture in the identity-of-being of the in-itself, a withdrawal by being in relation to itself and the appearance of presence to self or consciousness. It is only by making itself for-itself that being can aspire to be the cause of itself. Consciousness as the nihilation of being appears therefore as one stage in a progression toward the immanence of causality—*i.e.*, toward being a self-cause. The progression, however, stops there as the result of the insufficiency of being in the for-itself. The temporalization of consciousness is not an ascending progress toward the dignity of the *causa sui;* it is a surface flow whose origin is, on the contrary, the impossibility of being a self-cause. Also the *ens causa sui* remains as the *lacked,* the adumbration of an impossible *vertical* transcending which by its very non-existence conditions the movement of consciousness on the level; in the same way the vertical attraction which the moon exercises on the ocean has for its result the horizontal displacement which is the tide. The second clue which metaphysics can draw from ontology is that the for-itself is *effectively* a perpetual project of founding itself *qua* being and a perpetual failure of this project. Presence to itself with the various directions of its nihilation (the *ekstatic* nihilation of the three temporal dimensions, the twin nihilation of the dyad reflected-reflecting) represents the primary upsurge of this project; reflection represents the splitting of the project which turns back on itself in order to found itself at least as a project, and the aggravation of the nihilating hiatus by the failure of this project itself. "Doing" and "having," the cardinal categories of human reality, are immediately or mediately reduced to the project of being. Finally the plurality of projects *can* be interpreted as human reality's final attempt to found itself, resulting in the radical separation of being and the consciousness of being.

Thus ontology teaches us two things: (1) If the in-itself were to found itself, it could attempt to do so only by making itself consciousness; that is, the concept of *causa sui* includes within it that of presence to self—*i.e.*, the nihilating decompression of being; (2) Consciousness is *in fact* a project of founding itself;

that is, of attaining to the dignity of the in-itself-for-itself or in-itself-as-self-cause. But we cannot derive anything further from this. Nothing allows us to affirm on the ontological level that the nihilation of the in-itself in for-itself has for its meaning—from the start and at the very heart of the in-itself—the project of being its own self-cause. Quite the contrary. Ontology here comes up against a profound contradiction since it is through the for-itself that the possibility of a foundation comes to the world. In order to be a project of founding itself, the in-itself would of necessity have to be originally a presence to itself—*i.e.*, it would have to be already consciousness. Ontology will therefore limit itself to declaring that *everything takes place as if* the in-itself in a project to found itself gave itself the modification of the for-itself. It is up to metaphysics to form the *hypotheses* which will allow us to conceive of this process as the absolute event which comes to crown the individual venture which is the existence of being. It is evident that these hypotheses will remain hypotheses since we cannot expect either further validation or invalidation. What will assure their *validity* is only the possibility which they will offer us of unifying the *givens* of ontology. This unification naturally must not be constituted in the perspective of an historical becoming since temporality comes into being through the for-itself. There would be therefore no sense in asking what being was *before* the appearance of the for-itself. But metaphysics must nevertheless attempt to determine the nature and the meaning of this prehistoric process, the source of all history, which is the articulation of the individual venture (or existence of the in-itself) with the absolute event (or emergence of the for-itself). In particular the task belongs to the metaphysician of deciding whether the movement is or is not an initial "attempt" on the part of the in-itself to found itself and to determine what are the relations of this movement as a "malady of being" with the for-itself as a more profound malady pushed to nihilation.

It remains for us to consider a second problem: . . . If the in-itself and the for-itself are two modalities of *being*, is there not a hiatus at the very core of the idea of being? And is our understanding of it not severed into two incommunicable parts by the very fact that its extension is constituted by two radically heterogeneous classes? What is there in common between the being which is what it is, and the being which is what it is not and which is not what it is? What can help us here, however, is the conclusion of our preceding inquiry. We have just shown in fact that the in-itself and the for-itself are not juxtaposed. Quite the contrary, the for-itself without the in-itself is a kind of abstraction; it could not exist any more than a color could exist without form or a sound without pitch and without timbre. A consciousness which would be consciousness *of* nothing would be an absolute nothing. But if consciousness is bound to the in-itself by an *internal* relation, doesn't this mean that it is articulated with the in-itself so as to constitute a totality, and is it not this totality which would be given the name *being* or reality? Doubtless the for-itself is a nihilation, but as a nihilation it *is;* and it is in *a priori* unity with the in-itself. Thus the Greeks were accustomed to distinguish cosmic reality, which they called Τὸ πᾶν, from the totality constituted by this and by the infinite void which surrounded it—a totality which they called Τὸ ὅλον. To be sure, we have been able to call the for-itself a nothing and to declare that there is "outside of the in-itself" *nothing* except a reflection of this nothing which is itself polarized and defined by the in-itself—inasmuch as the for-itself is precisely the nothingness of *this in-itself*. But here as in Greek philosophy a question is raised: which shall we call *real*? To which shall we attribute *being*? To the cosmos or to what we called Τὸ ὅλον? To the pure in-itself or to the in-itself surrounded by that shell of nothingness which we have designated by the name of the for-itself?

But if we are to consider total being as constituted by the synthetic organization of the in-itself and of the for-itself, are we not going to encounter again the difficulty which we wished to avoid? And as for that hiatus which we revealed in the concept of being, are we not going to meet it at present in the existent itself? What definition indeed are we to give to an existent which as in-itself would be what it is and as for-itself would be what it is not?

If we wish to resolve these difficulties, we must take into account what is required of an existent if it is to be considered as a totality: it is necessary that the diversity of its structures be held within a unitary synthesis in such a way that each of them considered apart is only an abstraction. And certainly consciousness considered apart is only an abstraction; but the in-itself has no need of the for-itself in order to be; the "passion" of the for-itself only makes *there be* in-itself. The *phenomenon* of in-itself is an abstraction without consciousness but its *being* is not an abstraction.

If we wish to conceive of a synthetic organization such that the for-itself is inseparable from the in-itself and conversely such that the in-itself is indissolubly bound to the for-itself, we must conceive of this synthesis in such a way that the in-itself would receive its existence from the nihilation which caused there to be consciousness of it. What does this mean if not that the indissoluble totality of in-itself and for-itself is conceivable only in the form of a being which is its own "self-cause"? It is this being and no other which could be valid absolutely as that δλον of which we spoke earlier. And if we can raise the question of the being of the for-itself articulated in the in-itself, it is because we define ourselves *a priori* by means of a pre-ontological comprehension of the *ens causa sui*. Of course this *ens causa sui* is *impossible,* and the concept of it, as we have seen, includes a contradiction. Nevertheless the fact remains that since we raise the question of the being of the δλον by adopting the point of view of the *ens causa sui*, it is from this point of view that we must set about examining the credentials of this δλον. Has it not appeared due to the mere fact of the emergence of the for-itself, and is not the for-itself originally a project of being its own self-cause? Thus we begin to grasp the nature of total reality. Total being, the concept of which would not be cleft by a hiatus and which would nevertheless not exclude the nihilating-nihilated being of the for-itself, that being whose existence would be a unitary synthesis of the in-itself and of consciousness—this ideal being would be the in-itself founded by the for-itself and identical with the for-itself which founds it—*i.e.*, the *ens causa sui*. But precisely because we adopt the point of view of this ideal being in order to judge the *real* being which we call δλον, we must establish that the real is an abortive effort to attain to the dignity of the self-cause. Everything happens as if the world, man, and man-in-the-world succeeded in realizing only a missing God [*Dieu manqué*]. Everything happens therefore as if the in-itself and the for-itself were presented in a state of disintegration in relation to an ideal synthesis. Not that the integration has ever *taken place* but on the contrary precisely because it is always adumbrated and always impossible.

It is this perpetual failure which explains both the indissolubility of the in-itself and of the for-itself and at the same time their relative independence. Similarly when the unity of the cerebral functions is disrupted, phenomena are produced which simultaneously present a relative autonomy and which at the same time can be manifested only on the ground of the disintegration of a totality. It is this failure which explains the hiatus which we encounter both in the concept of being and in the existent. If it is impossible to pass from the notion of being-in-itself to that of being-for-itself and to reunite them in a common genus, this is because the *actual transition* from the one to the other and their reuniting cannot be effected. We know that for Spinoza and for Hegel, for example, if a synthesis is arrested before its completion and the terms fixed in a relative dependence and at the same time in a relative independence, then the synthesis is constituted at once as an error. For example, it is in the notion of a sphere that for Spinoza the rotation of a semicircle around its diameter finds its justification and its meaning. But if we imagine that the notion of a sphere is on principle out of reach, then the phenomenon of the rotation of the semicircle becomes *false*. It has been decapitated; the idea of rotation and the idea of a circle are held together without being able to be united in a synthesis which transcends them and justifies them; the one remains irreducible to the other. This is precisely what happens here. We shall say therefore that the $\delta\lambda o\nu$ we are considering is like a decapitated notion in perpetual disintegration. And it is in the form of a disintegrated whole that it presents itself to us in its ambiguity—that is, so that one can *ad libitum* insist on the dependence of the beings under consideration or on their independence. There is here a transition which is not completed, a short circuit. . . .

This question of the totality, however, does not belong to the province of ontology. For ontology the only regions of being which can be elucidated are those of the in-itself, of the for-itself, and the ideal region of the "self-cause." For ontology it makes no difference whether we consider the for-itself articulated in the in-itself as a well-marked *duality* or as a disintegrated being. It is up to metaphysics to decide which will be more profitable for knowledge (in particular for phenomenological psychology, for anthropology, etc.): to deal with a being which we shall call the *phenomenon* and which will be provided with two dimensions of being, the dimension in-itself and the dimension for-itself (from this point of view there would be *only one* phenomenon: the world), just as in the physics of Einstein it has been found advantageous to speak of an *event* conceived as having spatial dimensions and a temporal dimension and as determining its place in a space-time; or, on the other hand will it remain preferable after all to preserve the ancient duality "consciousness-being." The only observation which ontology can hazard here is that in case it appears useful to employ the new notion of a phenomenon as a disintegrated totality, it will be necessary to speak of it *in terms both* of immanence and transcendence. The danger, in fact, would be of falling into either a doctrine of pure immanence (Husserlian idealism) or into one of pure transcendence which would look on the *phenomenon* as a new kind of *object*. But immanence will be always limited by the phenomenon's dimension in-itself, and transcendence will be limited by its dimension for-itself.

After having decided the question of the origin for the for-itself and of the nature of the phenomenon of the world, the metaphysician will be able to attack various problems of primary importance, in particular that of action. Action, in fact, is to be considered simultaneously on the plane of the for-itself and on that of the in-itself, for it involves a project which has an immanent origin and which determines a modification in the being of the transcendent. It would be of no use to declare that the action modifies only the phenomenal appearance of the thing. If the phenomenal appearance of a cup can be modified up to the annihilation of the cup *qua* cup, and if the being of the cup is nothing but its *quality,* then the action envisaged must be capable of modifying the very being of the cup. The problem of action therefore supposes the elucidation of the transcendent efficacy of consciousness, and it puts us on the path of its true ontological relation with being. It reveals to us also, as a result of the repercussions of an act in the world, a relation of being with being which, although apprehended externally by the physicist, is neither pure externality nor immanence but which refers us to the notion of the Gestalt *form*. It is therefore in these terms that one might attempt a metaphysics of nature.

*Being and Nothingness, 617–625.*

# VI

---

## *Existential Ethics*

Ontology itself cannot formulate ethical precepts. It is concerned solely with what is, and we cannot possibly derive imperatives from ontology's indicatives. It does, however, allow us to catch a glimpse of what sort of ethics will assume its responsibilities when confronted with a *human reality in situation*. Ontology has revealed to us, in fact, the origin and the nature of *value;* we have seen that value is the *lack* in relation to which the for-itself determines its being as *a lack*. By the very fact that the for-itself *exists*, as we have seen, value emerges to haunt its being-for-itself. It follows that the various tasks of the for-itself can be made the subject-matter of an existential psychoanalysis, for they all aim at producing the synthesis which is lacking of consciousness and being in the form of value or self-cause. Thus existential psychoanalysis is *moral description,* for it presents to us the ethical meaning of various human projects. It indicates to us the necessity of abandoning the psychology of interest along with any utilitarian interpretation of human behavior—by revealing to us the *ideal* meaning of all human attitudes. These meanings are beyond egoism and altruism, beyond also any behavior which is called *disinterested*. Man makes himself man in order to be God, and selfness considered from this point of view can appear to be an egoism; but precisely because there is no common measure between human reality and the self-cause which it wants to be, one could just as well say that man loses himself in order that the self-cause may exist. We will consider then that all human existence is a passion, the famous *self-interest* being only one way freely chosen among others to realize this passion.

But the principal result of existential psychoanalysis must

be to make us repudiate the *spirit of seriousness*. The spirit of seriousness has two characteristics: it considers values as transcendent givens independent of human subjectivity, and it transfers the quality of "desirable" from the ontological structure of things to their simple material constitution. For the spirit of seriousness, for example, *bread* is desirable because it is *necessary* to live (a value written in an intelligible heaven) and because bread *is* nourishing. The result of the serious attitude, which as we know rules the world, is that the symbolic values of things are absorbed by their empirical idiosyncrasy as ink by a blotter; it brings to the fore the opacity of the object desired and posits it in itself as a desirable which is irreducible. Thus we are already on the moral plane but concurrently on that of bad faith, for it is an ethics which is ashamed of itself and does not dare speak its name. It has obscured all its goals in order to free itself from anguish. Man pursues being blindly by hiding from himself the free project which is this pursuit. He makes himself such that he is *expected* by all the tasks placed along his way. Objects are mute demands, and he is nothing in himself but the passive obedience to these demands.

Existential psychoanalysis will reveal to man the real goal of his pursuit, which is being as a synthetic fusion of the in-itself with the for-itself; existential psychoanalysis will acquaint man with his passion. In truth many have practiced this psychoanalysis on themselves and have not waited to learn its principles in order to employ them as a means of deliverance and salvation. Many, in fact, know that the goal of their pursuit is being; and to the extent that they possess this knowledge, they refrain from appropriating things for their own sake and try to realize the symbolic appropriation of their being-in-itself. But to the extent that this attempt still shares in the spirit of seriousness, to the extent they still believe that their mission of bringing the in-itself-for-itself into existence is engraved in things, they are condemned to despair; for they discover at the same time that all human activities are equivalent (for they all tend to sacrifice man in order that the self-cause may emerge) and that all are on principle doomed to failure. Thus it amounts to the same thing whether one gets drunk alone or is a leader of nations. If one of these activities is superior to the other, this will not be because of its real goal but because of the degree of consciousness which it possesses of its ideal goal; and in this case it will be the quietism of the solitary drunkard which is superior to the vain agitation of the leader of nations.

But ontology and existential psychoanalysis (or the spontaneous and empirical application which men have always made of these disciplines) should reveal to the moral agent that he is *the being by whom values exist.* It is then that his freedom will become conscious of itself and will reveal itself in anguish as the unique source of value and the nothingness by which the *world* exists. As soon as freedom discovers the quest for being and the appropriation of the in-itself as *its own possibles,* it will apprehend by and in anguish that they are possibles only on the ground of the possibility of other possibles. But hitherto although possibles could be chosen and rejected *ad libitum,* the theme which made the unity of all choices of possibles was the value or the ideal presence of the *ens causa sui.* What will become of freedom if it turns its back upon this value? Will freedom carry this value along with it whatever it does and even in its very turning back upon the in-itself-for-itself? Will freedom be reapprehended from behind by the value which it wishes to contemplate? Or will freedom by the very fact that it apprehends itself as a freedom in relation to itself, be able to put an end to the reign of this value? In particular is it possible for freedom to take itself for a value as the source of all value, or must it necessarily be defined in relation to a transcendent value which haunts it? And in case it could will itself as its own possible and its determining value, what would this mean? A freedom which wills itself freedom is in fact a being-which-is-not-what-it-is and which-is-what-it-is-not, and which chooses as the ideal of being, being-what-it-is-not and not-being-what-it-is.

This freedom chooses then not to *recover* itself but to flee itself, not to coincide with itself but to be always at a distance *from* itself. What are we to understand by this being which wills to hold itself in awe, to be at a distance from itself? Is it a question of bad faith or of another fundamental attitude? And can one *live* this new aspect of being? In particular will freedom by taking itself for an end escape all *situation?* Or on the contrary, will it remain situated? Or will it situate itself so much the more precisely and the more individually as it projects itself further in anguish as a conditioned freedom and accepts more fully its responsibility as an existent by whom the world comes into being? All these questions, which refer us to a pure and not an accessory reflection, can find their reply only on the ethical plane. We shall devote to them a future work.*

*Being and Nothingness, 625–628.*

* Sartre is anticipating *L'homme*, the announced, but never published, sequel to *L'être et le néant*. The place of *Man* in Sartre's system seems to have been partly usurped by the Social Anthropology of *La critique de la raison dialectique* (see below, p. 421). There is one reference in this work to a theory of value, and this reference suggests that *St. Genet* (see below, p. 378) can be regarded as the first phase in the elaboration of this theory.—Ed.

# CONSCIOUSNESS AND LITERATURE

# I

*Art and Action*

## 1 POETRY AND PROSE

Human action, in the real world, is dominated by needs and urged on by the useful. In this sense it is a *means*. It passes unnoticed, and it is the result which counts. When I reach out my hand *in order to* pick up my pen, I have only a fleeting [*glissante*] consciousness of my gesture; it is the pen which I see. Thus man is alienated by his ends. Poetry reverses the relationship: the world and things become inessential, become a pretext for the act which becomes its own end. The vase is there so that the girl may perform the graceful act of filling it; the Trojan War, so that Hector and Achilles may engage in that heroic combat. Detached from its purpose, which becomes faint, the action becomes a display of prowess or a dance. Nevertheless, however indifferent he might have been to the success of the undertaking, the poet, before the nineteenth century, remained in harmony with society as a whole. He did not use language for the end which prose seeks, but he had the same confidence in it as the prose-writer.

With the coming of bourgeois society, the poet puts up a common front with the prose-writer to declare it unlivable. His function at any period is to create the myth of man, but he now passes from white magic to black magic. Man is still presented as the absolute end, but by his success he is now sucked into a society which is utilitarian. Success will no longer allow transition to the myth; failure is now required. By putting a stop to the infinite series of his projects, failure restores him to himself in his purity. The world, as always for the poet, remains inessential, but it is now there as a pretext for his defeat. The purpose of the thing is to return man to himself by blocking his route. Moreover, it is not a matter of arbitrarily introducing defeat and ruin into the course of the world, but rather of paying no attention to anything else. The human undertaking has two countenances: it is both success and failure. . . . The man of action sees one and the poet sees the other. When the instruments are broken and unutilizable, when plans are thwarted and efforts useless, the world appears with a childlike and terrible freshness, unsupported and pathless. It has the maximum reality because it is crushing for man, and since action always has general significance, defeat restores to things their particular reality. But a reversal takes place, and defeat when considered as the final end, is both a challenge to, and an appropriation of, this world. A challenge because man is *worth more* than what crushes him; he no longer challenges things in their slight reality, like the engineer or the captain, but, on the contrary, in their excessive reality, by his very existence as a victim. He is the remorse of the world. An appropriation because the world, in ceasing to be the tool of success, becomes the instrument of failure. So there is the world, traversed by an obscure purposiveness; it is its coefficient of adversity, which functions the more humanly, the more hostile it is to man. The defeat itself turns into salvation. Not that it provides us with access to some transcendent; it shifts on its own and is metamorphosed. Thus, for example, poetic language emerges out of the ruins of prose. If it is true that the world is a betrayal and that communication is impossible, then each word by itself recovers its individuality and becomes an instrument of our defeat and a receiver of the incommunicable. It is not that there is *another thing* to communicate; but the communication of prose having miscarried, it is the very meaning of the word which becomes the pure incommunicable. Thus, the failure of communication becomes a suggestion of the incommunicable, and the thwarted project of utilizing words is succeeded by the pure disinterested intuition of the word.

Poetry is the loser winning. And the genuine poet chooses to lose, even if he has to die, in order to win. I repeat that I am talking of contemporary poetry. History presents other forms of poetry. It is not my concern to show their relations with ours. Thus if anyone insists on speaking of the commitment of the poet, let it be said that he is the man who commits himself to losing. This is the deeper meaning of that tough luck, of that malediction, which he always claims for himself and which he always attributes to an intervention from without; whereas it is his deepest choice, the source, and not the consequence of his poetry. He is certain of the total defeat of the human enterprise and arranges to fail in his own life in order to bear witness, by his individual defeat, to human defeat in general. Thus, he challenges, which is as we shall see what the prose-writer does too. But the challenging of prose is carried out in the name of some greater success; and that of poetry, in the name of the defeat hidden in every victory. . . .

The poet does not *utilize* the word, he does not choose among different senses; each of them, instead of appearing to him as an autonomous function, appears to him as a material quality which melts before his eyes into the other senses. Thus solely by the effect of his poetic attitude, he realizes in each word the metaphors which Picasso dreamed of when he wanted to make a matchbox which was completely a bat without ceasing to be a matchbox. Florence is city, flower, and woman. It is city-flower, city-woman, and girl-flower all at the same time. And the strange object which thus appears has the liquidity of the *river* [*fleuve*], the mild, tawny warmth of gold [*or*], and finally abandons itself with propriety [*décence*], and, by the continuous diminution of the silent *e*, prolongs indefinitely its reticent unfolding. To that must be added the insidious attempt at biography. For me, Florence is also a certain woman, an American actress who played in the silent films of my childhood, and about whom I have forgotten everything except that she was as long as an evening glove and always rather tired, and always chaste and always married and misunderstood and whom I loved and whose name was Florence. For the word, which snatches the writer of prose away from himself and throws him into the midst of the world, reflects for the poet, like a mirror, his own image. . . .

Usually the poet first has the scheme of the sentence in his mind, and the words follow. But this scheme has nothing in common with what one ordinarily calls a verbal scheme. It does not govern the construction of a signification. Rather, it is comparable to the creative project by which Picasso, even before touching his brush, prefigures in space the *thing* which will become a clown or a harlequin.

> *Flee, flee there, I feel that the birds are drunk*
> *But, oh, my heart, hear the song of the sailors.*\*

---

\* *Fuir, là-bas fuir, je sens que des oiseaux sont ivres*
*Mais ô mon coeur, entends le chant des matelots.*

This "but" which rises like a monolith at the threshold of the sentence does not tie the second verse to the preceding one. It colors it with a certain reticent nuance, with a qualification which penetrates it completely. In the same way, certain poems begin with "And." This conjunction no longer indicates to the mind an operation which is to be carried out; it extends throughout the stanza to give it the absolute quality of a *sequel*. For the poet, the sentence has tonality, a taste; through it, he tastes for their own sake the irritating flavors of protest, of reticence, of disjunction. He absolutizes them. He makes them real properties of the sentence, which becomes entirely a protest without being a protest against anything precise. He finds here relations of reciprocal implication . . . between the poetic word and its meaning; the cluster of words chosen functions as an image of the interrogative or restrictive nuance, and conversely the interrogation is an image of the verbal cluster which it delimits, as in the following superb verses:

> *Oh seasons! Oh castles!*
> *What soul is without fault?*\*

Here no one is questioned; no one is questioning; the poet is absent. And the question involves no answer, or rather it is its own answer. Is it therefore a false question? But it would be absurd to believe that Rimbaud "meant" that everyone has his faults. As Breton said of Saint-Pol Roux, "If he had meant it, he would have said it." Nor did he *mean* to say something else. He asked an absolute question. He conferred upon the beautiful word "soul" an interrogative existence. The interrogation has become a thing as the anguish of Tintoretto became a yellow sky. It is no longer a signification, but a substance. It is seen from the outside, and Rimbaud invites us to see it from the outside with him. Its strangeness arises from the fact that, in order to consider it, we place ourselves on the other side of the human condition, on the side of God. . . .

Prose is above all an attitude of mind. There is prose when, as Valéry would say, the word passes across our look as the glass across the sun. When anyone is in danger or in difficulty he grabs any instrument. When the danger is past, he does not even remember whether it was a hammer or a stick; moreover,

---

\* *O saisons! O châteaux!*
  *Quelle âme est sans défaut?*

he never knew; all he needed was a prolongation of his body, a means of extending his hand to the highest branch. It was a sixth finger, a third leg, in short, a pure function which he annexed to himself. This is the way with language: it is our carapace and our antennae; it protects us against others and informs us about them; it is a prolongation of our senses. We are within language as within our body. We *feel* it spontaneously while transcending it toward other ends, as we feel our hands and our feet; we perceive it when it is the other who is using it, as we perceive the limbs of others. There is the word which is lived and the word which is encountered. But in both cases it is in the course of an undertaking, either of my acting upon others, or the other upon me. The word is a certain particular moment of action and has no meaning outside of it. In certain cases of aphasia the possibilities of acting, of understanding situations, and of having normal relations with the other sex are lost.

At the heart of this aphasia the destruction of language appears only as the collapse of one of the structures, the most delicate and the most obvious. And if prose is never anything but the privileged instrument of a certain undertaking, if it must be left to the poet alone to contemplate words in a disinterested fashion, then one has the right to ask the prose-writer from the outset, "What is your purpose in writing? What undertaking are you launching; and why does it require your writing? . . ."

## 2 THE WRITER AND HIS AUDIENCE

One of the chief reasons for artistic creation is certainly the need of feeling that we are essential in relationship to the world. This appearance of the fields or the sea, this mood on someone's face, if I fix these on a canvas or in writing, I am conscious of producing them by condensing relationships, by introducing order where there was none, by imposing the unity of mind on the diversity of things. Thus I feel myself essential in relation to my creation. But now it is the created object which eludes me; I cannot discover and produce at the same time. The creation becomes inessential in relation to the creative activity. Even if it appears to others as definitive, the created object always seems to us in a state of suspense; we can always change this line, that shade, that word. Thus, it never *imposes* itself. A novice painter asked his teacher, "When should I consider my painting finished?" And the teacher answered, "When you can look at it in amazement and say to yourself, '*I'm* the one who made *that*.'"

Which amounts to saying "never." For it comes down to considering one's work with the eyes of another, and discovering what one has created. But it is obvious that the less conscious we are of the thing produced the more conscious we are of our productive activity. When it is a matter of pottery or carpentry, we work according to traditional norms, with tools whose usage is codified; it is Heidegger's famous "anyone" who is working with our hands. Then the result can seem to us sufficiently strange to preserve its objectivity in our eyes. But if we ourselves produce the rules of production, the dimensions, the criteria, and if our creative impulse comes from the very depths of our heart, then we never find anything but ourselves in our work. It is we who have invented the laws by which we judge it. It is our history, our love, our gaiety that we recognize in it. Even if we should look at it without ever adding any further touches, we never *receive* from it that gaiety or love. We put them into it. The results which we have obtained on canvas or paper never seem to us *objective*. We are too familiar with the procedures of which they are the effects. These procedures remain a subjective discovery; they are ourselves, our inspiration, our tricks, and when we seek to *perceive* our work, we create it again, we repeat mentally the operations which produce it; each of its aspects appears as a result. Thus, in the perception, the object is given as the essential thing and the subject as the inessential. The subject seeks to be essential in creation and succeeds, but then it is the object which becomes inessential.

This dialectic is nowhere more apparent than in the art of writing, for the literary object is a peculiar top which exists only in movement. For it to emerge, a concrete act is necessary which is called reading, and the object continues to exist only so long as reading continues. Otherwise there are only black marks on paper. But the writer cannot read what he writes, as the shoemaker can wear the shoes he has just made if they happen to be his size, or as the architect can live in the house he has built. In reading, one foresees; one waits. The reader foresees the end of the sentence, the following sentence, the next page. He waits for them to confirm or disprove his predictions. Reading is composed of a host of hypotheses, of dreams followed by awakenings, of hopes and disappointments. Readers are always ahead of the sentence they are reading in a merely probable future which partly collapses and partly is consolidated as they progress, which recedes from one page to the next and forms the moving horizon of the literary object. Without waiting, without a future, without ignorance, there is no objectivity.

Now the operation of writing involves an implicit quasi-reading which makes real reading impossible. When the words form under his pen, the author doubtless sees them, but he does not see them as the reader does, since he knows them before writing them down. The function of his look is not to awaken with a gentle touch the sleeping words waiting to be read, but to control the lining up of the signs. In short, his function is purely regulative, and he learns nothing from what he sees except when he observes some slip of the pen. The writer makes neither predictions nor conjectures. He projects. It often happens that he waits for inspiration, as the saying goes. But he does not wait the way he waits for others. If he hesitates, he knows that the future is not made, that he himself is going to make it, and if he still does not know what is going to happen to his hero, that simply means that he has not thought about it, that he has not decided upon anything. The future is then a blank page, whereas the future of the reader is two hundred pages filled with words which separate him from the end. Thus the writer encounters everywhere only *his* knowledge, *his* will, *his* plans, in short, himself. He touches only his own subjectivity; the object he creates is out of reach; he does not create it *for himself*. . . .

Thus it is not true that one writes for oneself. That would be the worst frustration. In projecting one's emotions on paper, one barely manages to give them a languishing extension. The creative act is only an incomplete and abstract moment in the production of a work. If the author existed alone he would be able to write as much as he liked, the work as *object* would never see the light of day and he would either have to put down his pen or his despair. But the operation of writing implies that of reading as its dialectical correlative and these two connected acts necessitate two distinct agents. It is the conjoint effort of author and reader which brings upon the scene that concrete and imaginary object which is the work of the mind. There is no art except for and by others. . . .

Since creation can find its completion only in reading, since the artist must entrust to another the task of carrying out what he has begun, since it is only through the consciousness of the reader that he can regard himself as essential to his work, all literary work is an appeal. To write is to appeal to the reader to bring into objective existence the discovery which I have undertaken by means of language. And if it should be asked *to what* the writer is appealing, the answer is simple. As the sufficient reason for the appearance of the esthetic object is never found either in the book (where we find merely solicitations to produce the object) or in the author's mind, and as his subjectivity, which he cannot get out of, cannot give a reason for the act of bringing into objectivity, the appearance of the work of art is a new event which cannot *be explained* by anterior data. And since this directed creation is an absolute beginning, it is therefore brought about by the freedom of the reader, and by what is purest in that freedom. Thus, the writer appeals to the reader's freedom to collaborate in the production of his work. . . .

Since the writer recognizes, by the very fact that he takes the trouble to write, the freedom of his readers, and since the reader, by the mere fact of his opening the book, recognizes the freedom of the writer, the work of art, from whichever side you approach it, is an act of confidence in the freedom of men. And since readers, like the author, recognize this freedom only to demand that it manifest itself, the work can be defined as an imaginary presentation of the world insofar as it demands human freedom. Thus there is no "gloomy literature," since, however dark may be the colors in which the writer paints the world, he paints it only so that free men may feel their freedom as they face it. Thus, there are only good and bad novels. The bad novels aim to please by flattering, whereas the good novel is a demand and an act of faith. But above all, the unique point of view from which the author can present the world to those freedoms whose concurrence he wishes to bring about is that of a world to be impregnated always with more freedom. It would be inconceivable that this unleashing of generosity provoked by the writer could be used to authorize an injustice, and that the reader could enjoy his freedom while reading a work which approves or accepts or simply abstains from condemning the enslavement of man by man. One can imagine a good novel being written by an American Negro even if hatred of the whites were displayed throughout, because it is the freedom of his race that he demands through this hatred. And since he invites me to adopt the attitude of generosity, the moment I experience my freedom, I cannot bear to identify myself with a race of oppressors. It is then against the white race and against myself as a member that I demand of all freedoms that they demand the liberation of the colored people. No one would suppose for a moment that it is possible to write a good novel in praise of anti-Semitism. For, the moment I experience my freedom as indissolubly linked with that of all other men, it cannot be required of me that I use it to approve the enslavement of some of them. Thus, whether he is an essayist, a pamphleteer, a satirist, or a novelist, whether he speaks only of individual passions or whether he attacks the social order, the writer, a free man addressing free men, has only a single subject—freedom.

> *Literature and Existentialism* [*What Is Literature?*], *35–37, 14–15, 16–18, 20–21, 39–43, 63–64.*

# II

———•———

## Art and Salvation

### 1  A VERTIGINOUS WORD

Genet is one of those people who live in the past. An accident riveted him to a childhood memory, and this memory became sacred. In his early childhood, a liturgical drama was performed, a drama of which he was the officiant: he knew paradise and lost it, he was a child and was driven from his childhood. No doubt this "break" is not easy to localize. It shifts back and forth, at the dictate of his moods and myths, between the ages of ten and fifteen. But that is unimportant. What matters is that it exists and that he believes in it. His life is divided into two heterogeneous parts: before and after the sacred drama. Indeed, it is not unusual for the memory to condense into a single mythical moment the contingencies and perpetual beginnings again of an individual history. What matters is that Genet lives and continues to relive this period of his life as if it had lasted only a moment.

To say "moment" is to say *fatal moment*. The moment is the reciprocal and contradictory envelopment of the before by the after. One is still what one is going to cease to be and already what one is going to become. One lives one's death, one dies one's life. One feels oneself to be one's own self and another; the eternal is present in an atom of duration. In the midst of the fullest life, one has a foreboding that one will merely survive, one is afraid of the future. It is the time of anguish and of heroism, of pleasure and of destruction. A moment is sufficient to destroy, to enjoy, to kill, to get oneself killed, to make one's fortune with a throw of the dice. Genet carries in his heart a bygone moment which has lost none of its virulence, an infinitesimal and sacred emptiness which concludes a death and begins a horrible metamorphosis. The plot of this liturgical drama is as follows: a child dies of shame; a hoodlum emerges in his place; the hoodlum will be haunted by the child. . . .

The child was playing in the kitchen. Suddenly he became aware of his solitude and was seized with anxiety, as usual. So he "absented" himself. Once again, he plunged into a kind of ecstasy. There is now no one in the room. An abandoned consciousness is reflecting utensils. A drawer is opening; a little hand moves forward.

*Caught in the act.* Someone has entered and is watching him. Beneath this gaze the child comes to himself. He who was not yet anyone suddenly becomes Jean Genet. He feels that he is blinding, deafening; he is a beacon, an alarm that keeps ringing. *Who* is Jean Genet? In a moment the whole village will know. The child alone does not know: in fear and shame he still hears the ringing of the alarm. Suddenly

> *a vertiginous word*
> *From the depths of the world abolishes*
> *the beautiful order. . . .*[*]

A voice declares publicly: "You're a thief." The child is ten years old.

That was how it happened, in that or some other way. In all probability, there were offenses and punishments, solemn promises and relapses. It does not matter. The important thing is that Genet lived and has not stopped reliving this period of his life as if it had lasted only a moment.

It is the moment of awakening. The sleepwalking child opens his eyes and realizes he is stealing. It is revealed to him that he *is* a thief and he pleads guilty, crushed by a fallacy which he is unable to refute; he stole, he is therefore a thief. Can anything be more evident? Genet, thunderstruck, considers his act, turns it over and over. No doubt about it, it is a theft. And theft is an offense, a crime. What he *wanted* was to steal; what he *did,* a theft; what he *was,* a thief. A timid voice is still protesting within him; he does not *recognize* his intentions. But soon the voice grows silent. The act is so luminous, so sharply defined, that there is no mistaking its nature. He tries to go back, to understand himself, but it is too late, he cannot find himself. The dazzlingly evident present confers its meaning on the past; Genet now *recalls* that he cynically decided to steal. What hap-

* Genet, *Poèmes*, p. 56.

pened? Actually, almost nothing: an action undertaken without reflection, conceived and carried out in the secret, silent inwardness in which he often takes refuge, has just *become objective*. Genet learns what he *is objectively*. It is this *transition* that is going to decide his entire life.

The metamorphosis takes place in a moment. He is nothing more than what he was before, yet he is now unrecognizable. Driven from the lost paradise, exiled from childhood, from the immediate, condemned to see himself, suddenly provided with a monstrous and guilty "ego," isolated, separated, in short changed into a bug. An evil principle dwelt in him unperceived, and now it has been discovered. It is this principle which is the source of everything. It produces the slightest impulses of his soul. The child lived at peace with himself; his desires seemed to him limpid and simple. Their transparency now appears to have been deceptive. They had a double bottom. Little Genet's shame reveals eternity to him. He is a thief by birth, he will remain one until his death. Time is only a dream in which his evil nature is refracted into a thousand gleams, a thousand petty thefts, but does not belong to the temporal order. *Genet is a thief;* that is his truth, his eternal essence. And, if he *is* a thief, he must therefore always be one, everywhere, not only when he steals, but when he eats, when he sleeps, when he kisses his foster mother. Each of his gestures betrays him, reveals his vile nature in broad daylight. At any moment the teacher may interrupt the lesson, look Genet in the eyes and cry out: "There's a thief!" It would be vain for him to think he deserved leniency by admitting his errors, by mastering the perversity of his instincts. All the impulses of his heart are equally guilty because all alike express his essence.

If only the vertiginous word had been uttered by his own father, the discovery would have taken place within the indestructible family unit, in other words within the unit of a single collective consciousness. The young culprit, isolated for a moment within that consciousness like an alien thought, would have soon been reabsorbed into it. One doesn't rob one's family. But though his foster parents' tenderness might at times have given Genet the illusion of his being their son, it is dissipated the moment they become his judges. Because he is regarded as a thief, Genet *becomes* a foundling. Father and mother unknown. Nobody wants to take responsibility for his birth. He seems to have produced himself, in defiance of everyone, in a burst of evil will: Evil is self-caused. At the same time, his faults are explained by dark forces whose origin antedate his birth: "That little thief, where does he come from? Only a slut would abandon her son. He must take after her." In short, everything fits together, everything becomes clear. Born of nothingness, the child has nothing, is nothing. His being has the substantiality of non-being. If it exists, it does so like a corrosive acid. Besides, does it exist? Is it not simply the foul beast that rushes through the troubled dream of an honest man?

Jouhandeau, another pariah, has aptly expressed what might be called the ontological curse: "The insult is perpetual. It is not only in the mouth of this person or that, explicit, but on all the lips that name me. It is in 'being' itself, in my being, and I find it in all the eyes that look at me. It is in all the hearts that have dealings with me. It is in my blood and is inscribed on my face in letters of fire. It accompanies me everywhere and always, in this world and in the other. It is myself, and it is God in person who proffers it in proffering me, who eternally gives me that execrable name, who sees me from that standpoint of wrath."

There is not even the possibility of shifting the blame to God by saying "since it's you who made me, *you're* the guilty one," for in this magical concept nature and freedom are one and the same: although the thief is enchained since he is unable to change, he is free since he is condemned. This is reminiscent of Calvinistic predestination which leaves the evildoer full responsibility for Evil while taking from him the possibility of doing Good. Being is here a subtle and radical perversion of freedom, a constant inclination to do evil, a kind of grace in reverse, a weighting of free-will which makes it always fall to the very bottom. In this counterpoint, freedom is responsible for Being and Being petrifies freedom. Although Genet is free to be guilty, he is not free to change. The reason is that the wrath of the just wants to perpetuate itself; if Genet became honest, it would lose its object. This virtuous anger is relentless. It is not enough for it to murder a child; it must also contrive a hopeless future for the monster it has just fabricated. He is told that prison and the penal colony are in store for him. Everything is decided; from an eternal cause derive irremediable consequences in the temporal order: "You'll end on the gallows!"

In a state of dazzlement Genet contemplates the ineluctable course of the universe and the interdependence of the circumstances that will lead him to capital punishment. Only yesterday everything was possible. He was perhaps the son of a prince; he would perhaps become a saint. He lived in an anarchy of desire, his heart was gladdened by chance graces, the future was still open. But now all is in order: he has been provided with a nature, a guilty freedom and a destiny. He is ten years old and he already knows to the last detail the life that he will have to sip drop by drop: "The order of this world, seen from the outside, appears so perfect in its inevitability that this world has only to disappear." . . .

The contempt and anger of decent people would be bearable if he could return blame for blame and hatred for hatred. And that is what he probably would have done if the "accident" had occurred a little later. Had he been called a thief at the age of seventeen, Genet would have laughed. That is the age at which one liquidates paternal values. He would have had a thousand ways and means at his disposal. He could have retorted that his accusers were themselves scoundrels, could have pointed to evil everywhere and have forced it, by means of its very excess, to be reabsorbed, along with good, into a kind of indifference and pathos; he could have challenged the principles of public morality in the name of a Nietzschean or anarchistic ethic, could have denied the existence of values and deigned to recognize only the law of force. But it is a child who has been caught, a very young child, timid, respectful, right-thinking, one who has had a religious upbringing, in accordance with the best principles, who has been imbued with so passionate a love of God that he desires saintliness rather than wealth. Nor can he resort to self-defense by accusing adults, for adults are gods to this religious little soul. He is trapped like a rat: he has been so thoroughly inculcated with the morality in whose name he is condemned that it is part of his very fiber. Now, whatever he does, right-thinking people have the initiative and will not lose it. They have penetrated to the very bottom of his heart and installed there a permanent delegate which is himself. It is he himself who will be both the court and the accused, the policeman and the thief. It is he who will commit the offense and who will deliver sentence and apply it. If he tries to withdraw into himself in order to escape the censure of those about him, he will find an even more severe censure, his own. He will be a zealous self-tormentor and will henceforth experience his states of mind, moods, thoughts, even his perceptions, in the form of a conflict. The simplest, most legitimate desire will appear to him as a thief's desire, hence as a guilty one. The adults triumph; they have found an accomplice who is none other than the accused. One isn't as lucky as that every day. In fact, the situation is even better: had the child developed normally, he would gradually have freed himself from this simple-minded morality, he would at least have made it more flexible, broader, would have perhaps replaced it by a religious ethic, by mysticism, by a liberal eclecticism or by anarchism, but he would have done so quietly, without turmoil, without inner catastrophe. But the terrible blow he has just received will forever prevent this amiable liquidation. Genet will not change. In his worst deviations he will remain faithful to the morality of his childhood. He will flout it, he will perhaps hate it, he will try to drag it with him through the mud, but "the original crisis" has burned it into him as with a red-hot iron. Whatever happens from now on, whatever he may do, whatever way out he may invent, one thing remains forbidden him: to accept himself. The law of his consciousness is conflict. Until the "crisis," he lived in the "sweet confusion" of the immediate, he was unaware that he was a person. He has learned this and, at the same time, that this person is a monster.

"Guilt," he will write later, "gives rise, first, to individuality." Beneath the accusing finger, it is all one, for the little thief, to discover that he is himself and that he is other than all. And no doubt many people have testified to the fact that, around the age of ten, they discovered their individuality with amazement or anguish. The child Gide wept in his mother's arms and screamed that he "was not like other children." But this discovery is usually made without much damage. Adults have nothing to do with it. The child is playing alone, a slight change in the landscape, an event, a fleeting thought, is enough to give rise to the reflective awareness which reveals our ego to us. And, as I have shown elsewhere, this ego is not yet anything to itself, except the empty and universal form of individuality. To be unlike the others is to be like everyone, since each is other than all and the same as itself. If the reflective operation takes place normally, it not only does not prevent reciprocal relationships, it produces them. I feel that I am other than Peter and I know that Peter resembles me because he feels he is other than I. However, the otherness that Genet discovers in himself excludes any reciprocity. It is not a case of an empty and universal form but of an individual difference that has to do with both form and content. There is Genet and there are all the others. And it is the height of irony that the child's dreadful loneliness occasions a finer understanding among those who condemn him: when decent people baptize an evildoer, they are enraptured; they huddle together, the better to block his way; they would even be willing to love each other. Genet quite realizes that he is an oblate and that his sacrifice serves as a bond among his sacrificers. *All the others*, whatever the differences separating them, recognize that they are fellow creatures in that they are not, thank God, thieves. *All the others*, whatever their conflicting interests, recognize their kinship because each reads in his neighbors' eyes the horror that Genet inspires in them; they constitute a single monstrous consciousness that judges and curses. It is horrible to recognize unanimity, to see suddenly that it is possible, that it is present, that one is touching it, that one has it, and to know at the same time that one has produced it, and to know at the same time that one has produced it against oneself. It would be pointless for him to turn back on the others and exclude them in turn, for there is not a square yard on earth from which he can chase them; he possesses nothing of his own. Thus, the loathing he inspires is one-way; he fills honest folk with loathing but cannot loathe them. The only feeling he retains in his heart is love, a humiliated, forbidden love which shamefully, humbly, seeks opportunities to manifest itself. Our Lady of the Flowers, in the criminal court, looks for the first time at the presiding magistrate who is going to condemn him to death: "It is so sweet to love that he could not keep from dissolving into a feeling of sweet, trusting tenderness for the judge. 'Maybe he ain't a pig!' he thought."

The child loves his judges, he tries to draw near them, to melt, even to the point of losing consciousness, into the unanimity which he has created. He finds no other way than to share the disgust he inspires in them, than to despise himself with their contempt. The trap works well. Genet tears himself apart with his own hands. He has now become an absolute object of loathing.

## Art and Salvation

Once upon a time in Bohemia there was a flourishing industry which seems to have fallen off. One would take children, slit their lips, compress their skulls and keep them in boxes day and night to prevent them from growing. This and similar procedures turned the children into amusing monsters who brought in handsome profits. A more subtle process was used in the making of Genet, but the result is the same: they took a child and made a monster of him for reasons of social utility. If we want to find the real culprits in this affair, let us turn to the decent people and ask them by what strange cruelty they made a child their scapegoat.

Any action modifies that which is in the name of that which is not yet. Since it cannot be carried out without breaking up the old order, it is a permanent revolution. It demolishes in order to build and disassembles in order to reassemble. From morning to night we heap up shavings, ashes, scraps. All construction entails an at least equal amount of destruction. Our unstable societies fear lest a false movement cause them to lose their balance. They therefore ignore the negative moment of our activities. We must love without hating the enemy of what we love, must affirm without denying the contrary of what we affirm, must elect without spurning those we have not elected, must produce without consuming. We rapidly cart away the dead, we stealthily recover waste, every day we mask, in the name of cleaning up, the destruction of the day before. We conceal the pillaging of the planet. The fear of knocking down the edifice is so great that we even take from ourselves our power of creating: we say that man does not invent, that he discovers. We reduce the new to the old. Upkeep, maintenance, preservation, restoration, renewal—these are the actions that are permitted. They all fall under the heading of repetition. Everything is full, everything hangs together, everything is in order, everything has always existed, the world is a museum of which we are the curators. Nevertheless, spirit, as Hegel says, is anxiety [*inquiétude*]. But this anxiety horrifies us: we must eliminate it and halt spirit by eliminating its mainspring of negativity. Unable to get rid of this malignant postulation completely, the right-thinking man castrates himself; he cuts the negative moment out of his freedom and throws away the bloody mess. Freedom is thus cut in two; each of its halves wilts away separately. One of them remains within us. It identifies forever Good with

Being, hence with what already is. As Being is the measure of perfection; an existing regime is always more perfect than one which does not exist. It is said to have demonstrated its worth. Anyone wishing to introduce the slightest improvement (and it is quite assumed that improvement is a pious notion which implies no destruction; it is a transition to a higher perfection which envelops and includes the prior perfection) is likewise required to demonstrate its worth and to give evidence, in all other respects, of an all the more profound attachment to Being, that is, to customs and traditions. To the right-thinking man, to be alone and to be wrong are one and the same; to isolate oneself is to withdraw deliberately into one's finiteness, therefore to will one's own nothingness. His dream is that history may end that there may come at last the time of happy repetition within the great sleep. No doubt he may fail, but if he does it is due to ignorance, omission, weakness; in short, to the trace of nothingness which remains in him and to which he submits, though detesting it. He will compensate for this particularity by strict obedience to the imperatives of the group. Moreover, to fail is *nothing*, literally: our failures are lacks of being and they are efficacious only through the Being which sustains them. The worst is not always certain.

The other half of his freedom, though cut out of him and thrown far away, does not, however, leave him quiet. Poor right-thinking man: he wanted, in the beginning, to concern himself only with the positive and with Being, to obey without faltering, to realize on his own little plot of ground a small, local end of history. But the fact is that history does not halt; Being is benumbed, surrounded by non-Being; and, in addition, man, man himself, be he respectful or scoffing, insolent or servile, cannot affirm without denying. If he poses a limit, he does so necessarily in order to transgress it, for he cannot pose it without at the same time posing the unlimited. Does he mean to respect a social prohibition? By the same impulse his freedom suggests that he violate it, for to give oneself laws and to create the possibility of disobeying them come to the same thing. The right-thinking man shuts himself up in a voluntary prison and locks the doors, but his stubborn freedom makes him leave by the window. "By the law," says St. Paul, "is the knowledge of sin." The decent man will make himself deaf, dumb, and paralyzed. It is he who has eyes that see not and ears that hear not. He is, by virtue of himself, the most abstract negation: the negation of negation. He will define himself narrowly by traditions, by obedience, by the automatism of Good, and will give the name *temptation* to the live, vague seething which is still himself, but a himself which is wild, free, outside the limits he has marked out for himself. His own negativity falls outside him, since he denies it with all his might. Substantified, separated from any positive intention, it becomes a pure negation that poses itself for its own sake, a pure rage to destroy that goes round in circles, namely Evil. Evil is the unity of all his impulses to criticize, to judge, to reject insofar as he refuses to *recognize* them and regard them as the normal exercise of his freedom and insofar as he relates them to an external cause. It is his dangerous inclination to develop his ideas to their ultimate limits when decency or discipline bids him stop midway. It is his anxiety, his fundamental disbelief or his individuality that comes to him from without, like Another himself, to tempt him. It is what he wants but does not want to want. It is the object of a constant and constantly rejected will which he regards as other than his "true" will. In short, it is the maxim, both in him and outside of him, of the Other's will. Not the will of some particular Other, nor even of all Others, but of that which in each individual is other than himself, other than self, other than all. Evil is the Other. And it is himself insofar as he is for himself Other than Self. It is the will to be other and that all be Other. It is that which is always Other than that which is. . . .

It is possible to trace with a certain accuracy the stages whereby Genet slowly transforms himself into a stranger to himself. And we shall see that it is simply a matter of progressively internalizing the sentence imposed by adults.

First of all, he wants to escape his destiny. He must awake from a nightmare. Caught, exposed, punished, he swears he will never do it again. Of course, in all sincerity. He does not recognize this act which has become objective and has suddenly revealed itself to be so terribly Other—simply because it is seen by the others; he hates it; he wishes it had never taken place. In hastily manifesting his will never to steal again, he tries to destroy symbolically his hardened, congealed act which encloses him in its carapace. Only a while ago he wanted to flee into the past, into the eternal, he wanted to die. Now he reverses the direction of his flight; his vow testifies to a wild impatience to escape into the future. Three or four years will go by during which he will not commit another theft; he has sworn not to. Already the years have gone by, he *is already* in the future, he turns upon this wretched present and confers upon it its true significance: it was only an accident. But at the same moment the Others' look again supervenes and cuts him off from himself. The Others have not the same reasons as he to believe in his vow, because, in the first place, their indignation also mortgages the future. If—which is unlikely—it were demonstrated that the child would not steal again, their sense of outrage would have to simmer down. In order to perpetuate itself—for, like all passions, it tends to persevere in its being—it must change into a prophetic transport. It therefore postulates the eternity of its object. What it is already aiming at through the child-thief is the adult, the hardened criminal, the habitual offender. Thus, in addition, this sacred emotion goes hand in hand with a legitimate mistrust. From a *practical* point of view, the owners must take precautions; they would be guilty in their own eyes if they did not lock the closets. But these precautions delineate a future that challenges Genet's vow. They are directed to a future that is both foreseeable and unforeseeable. Foreseeable: Genet has sinned, *therefore* he will sin. Unforeseeable: no one knows the hour or day of the next offense. Since the adults are unable to know the date of it, their vigilance confers upon the future theft a perpetual presence. It is in the air, in the silence of the grownups, in the severity of their faces, in the glances they exchange, in the locking of the drawer. Genet would like to forget about it, he buries himself in his work, but his foster mother, who tiptoed off, suddenly comes back and takes him by surprise: "What are you doing?" This is all that is needed: the forgotten theft comes to life again; it is present, vertiginous. Distrust and prophetic anger systematically project the past into the future; Genet's future fills with misdemeanors which are repeated at irregular intervals and which are the effect of a constant predisposition to steal. Obviously this predisposition is simply the reverse side of the adult's expectation. It is their vigilance, but turned around and projected into Genet, who in turn reflects it back to them. If they must be constantly on guard against his thefts, it is because he is constantly ready to commit them, and the greater their fear of being robbed, the greater seems to them his inclination to theft. Naturally, after that, how could he be expected not to succumb? It is the adults themselves who want him to relapse. He will fall into sin again, as often as they want him to.

So he now adopts the point of view of decent people. He docilely installs within himself the inclination attributed to him. But this inclination is, in its very form, *the Other's*. It is never within our own self that we discover the unforeseeable foreseeability of which I have spoken; we discover it in those who we are not. In our own eyes, we are neither foreseeable nor unforeseeable. I do not *foresee* that I shall take the train this evening—I decide to take it, and if there remains a wide margin of possibility in my plans, the reason is that they depend on others as much as on me. To be sure, I can at any moment change my plans, and I do not think of my versatility without a certain anxiety, but this anxiety comes from my feeling free and from the fact that nothing, not even my own vows, can enslave me. It is not a *fear* of a monster that might inhabit me and reduce me to slavery, but rather the opposite.

Genet the thief will await himself as the others await him, with *their* expectations. Foreseeable to others, he will attempt to foresee himself. He will be afraid of his future thefts. Unforeseeable to decent people, he will become unforeseeable to himself; he will wonder every morning whether the new day will be marked by a theft. He will take precautions against himself as if he were another, another whom he has been told to keep an eye on. He will be careful not to leave *himself* alone. He will voluntarily leave an empty room to join his parents in the next one. He will keep an eye on himself; he will watch for the crisis, ready to call the others to the rescue against himself. He fears himself as one fears a fire, a flood, an avalanche. His thefts become external events which he is powerless to oppose and for which he is nevertheless responsible. He observes himself, spies on himself, foils himself, as if he were an odd instrument that one must learn to use. He struggles against an angel within him, an angel of Evil. In this dubious combat everything is inverted. Being oneself becomes being-other-than-self. It is no longer even possible to believe in one's own vows; one distrusts them as one distrusts those of another. An alien future challenges and mocks the future one has given oneself. And this future is a Destiny, a Fatality, because it is the reverse side of *another freedom*. A freedom which is mine and which I do not know has prepared it for me, like a trap. In the depths of his consciousness Genet, like the animal in Kafka in the depths of its burrow, hears dull blows, scratchings. Another animal, a monster, is digging tunnels, is going to get at him and devour him. This other animal is himself. Yet he *never has seen it*.

For he never has seen it. A thief cannot have an intuition of himself *as thief*. The notion of "thief" is on principle incommensurate with the realities of the inner sense. It is of social origin and presupposes a prior definition of society, of the property system, a legal code, a judiciary apparatus and an ethical system of relationships among people. There can therefore be no question of a mind's *encountering* theft within itself, and with immediacy. On the other hand, the *Others*, all the Others, have this intuition at will; a thief is a palpable reality, like a tree, like a Gothic church. Here is a man being dragged along by two cops: "What has he done?" I ask. "He's a crook," answer the cops. The word strikes against its object like a crystal falling into a supersaturated solution. The solution immediately crystallizes, enclosing the word. In prose, the word dies so that the object may be born. "He's a crook!" I forget the word then and there, I see, I touch, I breathe a crook; with all my senses I feel that secret substance: crime. I did not, of course, witness the theft, but that doesn't matter! The guilty man's torn dusty clothes (he fell while trying to run away, he was beaten) contrast with the decent dress of the onlookers, with my own. They make me see that this man is beyond the pale. He is an untouchable *since* I cannot touch him without soiling my hands. The mud that stains his shirt and jacket is the mud of his soul *become visible*. He engages in a strange dance composed of false steps; he moves backward, forward, changes position by fits and starts; each of his movements is constrained. Quite simply because he is being taken to the police station by force and is resisting. But this constraint and force and vain violence manifest to my eyes that he is possessed. He is struggling against the Demon, and the incoherence of his gestures reveals his maladjustment: his foot stumbles on the sidewalk, he almost falls, and I know intuitively, by the simple contrast between his blundering haste and the slow, sure movements of the decent people about him, that he is an outcast, a ne'er-do-well who has never been able, or never wanted, to submit to any discipline. I can read on this body in its disarray that "Evil does not compromise." He has been struck and he is bleeding. His tormented face should tell me that he is weak, defenseless, that a pack has brought him to bay and bitten him. But I combine my loathing of Evil and my loathing of Blood. It is Evil that is bleeding, Crime is oozing from those wounds. And the look on his face expresses a state of daze (he has been half-killed), of fear ("What are they going to do to me?"), of anger ("They've hurt me!"), of shame ("All those people looking at me and yelling!"). But *to me* this state of daze is the sottishness of the alcoholic and the degenerate. Through his rage I touch Evil's inexpressible hatred of Good. His shame manifests consciousness in Evil. Five minutes before this fortunate encounter, Evil was still a merely abstract concept. A word was sufficient *to make me experience it.* A flesh-and-blood thief is crime accessible to all the senses.

Genet will never have this intuition. To be sure, he understands the meaning of the word. He has seen petty thieves being roughly handled by policemen. But he is condemned to read words in reverse. Decent people give names to things, and the things bear these names. Genet is on the side of the objects named, not of those who name them. I am aware that decent people are also objects to each other. I am given names: I am this fair-haired man who wears glasses, this Frenchman, this teacher. But if I am named, I name in turn. Thus, naming and named, I lived in a state of reciprocity. Words are thrown at me, I catch them and throw them at others, I understand, *in* others, what I am to them. *Genet is alone in stealing.* Later, he will know other thieves, but he will remain alone. We shall see that there is no reciprocity in the world of theft. This is not surprising, since these monsters have been fabricated in such a way as to be unable to make common cause. Thus, when he is given this vertiginous name, he cannot make out its meaning in the persons of those who name him. It is as if a page of a book suddenly became conscious and felt itself *being read aloud* without being able *to read itself.* He is read, deciphered, designated. The others feel his being, but he feels their feeling as if it were a hemorrhage. He flows into the eyes of others, he leaks, he is emptied of his substance. He has *vertigo,* in the strict sense of the word. When we stand on a precipice and suddenly feel dizzy, we feel that we are sliding away from ourself, that we are flowing, falling. Something is summoning us from the bottom of the abyss. That something is ourself, that is, our being

which is escaping from us and which we shall join in death. The
word is vertiginous because it opens out on an impossible and
fascinating task. I have shown elsewhere that certain extreme
situations are necessarily experienced as unrealizable. Well then,
Genet is unrealizable to himself. He repeats the magic word:
"Thief! I'm a thief!" He even looks at himself in the mirror, even
talks to himself as to someone else: "You're a thief." Is he going
to *see himself*, to feel a bitter, feverish taste, the taste for crime
that he gives off for others, is he at last going to feel his being?
Nothing changes: a child scowls at his own reflection, that is
all. . . .

Genet is relentless. "I'm a thief," he cries. He *listens* to his
voice; whereupon the relationship to language is inverted: the
word ceases to be an indicator; it becomes a *being*. It resounds,
it bursts upon the silence, one feels it running over one's tongue,
it is real, it is true. It is a casket, a box with a double bottom
which contains within it what Genet often calls "the mystery."
If one could crack this nut, one would find inside it the very
being of the thief; the being and the word are one and the same.
The states of consciousness are thus changed into signs. They
are a flickering that try to light up the darkness of the name.
The latter, which, on the other hand, is dark, massive, impenetrable, has become the being which is signified. "Such-and-such an
idea occurs to me, such-and-such a mood, desire, comes over
me. Is *that* what's called being a thief?" The word, which was
a means, rises to the rank of supreme reality. Silence, on the
other hand, is now only a means of designating language. The
trick is done: we have made a poet of the doctored child. He is
haunted by a word, a single word which he contemplates in
reverse and which contains his soul. He tries to see himself in it
as in a glass that has no backing; he will spend his life
meditating on a word. . . .

*St. Genet, 1–2, 17–26, 37–42.*

## 2 THE LANGUAGE OF CRIME

Let Genet use *words* as much as he likes; Society has put *things*
in safe-keeping. The vocables which he learns refer to forbidden
realities. Those for furniture, real estate, gardens designate the
property of others: the designated objects remain forever inaccessible to him, turn to others their true faces, in short, are in

themselves and on principle other than what they appear to him to be. Technical terms reflect an understanding among honest workers within an occupational group; but he will never share in this understanding, which was reached against him and his kind. The names that apply to the State, to national sovereignty, to the rights and duties of the citizens, concern realities which are thoroughly alien to him. Political and social problems are second-degree matters in that the integrated citizen decides which influences he will undergo, combat, and exercise in the collectivity. Those of Genet will never go beyond the first degree, since his very integration is in question. Our words turn their backs to him, designate absences, denote distances, name invisible things, refer to what is manifest to others and remains hidden from his eyes: they are repositories of unrealizable intuitions. No doubt he understands the "socialized" meaning of the vocables he uses, but this meaning remains abstract. . . .

Since this child is, for himself, another, language disintegrates and alters within him, becoming the language of the others. For him to speak is to steal words, and the latter retain, even in the depths of his throat, the indelible traits of their true owners: swindled [*truqué*] even in his inner monologue, Genet is a robber who has been robbed; he steals language and in return his thought is stolen from him. In our rapid, condensed, blunted, hacked soliloquies, words pass unnoticed, they serve as points of reference to guide our thoughts and gestures; in the case of Genet, the constant discrepancy [*décalage*] which separates words from what they name fixes his attention on them. He listens to himself speaking within himself, he does not have sufficient familiarity with language to dare cut into it, to abbreviate, to take shortcuts; it is not quite that he composes sentences: substantives march by in his head, pompously, rather stiffly, jerkily, like pictures projected by a magic lantern. These substantives indicate to an imaginary witness the action that the child is performing, without ever being quite able to express it. Little Culafroy turns on himself; there immediately appear in his head the noble and graceful words: "wheel around" [*vire-volte*]. But the torn shabby soles of his shoes slacken his pirouette: the words evoke an examplary reality that Genet does not succeed in imitating in his behavior. Whence the permanence of his astonishment: words, in him, are like foreign bodies; he observes them, examines them, puts them out of gear and runs them in neutral, just to see. As the designated objects are all equally tabu, myth and reality are equivalent: since they have taken the world from him, since everything is more remote and more fabulous than faraway Asia, it matters little whether Genet calls his prison a clink or a palace: it is equally impossible for him to live in a palace and to see a prison with the eyes of a judge or a taxpayer. What counts is the word's material presence, which symbolizes the signifying content that, for Genet, is none other than the being of the thing signified. To change words is to change being. His original crisis corresponded exactly to the intuitive crystallization that the word effected for other eyes: the word "thief" was an astringent. Haunted by this crisis, Genet aspires to provoke it, in turn, in other objects: he wants to name, not in order to *designate* but to *transform*. He looks at the walls of his cell, launches the word "palace" and waits: nothing happens, nothing ever happens. But why should this disturb him? In any case, he knows that he is denied the experience of intuitive crystallization: it will not take place if he says *palace;* nor will it if he says *prison.* As for the inner metamorphosis of the thing, since it is inner it will obviously escape him. The important thing is that the word be in his mouth: things—forbidden, remote, flowing—are the appearances of which words are the reality. There is no doubt but that the child makes himself an accomplice and a victim of a new mystification: the starving person is refused meat and bread but is given, instead, the word "steak"; let him amuse himself with it as much as he likes. In point of fact, if he merely repeats it in a low voice this act will certainly be followed by movements of his jaws, an abundant flow of saliva, contractions of the stomach accompanied by an emission of gastric juices, in short digestion with an empty stomach. Now, it is precisely this empty digestion and enjoyment, this exhausting delight of absence and nothingness, that Genet will later decide to prefer to all else.

But he now "makes himself" a thief: immediately the fissure spreads, multiplies in all directions. Language cracks from below; the virus attacks other verbal strata. That was to be expected: the decision to take upon himself what is imposed upon him and to launch out voluntarily on the only path that lies open to him can only hasten the course of his inner disturbances. It is he who becomes the agent of the disintegration of language: that is, without yet giving a name to his undertaking, without making it the object of a special act of will, he changes into a poet because he wills himself a thief. Since his adolescence he has had no "normal" relationship—that is, no prose relationship —with language. Two phases are to be distinguished: in the first, which goes as far as the solipsistic endeavor, the disturbances are not willed for their own sake; they are the consequence of the decision to steal. But in the second, that is, as soon as Genet undertakes to become his own companion, he takes the initiative and deliberately sinks into verbal disease.

Let us begin with the first phase. Genet the thief decides to lie. I do not quite know what he stole or how he went about things, but no matter. We can take the liberty of choosing as an example one of the thefts he committed when he was about thirty: the relationship to language does not change. Well then, he enters a bookshop with a rigged brief case and pretends that he wants to buy a rare book. While the bookseller goes to get the volume, Genet notices another on a table or a shelf and rapidly slips it into his brief case. When he addressed the bookseller, it was for the purpose of informing him of an intention which did not exist: he was not concerned with *buying* and probably did not have enough money on him to pay for anything; he wished only to get a troublesome witness out of the way. Yet he *communicated* with the other person. But it was a pseudo-communication which destroyed all possibilities of real communication. In short, like the surrealists who painted with the aim of destroying painting, but more effectively than they, he uses language to destroy language. The bookseller actually thinks that he is performing once again the act which he constantly repeats in the course of the day; it seems to him that his movements express his sustained will to do his job and to serve the interests of his employer. But the fact is that he is not acting, he is dancing: he goes to get *for nothing* a book that nobody wants to buy; his eagerness, his smile, which ordinarily aim at charming customers, are mere pantomime since there are no customers in the shop but only a thief who cannot be charmed. And the result of this pantomime is a denial of the real world to the advantage of a universe of pure appearance. He thinks he is going to the back of the shop to get a valuable article: he is actually going off to leave Genet a clear field. He has become a fake bookseller, a true accomplice of a thief. He thinks he has understood Genet's request, and, in point of fact, his senses have transmitted to him correct signs which his mind has correctly interpreted. Nevertheless, to understand was, in this case, not to understand, for thorough understanding would have implied that he had discerned the intention to deceive in the physiognomy or intonation of his fake client. The statement made him deaf, blind, ignorant: in short, it made of him a thing that one pushes out of the way. Let us note in passing the resemblance of the universe of theft to that of homosexuality: in both cases, inner reality becomes pure appearance without efficacy, and it is appearance, on the other hand, that becomes reality. In this fake world, language is used in the wrong way: although its function is to unite, to reveal and to harmonize, it separates, conceals, and estranges; although it is a body of signs which are meant to be offered to the intelligence of persons, it makes one of the speakers an unconscious instrument of the other.

Genet is aware that he is lying and knows that the object which is signified does not exist. He wants his statement, which for him is void of meaning, to offer the other an illusory plenitude. Signification exists *only for the other:* for the other, it transcends the words and aims at a certain object located in the back of the shop. Genet utters a sentence which he knows has meaning only for others. *For him* it is only a magical formula, the effect of which is to cast a spell on those who hear it and to make them do what they do not want to do by leading them to believe that they are doing what they want to do. In a sense, it is a cabalistic formula that is recited mechanically. And yet it is haunted by a signification that denies itself since Genet knows that the other understands it. The bookseller, who guides himself by means of the words, perceives Genet intuitively as a purchaser: proper clothing, relaxed attitude, these things tally with the statement and serve as a visible content. Thus, for Genet himself an intuitive meaning is present in the proposition, but *as another and for the other;* this meaning escapes him on principle, for he can no doubt know it in the abstract and by its effects on the person he addresses (he sees that the other smiles, walks away, etc.), but cannot enjoy it. From this point of view, it is a duplication of the original situation: the signification of the word "purchaser" is not given to Genet intuitively any more than was the word "thief." Here, however, the deformation is more serious, for this intuitive meaning is false while it is being lived by the other. The other just about manages, by his behavior, to impart to it an appearance of reality. There is thus, at the core of words, a concrete plenitude which refuses to give itself to Genet because it is lived by the other, and which is annihilated in the other, for it is only an illusion. When one tells a lie, language is isolated, stands out, imbibes its significations and constitutes an order apart: the order of the trap and the sham. But was it not actually that even before Genet dreamed of lying? Did not significations flee the child who wanted to grasp them? Was not speech already a breaking off of communication? Here as elsewhere Genet has merely adopted the given: cast out of language and out of the social world of tools, he uses instruments and words *in reverse;* the separative power of the Word became a power to lie when he decided to accept it and turn it to advantage. . . .

It may, however, be urged that there exists a community which has forged a language of its own against the bourgeois tongue—the community of tramps and crooks to which Genet belongs. With them, at least, communication is possible. In the reformatory, in prison, in the Court of Miracles, Genet can talk in prose: he has only to use argot.

But, to begin with, argot itself is a poetic language. And I am not, of course, asserting that its terms are noble or charming; I mean that this fabricated language represents the attempt of a parasitic society, which feels itself cut off from reality, to make good a huge verbal deficit by means of lyricism and the invention of words. Thieves and criminals are all more or less in the same situation as Genet: they have to use common words and these words are forbidden them. They must, of course, have a noun to designate a door or a train. But if they use the words "door" and "train," they are communicating among themselves by means of the language of the enemy; they are installing within themselves the words of the bourgeois, hence his thoughts, values and *Weltanschauung;* they are almost at the point of judging their crimes by his principles; a spy, a witness, a court of law are established in their hearts. Thus, their crimes and their will to form a unity of Evil create an immense gap in their verbal universe. For them the social act *par excellence* will be the invention of new conventions. They can, of course, distort customary words in accordance with certain rules, as in pig Latin. But this is still to concede too much to decent people: it is tantamount to admitting that the basic language remains the *white* language of the society of the just. Fake languages can serve them on occasion, when they want to talk without being understood by others. But they want *words of their own* in order to *remain among themselves*, in order to designate objects without resorting to the mediation of the society that hounds them. And as they have neither the leisure nor the means to invent a language, and as, in addition, the objects which they have to designate are not new realities which, in the manner of industrial inventions or scientific discoveries, require new denominations, they will be unable to avoid using the words of the dictionary. It is then that they hit upon what will become one of the fundamental procedures of argot. In order to name an object, they choose the terms of the common language which apply to lateral, secondary, or implicit properties of the object in question: most often these will be adjectives (*le dur* [the tough], *la lourde* [the door], *le grimpant* [the trousers]*) which they will transform into substantives.

In a certain sense, argot resembles the substitute language which is painfully reinvented by persons suffering from aphasia. For the aphasic, as for thieves, the *situation* is characterized by a heavy deficit, and he *reacts* by resorting to paraphrases. Argot is the aphasic language of crooks. The word of the common language designates the object by its essence: "infant," for example, goes straight to the essential characteristic of a child, to wit, that it does not speak. If man is defined as a reasonable or a political animal, it is a fact of prime importance that he is unable, at the beginning, to use reason, because he does not possess speech, or to communicate with his fellow men. And even if its etymology has been lost, at least the word corresponds to the entire thing and consequently caps the hierarchy of its properties. In rejecting the proper word, argot is thus compelled to use improprieties; it is a crooked language. In order not to give the name *infant* to the newborn child, it is reduced to calling it a *crapper*, that is, to referring to it by its intestinal incontinence; the slang word will be understood only with reference to the common language, that is, to a whole labor of definition, grouping, classification, and convention which allows the normal play of thought. The object of the slang word is not the naked thing but the thing with its name. A crapper is not simply a human offspring: it is *a human being already called*

* *Dur* = hard, *lourde* = heavy, *grimpant* = climbing.—Trans.

*an infant.* It is with things that have already been thought, classified, and named in a forbidden and sacred language that argot establishes its relations, just as those who speak it have contact only with matter that has already been worked. It feeds on the common language as tramps feed on the work of others. And the slang expression is poetic because it always refers to an absent reality (the essence named by the proper word) about which there is an unspoken agreement between interlocutors. . . .

*St. Genet, 278–283, 285–286.*

### 3 THE CRIME OF ART

Before writing, what is Genet? An insignificant little turd, a bug that scurries, unnoticed, between the slats of the floor. He has a feeling that he is horrifying all of Society, but he also knows that this horror is purely virtual and that, moreover, it relates to the thief *in general,* to *any* delinquent and not to Jean Genet. Society condemns theft: but it does so without thinking about it, by means of a specialized organ whose function is precisely to substitute systematic and general repression for diffuse repression, in short *to hush up scandal.* The culprit's crimes *never* come to the knowledge of the just man; the just man *never* thinks about the culprit; as a citizen of a democracy, he alone is qualified to punish, and the judiciary power emanates from him, as do all powers: but he has delegated his functions to the police, magistrates, and prison guards and no longer thinks about the matter. The contempt which these civil servants display for Genet in the name of the just man is not true contempt: it is impersonal, professional, like the smile of a salesclerk; they are paid to display it. As an anonymous object of an impersonal and, in general, virtual loathing, Genet is, in point of fact, ignored, forgotten: he squirms about in a shaft of light, blinded by the look that Society has been fixing upon him since his childhood; this look penetrates to his soul and sears all his thoughts; he is public, never alone with himself. But *at the same time* he knows that *nobody* is looking at him, that nobody, except a few cops, is aware of his existence. He would like to cry out to them: "Look at me I'm a criminal, it's you who have condemned me." No one hears him, people come and go, he calls out to them. Wasted effort. He will end by believing that he is invisible. If he has been dreaming since childhood of horrifying them *for good,* it is in order to be able to feel that he exists for someone and to transform these phantom witnesses into a real audience. He wants the dead look which enveloped him to sparkle, and, since the relationship which constitutes him in his very core is a relationship to all, he wants to actualize finally his dimension-for-the-Others. Whoever sees him despises him, but nobody sees him: how restful it must be to be seen: "The newspaper photo shows Nadine and her husband leaving the church where the priest has just married them. She is stepping across the swastika. The people of Charleville are looking at her with hostility. 'Give me your arm and close your eyes,' her husband must have murmured to her. She walks smilingly toward the French flags which are bedecked with crepe. I envy this young woman's bitter and haughty happiness." Genet steals so that people will think about him, so that he, too, can become a tabu object: *an object of loathing.* Loathing is closer to love than indifference. The perfidious solicitude that an examining magistrate shows for him in order to trip him up is, as we know, enough to make him confess to his crime: "a trifle would suffice" for that solicitude to become tenderness. When he was a child, other children spat in his face: "Yet, a trifle would have sufficed for that ghastly game to be transformed into a courtly game and for me to be covered with roses instead of spit. For as the gestures were the same, it would not have been hard for destiny to change every-thing: the game is being organized—the youngsters make the gesture of tossing—it would cost no more for it to be hap-piness. I awaited the roses. I prayed God to alter his intention ever so little, to make a false step so that the children would no longer hate me, would love me. I was then invested with a higher solemnity. I was no longer the adulterous woman being stoned. I was an object in the service of an amorous rite." When love is absent, blame and sanction are sacralizing rites. No sooner has Querelle killed than he belongs to all; he thus becomes a sacred object. What Genet wants is to become an accessory of the cult, a ritual object. But the more he steals, the less they are concerned with him. And furthermore, although he feels, in the scene related above, that he is being metamorphosed into an object, he has no perspective that would enable him to enjoy his objectivity: the latter is only a flight of all his being into the fathomless freedom of his tormentors. A later experience sug-gests another ruse to him: instead of becoming an object for the others, why not identify himself with a particular, material object that would be the butt of their hatred? He would then be able to see himself: he would see *the object that he is,* shining with their gobs of spit, shimmering in the light of their gazes. That is what happened once in Barcelona: the police arrest him; before jailing him, they search him and confiscate a tube of Vaseline that he used when making love. The ignominious accessory is taken from him and put on a table; it becomes Genet himself: firstly because it is his property, and secondly because it reveals and symbolizes his homosexuality. "I was in a cell. I knew that all night long my tube of Vaseline would be exposed to the scorn—a Perpetual Adoration turned into its opposite—of a group of strong, handsome, husky policemen. So strong that if the weakest of them barely squeezed two fingers together, there would shoot forth, first with a slight fart, brief and dirty, a ribbon of gum which would continue to emerge in a ridiculous silence. Nevertheless, I was sure that this puny and most humble object would hold its own against them; by its mere presence it would be able to exasperate all the police in the world; it would draw upon itself contempt, hatred, white and dumb rages. It would be slightly bantering—like a tragic hero amused at stirring up the wrath of the gods—indestructible, like him, faithful to my happiness, and proud." The tube of Vaseline, which is an effigy of Genet, flouts the cops *by its inertia.* Genet "in person" would be less able to resist them: he is sensitive, he can suffer. The inertia of the matter represents an invincible haughtiness, and yet this matter is haunted by a soul. Sheltered from blows and insults, Genet can peacefully dream in his cell about that obstinate little brute which he has delegated to receive them, in short he can take pleasure in himself.* How-

* The sticky tube of Vaseline reminds Genet of a beggar woman over whom he had wanted to "slobber." It is apparent that we are dealing here with a "constellation" of images: the child who was dripping with spit compared himself to a penis wet with sperm; and the tube which he uses to smear his penis with Vaseline makes him think of a face sticky with slaver. Finally he dreams of smearing the entire body of his lovers with Vaseline, and "their muscles bathe in that delicate transparence." Here we turn to a new theme: that of the transparent veil, of the gauze that puts objects into a kind of esthetic perspective. One can see the gradual transition from one term to the other. Spit, sperm, Vaseline: vitreous transparency which protects bodies and makes them shimmer. The basic image is sperm; but on the other hand, the insult appears as protecting pride; lastly, tulle—"voracious" beauty lends unreality, intruding between the look and things, like a transparent veil.

ever he remained passive during the operation: it was purely by chance that the policemen found the tube in his pocket.

But what if he gave himself, *by an act,* the power of existing elsewhere, in all his virulence, for horrified minds? What if he conferred ubiquity upon himself with his own hands? What if he deliberately invented a way of embodying himself in strange substances and forced the others to discover him there? Then the contempt of "all the police in the world" would no longer be undergone but demanded, and the bantering pride of the inanimate object would rightly express Genet's irony. Hidden behind a wall, this crafty hoodlum could enjoy at will the astonishment of decent people. He would *see* them *seeing* his image, and they would become objects for him precisely insofar as his reflection was an object for them. We have just defined the work of art according to Genet: it is an object of horror, or rather *it is Genet himself engendering himself by a criminal act as an object of universal horror and turning this horror into his glory because he has created himself in order to provoke it.* In *Our Lady of the Flowers* he says of a poem: "I have shat it out." Such is his esthetic purpose: to shit *himself* so as to appear as excrement on the table of the just. "Without disappointing the enthusiasm of the peasants" Sarah Bernhardt could have appeared in the shape of a little box of matches. Box of matches, tube of Vaseline, poem, they are all the same—wanton objects which embody persons. When one produces one of these objects, one is an artist, and when this object arouses horror, one is a criminal to boot. Haunted by the problem of the Other, which is *his* problem, Genet has spent his life meditating on the incarnation. He had to *make himself become* the Other that he already was for the Others. He had tried everything, he had attempted to make himself be reflected by a mirror, by the eyes of a lover, by those of the beloved, to have himself be possessed by the Other, by himself as Other: each undertaking ended in failure. Recourse to art in his final attempt: thus far he has been unable to be his own cause except in imagination, since it was the Others who had first, and spontaneously, affected him with this otherness. He now *realizes* this imagination in an object-trap which forces the Others to see him as he wants to be seen. He will be his own creature since his book is himself creating himself as Another and making the others breathe life into his creation. They made a thief of him; he now turns their formidable objectifying power against them and forces them to make him a fish, a flower, a shepherd, whatever he wishes. At last he sees himself, he touches himself: this big banned book that is pursued by the police is himself; if you open it, you are suddenly surrounded by characters, who are also himself. He is everywhere, he is everything, men and things, society and nature, the living and the dead. Imagine his joy: he lives alone, secretly; he hides from the police; he signs hotel registers with a false name; he effaces his footprints, all traces of his presence; he barely exists: yet he is everywhere; he occupies all minds, he is an object of horror. About his books one could say, without changing a word, what he said about his tube of Vaseline: "I was sure that this puny and most humble object would hold its own against them; by its mere presence it would be able to exasperate all the good consciences in the world; it would draw upon itself contempt, hatred, white and dumb rages. It would be slightly bantering—indestructible—faithful to my happiness and—exposed to scorn—a Perpetual Adoration turned into its opposite."

Will he succeed? Will his clandestine works be able to shock, whereas his thefts, which were more serious offenses, and more severely punished, went unnoticed?

Yes, because Society puts up more easily with an evil action than with an evil word. For specialists, magistrates, criminologists, sociologists, there are no *evil* acts: there are only punishable acts. For the man in the street, there *are* evil acts, but it is always the Others who commit them. Genet wants to reveal to the former that Evil exists and to the latter that its root is in themselves. . . .

Victim and tool of the decent citizen since childhood, Genet is now able to avenge himself at last: he is going to apply the *lex talionis*. He will make that innocent discover the Other in himself; he will make him recognize the Other's most indecent thoughts as his own; in short, he will make him experience with loathing his own wickedness. Poetic traps will captivate his freedom and will reflect it to him as being half his own and half alien. He will be forced to see himself and will be able neither to *recognize* himself nor to reject himself. It is with words that Genet will lay his traps. Words are the matter and weight of the soul; if they assemble within it to form evil thoughts, the soul is lost. It served as a refuge against threats and suffering: what will be its refuge against itself? The trap is a book, an object as stubborn and inert as a tube of Vaseline: black strokes on sheets of paper sewn together. Nothing more. And the object will remain that dead thing which is waiting for nothing, which fears nothing, which continues to grow until its owner himself decides to attend to it, to link up the signs, to project their meanings through the words, to organize the meanings among themselves. No sooner is it opened than an idea emerges, or a feeling, or a vague shape, and the reader knows that these furtive beings were already there in some way, but he also knows that they would not have appeared in that place and on that day without the complicity of his mind. He had only *not* to read, and moreover he can always stop reading. If he harnesses himself to the effort to understand, he constructs a complicated object which exists only through him and which will be dispersed in a multitude of black marks as soon as he turns his attention away: he is the one who is drawing these phantasms out of nothingness and maintaining them in being. To read is to carry out an act of guided invention. No doubt he does not adhere completely to what he reads; no doubt he waits until he has understood before giving or refusing his assent. But he has already circumvented himself: to understand is to accept; if later he wants to reject this alien sensibility, he will have to take himself in hand, will have to make a sharp break, will have to snatch himself back from the increasing vertigo. His freedom, which keeps the phrase supended in its illumination, looks everywhere for the thoughts, the memories which will facilitate an understanding of the text. If he reads that "beauty is Evil," the sentence has no meaning for him at first: if he wants to understand it, to breathe life into it, to adapt it for his personal use, he must recall the most beautiful faces, most beautiful paintings, that he has seen, those which he has been particularly fond of. No doubt he evokes them only as examples, but that is sufficient: he sees the Other's voracious thinking with his own most inward being, with his beautiful regrets, with his beautiful cares. The words are already hemming him in, giving him, despite himself, a past, a future which he does not recognize: if he wants to understand what he is reading, he must refer to what he has just read; thus, all the paradoxes which he condemns form, despite himself, his immediate past; he senses the existence of others which are on the horizon and which are making a new future for him. Invisible walls surround him; he is in a world which he would not have wanted to create and which would not have been if not for him. He spontaneously shapes his present thoughts and feels himself shaping them: they are indeed his own; and yet, despite their transparency, they have the disquieting depth of the thoughts of others since he does not hear them at first and has to decipher them. . . .

In order for Genet to struggle against the restive attention of his readers, in order to force them to have thoughts which are distasteful to them, there must be a categorical imperative—constantly lurking behind the words—that requires unconditional adherence. In short, the work must be beautiful. I have shown elsewhere that beauty presents itself as an absolute end: it is the free appeal that creative freedom addresses to all other freedoms. And as nothing can be created once and for all, except bridges and dams, since, as Mallarmé says, being has already happened, artistic creation is imaginary: through the work of art it presents the entire world as if it were produced and assumed for human freedom. Formerly the beautiful was an integral part of theodicy: the artist "showed" God his work as the enfeoffed vassal showed his lord the fief which the latter had just given him; he used his freedom to create appearances in order to reflect the supreme freedom which had devoted itself to creating being. Today God is dead, even in the heart of the believer, and art becomes an anthropodicy: it makes man believe that man created the world; it presents his work to him and justifies his having made it. There is an ethic of Beauty; it requires of us a kind of demiurgic stoicism: optimism without hope, acceptance of Evil as a condition of total unity, affirmation of human, creative reality over and above its failures, of a universe that crushes it, assumption by freedom of suffering, crimes and death; we must will being as if we had made it. . . .

"My victory is verbal, and I owe it to the sumptuousness of the words." In point of fact, Genet's victory is complete: he escapes from poverty, from prison, from horror; decent people support him in style, seek him out, admire him; even those who still censure him have to accept him since he has filled their minds with obsessive images. What does he give in return? Nothing. A moment of horror, a suspect beauty that disappears: he has spoken at length about a sinister and iniquitous world and yet has managed to say nothing about it. His extraordinary books are their own rebuttal: they contain both the myth and its dissolution, the appearance and the exposure of the appearance, language and the exposure of language. When we finish them, the reading leaves a taste of ashes since their content cancels itself. The good conscience dreamed of fullness, of being; Genet disturbs it by giving it "the notion of an escaping object that is missing." This happens because he has not called anything into question nor created new values. He has entered the readers' hearts and imparted to them his infernal lightness. He will henceforth be in them this sudden suspicious lifting [*allégement louche*], this emptiness; he has restored *negativity* to them. . . .

Genet plays loser wins with his work and you are his partner: so you will win only by being ready to lose. Let him cheat; above all do not defend yourself by adopting attitudes: you have nothing to gain by putting yourself into a state of Christian charity, by loving him in advance and by accepting the pus of his books with the abnegation of the saint who kisses the leper's lips. The high-minded have brooded over this infected soul; it thanked them with a fart, and they deserved it, for their benevolence was only a precaution for disarming his wiles. You will deplore the misfortunes he suffers only in order to hide from yourself his free-will to do harm. In that case, you are helping a thief by trying to find excuses for him; to find excuses for the poet is to wrong him. Furthermore, do not take refuge in estheticism; he will drive you from under cover. I know people who can read the coarsest passages without turning a hair: "Those two gentlemen sleep together? And then they eat their excrement? And after that, one goes off to denounce the other? As if that mattered! It's *so* well written." They stop at Genet's vocabulary so as not to enter his delirium; they admire the poem so as not to have to *realize* the content. But form and content are one and the same: it is *that* content which requires *that* form. So long as you play at amoralism you will remain at the threshold of the work. So? So you must not resist, you must let yourself be fooled, must remain yourself, must let yourself be naïvely indignant. Do not be ashamed of being taken for a fool. Since this fanatical challenging of all man and all his loves is expressly meant to shock, then be shocked, do not fight against the horror and uneasiness that the author wants to arouse in you. You will appreciate the snares of this sophist only if you fall into them. . . .

What will remain when the book has been shut? A feeling

of emptiness, of darkness and of horrible beauty, an "eccentric" experience which we cannot weave into the fabric of our life and which will forever remain "on the edge," unassimilable, the memory of a night of debauchery when we gave ourselves to a man and came off. There are books which address themselves, in each individual, to all, and we feel that we are *the* crowd when we enter them. Those of Genet are brothels into which one slips by a door which is ajar, hoping not to meet anyone; and when one is there, one is all alone. Yet it is from this refusal to universalize that their universality is due: the universal and incommunicable experience which they offer to all as individuals is that of solitude. . . .

We usually live in a sort of familiar and unthinking vagueness, we are not quite objects and not quite subjects. The Other is that instrument which obeys the voice, which regulates, divides, distributes, and it is, at the same time, that warm, diffuse atmosphere which envelops us; and that is what we, too, are for others and consequently for ourselves. However, this immediate vagueness contains the germ of disequilibrium: you are with all, you write for all, you take God to witness, or the human race, or history, or your next-door neighbors; you are the docile instrument of a family, of a social group, of a profession, of a party, of a church; you receive your thoughts from the outside by means of newspapers, the radio, lectures and speeches and immediately redistribute them; not a moment goes by without your speaking and listening, and whatever you say or hear is what anyone would have said or heard in your place; from morning to night you submit to the tyranny of the human face, you have no secrets, no mystery, nor do you want to have any—and yet, in a certain way, you are alone. And I do not locate this solitude in our private life, which is only a sector of public life, nor in our tastes, which are social and shared: I find it everywhere. Being a negation, it is the negative of our loves, of our actions, of our personal or political life. It is neither subjectivity, in the strict sense of the word, nor objectivity, but the relationship between the two when it is experienced as a failure. It is born within communication itself, as poetry is within all prose, because the most clearly expressed and understood thoughts conceal an incommunicable element: I can make them be conceived as I conceive them but am unable to make them live as I live. This solitude is found within mutual love: when you are unable to make your wife share a taste which you have in common with thousands of other people, when you remain separated from her within pleasure. In these examples, subjectivity does not succeed in dissolving objectivities. But we are *also* alone when we cannot *become objects sufficiently:* surrounded, supported, fed, re-created by your party, you may want to be only a cell of that great organism and yet you feel your solitude for the simple reason that it always remains possible for you to leave the party and that your very loyalty is deliberate, or else out of fear of being led one day to criticize the leaders and to refuse obedience, in short, because of the anxiety you feel when confronted with your freedom and exactly insofar as you are not the stick or corpse which you are making an effort to imitate; the victor is alone because he cannot identify himself completely with the fine object which is being led in triumph: because of his hidden defeat. This vague sense of a want of exact correspondence between the subjective and objective would still be nothing, for we spend our time hiding the fact from ourselves; but our professional mistakes, our thoughtless acts, our blunders and our mishaps suddenly exasperate it: the error, the slip, the foolish act creates a vacuum around us; suddenly the others *see* us, we emerge from the original indistinctness, we have become objects; at the same time, we *feel ourselves being looked at*, we feel ourselves blushing and turning pale: we have become subjects. In short, our solitude is the way we feel our objectivity for others in our subjectivity and on the occasion of a failure. Ultimately, the criminal and the madman are pure objects and solitary subjects; their frantic subjectivity is carried to the point of solipsism at the moment when they are reduced for others to the state of a pure, manipulated thing, of a pure *being-there* without a future, prisoners who are dressed and undressed and taken care of. On the one hand the dream, hallucination, absence; on the other the world of the concentration camp; on the one hand, shame and the impotent hatred that turns against itself and vainly defies the heavens, and on the other the opaque being of the stone, of "human material." The individual who becomes aware of this explosive contradiction within himself knows true solitude, that of the monster; botched by Nature and Society, he lives radically, to the point of impossibility, the latent, larval solitude which is ours and which we try to ignore. One is not alone if one is right, for Truth will out; nor if one is wrong, for it will suffice to acknowledge one's mistakes for them to be forgotten. One is alone when one is right and wrong *at the same time:* when one declares oneself right as subject—because one is conscious and lives and because one cannot and will not deny what one has willed—and when one declares oneself wrong as object because one cannot reject the objective condemnation of all of Society. There is only one path leading down to the solitude of the unique, the path that leads, through impotence and despair, to error and failure. You will be alone if you know that you are in the eyes of everyone, a guilty object, while your conscience continues, despite itself, to approve of itself; you will be alone if Society ignores you and if you cannot annihilate yourself: Genet's "impossible nullity" is solitude. . . .

Since every thought divides as much as it unites, since every word draws one closer by virtue of what it expresses and isolates by virtue of what it does not say, since a fathomless abyss separates the subjective certainty which we have of ourselves from the objective truth which we are for others, since we do not cease to judge ourselves guilty even though we feel innocent, since the event transforms our best intentions into criminal desires not only in history but even in family life, since we are never sure of not becoming traitors retrospectively, since we constantly fail to communicate, to love, to be loved, and since every failure makes us feel our solitude, since we dream at times of effacing our criminal particularity by humbly acknowledging it and at times of affirming it defiantly in the vain hope of assuming it entirely, since we are conformists in broad daylight and defeated and evil in our secret soul, since the one resource of the guilty person and his only dignity is obstinacy, sulkiness, insincerity, and resentment, since we cannot escape from the objectivity that crushes us nor divest ourself of the subjectivity that exiles us, since we are not allowed even to rise to the plane of being or sink into nothingness, since we are, in any case, *impossible nullities,* we must listen to the voice of Genet, our fellow man, our brother. He pushes to the limit the latent, masked solitude which is ours; he inflates our sophisms until they burst; he magnifies our failures to the point of catastrophe; he exaggerates our dishonesty to the point of making it intolerable to us; he makes our guilt appear in broad daylight. Whatever the society that succeed ours, his readers will continue to declare him wrong, since he opposes *all* society. But that is precisely why we are his brothers; for our age has a guilty conscience with respect to history. There have been times that were more criminal, but they didn't care about posterity; and others made history with a clear conscience; men did not feel that they were cut off from the future; they felt that they were creating it and that their children would agree with them; the succession of generations was an environment in which they felt at their ease. Revolutions are now impossible. We are being threatened by the bloodiest and most stupid of wars. The proper-tied classes are no longer quite sure of their rights, and the working class is in retreat. We are more aware of injustice than ever, and we have neither the means nor the will to rectify it. But the lightning progress of science gives future centuries an obsessive presence; the future is here, more present than the present: men will go to the moon, perhaps life will be created. We feel that we are being judged by the masked men who will succeed us and whose knowledge of all things will be such that we cannot have the slightest inkling of what it will be; our age will be an object for those future eyes whose look haunts us. And a guilty object. They will reveal to us our failure and guilt. Our age, which is already dead, already a *thing*, though we still have to live it, is *alone* in history, and this historical solitude determines even our perceptions: what we see *will no longer be;* people will laugh at our ignorance, will be indignant at our mistakes. What course is open to us? There is one which I perceive and which I shall discuss elsewhere. But the course which one usually takes is to install oneself in the present moment of history and to will it defiantly with the stubbornness of the vanquished; one invents sophisms in order to maintain principles which one realizes are going to disappear and truths which one knows will become error. That is why Genet the sophist is one of the heroes of this age. He is held up to obloquy before our eyes as we are before the look of future centuries; the Just will not cease to cast blame on him nor will History cease to blame our age. Genet is ourselves. . . .

If there is still time to reconcile, with a final effort, the object and the subject, we must, be it only once and in the realm of the imaginary, realize this latent solitude which gnaws away at our acts and our thoughts. We spend our time fleeing the objective into the subjective and the subjective into objectivity. This game of hide-and-seek will end only when we have the courage to go to the limits of ourselves in both directions at once. At the present time, we must bring to light the subject, the guilty one, that monstrous and wretched bug which we are likely to become at any moment. Genet holds the mirror up to us: we must look and see ourselves there.

*St. Genet*, *486–490*, *495–497*, *585–586*, *589*, *591–592*, *597–599*.

# CONSCIOUSNESS
# AND SOCIETY

# I

## Actions and Meanings

Man is, for himself and for others, a signifying being, since one can never understand the slightest of his gestures without transcending the pure present and explaining the gesture by reference to the future. Furthermore, he is a creator of signs to the extent that—always ahead of himself—he uses certain objects to designate other absent or future objects. But both operations are reducible to a pure and simple transcending. To transcend present conditions toward their later change and to transcend the present object toward an absence are one and the same thing. Man constructs signs because in his very reality he is signifying; and he is signifying because he is a dialectical transcending of all that is simply given. What we call freedom is the irreducibility of the cultural order to the natural order.

To grasp the meaning of any human performance we must employ what German psychiatrists and historians have called "understanding" [*verstehen*].* But this involves neither a particular talent nor a special faculty of intuition; it is simply the dialectical movement which explains the act by arriving at its terminal signification from its starting conditions. The movement is originally progressive. If my companion suddenly goes toward the window, I understand this gesture in terms of the material situation in which we both are. It is, for example, because the room is too warm. He is going "to let in some air." This action is not inscribed in the temperature; it is not "set in motion" by the warmth as by a "stimulus" provoking a series of reactions. There is present here a synthetic mode of be-

---

* *Cf.* above p. 296, where the translation "comprehension" was used.—Ed.

havior which, in unifying itself, unifies before my eyes the practical field in which we both are. The movements are new, they are adapted to the situation, to particular obstacles. This is because psychological sets are *abstract* adjustments which are insufficiently determinate; they become determined within the unity of the undertaking. It is necessary to avoid that table; then the window is of the casement type or a sash window or a sliding one or perhaps—if we are in a foreign country—of a type not yet known to us. In any case, if I am to transcend the succession of gestures and perceive the unity which they give themselves, I must myself feel the overheated atmosphere as a need for fresh air; that is, I must myself experience the transcending of our material situation. Within the room, doors and windows are never entirely passive realities; the work of others has given them their meaning, has made out of them instruments, possibilities *for an other* (any other). This means that I *understand* them already as instrumental structures and as products of a directed activity. But my companion's movement makes explicit the crystallized indications and designations in these products; his behavior reveals the practical field to me as a "hodological space," and conversely the indications latent in the instruments become the crystallized meaning which allows me to understand his undertaking. His behavior *unifies* the room, and the room defines his behavior.

What we have here is so clearly an enriching transcending *for both of us* that this performance, instead of being first clarified by the material situation, can reveal the situation to me. Absorbed in our work or discussion, I had experienced the warmth as a confused, unnamed discomfort; in my companion's gesture, I see at once both his practical intention and the meaning of my discomfort. The movement of understanding is at once progressive (toward the objective result) and regressive (I go back toward the original condition). Moreover, it is the act itself which will define the heat as unbearable; if we don't lift a finger, it is because the temperature can be tolerated. Thus the rich, complex unity of the undertaking emerges from the most meager condition and turns back upon it to clarify it. Furthermore, at the same time but in another dimension, my companion reveals himself by his behavior. If he gets up deliberately and opens the window a crack before beginning the work or the discussion, this gesture refers to more general objectives (the will to show himself methodical, to play the role of an orderly man, or his real love of order). He will appear very different if he suddenly jumps to his feet and throws the casement window wide open as if he were suffocating. Here also if I am to be able to understand him, it is necessary that my own behavior in its projective movement should inform me about my own depths—that is, about my wider objectives and the conditions which correspond to the choice of these objectives. Thus *understanding* is nothing other than my real life; it is the totalizing movement which gathers together my neighbor, myself, and the environment in the synthetic unity of an objectification in process.

Precisely because we are a *pro-ject,* understanding may be entirely regressive. If neither one of us has been aware of the temperature, a third person coming in will certainly say: "Their discussion is so absorbing that they are about to suffocate." This person, from the moment he entered the room, has experienced the warmth as a need, as a wish to let in some fresh air; suddenly the closed window has assumed for him a signification, not because it was going to be opened, but, quite the contrary, because it had not been opened. The close, overheated room reveals to him an act which has not been performed (and which was indicated as a permanent possibility by the work deposited in the present instruments). But this absence, this objectification of non-being, will find a true consistency only if it serves to reveal a positive undertaking. Through the act to be performed and not yet performed, this witness will discover the passion which we have put into our discussion. And if he laughingly calls us "bookworms," he will be finding still more general significations in our behavior and will illuminate our depths.

Because we are men and because we live in the world of men, of work, and of conflict, all the objects which surround us are signs. By themselves they indicate their use and scarcely mask the real project of those who have made them such *for us* and who address us through them. But their particular arrangement, under this or that circumstance, retraces for us an individual action, a project, an event. The cinema has so often used this process that it has become a convention. The director shows us the beginning of a dinner, then he cuts; several hours later in the deserted room, overturned glasses, empty bottles, cigarette stubs littering the floor, indicate by themselves that the guests got drunk. Thus significations come from man and from his project, but they are inscribed everywhere in things and in the order of things. Everything at every instant is always signifying, and the significations reveal to us men and relations among men mediated by the structures of our society. But these significations appear to us only insofar as we ourselves are signifying. Our understanding of the Other is never contemplative; it is only a moment of our *praxis*, a way of living—in conflict or in complicity—the concrete, human relation which unites us to him.

Among these significations there are some which refer us to a lived situation, to a specific action, to a social event. Thus those broken glasses are charged, on the screen, with retracing for us the story of an evening's orgy. Others are simply signs—such as an arrow on the wall in a subway corridor. Some refer to "collectivities." Some are symbols, the reality signified is present in them as the nation is in the flag. Some are announcements of instrumentality: certain objects offer themselves to me as *means* —a pedestrian crossing, a shelter, etc. Still others, which we usually, but not always, apprehend through the actual overt behavior of real men, are quite simply ends.

We must resolutely reject the so-called "positivism" which imbues today's Marxist and impels him to deny the existence of these last significations. The supreme mystification of positivism is that it pretends to approach social experience without any *a priori*, when in fact it has decided from the start to deny one of its fundamental structures and to replace it by its opposite. It was legitimate for the natural sciences to free themselves from the anthropomorphism which bestows human properties on inanimate objects. But it is perfectly absurd to introduce by analogy the same scorn for anthropomorphism in anthropology. In the investigation of man, what procedure can be more exact and rigorous than to recognize his human properties? Ordinary observation of the social field should have led to the discovery that the relation to ends is a permanent structure of human undertakings and that it is *on the basis of this relation* that real men evaluate actions, social and economic institutions. It should have been ascertained that our understanding of the Other is necessarily attained through ends. Someone who from a distance watches a man at work and says: "I don't understand what he is doing," will find insight comes when he can unify the disjointed moments of the activity he is watching, by anticipating the result aimed at. A better example—in order to fight, to outwit the opponent, a person must have at his disposal several systems of ends at once. In boxing, one will grant to a feint its true finality (which is, for example, to force the opponent to lift his guard) if one discovers and rejects at the same time its pretended finality (to land a left hook on the forehead). The double, triple systems of ends which others employ condition our activity as strictly as our own end. A positivist who clung in his practical life to his blindness to the teleological would not live very long.

It is true that in a society which is wholly alienated, in which "capital appears more and more as a social power of which the capitalist is the functionary,"* the manifest ends can mask the profound necessity behind an evolution or a mechanism already in operation. But even then the end as the signification of the lived project of a man or of a group of men remains real, to the extent that, as Hegel said, the appearance possesses a reality as appearance. Its role and its practical efficacy, in this last case as well as in the preceding, need to be specified. . . . The stabilization of prices in a competitive market *reifies* the relation between seller and buyer. Courtesies, hesitations, bargaining, all this activity is pointless, since the chips are already down. And yet each of these gestures is lived by its author as an act. Doubtless this activity lapses into the realm of mere appearance. The permanent possibility that an end may be transformed into an illusion is characteristic of the social field and the modes of alienation, but it does not deprive the end of its irreducible structure. Rather the notions of alienation and mystification retain their meaning only to the extent that they steal ends and disqualify them. There are accordingly two conceptions which we must be careful not to confuse. The first, which is held by numerous American sociologists and by some French Marxists, stupidly substitutes for what is given in experience an abstract causalism or certain metaphysical forms or concepts, such as motivation, attitude, or role, which have no meaning except in conjunction with an end. The second recognizes the existence of ends wherever they are found and restricts itself to declaring that certain among them can be neutralized

* Marx: *Das Kapital*, III, 1, p. 293.

in the historical process of totalization.* This is the position of genuine Marxism and of existentialism. . . .

*Search for a Method, 152–159.*

* The contradiction between the reality of an end and its not actually existing is a fact of everyday life. To cite only the commonplace example of a fight—the boxer who, deceived by a feint, lifts his guard to protect his eyes, is really pursuing an end; but for his opponent, who wants to punch him in the stomach, this end—in itself or objectively—becomes the *means* for carrying through the punch. By making himself a subject, the awkward boxer has realized himself as an object. His end has become the accomplice of his opponent's. It is at once end and means. . . .

# II

———————•———————

## Individual Actions and Social Consequences

### 1 DIALECTICAL REASON

Totality is defined as a being, radically distinct from the sum of its parts, which is complete—in one form or another—in each of these parts, and which relates to itself either through its relation to one or several of its parts, or else by its relation to the connections that all, or several, of these parts maintain among themselves. But when, by hypothesis, this reality is *made* (a painting or a symphony are examples where the integration is pushed to its limits), it can exist only within the imaginary—that is, as the correlative of an act of the imagination. By its very definition, it claims the ontological status of the in-itself, or the inert. The synthetic unity which will produce its appearance of totality cannot be an act, but only what remains of a past action (in the way that the unity of a medal is the passive residue of its minting). By its being-in-externality, the inertia of the in-itself gnaws away at this appearance of unity; the passive totality is, in fact, gnawed away by an infinite divisibility. Thus, as the active power of holding together its parts, it is merely the correlative of an act of the imagination; *the* symphony, *the* painting are—as I have shown elsewhere—imaginaries projected through the complex of dried pigments or the collection of sounds which serve as their *analogue*.* And when practical objects—machines, instruments, consumer goods, etc.—are concerned, our present action is what gives them the appearance of totalities by reviving, in one way or another, the *praxis* which attempted to totalize their inertia. We shall see below that these inert totalities have a major importance, and that they create among men that type of relation which later will be called the practico-inert. These *human* objects should

* See above, p. 80.—Ed.

421

be studied in the human world where they receive their practico-inert status; that is, they weigh upon our destiny through that contradiction within them which opposes *praxis* (the labor that has made them and the labor that makes use of them) and in-ertia. But these comments show that they are products, and that the *totality*—contrary to what we might believe—is merely a regulative principle of totalization (and can at the same time be reduced to the inert whole of its temporary creations).

If, indeed, something must exist which presents itself as the synthetic unity of the diverse, this can only be a unification in process, that is, an act. That synthetic unity of a habitat is not simply the labor that has produced it, but also the act of inhab-iting it; left to itself it returns to the multiplicity of inertia. Thus the totalization has the same status as the totality: through the multiplicities, it continues that synthetic labor which makes of each part a manifestation of the whole, and which relates the whole to itself through the mediation of the parts. But this is an act *in process*, one which cannot stop without the multiplic-ity returning to its original status. This act delineates a prac-tical field which, as the undifferentiated correlative of the *praxis*, is the formal unity of the whole which is to be integrated; inside this practical field, the act attempts to carry out the most rigorous synthesis of the most highly differentiated multiplicity: thus, by a double movement, the multiplicity multiplies itself to infinity, every part opposes itself to every other part and to the whole which is in the process of forma-tion, while the totalizing activity tightens all the bonds, making of each differentiated element its immediate expression and its mediation as well in relation to the other elements. From this point on, the intelligibility of the dialectical reason can easily be established; it is none other than the very movement of to-talization. Thus, to take only one example, it is in the context of totalization that the negation of negation become affirma-tion. Within the practical field, the correlative of the *praxis*, all determination is negation: by differentiating certain groups, the *praxis* excludes them from the grouping formed by all the others, and the unification in process appears *simultaneously* in the most differentiated products (which indicate the direction of the movement), in the less differentiated products (which indicate continuities, resistances, traditions, and a stricter but more superficial unity), and in the conflict between the two (which reveals the present state of the totalization in process).

By determining the least differentiated groups, the new negation will raise them to the level of the others, and will necessarily do away with the negation which was making every group into the antagonist of every other. Thus, it is within a unification in process (a unification which, moreover, has already defined the limits of its field), and there alone, that a determination can be called a negation, and that the negation of negation must necessarily be an affirmation. If the dialectical reason exists, it can only be (from the ontological viewpoint) the totalization in process, taking place where the totalization occurs; and (from the epistemological viewpoint) the permeability of that totalization by a knowledge whose approach is, in principle, totalizing. But, since it is inadmissible that the totalizing knowledge arrive at the ontological totalization as a new totalization of the latter, the dialectical knowledge must be a moment of totalization or, if you prefer, the totalization must include its reflective retotalization within itself, as an indispensable structure and as a totalizing process within the process as a whole.

Thus the dialectic is a totalizing activity. It has no laws other than the rules that are produced by the totalization in process; these are obviously concerned with the relations between the unification and the unified—that is, the modes of *effective* presence of a process of becoming which totalizes those parts which are totalized. And knowledge—which itself is totalizing —is the totalization itself, insofar as the latter is present in certain partial structures of a specific character. In other words, if the totalization is consciously present to itself, this cannot be such that the latter is the still formal and faceless activity which unifies synthetically; rather, it is through the mediation of differentiated realities that it unifies, realities which embody it effectively insofar as they totalize *themselves* by the very movement of the totalizing act. These comments permit us to define a primary characteristic of the *critical experience:* it goes on *inside* the totalization, and cannot be a contemplative grasp of the totalizing movement; nor can it be a singular and autonomous totalization of the known totalization. Rather, it is a real moment of the totalization in process, insofar as this latter embodies itself in all its parts, and is realized, through the mediation of certain of these, as the synthetic knowledge of itself. In practice, this means that the critical experience can and should be the reflective experience of anyone at all.

Yet we must deepen, and at the same time restrict, the terms

423

we have just been using. Indeed, when I say that the experience must be *reflective*, I mean that it is no more distinguishable, in the singularity of its moments, from the totalization in process than the reflection is distinguishable from the human *praxis*. I have shown elsewhere that one must think of reflection, not as a parasitical and separate consciousness, but as the particular structure of certain "consciousnesses." If the totalization is in process in any sector whatever of reality, this totalization can only be a singular adventure under singular conditions, and, from the epistemological point of view, it produces universals which illuminate it, and *singularizes* these by making them internal (indeed, in this manner every concept forged by history, including that of man, is a singularized universal having no meaning apart from *that* singular adventure). The critical experience can be but a moment of that adventure, or, if you prefer, that totalizing adventure produces itself as the critical experience of itself at a certain moment of its development. And this critical experience grasps, through reflection, the singular moment; this means that it is the singular moment in which the act endows itself with the reflective structure. Thus the universals of the dialectic—its principles and its laws of intelligibility —are singularized universals; all attempts at abstraction and universalization would only result in proposing schemes that remained valid *for that adventure*. We shall see to what degree formal extrapolations are conceivable (in the abstract hypothesis where other, still unknown, ontological sectors are *also* totalizations) but, in any case, these extrapolations cannot claim to be knowledge; their sole utility, when they are possible at all, is the better to reveal the singularity of the totalizing adventure in which the experience occurs.

*Critique de la raison dialectique, 138–141.*

## 2 ANYONE AT ALL

This makes clear in what sense we should take the expression "anyone at all" [*n'importe qui*]. If the totalization claims a moment of the critical consciousness, as the necessary avatar of the totalizing *praxis*, it goes without saying that this moment cannot appear at any time, or any place, whatever. It is conditioned, in its deep reality as well as in the modes of its appearance, by the synthetic rule characterizing *this* totalization, as well as by the prior circumstances which it must transcend and retain within itself according to that very rule. To make myself more easily understandable, let me say that—if, as is the hypothesis, our sector of totalization is human history—the critique of the dialectical reason cannot appear *before* the historical totalization has produced that singularized universal which we call dialectical, that is, before it is established, through the philosophies of Hegel and of Marx. Nor can it appear *before* the *abuses* which have obscured the very notion of dialectical reality and have produced a new schism between the *praxis* and the knowledge which illuminates it. Indeed, the *Critique* takes its etymological meaning and its origin from the real need to separate true from false, to set limits to the scope of totalizing activities in order to restore to them their validity. In other words, the critical experience could not take place *in our history* before Stalinist idealism had rigidified both epistemological practices and epistomological methods. It can take place only as the intellectual expression of the straightening out which, in this "one world" of ours, characterizes the post-Stalinist period. Thus, when we discover that *anyone at all* may realize the critical experience, this does not mean at any period. We are talking about anyone at all *today*. What, then, does this "anyone at all" mean? We understand this expression as meaning that any one human life whatever, if the historical totalization must be able to occur, is the direct and indirect expression of the whole (the totalizing movement) and of every life, to the exact extent to which this one life opposes itself to everything and everyone. Consequently, in any life whatever (but more or less explicitly, depending upon the circumstances) the totalization realizes the divorce between the blind and principle-less *praxis* and the rigidified thought, or, in other words, that obscuring of the dialectic which is a moment of the totalizing activity and of the world. By this contradiction—lived through in uneasiness and sometimes as heart-rending—the totalization ordains for everyone, as his individual future, the re-evaluation of his intellectual tools; this represents, in effect, a new moment, more detailed, integrated, and rich, of the human adventure. In fact we see *today* the birth of numerous attempts—all interesting and all (including, of course, the present one) debatable—to question the dialectic about itself. And this means not only that the ori-

gin of the critical experience is itself dialectical, but also that
the appearance in each person of the reflective and critical consciousness defines itself as an individual attempt to grasp,
through one's own real life (conceived as an expression of the
whole), the moment of historical totalization. Thus, in its most
immediate and superficial character, the critical experience of
totalization is the very life of the investigator, insofar as this
life criticizes itself reflectively. In abstract terms this means
that only a man living inside a sector of totalization may grasp
the internal relations which unite him with the totalizing movement.

These comments . . . remind us, too, that the epistemological point of departure must always be consciousness, as the
apodictic certainty (of) itself and as consciousness *of* such and
such an object. But we are not concerned, at this point, with
questioning consciousness about itself: the object that it ought
to claim is precisely *life*, that is, the objective being of the investigator in the world of Others, inasmuch as this being has been
totalizing itself since birth and will do so until death. From that
point on the individual disappears from historical categories—
alienation, the practico-inert, the series, groups, classes, components of history, labor, the individual and the common *praxis*
—he has lived, he lives, all of that internally. If the movement
of the dialectical reason exists, this movement produces that
life, that affiliation with a certain class, certain surroundings,
certain groups; it is the totalization itself which has caused
his successes and his failures, through the vicissitudes of his
community, his particular joys and sorrows; the dialectical
links are disclosed through his amorous or familial ties, through
his friendships, through the "relations of production" which
have left their imprint on his life. From that point onward, his
comprehension of his own life must go so far as to deny its singular determination, in order to seek its dialectical intelligibility in the whole of the human adventure. And I am not considering here that coming to awareness which would make him
grasp the *content* of that life starting from concrete history of
the class to which he belongs, the contradictions characteristic
of that class and its struggles against the other classes. We are
not trying to reconstruct the real history of the human species;
rather, we are attempting to establish the *Truth of History*.
Hence, it is a question of the critical experience being brought
to bear upon the nature of the links of interiority (if they exist)

starting from the human relations which define the investigator. If he is to be totalized by history, what is important here is to relive his affiliations with human groups of different structures, and to determine the reality of these groups, through the links that constitute them and the practices that define them. And to the very extent that he, personally, is the living mediation between these heterogeneous groups (as, also, is any individual whatever), his critical experience must discover if this mediating bond is itself an expression of totalization. In a word, the investigator must, if the unity of history exists, grasp his own life as the Whole and the Part, as the link between the Parts and the Whole, and as the relation of the Parts among themselves, in the dialectical movement of Unification. He must be able to make the leap from his own singular life to History, by the simple, practical negation of that negation which determines it. From this point of view, the sequence of the experience is now clearly apparent to us: it must be regressive. Inverting the synthetic movement of the dialectic *as method* (that is, inverting the Marxist movement of thought which goes from production and relations of production to the structures of the groups, then to the interior contradictions of the latter, then to the milieu and, should the occasion arise, to the individual), the critical experience will start out from the immediate, that is, from the individual attaining himself in his abstract praxis,* to rediscover, through deeper and deeper conditionings, the totality of his practical links with others, and thereby the structures of the diverse practical multiplicities and, through the contradictions and struggles among these, the concrete absolute: historical man. That is tantamount to saying that the individual— the questioner who is questioned—*is myself* and is no one. There remains the link between collectivities and groups; through the lived relationship of affiliations we shall grasp— in this self which is disappearing—the dynamic relations of the different social structures, insofar as they are transforming themselves through history.

*Critique de la raison dialectique, 141–143.*

---

* I understand "abstract" here in the sense of "incomplete." From the point of view of his singular reality, the individual is not abstract (one might say that he is the concrete itself), but *on condition that* more and more profound determinations have been discovered which constitute him in his very existence as an historical agent, and, at the same time, as a product of history.

## 3 NEED

The major discovery of the dialectical experience . . . is that man is "mediated" by things to the exact extent that things are "mediated" by man. We shall have to bear in mind the whole of this truth, in order to develop all its consequences. It is what is called dialectical *circularity;* it ought, as we shall see, to be established by the experience, but were we not already dialectical beings, we could not even understand it. I present it at the outset, not as a truth or even as a conjecture, but as the type of thinking which ought to be adopted *prospectively,* in order to shed light upon an experience which is developing on its own.

On the most familiar and superficial level, the experience *first* reveals, in the unity of dialectical relations, unification as a movement of the individual *praxis,* plurality, the organization of plurality, and the plurality of organizations. To see this, one need only open one's eyes. The problem is that of their relationships. If there are individuals, *who* totalizes? or *what?*

The immediate, but inadequate, answer is that there would be not even an adumbration of partial totalization if the individual were not, *by himself,* totalizing. *The whole historical dialectic rests upon the individual praxis, insofar as the latter is already dialectical*—that is, to the extent that action is, by itself, the negating transcending of a contradiction, the determination of a present totalization in the name of a future totality, the real and effective labor upon matter. We know all that; subjective and objective experience taught us so a long time ago. Our problem is this: what shall *the* dialectic be, if there is nothing but men and if these men are all dialectical? But I have said that the experience itself would furnish its own intelligibility. We must, then, see at the level of the individual *praxis* (it matters little for the moment what collective constraints create it, restrict it, or deprive it of its effectiveness) what, strictly speaking, is the rationality of action.

Everything is discoverable in *need* [*besoin*]: this is the first totalizing relation between that material being, a man, and the material group to which he belongs. This relation is *unilateral,* a relation of *interiority.* Through need, as a matter of fact, there appears in matter the first negation of negation and the first totalization. Need is negation of negation to the extent that it exposes itself as a *lack* inside the organism; it is positivity to the extent that, through it, the organic totality tends to conserve itself *as such*. Indeed, the primitive negation is a first contradiction between the organic and the inorganic, in the double sense that lack defines itself *for a totality*, but that a *lacuna*, a *negativity* has, as such, a *mechanical* type of existence; and that, in the last analysis, *what is lacking* can be reduced to unorganized or less organized elements or, simply, to dead flesh, etc. From this point of view, the negation of this negation comes about by transcending the organic toward the inorganic. Need is the link of *unilateral immanence* with the surrounding materiality, insofar as the organism is seeking to *feed itself*. It is already totalizing, and doubly so: for it is nothing but the living totality, revealing itself as a totality and disclosing the material environment, to infinity, as the total field of the possibilities of satisfaction. On the level that concerns us, this transcending through need holds no mysteries, since the original behavior of, for example, the need for food repeats the elementary behavior of nutrition: chewing, salivation, stomach contractions, and so forth. Transcendence is evinced here as the simple unity of a total function. Without the unity of elementary behavior within the whole, hunger would not exist; there would be only a scattering of distracted and disconnected actions. Need is a function which presents itself for what it is, and which totalizes itself, as function, because it is reduced to becoming a gesture, functioning for itself and not within the integration of organic life. And, through this isolation, the organism as a whole runs the risk of disintegration—that is, the danger of death. This first totalization is *transcendent* to the extent that the organism finds its being outside itself—immediately or mediately—in the inanimate being; need introduces the *first contradiction*, since the organism depends, for its very being—directly (oxygen) or indirectly (food)—upon the unorganized being; and since, conversely, the control of reactions imposes upon the inorganic a biological status. In fact it is a question of a different status being imposed on the same materiality; for, as everything leads us to believe, living bodies and inanimate objects are composed of the same molecules. Yet their status is mutually contradictory, for the one assumes a link of interiority between the whole, as unity, and molecular relations; whereas the other is a status of pure exteriority. Nevertheless, negativity and contradiction attain the inert through organic totalization. Once there is the appearance of need, the surrounding matter receives a passive unity, owing to the single fact that a totalization in process reflects itself there as a totality. Matter revealed as passive totality by an organic being trying to find its being there—such is nature, in its first form. Already, it is from the starting point of the total field that need seeks there its possibilities of being satisfied; and it is the totalization which will reveal, in the passive totality, its own material being as abundance or as scarcity.

But at the same time that Nature, through the mediation of need, appears as a false organism, the organism exteriorizes itself in nature as pure materiality. Within the organism, in fact, the biological status superimposes itself upon the physicochemical one. Now even if it is true that, in the interiority of nutritive assimilation, the molecules are controlled and filtered into an intimate relationship with the permanent totalization, still when the living body is revealed from the viewpoint of exteriority, it satisfies all external laws. In this sense, one could say that matter, outside of the body, reduces the body to inorganic status to the same degree that the body transforms matter into a totality. Through just this, the body is *in danger* in the universe; it too harbors the possibility of the organism's *nonbeing*. Conversely, the organic totality, in order to find its being in nature or to protect itself against destruction, must become inert matter, for it is as a mechanical system that it can modify the material environment: the man in need is an organic totality who perpetually makes himself his own tool in the realm of exteriority. The organic totality acts upon inert bodies through the intermediary of the inert body *which it is*, and which it *makes itself be*. It *is* inert inasmuch as it is already subject to all the physical forces which expose it to itself as pure passivity; it *makes itself be* its being to the extent that a body can act upon another body, in the realm of exteriority, through inertia itself and from without. The action of the living body upon the inert can exert itself either directly or through the mediation of another inert body; in the latter case we call this intermediary a tool. But once the organized body takes its own inertia as the mediation between inert matter and its own need, the instrumentality, the end, and the labor are given together; the totality to be conserved is in fact projected as a totalization of the movement by which the living body utilizes its inertia to overcome the inertia of things. At this level, transcending exteriority toward interiorization has the simultaneous character of existence and of *praxis*. Organic function, need, and *praxis* are strictly linked in a dialectical sequence; with the organism, in fact, dialectical time enters into being, since the living being can survive only in renewing itself. This *temporal* relation between the future and the past, through the present, is nothing but the functional relation of the totality to itself; the totality is its own future, seen across a present of reintegrated disintegration. In a word, living unity is characterized by the decompression of the momentary temporality; but the new temporality is an elementary synthesis of change and identity, since the future governs the present to the extent that this future identifies itself narrowly with the past. The cyclical process—which characterizes both biological time and that of the earliest societies—is broken *from without*, by the environment, simply because scarcity, as a contingent and ineluctable fact, interrupts the exchanges. This interruption is lived *as a negation*, in the simple sense that the cyclical movement or function reproduces itself to no effect, and by just this denies the identification of future with past and falls back to the level of a circular organization that is *present* and is conditioned by the past. This lag [*décalage*] is the condition necessary for the organism to be, no longer the locale and destiny of the function, but its end; indeed, the only difference between the primitive synthetic temporality and the time of the elementary *praxis* results from the material environment, which—through the absence of what the organism is seeking there—transforms the totality as future reality into *possibility*. As the negation of negation, need is the organism itself, living itself in the future through present disorders, as its own possibility and, consequently, as the possibility of its own impossibility; and the *praxis*, at first, is nothing other than the relation of the organism, as external and future end, to the present organism, as threatened totality: this is function exteriorized. The real difference does not lie between the function as internal assimilation, and the construction of tools with an end in view. Indeed, many animal species make tools of themselves; that is, organized matter produces, by itself, the inorganic or the pseudo-inert. I have said that the organism can act upon the environment only by falling provisionally back to the level of inertia; the animals-tools make themselves permanently inert to protect their life, or if you prefer, instead of utilizing their own inertia they protect it behind a fabricated inertia. At this ambiguous level one may see the dialectical passage from function to action. The *project* as transcendence is only the exteriorization of immanence. Actually the transcendence is already there, in the functional fact of feeding and discharge, since we discover in this a relation of unilateral interiority between two states of materiality. And, conversely, the transcendence contains immanence within itself, since its link with its end and with the environment rests upon externalized interiority.

Hence, although *at first* the material universe can render man's existence impossible, it is through man that negation attains man and matter. On this basis we may understand the crude intelligibility of the famous law of the "negation of negation" which Engels is wrong in giving as, fundamentally, an irrational "abstraction" from natural laws. In fact, the dialectic of Nature—whether one seek it in "changes of state" generally, or make of it the *dialectic operating from without* in human history—is incapable of answering two essential questions: Why is there something like a negation in, the natural world or in human history? and Why, and in what definite circumstances, does the negation of negation yield an affirmation? Indeed, one cannot see why the transformations of energy . . . could be considered as negations, unless they are so considered by man for the purpose of conventionally indicating the direction of the process. There is no doubt that matter passes from one state to another; this means that there is change. But a material change is neither affirmation nor negation. It has not *destroyed,* because nothing was *constructed;* it has not *broken resistances,* because the confronting forces have very simply given the result that they were to have given—it would be just as absurd to assert that two opposing forces acting upon a membrane *negate themselves,* or to say that they *collaborate* to determine a certain tension. All one can do is to utilize the *negative sequence* to distinguish one direction from the other.

*Critique de la raison dialectique*, *165–169.*

# 4 SCARCITY

Scarcity—as the lived relation of a practical multiplicity with the materiality environing it and within it—is the foundation of the possibility of human history. This implies two explicit reservations: it does not found, for an historian living in 1957, the possibility of *all* History; for we have no means of knowing whether—for other organisms on other planets or for our descendants, in the event that technical and social transformations should destroy the context of scarcity—another History, constituted on another basis, with other motivating forces and other inner schemes, is or is not logically conceivable. (By this I mean not only that we do not know if, elsewhere, the relation of organic beings to unorganized ones can be other than that of scarcity, but also that if these beings should exist, it is impossible to decide *a priori* whether their temporalization would or would not take the form of a history.) But to say that our History is a history of men, and to say that it emerged and developed in the permanent context of a field of tension engendered by scarcity—these are the same thing. The second reservation: scarcity founds the possibility, not the reality, of human history; in other words, it makes History possible, and other factors (which we shall have to determine) are necessary in order for it to occur. The reason for this restriction is that there are backward societies which suffer, in a sense, more than others from famine or from the seasonal deprivation of food resources, and yet which are rightly classed by ethnographers as history-less societies, based on repetition.* This means that scarcity can be great, provided an equilibrium is established for a given mode of production, and if it preserves itself from one generation to the next, it does so as *exis*, that is, both as the physiological and social determinism of human organisms, and also as the practical project of maintaining institutions and corporate development at this stage. This corresponds ideologically to a decision about human "nature": *man* is that stunted being, misshapen but hardened to suffering, who lives to labor from dawn to dusk with *these* (rudimentary) technical means, upon

---

* Actually, we shall see that they are beginning to interiorize *our* History, for they have submitted passively to colonial activity as to an historical event. But it is not a reaction to *their* scarcity, which historializes them.

an unproductive and forbidding earth. Later we shall see that certain scarcities condition a moment of History when, in the context of techniques which themselves are changing . . . , they occur themselves of their own accord, in the form of a sudden change in the standard of living. History is born out of a sudden imbalance which fissures society at every level; scarcity is the foundation of the possibility of human history, its possibility only in the sense that it can be lived (through internal adaptations of the organisms) within certain limits, as an equilibrium. As long as we remain within this realm, there is no logical (*i.e.*, dialectical) absurdity in conceiving a History-less earth, where human groups would vegetate and remain within a cycle of repetition, making their living through rudimentary techniques and tools, and knowing absolutely nothing of one another. I am well aware that it has been said that these History-less societies are actually societies where History has stood still. This is quite possible, since in fact they have a technology at their disposal and since—primitive as its tools may be—it took a temporal process to lead them to *that* degree of efficiency, through social forms which themselves, despite everything, present in relation to that process a certain differentiation; hence these, too, reflect that temporalization. This point of view, in effect, conceals the *a priori* will of certain ideologists (who can be found among idealists as well as Marxists) to establish History as essential necessity. In this perspective, the non-historical societies would be, in contrast, certain exceptional moments in which historical development brakes itself and stops short, turning its own forces against itself. From the *critical* point of view, it is impossible to accept this conception, extremely congenial as it may be (since it introduces necessity and unity into everything), simply because it claims to be a conception of the world, without being capable of invalidation or confirmation by the facts. (True, many groups stabilized in repetitiveness have a legendary history; but this proves nothing, since that legend is a negation of History; its function being to introduce the *archetype* into the sacred moments of repetition.) The only thing we are able to conclude, insofar as we are examining the validity of a dialectic, is that scarcity in any case is not of itself sufficient to bring about historical development or the bursting, in the course of its development, of a bottleneck which is transforming History into repetition. On the contrary, it is scarcity—as the real and perpetual tension between man and environment, man and man—which *in any case* takes fundamental structures (techniques and institutions) into account: not in that it would have produced them as a real force, but in that these have been brought about *in the environment of scarcity** by men whose *praxis* interiorizes this scarcity even as it desires to go beyond it.

Abstractly, scarcity can be considered as a relation of the individual to the environment. Practically and historically—that is, insofar as we are situated—the environment is an already constituted practical field, which reflects for each person the collective structures (we shall see later what this means), of which the most fundamental is precisely scarcity, as the negative unity of the multiplicity of men (of *this* concrete multiplicity). This unity is negative in relation to men, since it reaches man through matter, *insofar* as it is inhuman (that is, insofar as his human presence *is not* possible without struggle on this earth). This means, then, that the first totalization by materiality appears (within a determined society and among autonomous social groups) as the possibility of their common destruction, *and* as the permanent possibility for everyone that this destruction by matter may happen to him' through the *praxis* of other men. This first aspect of scarcity *can* condition the union of the group, in the sense that the group, collectively viewed, can organize itself to react collectively. But this dialectical and strictly human aspect of the *praxis* can in no way be confined to the relation of scarcity itself, precisely because the dialectical and positive unity of a common action is the negation of the negative unity, as the environing materiality turning back upon the individuals who have totalized it. In actual fact scarcity, as tension and as field of forces, is the expression of a quantitative fact, more or less strictly defined: any natural substance or manufactured product exists, in a specific social field, in insufficient number, *given* the number of members of the groups, or that of the region's inhabitants: *there is not enough for everyone*. Thus for each person, everyone (the group) exists insofar as the consumption of a certain product there, by others, deprives him *here* of an opportunity to find and

* As we shall see, *scarcity* is environment insofar as it is the unitary relation of a plurality of individuals. In other words, it is an individual relation and a social environment.

consume an object of the same order. In examining the vague and universal relation of indeterminate reciprocity, it may be noted that men can be united with each other indirectly in a "series," * without even suspecting the existence of this or that other person. But in the realm of scarcity, in contrast, even if individuals were unaware of each other, even if social stratifications and class structures were to break off reciprocity completely, still each person within the definite social field exists and acts in the presence of each and every one. *This* member of *this* society does not, perhaps, even know the number of individuals who compose it; perhaps he is unaware of the exact connection between man and the natural substances, the human instruments and products, which define scarcity; perhaps he explains the present poverty by absurd and quite untrue reasons. For all this, it is no less true that the other men of the group exist *together* for him, insofar as each of them is a threat to his life or, if you prefer, insofar as the existence of each is the interiorization and assumption, by a human life, of the environment as the negation of men. But if the individual member we are considering recognizes himself, through his need and his *praxis,* as being *among men,* he discloses each of them in the perspective of the object of consumption or the manufactured product; and—on the elementary level on which we are—he discloses each of them as the simple possibility of consuming an object that he needs. In short, he discovers each of them as the material possibility of his own annihilation through the material annihilation of an object of primary necessity.

*Critique de la raison dialectique, 202–205.*

## 5 EXPENDABLES

One must, of course, view these comments as describing a still very abstract moment of our regressive experience; all social antagonisms are actually qualified and structured in a given society, which itself defines, at least to a certain degree, the limits of scarcity for each of the groups that constitute it, and defines itself in the fundamental context of collective scarcity (that is, of an original connection between productive forces and the relations of production). What is important to us just

* See below, p. 459.—Ed.

now is only to set out *in sequence* the structures of dialectical intelligibility. Now, from this point of view we immediately grasp that totalization by scarcity spirals. In fact, scarcity does not express the radical impossibility of the human organism's existence (although, as I have shown, one may wonder whether the expression might not be true in this form: the radical impossibility of the human organism's existence without labor); but in a given situation, be it of the raft of the *Medusa,* an Italian city in a state of siege, or a contemporary society (which, as we know, discreetly chooses its dead, and which, in its deepest structures, is already a selection of who is to be secure and who underfed), scarcity realizes the passive totality of the individuals of a collectivity as the impossibility of coexistence. The group in the nation is defined *by its expendables* [*excédentaires*]; it must reduce itself numerically to stay alive. Note that this *numerical reduction,* always present as a practical necessity, does not necessarily take the form of murder. One can let people die (as was the case when there was a surplus of children during the Ancien Régime); one can practice birth control; in the latter case it is the unborn child, as future consumer, which is designated undesirable—that is, it is regarded either as, in the bourgeois democracies, the impossibility of feeding its brothers in the individual family or else, as in a socialist nation, China for example, as the impossibility of maintaining a certain rate of population growth so long as a certain rate of production growth cannot be surpassed. But when it is not a matter of controlling birth, the negative requirement of materiality reveals itself solely under a *quantitative* aspect. That is, one can determine the number of expendables, but not the particular individuals.\* Strongly evident here, is that *commutativity* whose full importance we shall appreciate later, and which reveals each member of the group *simultaneously* as a possible survivor, and as an expendable to be disposed of. And thus, every person's objectivity is constituted by himself and by everyone. The direct movement of need affirms him unconditionally, as having to survive; this is the practical evidence of hunger and

---

\* I have said, and I repeat, that we shall later see social institutions as the stratified and inert choice that a society makes of its dead (naturally this is *only one* of the aspects of the institution). But even when this choice is exercised, even when an oppressed and exploited class must bear it, the indeterminacy remains within that class and at the level of the individuals.

work; no direct challenge of this evidence can be conceived, for it itself translates the transcendence of a radical challenge to man by matter. But at the same time the individual is challenged by each person *in his being*, and by the same movement which transcends every challenge. Thus *his own activity* turns back against him, and reaches him *as Other* through the social environment. Through socialized matter and through material negation as inert unity, man constitutes himself as Other than man. For each person, man exists as *inhuman man*, or if you prefer as an alien species. And this does not necessarily mean that the conflict is interiorized and lived *already*, in the form of a struggle for life, but merely that the *simple existence* of each person is defined by scarcity, as the constant risk of non-existence *for another and for everyone*. Rather, I do not discover this constant risk of the annihilation of myself and of everyone only in *Others*; rather, *I myself am* that risk insofar as I am Other, that is, insofar as I am designated *with the Others* as a possible expendable by the material reality of the environment. We are concerned with an objective structure of my being, since *really* I am dangerous for the *Others*, and through the negative totality for myself, in that I form a part of that totality. . . .

When I say that man exists as Other, under the aspect of the inhuman man, one must obviously understand this for all the human occupants of the social field, considered for others and for themselves. Or in other words, each person *is* the inhuman man for all the Others; he considers all the Others as inhuman man; and he really treats the Other with inhumanity. . . . But one must understand these comments in their true sense, that is, in the perspective which recognizes that there is no human *nature*. Yet up to this moment, at least, of our prehistory, scarcity—whatever form it may take—dominates all *praxis*. Thus one must understand *both* that man's inhumanity does not come from his nature—that, far from excluding his humanity, his nature can be understood only through it—*and yet* that, as long as the sway of scarcity is not yet ended, there will be *in each man and in everyone* an inert structure of inhumanity which, in short, is nothing other than the material negation insofar as it is interiorized. Let us, in fact, understand that inhumanity is a relation of men among themselves, and cannot be anything *but that;* one can be cruel, no doubt, and uselessly so, to this or that particular animal; but it is in the name of human relations that this cruelty is blamed or punished. Who, indeed, will believe that the carnivorous species which trains hundreds of millions of animals in order to kill them, or to use their strength, and systematically destroys other animals (either for hygiene or for self-protection, or, quite gratuitously, for sport)—who will believe (unless he refers to gelded and domesticated animals and relies on too simple a symbolism) that this predatory species has placed its values and its real self-definition in its relations with animals? Now *human* relations (positive or negative) are relations of reciprocity; this means that one individual's *praxis* in its practical structure *recognizes*, in order to accomplish its purpose, the *praxis* of the other. That is, basically, it judges the duality of activities as an inessential characteristic, and the unity of the *praxes,* such as they are, as their essential character. In reciprocity, the *praxis* of my reciprocal is, as it were, fundamentally *my praxis,* separated in two by accident; each truncated part becomes a complete *praxis* again, but each preserves, from its original indifferentiation, an appropriateness to and an immediate understanding of the other. I am not claiming that the relation of reciprocity has ever existed in man *before* the relation of scarcity, since man is the historical product of scarcity. But I do say that, without this human relation of reciprocity, the inhuman relation of scarcity would not exist. Indeed, scarcity, as a unilateral relation of each and every one to matter, finally becomes the objective and social structure of the material environment and thereby designates, with its inert finger, each individual as a factor and a victim of scarcity. And each individual interiorizes this structure, in the sense that, by his behavior, he becomes *the man of scarcity.* His relation with the Other, *insofar as* it derives from matter, is a relation of exteriority; in the first place, because the Other is the pure possibility (vital but abstract) that the necessary product may be destroyed, and then, because it is defined in exteriority as a threatening but contingent possibility of the product itself, as external object; in the second place, because scarcity, as a fixed scheme of negation, organizes, through each person's *praxis,* each group of possible expendables as a totality *to be denied,* inasmuch as it is a totality that denies all that is not itself. Thus, through matter, the negative unity results in the false—that is, inert—totalization of men, as molecules of wax are inertly united, *from without,* by a seal. But since the relations of reciprocity have not been, for all that, removed, it is *into them* that exteriority slides. This means that each person's understanding of the Other's *praxis* remains, but that this other *praxis* is understood from within, to the exact extent that the materiality interiorized within the agent who understands constitutes the Other, as an inert molecule separated from all other molecules by a negation of exteriority. In pure reciprocity, what is Other than me *is also the same.* In reciprocity *modified by scarcity,* the same appears to us as the counter-man, insofar as *this same man* appears as radically Other (that is, as the bearer for us of the threat of death). Or, if you like, we understand roughly his ends (they are ours), his means (we have the same ones), the dialectical structures of his acts; but we understand them as if they were the characteristics of *another species,* our demoniac counterpart.

*Critique de la raison dialectique, 205–208.*

## 6 VIOLENCE

Nothing, in fact—neither wild beasts nor microbes—can be more terrible for man than a species that is intelligent, flesh-eating, cruel, a species which would be able to understand and to thwart the human intelligence, a species whose goal would be precisely the destruction of man. That species is obviously ours, taking hold of every man among others in the environment of scarcity. In any case, whatever society may be, this is the abstract and fundamental matrix of all the reifications of human relations. At the same time, it is the first stage of the *ethical,* insofar as this is only the *praxis* casting light upon itself on the basis of given circumstances. The first movement of the ethical, here, is the constitution of radical evil and of manichaeanism; it appraises and evaluates (we cannot linger here over the production of the values) the rupture of the reciprocity of immanence by interiorized scarcity; but it does so by grasping it as a product of the *praxis* of the Other. The counter-man, in fact, seeks the liquidation of men by sharing their goals and adopting their means; the rupture appears at the moment when this deceitful reciprocity unveils the danger of death it disguises—or, if you prefer, the impossibility for those men involved in reciprocal ties of *all* remaining upon the soil which bears and feeds them. And let us not make the mistake of thinking that this interiorized impossibility characterizes individuals *subjectively:* quite to the contrary, it makes each person *objectively dangerous* for the Other, and endangers the concrete existence of each person in that of the Other. Thus man is objectively constituted as inhuman, and this inhumanity is translated into the *praxis* by the grasp of evil as the structure of the Other. This is why the clashes—of highly ambiguous origins and rather confused nature—in which nomadic tribes indulge when, by accident, they encounter one another, have allowed the historians and ethnographers to question some elementary truths of historical materialism. It is in fact true that the economic motive is not always essential, and even, sometimes, that it cannot be found at all; these wandering groups have the whole plain to themselves alone, they *do not bother* one another. But this is not the question. It is not always necessary for scarcity to be explicitly involved; rather, it is that, in each of those tribes, the man of scarcity encounters in the other tribe the man of scarcity in the aspect of the counter-man. Each person is constituted in such a manner, by his struggle against the physical world and against men (often within his own group), that the appearance of strangers—bringing up, for him, both the link of interiority and the link of absolute exteriority— makes him perceive man in the form of an alien species. The strength of his aggressiveness, of his hate, *resides in need,* but it matters little that this need has just been satisfied; its perpetual rebirth and the anxiety of each person result, every time a tribe appears, in constituting its members as famine overtaking the other group in the form of a human *praxis.* And, in the clash, it is not the simple danger of scarcity which each antagonist wishes to destroy in the other; rather it is the *praxis* itself, insofar as it is a betrayal of man in the interest of the counter-man. Thus we consider, at the very level of need and through need, that scarcity lives itself, in practice, through manichaean activity, and that the ethical reveals itself as a destructive imperative: evil *must* be destroyed. It is at this level, too, that one must define *violence* as a structure of human action under the sway of manichaeanism and in the context of scarcity. Violence claims always to be a *counter-violence,* that is, retaliation to the violence of the Other. This *violence of the Other* is an objective reality only to the extent that it exists in all as the universal motivation of counter-violence; and it is very simply the intolerable fact of the reciprocity which has been broken, and of the systematic utilization of man's humanity for effecting the destruction of the human. Counter-violence is exactly the same thing, but in the role of a process of restoring one's rights, in the role of a response to provocation: in destroying the inhumanity of the counter-man in the antagonist, I can, in fact, only destroy in him the humanity of the man, and realize his inhumanity within myself. Whether it is a question of killing, torturing, enslaving, or merely mystifying, my goal is to do away with alien liberty as a hostile force, that is, as that force which can repulse me from the practical field and make of me an individual who is "superfluous" [*de trop*], condemned to death. In other words it is man *qua* man, that is, as free *praxis* of an organized being, that I am attacking; it is man, and nothing else, that I hate in the enemy—that is, myself as Other, and it is certainly I whom I wish to destroy in him, in order to prevent him from destroying me, actually, in my body. But these relations of exteriority in reciprocity are complicated by the development of the *praxis* itself, which re-establishes the reciprocity in its negative form, as antagonism, beginning at the moment when a real struggle is developing. Reckoning from the concrete necessities of strategy and tactics, one is obliged to lose out if one does *not recognize* the antagonist as another human group capable of inventing snares, of foiling one's own snares, of letting itself be caught in some of them. The conflicts of scarcity (from wars between nomads to strikes) perpetually oscillate between two poles: the one makes of the conflict the manichaean struggle of men against their terrible counterparts, while the other reduces it to the human proportions of a dispute that is resolved by violence because conciliations are exhausted, or because mediations are lacking. What is important here is that the *praxis*, once it constitutes itself as the activity of an army, a class, or even a more restricted group, transcends *in principle* the reifying inertia of the relations of scarcity. I mean by this that the inert morality of manichaeism and radical evil implies a distance suffered, an impotency lived, a certain manner of discovering scarcity as destiny—in short, a veritable domination of man by the interiorized material environment. It is not, then, a question of a permanent structure, in the sense in which it would remain fixed and inert at a certain level of human density, but rather of a certain moment of human relations, always transcended, and partially liquidated, always reviving. In truth, this moment is located between the liquidation, by the scarcity of positive reciprocities (to whatever degree of the human *praxis* this liquidation is produced), and the reappearance, under the dominion of the same scarcity, of negative and antagonistic reciprocities. And this intermediary moment is precisely the first moment, and the productive scheme, of the complex process of reification. In this moment, the individuals of a social field live with the environment in a false relation of reciprocity (that is, they designate what they are, and what others are, through matter, as pure quantity), and carry this relation into the social realm by living their reciprocity of human beings as a denied interiority—or, if you prefer, by living it falsely in exteriority.

It will be said that we must still explain how matter as scarcity can unite men in a common practical field, while the free human relations, taken outside of economic constraint, reduce themselves to constellations of reciprocity. In other words, since the totalizing power derives from the *praxis*, how does matter govern *the totalizing actions* by scarcity, in such a way as to make them effect the totalization of all the individual totalizations? But the answer lies in the question itself: one must, in fact, conceive that neighboring groups, even those of differing structure—for example, Chinese peasants and nomads, on the frontiers of China during the T'ang dynasty—are materially united in a single place, defined simultaneously by a certain material configuration, a certain state of techniques and of communications. The nomads have a restricted area of travel—they remain, after all, at the edge of the desert; the Chinese peasants, that army of pioneers, advance step by step, each day wresting a little arable land from the unproductive desert. The two groups know one another, an extreme tension opposes them and unites them; for the Chinese the nomads are looters who know how to do nothing but steal the fruits of others' labor; for the nomads the Chinese are veritable colonists who are pushing them back little by little into an uninhabitable desert. Each group, insofar as it is *praxis* (we shall return to the group), makes the Other figure as an object in the unity of its practical field; each one knows that he figures as an object in the group of the Other. This utilitarian knowledge will express itself, for example, in the precautions that the peasants will take against surprise attacks, in the care the nomads put into preparing their next raid. But it is *just this* which prevents the two movements of practical unification from constituting, with the same environment, two *different fields of action*. For each, the existence of the Other, as the object of which it is the object, simply constitutes the material field as undermined, or in other words as having a double foundation. In this coexistence, there is no duality unless it exist as the double meaning of each material object. The field constitutes itself practically as a means capable of being utilized by the Other; it is a mediation between the two groups, to the extent that each makes of it a means against the means of the Other. Everything is, at the same time, snare and feint; the hidden reality of the object is what the Other will make of it. At the same time that the pure materiality of the environment becomes the contradictory unity of two opposed totalizations, each group, insofar as it is an object among objects—that is, insofar as it is the means chosen by the Other to attain its ends—finds itself objectively totalized as a material fragility with all the other material structures of the field. Insofar as it is a transcended, foiled *praxis*, a deceived liberty used against its will . . . , each individual and each village realize themselves as being objectively characterized by the inertia of what surrounds them; and this objective character will show itself the more definitely, the more the peasants who fear the raid take more precise measures to avoid it by transcending their environment. In the solitary *praxis,* as we have seen, the cultivator makes of himself an inert object for acting upon the soil; now his inertia reappears, coming to him through other men. But if, in an engagement, the relation of forces is favorable to him, he perceives his new labor (war is a labor of man upon man) in the guise of a *power*. By that, we must understand something entirely new, that is, the effectiveness of a human *praxis*, through matter, against the *praxis* of the other, and the possibility of transforming an objectivizing object into an absolute object. But what particularly interests us, from our point of view, is that each square foot of the practical field totalizes the two groups and their two activities for each of their members, insofar as the terrain presents itself as the permanent possibility of alienation for each and for all. The negative unity of scarcity, interiorized in the reification of reciprocity, re-exteriorizes itself for us all in the unity of the world as the common ground of our oppositions; and we re-interiorize this unity into a new negative unity: we are united by the fact that we all inhabit a world defined by scarcity.

*Critique de la raison dialectique, 208–211.*

## 7 LABOR

It goes without saying that scarcity can be the occasion for the realignment of social groups with the project of combating it. In fact, man makes his living in the midst of other men who are making theirs, too (or who are having it made by others)—that is, in the social field of scarcity. It is not my intention to study the type of groups and institutions which form themselves within this social field; we are not concerned with reconstituting the moments of History or the descriptions of sociology. Besides, this is not the moment to discuss human fields insofar as they unify themselves under the impetus of an active organization of multiplicity, with differentiated functions; instead we must pursue our experience in the regressive order, and return to materiality as the inert synthesis of human plurality. However, we shall not leave this stage without having commented upon these unified and differentiated groups, but we shall do so only insofar as they are struggling against scarcity, and insofar as scarcity conditions their structures. They constitute and institutionalize themselves—not insofar as scarcity appears to each in need, through the need of Others, but insofar as it is denied, in the unified field of the *praxis, by labor.* Obviously, we must understand by this that labor is, as we have seen, *first of all the organism* reducing itself to an inertia directed to act upon inertia and to satisfy itself as need. This does not in itself mean . . . that labor must be defined as a struggle against scarcity. But in a social field defined by scarcity—that is, in the human and historical field—labor defines itself necessarily, for man, as the *praxis* aiming to satisfy its need *in the context of scarcity,* and by a special negation of the latter. In hunting, for example, where it is not a question of the systematic production of a tool but of *finding* animals that already exist in the field, one must not forget that the speed of the "game," the *average* distance it keeps (a flock of migrating birds in the sky, etc.), dangers of all kinds, constitute *factors of scarcity*. Thus the hunting rifle appears as creator, in the sense that, negatively, it partially destroys the distance, it opposes its speed to the speed of the hunted animal; and, positively, it multiplies, for the hunter, the number of his possible prey, or (in the end the same thing) the opportunities for hitting one of them. And—what is important within the chosen perspective—it is the same thing *here* to declare that the number of opportunities for an individual or family to be fed is multiplied by the tool in a given practical field (for this practical field, at the level at which we are considering it, is not *really changed* by the tool), or at least, conversely, that the tool brings a transformation of the practical field for the populations that live from hunting and fishing—if not perhaps in its amplitude, then in its differentiation and its abundance. Thus the human labor of the individual (and consequently of the group) is conditioned in its end, and thus in its movement, by man's basic project of transcending scarcity —for himself or for the group—as the danger of death, the present suffering and the primitive relation which *simultaneously* constitute Nature by man and man by Nature. But *precisely for this reason*, scarcity—without ceasing to be that basic relation —will qualify the whole group or the individual combating this scarcity by *making themselves scarce to destroy scarcity*. In certain special historical conditions, if technique enables a certain stage of scarcity to be transcended—in other words, if the environment worked by preceding generations and the number and quality of the tools available allow a definite number of workers to increase production in definite proportions—it is the men who become scarce, or risk becoming so. . . . It is the scarcity of products that designates men as scarcity in a social field (but not in all of them), *at the same time* that it continues to designate them commutatively as expendables insofar as they are men of need. And naturally, this scarcity of men can designate one structure of organization as well as another (lack of manpower, lack of professional workers, lack of technicians, lack of trained personnel). In any case, what is important is that within a given group, the individual is constituted in his humanity by other individuals, *simultaneously* as expendable and as scarce. His expendable aspect is immediate. His aspect as *scarce object* appears in the most primitive forms of practical association, and creates a perpetual tension in a particular society. But in particular societies, with certain modes of production, the scarcity of man with respect to the tool can transform itself, under the effect of its own effects, into the scarcity of the tool with respect to man. The heart of the question remains the same: for a given society the number of tools designates, by itself, the producers; and, at the same time, the sum of producers and of means of production defines the limits of production and the margin of nonproducers (that is, of rejected producers) which society can permit itself. The extra nonproducers represent an expendable which can either vegetate in malnutrition or can disappear. It goes without saying that this new form of scarcity presupposes a society which rests upon *particular* kinds of work, carried out in common by an organized group. But by that we have not defined a particular historical society; Chinese society in imperial times (in that it is conditioned first of all by the flow of its rivers), like Roman society (in that it assures its domination over the Mediterranean world by the construction of an immense communications system), answers the requisite conditions as well as does capitalism, although this type of scarcity is essentially developed during the course of the movement of modern industrialization. But in the same manner, in certain structured historical circumstances, the institutionally established inequality of classes and of conditions may draw along in its wake a total reversal of the situation, that is, *a scarcity of the consumer with respect to the object produced.* Granted this is a question of a relative scarcity, explained *at one and the same time* by a certain material rigidity of production (which cannot be dropped below certain limits) and by an institutionalized social choice of the consumers (or rather, of the hierarchy of consumers, which itself betrays the social structures crystallized about the mode of production—what the Marxists call "the relations of production)." It is all too clear that this reversal is particularly characteristic of our capitalistic society, and represents an expression of its basic contradiction: overproduction. But it is the absence of an internal market capable of absorbing all the production which, since antiquity, has compelled maritime societies to trade by sea (that is, to search for new products or for raw materials, and especially to organize reciprocal markets); it is this which has forced the Continental powers into military imperialism.

But this scarcity of men with respect to the product, the ultimate turning back on itself of the dialectic of scarcity, presupposes, as an essential condition, the scarcity of the product with respect to man. This scarcity exists as man's fundamental determination: we know that socialization of production does not abolish it, unless this be in the course of a long dialectical process whose outcome we cannot anticipate. The scarcity of the consumer, with respect to this product or that, is conditioned by the scarcity of all products with respect to all consumers. It is, in fact, on the basis of this fundamental scarcity, beginning with the mode of production, that certain relations of production are defined, relations which institutionally exclude certain social groups from full consumption and which reserve this consumption for other groups (insufficient in number to consume everything). It is perfectly useless to expound here the dialectic of "overproduction" and the crises it engenders; all that is important is to indicate that, in the process as a whole, it ruins capitalism—by a lack of outlets in a regime of competition—in the same degree that it augments the scarcity, for the proletariat, of objects of primary necessity. It is perfectly logical, at this level of the contradiction, to see the same society liquidate a part of its members as expendable, and destroy a part of its products because production is expendable with respect to consumption. It would, besides, be distributing these products for nothing, to those very people it is permitting to die; moreover, we know that in so doing it would not help their plight at all. In fact, the change should take place at the level of the mode of production and the fundamental relations it engenders, in order that the possibility of the scarcity of consumers be in any case excluded, and that the fundamental reality be eliminated in a long-term process. What interests us, from the point of view of the logical structures of History, is that the historical process constitutes itself through the field of scarcity; if it actualizes all of this field's dialectical possibilities, it does so by its contingent *de facto* materiality, the outcome of a primary contingency. . . .

*Critique de la raison dialectique, 211–214.*

We must clearly understand here that the rediscovery of scarcity in experience does not claim at all to contradict the Marxist theory, nor to complete it. It is of another order. The essential discovery of Marxism is that labor, as historical reality and as the utilization of determined tools in an already determined social and material sphere, is the real basis of the organization of social relations. This discovery *can no longer* be challenged. What *we* are showing is this: the possibility that these social relations become contradictory itself proceeds from an inert and material negation, which is re-interiorized by man. We are also showing that *violence,* as the negative relation of one *praxis* to another, characterizes the immediate relation of all men, not as real action but as the inorganic structure re-interiorized by organisms; also, that the possibility of reification is given in all human relations—even in a pre-capitalist period, even in relations between family members or friends. As for scarcity itself, it has a formal dialectic that we have sketched out: the scarcity of the product, the scarcity of the tool, the scarcity of the worker, the scarcity of the consumer; also, it has an historical and concrete dialectic, of which we have nothing to say, since it is for the historians to retrace these stages. In fact, it would be necessary to show a double transition under the influence of production itself. On the one hand, there is a transition from scarcity as the expendable character of each person with respect to all, to scarcity as society's designation of groups of underconsuming producers. (At this moment the relation becomes *violence* between the groups, not because it has been necessarily established by violence—Engels is right—but because it *is* in itself a relation of violence, between violent men.) On the other hand, there is a transition from the absolute scarcity, as a certain impossibility of existing together in certain material conditions determined for all the members of the group, to relative scarcity as the impossibility, in given circumstances, for the group to grow beyond a certain limit without the mode or relations of production changing (*i.e.*, scarcity reassumed as the discreet liquidation of the unproductive, within a given society and according to certain rules *at the same time as* the choosing of undernourished producers). This relative scarcity which itself has an historical dialectic (that is, an intelligible history) passes into the rank of *institution*, in societies divided into classes. The analytic study of the relations of scarcity is called political economy. All this is tantamount to saying that in restoring to scarcity its importance, one does not revert to some pre-Marxist theory asserting the supremacy of the "consumption" factor; rather, one brings out negativity, as the implicit motive of the historical dialectic, and gives it its intelligibility. In the *environment of scarcity*, all the structures of a determined society rest upon its mode of production. . . .

*Praxis* is above all the instrumentalization of material reality. It envelops the inanimate thing in a totalizing project which imposes a pseudo-organic unity upon it. By this I mean that this unity is indeed that of a whole, but that it remains social and human, it does not attain *in itself* the structures of exteriority which constitute the molecular world. If, on the other hand, the unity persists, it is *through material inertia*. But since this unity is nothing but the passive reflection of the *praxis*— that is, of a human undertaking carried out under determined conditions, with well-defined tools and within an historical society at a certain stage of its development—the object produced reflects the entire collectivity. Only it reflects the collectivity in the dimension of passivity. Let us take the example of the act of *sealing:* it is done on the occasion of certain ceremonies (treaties, contracts, etc.), by means of a certain tool. The wax *reproduces* [*retourne*] this act; its inertia reflects the *action* as pure *being-there*. At this level, the practice absorbed by its "material" becomes the material caricature of the human. The manufactured object proposes to, and imposes upon, men. It designates them and indicates to them how it is to be used. This complex of signs could be introduced into a general theory of meaning, by saying that the tool is meaningful [*signifiant*] and that man is here a *meant* [*signifié*]. In actual fact, the meaning came to the tool through the labor of man, and man can mean only what he knows. In a sense, then, it seems that the tool reflects for individuals only their own knowledge. This can be seen in the routine of the artisan, who grasps, through the tool he himself has made, the eternal recurrence of the same gestures that define a permanent status within the corporation or the town, with respect to an unvarying clientele.

But precisely because the meaning has taken on the character of materiality, it enters into relation with the entire universe. This means that an infinity of unpredictable relations is established, through the intermediary of social practice, between the matter that absorbs the *praxis* and the other materialized meanings.

The inert *praxis* permeating matter transforms natural forces without meaning into quasi-human practices—that is, into passified actions. Grousset correctly notes that the Chinese peasants are colonists: for four thousand years they have conquered the arable soil at the borders of the country, at the expense of nature and the nomads. One aspect of their activity is the deforestation which has gone on, century after century. This *praxis* is living and real, and retains a traditional aspect: even recently, the peasant was ripping out bushes to clear a place for millet. But at the same time, the *praxis* leave its mark upon nature, both positively and negatively. Its positive aspect is that of the soil and its apportionment to cultivation. Its negative aspect is a meaning not grasped by the peasants themselves, precisely because it is an absence: *the absence of trees*. This characteristic immediately strikes any European who *today* flies over China in an airplane: the present government has become aware of it and knows the seriousness of the danger. But the traditionalist Chinese of past centuries could not grasp it, for their goal was the conquest of the soil; they saw the plenty represented by the harvest, and were not alert to *that lack* which was for them, at the most, only a liberation—the elimination of an obstacle. From this viewpoint, deforestation—as passified pratice that has become *characteristic* of the mountains, in particular of those that dominate Szechwan—transforms the physico-chemical sector that might be called "wild" because it starts where human practice ends. To begin with, this wild sector is human to the exact extent to which it reveals, for society, its historical limit at a determined moment. But above all, deforestation as the elimination of obstacles becomes, negatively, the absence of protection: since the loess of mountains and of peneplains is not held by the trees, it fills the rivers, raises them above the level of the plain and, in the lower parts of their courses, blocks them up like a cork so that they overflow. Thus, the whole process of the terrible Chinese floods appears as a deliberately constructed mechanism. If some enemy of mankind had wanted to persecute the workers of Great China, he

would have ordered mercenary troops systematically to defor-
est the mountains. The positive system of cultivation is transformed into an infernal machine. Now, the enemy who brought
the loess, the river, the gravity, the whole hydrodynamics, into
this destructive apparatus—is the peasant himself. But his activity, taken in the moment of its living development, does not
warrant, by intention or in reality, this reversal: in *this* place, for
*this* man who is farming, there exists only an organic link between the negative (elimination of the obstacle) and the positive (enlargement of the arable sector). For counter-finality to
exist, it is necessary above all that a sort of *disposition* of matter (here, the geological and hydrographic structure of China)
adumbrate it in advance. . . .

Matter alone carries meanings. It retains them in itself, like
engravings, and gives them their real effectiveness: in losing
their human properties, man's projects are engraved in Being
—their translucency becomes opacity, their superficiality becomes density, their volatile lightness becomes permanence;
they *come into Being* as they lose their character of lived
event. Insofar as they are Being, they refuse—even if they are
deciphered and known—to be dissolved themselves into knowledge. Only matter itself, knocking against matter, can disintegrate them. The meaning of human labor is that man reduces
himself to inorganic materiality, in order to act materially
upon matter and to change his material life. Through tran-
substantiation, the project that our bodies engrave in the thing
assumes the substantial characteristics of that thing, without
entirely losing its original qualities. Thus it comes to possess
an inert future, within which we shall have to determine our
own future. The future comes to man through things, to the extent that it has come to things through man. Meanings as passive impenetrability become, in the human universe, the surro-
gates for man: to them he delegates his powers. By contact,
and by passive action *at a distance*, they modify the whole of
the material universe. This means both that they have been
engraved into Being, and that Being has been poured into the
world of meanings. But in addition, this means that these
heavy and inert objects are situated at the base of a community whose relations are *from one side* relations of interiority.
It is through this interiority that a material element can modify,
at a distance, another material element (for example, the reduc-

tion in the output of the mines in the Americas checked inflation in the Mediterranean countries in the mid-seventeenth century). But by this very modification, it helps to break the link of interiority that unites men among themselves. From this point of view, one can accept both Durkheim's formula: "Treat social facts as things," and the answer of Weber and of contemporaries: "Social facts are not things." Or, if you prefer, social facts are things to the extent that *all things*, directly or indirectly, are social facts.

*Critique de la raison dialectique,*
*224–225, 231–233, 245–246.*

## 9 THE TOOL

The project reawakens the meanings; it restores to them, for a moment, their vigor and their true unity in the process of transcendence which ends by engraving this totality in an already meaningful and perfectly inert material—be it iron, marble, or language—but a material that others, from beneath, animate with their movement like those stagehands who make waves by crawling about under a canvas. Everything changes, becomes jumbled; the different meanings pile up and intermingle in a passive recomposition which substitutes the fixity of Being for the unlimited progress of the totalization in act, and encloses the totality-object in its limits and produces the set of contradictions that will oppose it to the Universe. For it is not the understanding that solidifies meanings, it is Being; in this sense, the materiality of the thing or of the institution is the radical negation of invention or creation; but this negation reaches Being through the project that denies prior negations. In the pair, "matter-undertaking," man becomes denied by matter. Depositing his meanings (that is, the pure totalizing transcendence of the former Being) in matter, he lends his negative power, which impregnates materiality and transforms itself into destructive power.\* . . .

---

\* This is what primitive man immediately grasps, when he dreads and reveres, in the arrow or the ax, his own power become maleficent and turned against him. In this sense there is nothing surprising in those religious ceremonies in which a supernatural power is conferred upon the weapons whose effectiveness is revealed every day by technique and experience. For this effectiveness is

Man is still the man of need, of *praxis*, and of scarcity. But, insofar as he is dominated by matter, his activity no longer derives directly from need, although that is its fundamental basis. It is awakened in him from without, by processed matter as the practical requirement of the inanimate object. Or, if you prefer, it is the object that designates its man, as he of whom a certain behavior is expected. If we are, in fact, concerned with a restricted social and practical field, the need of the worker and the necessity of making his living (or of selling his labor force to purchase provisions) suffice to create, for each person, the unifying and totalizing tension of the field. But this need is not necessarily present "in person": it is simply that to which the *praxis* entirely refers. On the other hand, insofar as this social field (factory or workshop, for example) is unified by all the others, through an already constituted hierarchy, the individual worker is subject to this unification in the things themselves, as an alien force and, at the same time, as his own force (this is outside of the structure of alienation, strictly speaking, insofar as it is linked to capitalistic exploitation). And this unification that refers him to the Others, and to himself as Other, is quite simply the collective unity of labor (of the workshop or factory), insofar as he can grasp this unity concretely only in the perspective of his own work. Actually, if he *sees* other workers laboring, the unification of their movements is an abstract knowledge, but he experiences his own labor as the labor of Others, of all the Others of whom he is one—insofar as the general movement of the collective *praxis* reawakens the practical meanings that work already performed, in other times and places, has deposited in the tools. In actual fact, a tool is a *praxis* crystallized and inverted by the inert that sustains it, and this *praxis* in the tool is directed to anyone at all: a brace and bit, a monkey wrench designate me just as well as they do my neighbor. Only these designations, when directed to me, remain generally abstract and

---

**simultaneously** the crystallization of a human labor (the labor *of another*) and the congealed indication of a future performance. This fusion of Other and oneself in a sort of eternity, this possession of the hunter by the technical talents of the blacksmith, and finally this petrification of the one and of the other—in these primitive man sees at the same time a beneficent power and a threat; beneath the *instrumentality* of processed matter [*matière ouvrée*] he suspects its secret hostility. This contradiction, as has long been known, characterizes the relation to the holy.

purely logical, because I am a petty-bourgeois intellectual or, if you prefer, I am designated as a petty-bourgeois intellectual by the very fact that these relations remain purely dead possibilities. The skilled worker, on the other hand, in the practical field of common labor and in act, is really and directly designated by the tool or the machine by which he is affected. In actual fact, the *method for use*—such as the machine's producer established it in the past—does not designate him any more than it does me; it is only a certain way of making itself used which constitutes the object itself, whoever the user may be. But through this dead designation of inertia, the group at work designates it, to the very extent that the work of all depends upon the work of each. But as Marx has shown, the machine, as passive materiality, realizes itself as *negation* of this human interdependence, interposing itself between the workers, to the exact extent that it is the indispensable means of their work; the living solidarity of the group is destroyed before it has even been able to form. What a man expects of another man, when their relation is human, defines itself in reciprocity, for expectation is a human act. There could be no question of their relation imposing a *passive requirement* [*exigence*] except when, in a complex group, the divisions, the separations, and the rigidity of the organs of transmission replace the living relations by a mechanical status of materiality (we shall deal with this later); for the *praxis*, as such, can unite itself to *praxis* in reciprocal action, and each man can decide his end to the extent to which he recognizes that of the Other; but no *praxis* as such can even formulate an imperative, simply because requiredness does not enter into the structure of reciprocity.*

*Critique de la raison dialectique*, 249, 252–253.

* We shall see later the individual affecting himself with inertia through the oath. Requiredness becomes possible.

# III

·

## Social Structures

### 1 SOLITUDE

Consider a group of people on the place Saint-Germain. They are waiting for a bus, at the bus stop in front of the church. I use the word "group" here in its neutral sense: as yet I do not know whether this gathering we are concerned with is, as such, the inert result of separate activities; or whether it is a common reality, regulating the acts of each person; or whether it is a conventional or a contractual organization. These people—whose age, sex, class, and social milieu are different—realize, within the commonplace life of everyday, the relation of solitude, reciprocity, and unification from without (and massification from without) that characterizes, for example, the residents of a big city insofar as they are united without being integrated through work, struggle, or any other activity within an organized group common to them all. We must, in fact, note first of all that we are concerned with a plurality of solitudes: these people do not care about one another, do not speak to one another, and in general do not look at one another; they exist side by side, around a signpost. At this level, I might note that their solitude is not an inert status (or the simple reciprocal exteriority of organisms); rather, it is lived, *in actual fact,* in the project of each, as his negative structure. Or, if you wish, the solitude of the organism, as the impossibility of uniting with the Others in an organic totality, reveals itself through the solitude lived by each person as the provisory negation of reciprocal relations with the Others. This man is isolated not only by his body, as such, but by the fact that he turns his back on his neighbor—who, moreover, has not even noticed him (or has discovered him in his practical field, as a general individual defined by waiting for the bus). And this attitude of semi-unawareness has as its practical condi-

456

tions the real affiliation with other groups: it is morning, he has just got up, left his dwelling; he is still involved with his children, who are sick, etc. Furthermore, he is going to the office; he has an oral report to make to his superior. He is preoccupied with its phrasing, rehearsing it under his breath, etc. Another practical condition is his being-in-the-inert (*i.e.*, his interest). This plurality of separations can, then, express itself, in a certain fashion, as the negative of the individuals' integration into separate groups (or groups that are separated *at this time* and *at this level*); and, through this, as the negative of each person's projects insofar as they determine the social field on the basis of given conditions. But conversely, if the question is examined from the standpoint of the groups, interests, etc.—in short, the social structures insofar as they express the fundamental set-up of society (mode of production, relations of production, etc.) —one can, on the other hand, define each solitude from the standpoint of the forces of disintegration which the social group exercises on individuals (forces which are, of course, the correlatives of forces of integration, which we shall discuss soon). Or, if you wish, the intensity of solitude, as a relation of exteriority between the members of a temporary and contingent gathering, expresses *the extent of massification* of the social group, insofar as it is produced on the basis of given conditions. At this level, the reciprocal solitudes, as negation of reciprocity, signify the integration of the individuals into the same society and, *in this sense*, can be defined as a certain manner (conditioned by the totalization in process) of living, in interiority and as reciprocity, within society, the exteriorized negation of all interiority: "No one helps anyone, it's every man for himself"; or, on the other hand, in sympathy, as Proust wrote: "Every person is very much alone." Ultimately, in our example, solitude becomes—for every man and through him, for him and for the others—the real and social product of big cities. Actually, for every member of the group waiting for the bus, the big city is present . . . as the practico-inert group in which there is a movement toward the interchangeability of men and of their instruments; the city has been there since morning, as requirement, as instrumentality, as social milieu, etc. And, in terms of the city, we are aware of the millions of people who are the city, and whose perfectly invisible presence makes of each person a polyvalent solitude (with millions of facets), and, *at the same time*, an *integrated* member of the city (the *"vieux Parisien,"* the *"Parisien de Paris,"* etc.). Let us add to this the fact that the mode of life awakens in each individual modes of behavior which are *solitary*—buy the paper as you leave the house, read it on the bus, etc.—which often are *operations* for making the transition from one group to another (from family intimacy to the public life of the office). Thus solitude is a project. As such, moreover, it is relative to certain individuals and to certain moments: to isolate oneself by reading the paper is to utilize the national collectivity and, in the end, the totality of living men, insofar as one figures among them and is dependent on all of them, to separate oneself from the hundred people who are waiting for or using the same vehicle in common. Organic solitude, experienced solitude, lived solitude, solitude-behavior, solitude as a social status of the individual, solitude as the exteriority of the groups conditioning the exteriority of the individuals, solitude as a reciprocity of isolations in a society that creates *masses:* all these forms, all these oppositions come together at once in the little group we are considering, insofar as isolation is an historical and social means of man's behavior among a gathering of men.

But at the same time, the relation of reciprocity remains in the gathering itself, and among its members; the negation of solitude by the *praxis* preserves it in its denial: it is, in fact, the pure and simple practical existence of men among men. Not only do we find it as a lived reality—since each person, even though he turns his back on the Others, even though he knows neither their number nor their appearance, knows that they exist as a finite and indeterminate plurality *of which he is a part*—but, even outside each person's real relation to the Others, the sum of *solitary* behaviors, insofar as they are conditioned by the historical totalization, presupposes, at every level, a structure of reciprocity: it must be the most conscious possibility and the most immediate reality, in order that the social patterns in usage—clothing, haircut, demeanor, etc.—be adopted by each (although this is certainly *not all* that is necessary), and in order that each person, noticing something out of order in his dress, repair it hastily and, if possible, in secret. This means that solitude does not lift one out of the visual and practical field of the Other, and that it realizes itself objectively in this field.

*Critique de la raison dialectique, 308–310.*

At this level, we can once again recognize the same society (which we just saw as an agent of massification), insofar as its practico-inert being serves as an environment conducive to inter-individual reciprocities: for these separate men form a group, *insofar as* they are all standing on the same sidewalk protecting them from the cars crossing the square, *insofar as* they are grouped around the same bus stop, etc. And especially, these individuals form a group in that they have a *common interest*, that is, insofar as, separated as organic individuals, a structure of their practico-inert being is common to them, and unites them from without. They are all—or almost all—employees, users of the bus line, knowing the timetable and frequency of the buses; consequently they are waiting for the *same* vehicle: the 7:49 bus. This object, insofar as they are dependent upon it (breakdowns, failures, accidents), is *their present interest*. But this present interest—since they all live in the same district—goes back to fuller and deeper structures of their general interest: improvement of public transportation, stabilization of fares, etc. The bus they wait for unites them, as being their interest as individuals who *this morning* have business on the other side of town; but already, as the 7:49, it is *their interest as users*: everything is temporalized. The individual passenger recognizes himself as *resident* (that is, he reflects the five or ten preceding years), and at the same time, the vehicle is characterized by its daily, eternal return (actually it is, in fact, *the same*, with the same driver and conductor). The object acquires a structure which exceeds its pure inert existence; it is provided, as such, with a passive future and past, which present it to the passengers as a small fragment of their destiny.

However, to the extent to which the bus designates the present users, it constitutes them in their *interchangeability*: each person, in fact, is produced by the social group as united to his neighbors, insofar as he is narrowly identical with them. In other words, their external-being (that is, the interest they have as users of the bus line) is unique, insofar as it is a pure and indivisible abstraction, not a rich, differentiated synthesis; it is a simple identity, designating the user as an abstract generality by a definite *praxis* (signal the bus, climb aboard, pay the fare, and sit down), in the development of a large and synthetic *praxis* (the undertaking which, each morning, unites driver and conductor in this temporalization that is *one* particular ride through Paris at a certain hour). At this moment of the experience, the group has its unique being outside of itself, in an object to come, and each individual insofar as he is determined by the common interest differentiates himself from each other only by the simple materiality of the organism. And already, if the group is characterized in its temporalization as waiting for its being, insofar as it is the being of all, the abstract unity of the common being-to-come [*à-venir*] reveals itself as *being-other* with respect to the organism which it *is concretely* (or if you prefer, which it *exists*). This moment cannot be that of conflict, and is already no more than that of reciprocity; it must be regarded, quite simply, as the abstract stage of identity. Insofar as *they have the same objective reality* in the future (a moment longer, the same moment for all, and the vehicle will appear around the corner), the *unjustifiable* separation of these organisms (insofar as it arises from other conditions, and another region of being) is determined as *identity*. There is *identity* when the *common* interest (as determination of generality by the unity of an object, in the context of defined practices) is revealed, and when the plurality is defined exactly *with respect to that interest*. In that moment, in fact, it matters little that the passengers are differentiated by biological or social characteristics; insofar as they are united by an abstract generality, they are, as separate individuals, identical. Identity is the practico-inert unity to come, insofar as it is determined itself in the present moment as *meaningless separation*. And since all the lived characteristics which might serve as a differentiation of interiority fall outside of that determination, the identity of each person with each Other is their unity over there, as being-other; here and now, it is their common otherness. Each person is the same as the Others insofar as he is Other than himself. And identity as otherness is the *separation of exteriority*, or if you prefer, the impossibility of realizing, through the body, the transcendent unity to come, insofar as one feels this unity as irrational necessity.*

It is precisely at this level that the material object will deter-

---

* It is, in fact, perfectly rational, if one reconstructs the stages of the entire process. Just the same, the conflict between interchangeability and existence (as unique, lived *praxis*) must be lived, at a certain level, as an absurdity which is *shocking*.

mine the serial order as the social reason for the separation of individuals. The practico-inert requirement emerges, here, out of scarcity: *there is not room enough for everyone*. But, in addition to scarcity as the contingent but fundamental relation of man to Nature, there remains the context of the whole experience; *this* particular scarcity is an aspect of material inertia. Whatever be the demands, the object remains passively what it is; nor must it be believed that the material requirement is necessarily a special and directly experienced scarcity; we shall see other practico-inert structures of the object, *as being individuated by the generality*, conditioning other serial relations. I have merely chosen this example for its simplicity. The particular scarcity, then—the number of people in proportion to the number of seats—would designate without any particular practical arrangement, each person as in excess; that is, the Other would be the rival of an Other by the very fact of their identity; the separation would turn into contradiction. But, except in instances of panic—where, indeed, everyone fights against *himself in the Other*, turning in panic from an abstract unity and a concrete but unthinkable singularity—the relation of reciprocity, being, emerging or re-emerging in the exteriority of identity, establishes the interchangeability as the impossibility of deciding, *a priori*, who is in excess; it encourages an arbitrary procedure whose only purpose is to avoid, through some order, conflicts or unfairness. The passengers, waiting for the bus, have lined up in the order of arrival. This means that they accept *the impossibility of deciding who is in excess in terms of the intrinsic qualities of the individual;* in other words, they remain upon the terrain of the common interest, of the identity of separation as meaningless negation; positively, this means that they seek to differentiate each Other from the Others without adding anything to his *character of Other* as unique social determination of his existence. The *serial unity*, then, as common interest, imposes itself as requirement and destroys all opposition.

*Critique de la raison dialectique*, *310–312.*

### 3 ALIENATION

To be alienated or simply altered, the individual must be an organism susceptible of dialectical action; and it is through the free *praxis* that necessity is revealed as a transformation of his product and himself by his product in the Other. The constraints of need, the requirements of the processed Thing, the imperatives of the Other, his own powerlessness—his *praxis* reveals all these to him, and interiorizes them. His free activity, in its freedom, takes upon itself everything that crushes him: exhausting work, exploitation, oppression, rising prices. This is tantamount to saying that his freedom is the means chosen by the Thing and the Other to crush him, and to transform him into a processed Thing. Thus the period of the free contract by which, in the nineteenth century, the isolated worker, prey to hunger and poverty, sells his labor strength to a powerful employer who imposes his own prices—this is both the most shameless mystification and a reality. Certainly he has no other out; the choice is impossible, he has not the ghost of a chance of finding better-paid work, and besides he does not even ask himself the question: what is at stake? He goes to sell himself at the factory every morning (during the *belle époque*, they made daily contracts to retain workers), by a sort of somber and resigned *exis* which scarcely resembles a *praxis*. And yet, after all, a *praxis* is involved: habit is directed, organized, in the end settled; the means are chosen (if he learns that many workers will be presenting themselves for hire, he will get up an hour earlier to be there before the others); in other words, the ineluctable destiny that is overwhelming him goes through him. Those factory girls ruminating a vague dream, are at the same time pulsating with a rhythm *external to them*—a rhythm which is the work of all *as other*. It is correct to claim that the semi-automatic machine is dreaming through them. But at the same time, these dreams are a mute and personal behavior, which realizes the machine's verdict by pursuing its own ends (stabilization of the physical person against devaluation by the alien universality of what is required, etc.). And, *with respect to this rhythm*, which was so alien to the girl's vital personal rhythms that during the first few days it seemed unendurable: she wanted to adapt herself to it, she *made an effort*, followed her friends' advice, invented a personal relation of interiority valid for herself alone (given her height, strength, other physical characteristics, etc.), which is, if you like, the best means of individual adaptation. To do this, it is *entirely obvious* that she gave herself to the machine, and that the latter, insofar as it is the work of Others, in the negative unity of

a destiny, takes possession of her work and makes it other; ultimately, the total adaptation to semi-automatism is the destruction of the girl's organic rhythms, and the interiorization of a
rhythm which is absolutely other. But the moment in which the
girl reveals herself as the *object of the machine*—that is, the moment the mystification reveals itself as objective alienation—
is also the moment that she is successful in her adaptation
(within the narrow limits assigned her). There was nothing she
could have avoided (short of, perhaps, failing to adapt and
finding herself eliminated, first from the labor market, finally,
as in excess, from society, through sickness); the constraints at
the outset (the impossibility of her family staying alive, unless
at least *three people* work at the factory), the constraints that
find her in the factory, in front of the production line, etc.—
these are ineluctable, and each reinforces the others. But these
constraints do not derive from things, except to the extent that
things make themselves the relays of human actions; behind
these, there is the multiplicity of workers and their false unity
through the factory—that is, through a destiny to be denied
and experienced together. Besides, these are requirements, not
purely material constraints, insofar as a free *praxis* is defined
according to these stony voices. In other words, freedom, here,
does not mean the possibility of choice, but the necessity of living
the constraint, in the form of a requirement to be fulfilled by a
*praxis*. . . .

When the free individual *praxis* develops as an undertaking
that is temporalizing through the course of a life, its motivations are never "psychical" or "subjective": they are the things,
the real structures, insofar as they are revealed by the project
through its concrete ends and from the standpoint of these ends.
Also most of the time, there is no *explicit consciousness:* the
situation is known through the act that it motivates, and this act
already denies it. But *precisely* because the Others are brought
into operation through things, and because their freedom is
relevant to my freedom as Other—that is, as freedom-thing, or
as freedom of this thing or that—the structure of the situation
remains, nonetheless, *requirement*. It is negligible in the instance that concerns us, but this authoritarian structure of passivity has a variable and sometimes major importance, depending upon the extent to which the free *praxis* of the individual
re-actualizes this structure by constituting itself, and exhausts

itself by surrendering its own sovereignty to this piece of matter—which, as we have seen, turns his sovereignty against itself and converts it into inertia, because the matter cannot be transcended. But this inertia itself alters the *praxis*, insofar as it is *praxis;* it gives its status of thing to a free activity, not to another thing.

*Critique de la raison dialectique*, 364–365, 366.

## 4 THE GROUP

The upheaval that rends a collectivity [*collective*] of individuals by the lightning stroke of a common *praxis* obviously originates in a synthetic—and consequently, material—transformation, which occurs in the context of scarcity and of existing structures. For organisms whose risk and practical movement, and suffering as well, reside in need, the driving force is danger, at every level of materiality (*i.e.*, be it hunger or the bankruptcy *whose meaning* is hunger, etc.) or transformations of instrumentality (the requirements and the scarcity of the tool replace the scarcity of the immediate object of need, the modifications of the tool, grasped in their ascending meaning, as necessary modifications of the collectivity). In other words, without the original tension of need as a relation of interiority with Nature, the change would not take place; and, conversely, there is no common *praxis*—at whatever level it is situated—whose regressive and descending meaning does not relate directly or indirectly to this original tension. Thus one must understand *above all* that the origin of any restructuring of collectivity into group is a complex fact that occurs *simultaneously* at every stage of materiality, but a fact that is transcended, as organizing *praxis*, at the level of serial unity. But the event, universal as it may be, cannot be lived as its own transcendence toward the unity of all, unless its universality is objective *for each person;* or, if you prefer, unless it creates in each person a unifying structure of objectivity. Up to this point, in fact—in the dimension of the collectivity—the real had defined itself by its impossibility. Indeed, what we call the *meaning of realities* refers precisely to the meaning of what is, by its principle, forbidden. The transformation, then, is effected when impossibility itself is impossible—or, if you prefer, when the synthetic event reveals the impossibility of changing as impossibility of living.* This has the direct result of making the *impossibility of changing* the very object to be transcended, in order to continue life. In other words, we have emerged into a vicious circle; the group constitutes itself on the basis of a need or a common danger, and defines itself by the common objective that determines its common *praxis.* Yet neither the common need, nor the common *praxis,* nor the common objective can define a community, unless the latter makes of itself a community by feeling individual need as common need, and by projecting itself, in the internal unification of a common integration, toward the objectives that it produces as common. Without famine, this group would not have constituted itself; but how is it that it defines itself as common struggle against a common need? Why do not the individuals—as also happens—in a particular case quarrel among themselves over food like dogs? That is the same as asking how a synthesis occurs when the power of synthetic unity exists simultaneously everywhere (with every individual, as the free unification of the field) and nowhere (insofar as it would concern a free transcendent unification of the plurality of individual unifications). Indeed, let us not forget that the *common object,* as the unity of the multiple outside of itself, is above all the producer of serial unity, and that it is on the basis of this double determination that the antidialectical structure of the collectivity—or *otherness*—is constituted.

But this last observation can help us. If, indeed, the object

* It is obvious that anglers do not form their clubs, nor old ladies their circulating libraries, under the threat of mortal danger; yet these groups—which, incidentally, answer very real needs, and whose objective meaning relates to the total situation—are superstructures or, if you prefer, groups constituted in the general and permanent activity of the regroupment of collectivities (class structures, class against class, national and international organizations, etc.). Beginning at that moment when the stage of the dialectical regrouping of dialectics is attained, the totalizing activity *itself* becomes a factor, setting, and reason of the secondary groups. They are its living determination, and take a part in the negation; but, at the same time, they contain it entirely within itself, and their dialectical conflicts take place through it and by means of it. In this way . . . they can be studied either horizontally (and empirically) insofar as they determine themselves in a setting where the structure of the group is already given objectively, or vertically insofar as each one of them expresses, in its concrete richness, the whole of human materiality and the whole of the historical process. Thus, I have only to concern myself here with the fundamental fact of the grouping as the *praxis*' conquest, or reconquest, of the collectivity.

itself produces itself, as the link of otherness between the individuals of the collectivity, the serial structure of multiplicity depends, basically, upon the fundamental characteristics of the object itself, and upon its original relation with all and with each person. Thus it is that the complex of means of production, insofar as they are the property of *Others*, gives to the proletariat its original structure of seriality, because this complex is an undefined group of objects whose requirements themselves reflect the *demand* of the bourgeoisie as seriality of the Other. But on the other hand, one can consider, in the experience, the common objects, which by themselves and *in the practico-inert field* constitute the rough delineation of a totality (as totalization of the multiple by the Other, through matter), and can ask oneself if they, too, should constitute the multiple envisaged as seriality.

Since the twelfth of July, the people of Paris have been in a state of insurrection. Its wrath has deep causes, but these causes as yet have reached the lower classes only in their common powerlessness (cold, hunger, etc., everything experienced in resignation, that serial behavior which presents itself falsely as individual virtue, or in unorganized outbursts, riots, etc.). On the basis of what external circumstances will groups constitute themselves? . . .

*Critique de la raison dialectique, 384–386.*

## 5 ENCIRCLEMENT

From the exterior, the government constitutes Paris as a totality. As early as July eighth, Mirabeau reported to the National Assembly (but his speech is known at the same time to the Parisians) that thirty-five thousand men are divided between Paris and Versailles, and twenty thousand more are to come. And Louis XVI answers the deputies: "It is necessary that I use my power to restore and maintain order in the capital. . . . These are the reasons that have led me to have troops assembled around Paris." And the morning of Sunday the twelfth, the city is designated to itself, internally, by posters "by order of the king" which announce that the concentration of troops around Paris is intended to protect the town against brigands. Thus, as practico-inert tension and as *exis* of the Parisian gathering, the place is constituted by an exterior *praxis*, organized as a totality.

This totality, moreover, as object of *praxis* (city to surround, disturbances to prevent) is by itself a determination of the practico-inert field; the city is simultaneously the place, in its totalized and totalizing configuration (the state of siege sketching itself out determines it as containing) and the population designated under the form of materiality sealed by the military act which produces it as an enclosed crowd. The *rumors*, the *posters*, the *news* (especially that of Necker's departure), relay to each individual his common designation: *he is a particle of a sealed materiality*. At this level, it might be said that the totality of the encirclement is lived *in seriality*. This is what is called effervescence: people are running in the streets, shouting, gathering in groups, burning the gates of the tollhouses. The link of individuals among them is, under the diverse real forms that it can take, that of otherness as the immediate revelation of oneself in the Other. *Imitation*—which I have described elsewhere* —is one of the manifestations of this otherness of quasi-reciprocity. This structure of otherness is constituted by the *common fate as totality*. That is, the common fate appears as the practical objective of the royal armies;† here it is a totality of destruction, insofar as the individuals are designated by their identical affiliation with the same city. By threatening to destroy the seriality by *the negative order of massacre*, the troops, as practical unities, give this totality experienced as a negation in each —but a *possible* negation—seriality. It is thus, by the coexistence of the two structures, the one being the possible and future negation of the other (and simultaneously the negation of all in each), that each person continues to see himself in the Other, but he sees himself there as *himself*—that is, here, as the totalization in himself of the Parisian population, by the saber slash or the gunshot that will wipe him out. And this *situation* establishes what is improperly called contagion or imitation, etc.: in

* See above, p. 81.—Ed.

† The government seems to have had no precise intentions. It did not really know what it wanted, nor what it was capable of. But that has no importance: the deploying of troops and the beginning of the encirclement carried their objective meaning in themselves, that is, they designated the Parisian populace as the sole object of a systematic and synthetic undertaking of annihilation. It is useless to say that no one at court wanted that slaughter; it became, of itself and because of the relevance of an army's general function to that particular situation, an immediate possibility which was actually no longer dependent upon *an intention* of the leaders.

this behavior, indeed, each sees in the Other his own future, and discovers, on that basis, his present act in the act of the Other. *To imitate*, in these still inert movements, is *to discover*, simultaneously, *oneself* in the process of performing one's own action over there in the Other; and performing here, in oneself, the action of the Other, fleeing in one's own flight and that of the Other,* attacking with a single attack in the Other and with his own fists; without agreement or accord (in fact, exactly the opposite of an agreement), but realizing and living the otherness on the basis of the synthetic unity of a totalization, organized and *to come*, of the gathering [*rassemblement*] by an exterior group.

Then incidents occur in Paris itself, at the gates and in the Tuileries garden, between military detachments and groupings produced by imitation. The outcome is a new thrust of serial and defensive violence: the arms depots are looted. This revolutionary response to a situation which was deteriorating every minute has, certainly, the historical importance of a common and organized act. But in fact it is not that. It is a collective performance: each person is determined to arm himself by the effort Others make to find arms, and each person tries to arrive before the Others since, in the context of the newly emerged scarcity, each individual's effort to take a gun becomes the Other's danger of remaining unarmed. At the same time, the performance is constituted by relations of imitation and of contagion; each finds himself in the Other by the very manner in which he starts out. However these violent and effective gatherings are perfectly inorganic; they lose their unity and find their unity again, without anything being changed with respect to what one might call (as did Durkheim, though in a totally different sense) the "mechanical solidarity" of their members. Moreover, they run the danger of quarreling among themselves soon over a gun (the rupture of the collective into reciprocities of antagonism). If the meaning of this passive activity is revolutionary, it is above all to the extent that, under the pressure of an exterior *praxis*, the unity of powerlessness (that is, the inertia) transforms itself into a massed crowd, into *weight of number*. For this crowd, which is still structured within itself in otherness, finds in its very disorganization an irresistible me-

---

* He who sees someone run, runs: not that he is learning *what must be done;* he discovers *what he is in the process* of doing. And, of course, he cannot discover it *except by doing it. . . .*

chanical force for breaking the sporadic resistances of those in charge of the arms depots. But the other factor which will soon create the revolutionary *praxis* of the group is that the individual act of *arming oneself,* insofar as in itself it is a complex process whose end is, for each individual, the defense of his own life, and whose driving force is seriality—this act, *by itself* and in its result, turns into freedom in a double sense. Insofar as everyone wants to defend his life against the dragoons—or, if you like, insofar as the government is attempting a policy of force and insofar as this attempt at an organized practice determines the whole of the field as practical, with whatever *promotes* this policy and whatever can oppose it—the result *in the field of the praxis* is that *the people of Paris have taken arms against the king. . . . A united group has produced a concerted action.* This is the case not only for the leaders of the army who know it, but for the Parisian population, which re-interiorizes this knowledge as a structure of unity. The unity, here, is still *elsewhere,* that is, is still past and future. Past: *the group has performed an act* and the collectivity observes this with surprise, as a moment of its passive activity; *it has been a group.* And this group has defined itself by a revolutionary action that renders the process irreversible. Future: the arms themselves, to the extent that they have been taken in order to oppose the concerted action of the military troops, adumbrate in their very materiality the possibility of a concerted resistance.

The uneasiness of the electors is going to create institutional groups inside the gathering, as *negative unities.* They decide, in fact, to re-establish a militia of forty-eight thousand citizens, and instruct the districts to implement the decision. The avowed end is to avoid public disturbances. In this new moment, the future militia appears as levied from the gathering with the intention of combating it, while the majority of the population has no fear of "uprisings" and, with justification, sees real danger only in the troops billeted around the capital. . . .

The violent contradiction between the militia and the people, being produced within the people, produces the possibility of an internal unity, as the negation of the unity of exteriority. The militia, insofar as it is still a *seal* applied to a multiplicity, cannot contradict and dissolve itself except in a *free organization.* Freedom—as the simple positive determination of the *praxis,* organized on the basis of its real objectives (defending oneself against the soldiers of the Prince of Lambesc)—manifests itself as the necessity of dissolving necessity. On the basis of that, a dialectic is set up at the Hôtel de Ville, between the constituted authorities who do not want to supply weapons, who beat about the bush and find loopholes, and the crowd, becoming more and more menacing, revealing itself through the behavior of the electors, the provost of merchants, etc., as *unity-exis*. When rags are found in the cases of weapons promised by Flesselles, the crowd considers itself to be *deceived*, that is, it interiorizes the behavior of Flesselles and grasps it *not in seriality* but against seriality, as a sort of passive synthesis. In fact, *deception*, as procedure, is located in the context of an antagonistic relation of reciprocity. In deceiving the crowd,* Flesselles confers upon the flight in otherness a sort of *personal* unity; and this personal unity necessarily characterizes the reaction of wrath that translates it, and, for the gathering itself reveals it. Each individual reacts in a new fashion: not as individual or as Other, but as singular incarnation of the common person. This new reaction in itself has nothing magical in it: it merely translates the re-interiorization of a reciprocity.

*Critique de la raison dialectique*, 387–391.

## 6 APOCALYPSE

From this moment on, something is given which is neither the group nor the series, but what Malraux, in *L'Espoir,* has called the Apocalypse—that is, the dissolution of the series into the group in fusion. And this group, still unstructured—that is, completely *amorphous*—characterizes itself as the immediate contrary of otherness. In the serial relation, in fact, unity as the Reason of the series is always *elsewhere;* in the Apocalypse, although the seriality remains at least as a process on the way to liquidation—and although it can always reappear—the synthetic unity is always present *here.* Or, if you prefer, in every place in the city at every moment, in every partial process, the part comes entirely into play and the movement of the city finds there its fulfilment and its meaning. "By evening," writes Montjoye,†

---

* It seems that he acted in good faith, but this makes little difference. The crowd did not *believe itself* deceived: it *was* deceived.
† In *L'Ami du Roi,* Part III, p. 70.

"Paris was a new city. Cannon shots, fired intermittently, warned the people to be on their guard. To the noise of the cannons was added that of the bells, which kept sounding the alarm. The sixty churches where the residents were gathered overflowed with people. Everyone there was an orator."

The city is the group in fusion; we shall soon see how the latter is to be distinguished from seriality. However, first we must make it clear that it will congeal into a collectivity if it is not structured in a temporal development whose speed and duration obviously depend upon the circumstances and the situation. Actually, the group in fusion is still the series, denying itself by re-interiorizing the exterior negations; or, if you wish, there is no difference in this moment between the positive itself (group in the process of formation) and that negation which denies itself (series in dissolution). We can point out that the first structuring (insofar as it comes from the group itself) reaches *one* district, as the part of an entirely fluid whole, *of its practico-inert structure*. The Saint-Antoine district has always lived *in the shadow* of the Bastille; that black fortress is a threat, not so much because it is a prison as because of its cannons. It is the symbol of repressive force, as the boundary of a poverty-stricken and agitated district. Furthermore, clashes and repressed uprisings —in particular the bloody repression during the month of April, the Reveillon affair—remained inside the gathering itself, as an *exis*. . . . What interests us now, from the standpoint of the genesis of an active group, is that this *exis in fact* structures a route; it is first of all the hodological determination of the lived space of the district. And this route is negative: it is the possibility of the troops entering the district, by coming from the west and the northwest, to carry out massacres there (as in April). In other words, the practico-inert unity of the field is determined, at the moment in which seriality is in the process of dissolution, as a possible act of penetration by the Other, that is, by a free enemy organization. At the same time, this possibility actualizes the threat of the Bastille: it is the possibility, for the district's inhabitants, of being *caught in the crossfire*. . . .

And the Bastille, in turn, in the context of scarcity, reveals the primary requirement of common freedom: in order to defend the district against the soldiers, weapons are necessary; now these are lacking *in the district*, but they are present in the Bastille. The Bastille becomes the common interest insofar as it *can and must,* at one and the same time, be disarmed, be a source of supply of weapons, and, perhaps, be turned against the enemies coming from the west. Urgency derives, then, from the scarcity of time: the enemy is not there, but it might arrive at any minute. The operation defines itself for everyone as the urgent discovery of a terrible common freedom. . . .

The essential characteristic of the group in fusion is the sudden restoration of freedom. Not that freedom has ever ceased to be the condition of the act, and the mask that dissimulates alienation; but we have seen that it has become, in the practico-inert field, the mode in which alienated man must live his own servitude in perpetuity, and, finally, the sole means he has to reveal the necessity of his alienation and his powerlessness. The explosion of the revolt, as liquidation of the collectivity, does not *directly* draw its sources from the alienation, revealed by freedom, nor from freedom suffered as powerlessness; a conjunction of historical circumstances is needed; an historical change in the situation, a risk of death, violence.

*Critique de la raison dialectique,*
*391–392, 393–394, 425.*

## 7 THE OATH

The group in fusion found its unity quite simply in real common activity, that is, just as much in its undertaking as in that of the adversary and in the violent, dangerous, sometimes mortal effort to destroy the common danger. The totalization of the group had nothing ideal about it, it came about through sweat and blood; it objectivized itself through destruction, perhaps through the slaughter of enemies (as witnessed by the summary executions after the taking of the Bastille). At the same time, although constituting itself as a means of acting, the group did not posit itself for itself: it posited the objective, and it *became praxis.* But if the grouped multiplicity should survive the realization of its immediate objectives, the urgency becomes distant. . . . The differentiations of the group, during the skirmish, the group's transformations and its real intentions, occurred under the almost unbearable pressure of the enemy group, and they were determined as negations of that pressure. In this sense, they might have been called "adaptive behavior"; the structure of the fighting group is, after all, that of the enemy, *apprehended in replica*. In absence, the new differentiations are, to be sure, narrowly defined with respect to the totality of objective circumstances; it is no less true that the group determines itself in accordance with a future unification (unification through the enemy's return), and of a past unity (its group-being as transcended past, or, in other terms, its practical reality insofar as it *has been* and insofar as it is objectivized in materiality). This means that it has no way of acting upon the enemy, tomorrow or even tonight, other than by presently acting upon itself. This structure of common action already existed implicitly in the fusion, since the original differentiations are, in fact, internal transformations of the group. Yet active and passive were closely mingled, such that, often, one could not know whether the group differentiated itself by its struggle, or whether it was differentiated by the enemy maneuver.* In contrast, the differentiation —when the enemy is not realized as a force undergone—becomes, within the group, the action of the group upon itself. In other words, the group becomes the means of future action, by becoming its own immediate objective. We can speak here of *reflection*, in the strictly practical sense: the group, waiting for the attack, seeks positions to occupy, separates in order to be able to fill all of them, distributes the weapons, assigns patrols to some, and to others the job of scouting or of guarding a certain post, establishes communications—even of the crudest sort, a mere cry of warning—and through this, in the free exploitation of place and resources, it is constituted for itself as a group. Its objective is certainly a new status, in which individuals and subgroups assume—in it, by it, and for it—various functions which intensify its power and tighten its unity. It is impossible to deny it *posits itself for itself* once it has survived its victory; or, if you prefer, a new structure must be taken into account—*the group consciousness*. . . .

The group comes *to see itself* revealed in *its* already past victory; that is, it takes itself as its own end, at first implicitly (we will see the Bastille conquered, that fortress finally reduced to powerlessness) and then explicitly (the lowered drawbridges,

---

* Or by *false maneuver:* by throwing itself blindly on one part of the group, without seeing the other elements pouring out from other streets, the troop of soldiers or police constitutes these newcomers as those who *surround* it, or else defines them by the opportunity it has given them of attacking it *from the rear.*

the prisoners, the free movement in courtyards and halls, all reflect, in the practico-inert, the action that changed their status). To this extent, then, reflexivity comes to the group from its past *praxis*, insofar as the object produced designates the group to itself as a group—to the very extent that that object belongs only to an unfolding *praxis* of the group. But this object designates it to every third party in a synthetic opposition between what the group is and what it is becoming: the group—externalized, past, inert, inscribed in the thing—is already made of marble or steel; its object-being (the Bastille) is the real conservation of its past-being (the practical struggle and the victory) to the extent that this past being is, in itself, inert (being transcended). But, insofar as its *praxis* of revelation is a common *praxis* and insofar as the common object reflects this community, the practical relationship appears as a process of disintegration. Indeed, from one point of view, the only *reason* for the regrouping here is the common object, insofar as it demands to be apprehended in common. Thus the immense pressures that determined the liquidation of the serial relationship have temporarily disappeared. . . . The group becomes, in each person, the common objective: its *permanence* must be salvaged. . . .

When freedom becomes a common *praxis* in order to establish the group's permanence, producing its own inertia by itself and in mediated reciprocity, this new status is called *the oath*. It stands to reason that this oath can take many different forms, from the explicit act of swearing (the Tennis-Court Oath, the oath as synthetic link among members of the medieval community), to the oath implicitly assumed as an already existing reality of the group (for example, for those who are born into the group and grow up among its members). In other words, the *historical act* of taking an oath in common—although it is in universal practice, and *in every case* corresponds to the surviving group's resistance to the separating action of differentiation and (spatio-temporal) estrangement—is not the necessary form of the common oath, insofar as the latter is a warranty against the future, an inertia produced in immanence and by freedom, a basis of all differentiation. If, for example, we examine it as a communal link in the Middle Ages— in its explicit reality as an historical act—it simply presents itself *as such*, and reveals its structures more easily.

The oath is a mediated reciprocity. All its derivative forms—

for example, the legal oath of the witness, the individual oath sworn upon the Bible, etc.—acquire meaning only on the basis of that original oath. But one must beware of confusing it with a *social contract*. Here it is by no means a question of seeking any basis whatever in this society or that—an undertaking whose absolute absurdity we shall see later on—but of showing the necessary transition from one form of the group, immediate but in danger of being dissolved, to another form, one that is reflexive but permanent.

*Critique de la raison dialectique,*
*434–436, 437, 439.*

## 8 TERROR

If we look at it closely, we see that the basis of terror is the fact that the group has not, and cannot have, the ontological status that it claims in its *praxis:* conversely, it is the fact that each and every person is produced and defined on the basis of this non-existent totality. There is a sort of interior emptiness, an indeterminate and unbridgeable distance, of uneasiness in each community, large or small; this uneasiness gives rise to a reinforcement of the practices of integration, and increases proportionately with the increased integration of the group. . . .

Of the two negations of the group—the individual *praxis* and seriality—the former, as we have seen, is accompanied by the realization of the common undertaking; it is the ontological negation and the practical realization. The latter is definitive, and it is in opposition to this seriality that the group was originally consituted. However, it is the individual *praxis* that constitutes the suspect for the apparatus of terror. But this is because terror is itself, in its own eyes, suspect, insofar as it becomes, in fact, the function and power of certain subgroups and certain common individuals (public prosecutors, juries, judges of the revolutionary tribunal, Committee of Public Safety, etc.), it is realized by deliberations and decisions that themselves create recurrence, and at the same time, by processes that are realized in the tension of transcendence-immanence. By the purge—of whatever sort, whether exclusion or execution—the purger is constituted as suspect, and is always likely to be purged; he produces himself as such *in his own eyes.* . . .

On the basis of well-defined exterior circumstances (invasion, provincial disturbances, the revolt in La Vendée, the social up-risings, and the danger of famine), the Terror has already estab-lished itself as the sole means of governing. And—in whatever historical circumstance we may be considering—it arises out of opposition to seriality, not freedom. Indeed, in its origin, and in its manifestation as well, it is freedom liquidating, by means of violence, the indefinite flight of the Other, that is, powerless-ness. At the Convention, the Terror is born of the objective con-tradiction between the necessity for a common *praxis*, free and indivisible, and the objective but elusive—and, moreover, unfor-mulated—divisions of a governing Assembly which remains in turmoil, *altered* by the violence it has experienced. In this fun-damental atmosphere, the free *praxis* is suspect: seriality me-diated by freedom is revealed, then, as passive otherness, and consequently practical freedom is denounced as creator of otherness. All this can be lived as the diffuse reality of the group (integration refused to *him who has just come in;* in all the narrow spheres of prisons, houses of detention and of cor-rection, etc. Genet has undergone and defined the permanent ex-perience of terror; fraternity was realized in only one way: against him). The experience can also occur insofar as one *ex-periences upon oneself* the *praxis* (surveillance, police control, threats, arrests, etc.) of specialized apparatus. In any case, each person is purger and purged; the Terror is *never* a system estab-lished by the will of a minority, but rather the reappearance—under definite circumstances—of a fundamental relation of the group as an interhuman relationship. . . .

The fundamental modification consists in the total transfer of the *common being of the group*—regulative freedom and the impossible ontological unity—to the *praxis* of the group as such. The group *praxis*, and this alone, creates the common unity, and the group claims ontological status all the more force-fully as the reawakening seriality risks dissolving the group. Con-sequently, each person's reciprocal work consists in projecting the ontological unity onto the practical unity: the *praxis* be-comes the group's being and its essentiality; it will produce in the *praxis* its men as the inorganic instruments it needs for its evolution. And freedom lies *in the praxis,* not in each individual action. This new structure of the group is simultaneously the practice of the Terror and a reaction of defense against the Ter-ror; it consists in a double relation of mediated reciprocity. Each person is construed by the Other, through everyone, as the inorganic tool by means of which action is realized; each person constitutes action as freedom itself, in the form of terror-imperative. It is this freedom that gives a little borrowed freedom to its own tools. Yet this borrowed freedom is not disturbing; rather, it is the reflection of the common freedom upon a particular inorganic object, not the practical freedom of a single agent. At this level the institution is defined.

*Critique de la raison dialectique,*
*567–568, 578–580.*

## 9 THE INSTITUTION

The institution cannot be produced as practice's free determination of itself. And if practice again takes charge of the institution as a defense against terror, this is to the extent that this petrification of itself is an induced metamorphosis, whose origin is elsewhere. We are familiar with this origin: it is *precisely* the re-emergence of seriality. For the institution has that contradictory characteristic, often pointed out by sociologists, of being both *praxis* and thing. As *praxis*, its teleological meaning can be obscured; but this is because the institution is nothing but a carcass, or because those who are institutionalized have a real comprehension of the institution's end, and cannot or do not want to communicate it; indeed, every time we have the means of deciphering it (for example, every time we examine those institutions of a contemporary industrialized society), we discover its teleological characteristics, that is, a solidified dialectic of alienated ends, liberating ends, and the alienation of these new ends. On the other hand, however, the institution as such possesses a considerable force of inertia, not only because it is a part of an institutional whole, and cannot be modified without all the other parts being modified, but particularly, and in itself, because it posits itself, by and in its inert-being, as essentiality, defining men as the inessential means of its perpetuation. But this inessentiality comes neither from the institution to the individual, nor from the individual to the institution; in actual fact, what becomes isolated is the practice, insofar as it is produced in a common setting defined by new human relationships. These relationships are quite simply based upon serial powerlessness: if

I apprehend the institution as fundamentally unchangeable, it is because my *praxis* itself is determined in the institutionalized group as incapable of changing the institution; and this power-lessness originates in my relation of circular otherness with the other members of the group. . . .

*The institution's being*, as the geometrical center of the inter-sections of the collective and the common, is the non-being of the group, produced as a relationship among its members. The unity of the institution is the unity of otherness, insofar as it is introduced into the group, and insofar as the group uses it to re-place its own missing unity. But its relation to each individual is one of interiority, although it can be defined as the *praxis* in exteriority: indeed, it determines each individual as inertia and as practical obligation. In fact, it transcends each person inso-far as it resides in all the Others, and insofar as it is, there, un-predictable and other, and is dependent upon this unpredictable-ness. But on the other hand, insofar as it is institutionalized *praxis,* it remains *a power over each individual* (in the name of his oath of loyalty), or, if each person represents and maintains it, it is *his free power over the Others*. At present this free power is challenged: for each individual and his power appears to each individual in the contradictory unity of the same and of the Other. Consequently recognition is challenge, but challenge is recognition. . . . Thus everywhere, even in the army (a type of institutional group), the new status of power is revealed: in the organized group it can be defined as the right to do one's duty; here, it should be defined as the duty of doing one's best in order that one's right to do one's duty be recognized. Institutional man must obtain this *recognition* through two opposed and simul-taneous practices: on the one hand, when his institutional power is not directly in question, the general tactic is to liquidate the Other in himself in order to liquidate it in the Others (the officer living in the midst of his men, regulating his whole life by theirs); on the other hand, when the moment of exercising power arrives, institutional man is suddenly constituted as the absolute Other, through his playing of a role and wearing of a uniform. He establishes the tenacity of exercised power, decisions taken, etc., upon his *institution-being,* that is, upon the inertia and the total opacity of otherness, which has become the particular insti-tution's presence in him, and hence the group's presence as com-mon *praxis.* Indeed, at this level the mystification is easily achieved: since the institution remains practice and the group has not dissolved, the former, in its negative being (which, fundamentally, is merely the ubiquity of non-being) is revealed in the appropriate circumstances as the ontological status of the community. This means that it refers to the whole of the institutional system as the relational totality of the grouped multiplicity's synthetic determinations. Through the power-man, who reveals himself—through familiar rituals and dances—as institution-being, the organized individual believes he apprehends himself as integrated into the group through the institutional whole (and, as a matter of fact, this is what every citizen believes and says), while actually the institution can appear only at a determined moment of the group's involution, and appear as the precise index of its disintegration. . . . Powerlessness and imperative, terror and inertia, are reciprocally established. The institutional moment, in the group, corresponds to what might be called systematic self-domestication, that of man by man. The end is, in fact, to create men such that (as common individuals) they are defined in their own eyes and among themselves by their fundamental relation (mediated reciprocity) to institutions. More than half the work is done by circular seriality; a systematic activity of each person upon himself, and of each person through all, will result in the creation of the rigorous correlative of the institution-man, that is, the institutionalized man. To the extent that the ossified *praxis* (the institution) receives its ossification from our powerlessness, it constitutes—for each person and for all—a definite index of *reification*. This does not necessarily mean that we experience it as a constraint, but rather that it is our own inorganic inertia in the social sphere. But the moment of common degradation at which the institution appears is precisely that in which each person claims to reject freedom for himself, in order to realize, as a thing, the imperiled unity of the descending group. Thus at this level of involution (under the pressure of external circumstances), the common individual wants to become a thing held against other things by the unity of a seal; the model of the institutional group will be the *forged tool.* And each person, as such, is an accomplice of institutionality. But, conversely, this is also because he is its victim, *even prior to his birth.* The previous generation had defined, even before he was born, the institutional future of his generation, its exterior and mechanical destiny, that is, as determination of untranscendability (or as determination *of its being*). Military, civic, professional, etc., "obligations" constitute, in advance, an untranscendability deep inside each person (if he is born within the group); naturally, one must *fulfill* these obligations (and not "play these roles" or "preserve these attitudes," as the cultural analysts say, indiscriminately confusing material conditions, possibilities defined by the historical whole on the basis of these conditions, and institutional obligations). These births into the group are oaths (reiterated by *rites de passage*), and these oaths become an assumption of the institutional inertia with which the others have marked the child under the form of the free commitment to *realize the institution*. From this point of view, the institutional being is, in each person, a prefabricated inertia of inorganic being, which will be transcended through a practical freedom whose sworn function is to objectify itself in that same being as the inert determination of the future. The institution produces its agents (the organizers and the organized) by marking them in advance with institutional determinations; and reciprocally the institutionalized agents, in their relationships of directed otherness, identify themselves in turn with the practical system of institutional relationships, insofar as this system is necessarily inscribed in a group of processed objects whose origin is inorganic. Thus the institution, as stereotyped *praxis* (although often, under the pressure of such circumstances, its efficacy consists in stereotyping), in its rigidity is an adumbration of the future. As the inert persistence of a reified organization within a grouping which, in another connection, may very well reorganize itself, it is constituted as the elementary and abstract permanence of the social past *as being*, even and especially if the alterations in process reveal the perpetual change of this same past *as meaning*.

*Critique de la raison dialectique*,
*581, 583–586.*

## 10 THE SCANDAL

The scandal is not, as Hegel believed, the mere existence of the Other, which would throw us back upon an unintelligible situation. It lies in violence undergone (or threatened), that is, in interiorized scarcity. In this, although the original fact is logically and formally contingent (scarcity is merely a *material given*), its contingency does not hinder the intelligibility of violence—on the contrary. What is important, in fact, for the dialectical understanding of the Other, is the rationality of his *praxis*. Now this rationality appears in violence itself, insofar as the latter is not a contingent ferocity of man, but an understandable re-interiorization *in each person* of the contingent fact of scarcity; human violence is *meaningful*. And as this violence is, in each person, a negation of the Other, negation, in its reciprocity, becomes meaningful in and for each person as scarcity which has become a practical agent, or, if you prefer, as scarcity-man. Thus practical negation is constituted as negation of the scandal-negation, simultaneously insofar as the latter is the Other in each individual, and insofar as this Other is interiorized scarcity. From this point of view, what is indissolubly denied by the *praxis* is negation as a condition of man (that is, as conditioning reassumed in violence by the conditioned), and as the freedom of an Other. And it is precisely the scandal of the presence (as a sign of my object-being) of the Other's freedom in me, as negation-freedom of my freedom, is itself a determination in rationality to the extent that this negative freedom realizes in practice the impossibility of our coexisting in a field of scarcity. In short, on the basis of scarcity and in the perspective of the Other's annihilation, each person's struggle is a deeper understanding of others. Indeed, to understand, in the immediate sense, is to apprehend the *praxis* of the Other, in its ends and its means, as a simple objective and transcendent temporalization. To understand in struggle is to apprehend the Other's *praxis* in Immanence, through its own objectivity and in a practical transcendence. This time, I understand the enemy *in terms of myself* and I understand myself *in terms of the enemy:* his *praxis* is not revealed as a pure transcendent temporalization which I reproduce without participating in it; I understand it directly and from within, through the action I produce to defend myself against it. Urgency forces me to discover my objectivity and to assume it in every detail; it forces me to penetrate, as far as the concrete circumstances permit, the activity of the enemy. Understanding is an immediate fact of reciprocity. But however much this reciprocity remains positive, understanding remains abstract and external. Struggle, in the field of scarcity, as negative reciprocity, engenders the Other as Other than man, or counter-man; but at the same time I understand him, at the very sources of my *praxis*, as the negation of which I am the concrete and practical negation, and the danger of my death.

For each of the two adversaries, the struggle is intelligible; or rather, at this level, it is intelligibility itself. Were it not, the reciprocal *praxis* would, on its own, be stripped of meaning and of goals.* But what concerns us is the general problem of intelligibility, most particularly at the concrete level. Now *if a concrete dialectic [dialectique située]* is to be possible, a social conflict, a battle, an extraordinary conflict as complex event produced by the practices of the two individuals' or two multiplicities' reciprocal antagonism, must be *in principle* understandable to the third parties who depend upon it without participating in it, or to the witnesses who watch it from outside without being in the least involved in it. From this point of view, then, nothing is certain *a priori;* we must continue our experience. Indeed, each adversary *realizes* the intelligibility of the conflict because he totalizes it for *himself* in and by his own *praxis;* but the reciprocal negation is, for the third party, the very reality of the struggle. This third party, by its mediation, realizes the transcendent and objective unity of the positive reciprocities. Does this unity remain possible when each action aims at destroying that of the other, and when the observable results of this double negation are nil, or else—what most often happens—when the teleological meanings inscribed in each action by both adversaries have been semi-obliterated or transformed by the Other, to the point that no trace of concerted activity is any longer decipherable? In the same fashion, to take the simple example of a struggle between only two adversaries, each blow dealt by the one is dodged or parried or blocked by the other; never completely, however, un-

---

* Granted this formal characteristic does not preclude the existence of degrees in the reciprocal understanding of adversaries. Circumstances decide this, and one may be "handled like a child," "manipulated," etc.; or else one may take part in absurd wars (as happened in the late Middle Ages) in which the contradictions characteristic of the period result in the mutual incomprehension of the armies (who were trying not to meet). Also the result of the failure to understand the significance of a technical improvement was that the French nobility was decimated by the English bowmen. This is obvious: the enemy always counts upon a new weapon, an unpredicted, uncomprehended maneuver, to win its victory. But *precisely because of this*, we should understand that struggle as reciprocity is a function of the reciprocity of understanding. If one of the adversaries ceases to understand, he is the *object of the Other*.

less there be a considerable difference of strength or skill between them. And the same observation . . . would be valid for most of the historic "days of decision": often they end in indecision. Thus the results obtained cannot entirely be attributed either to the action of the insurgents or to that of the governmental forces; we must understand them not insofar as they are the realization of a project, but precisely as the action of each group (and also of chances, accidents, etc.) has prevented them from realizing that of the Other—that is, to the extent that they *are not* practical meanings, to the extent that their mutilated and truncated meaning does not correspond to anyone's practical plans and, in that sense, they fall short of the human.

*Critique de la raison dialectique, 752–754.*

# IV

---•---

## The Verdict of History

VOICE OF FRANZ (*from the tape recorder*)  Centuries of the future, here is my century, solitary and deformed—the accused. My client is tearing himself open with his own hands. What you take for white lymph is blood. There are no red corpuscles, for the accused is dying of hunger. But I will tell you the secret of these multiple incisions. The century might have been a good one had not man been watched from time immemorial by the cruel enemy who had sworn to destroy him, that hairless, evil, flesh-eating beast—man himself. One and one make one—there's our mystery. The beast was hiding, and suddenly we surprised his look deep in the eyes of our neighbors. So we struck. Legitimate self-defense. I surprised the beast. I struck. A man fell, and in his dying eyes I saw the beast still living—myself. One and one make one—what a misunderstanding! Where does it come from, this rancid, insipid taste in my mouth? From man? From the beast? From myself? It is the taste of the century. Happy centuries, you who do not know our hatreds, how could you understand the atrocious power of our fatal loves? Love. Hatred. One and one. . . . Acquit us! My client was the first to know shame. He knows he is naked. Beautiful children, you who are born of us, our pain has brought you forth. This century is a woman in labor. Will you condemn your mother? Eh? Answer! (*Pause*) The thirtieth century no longer replies. Perhaps there will be no more centuries after ours. Perhaps a bomb will blow out all the lights. Everything will be dead—eyes, judges, time. Night. Oh, tribunal of the night—you who were, who will be, and who are—I have been! I have been! I, Franz von Gerlach, here in this room, have taken the century upon my shoulders

484

and have said: "I will answer for it. This day and forever."
What do you say?

CURTAIN

*The Condemned of Altona, 177–178.*

# Selective Bibliography

*The numbers in brackets indicate material found in this anthology.*

### PHILOSOPHICAL WRITINGS

"La transcendance de l'ego: Esquisse d'une description phénoménologique," *Recherches philosophiques* VI (Paris: Boivin, 1936); translated by Forrest Williams and Robert Kirkpatrick as *The Transcendence of the Ego* (New York: Noonday, 1957). [51-57]

*L'imagination* (Paris: Alcan, 1936; 2nd ed. Presses Universitaires de France, 1948); translated by Forrest Williams as *Imagination* (Ann Arbor: University of Michigan Press, 1962).

*Esquisse d'une théorie des émotions* (Paris: Hermann, 1939); translated by Bernard Frechtman as *The Emotions: Outline of a Theory* (New York: Philosophical Library, 1948), and by Philip Mairet as *Sketch for a Theory of the Emotions* (London: Methuen, 1962. [74-76]

*L'imaginaire: Psychologie phénoménologique de l'imagination* (Paris: Gallimard, 1940); translated by Bernard Frechtman as *Psychology of the Imagination* (New York: Philosophical Library, 1948). [77-97]

*L'être et le néant: Essai d'ontologie phénoménologique* (Paris: Gallimard, 1943); translated by Hazel Barnes as *Being and Nothingness* (New York: Philosophical Library, 1956). [101-181, 188-230, 242-365]

*L'Existentialisme est un humanisme* (Paris: Nagel, 1946); translated by Bernard Frechtman as *Existentialism* (New York: Philosophical Library, 1947).

*Réflexions sur la question juive* (Paris: Mortihien, 1946); translated by George Becker as *Anti-Semite and Jew* (New York: Schocken Books, 1948), and by Eric de Mauny as *Portrait of of the Anti-Semite* (London: Secker and Warburg, 1948).

## SELECTIVE BIBLIOGRAPHY

*Baudelaire* (Paris: Gallimard, 1947); translated by Martin Turnell (New York: New Directions, 1950).

*Saint Genet, comédien et martyr* (Paris: Gallimard, 1952); translated by Bernard Frechtman as *Saint Genet, Actor and Martyr* (New York: Braziller, 1963). [378-411]

*Critique de la raison dialectique,* preceded by *Question de méthode* (Paris: Gallimard, 1960); *Question de méthode* translated by Hazel Barnes as *Search for a Method* (New York: Knopf, 1963); selections translated for this volume by Starr and James Atkinson. [415-483]


### NOVELS

*La Nausée* (Paris: Gallimard, 1938); translated by Lloyd Alexander as *Nausea* (New York: New Directions, 1949), and as *The Diary of Antoine Roquentin* (London: John Lehmann, 1949). [58-73]

*Les Chemins de la Liberté*

    I. *L'âge de raison* (Paris: Gallimard, 1945); translated by Eric Sutton as *The Age of Reason* (New York: Knopf, 1947).

    II. *Le sursis* (Paris: Gallimard, 1945); translated by Eric Sutton as *The Reprieve* (New York: Knopf, 1947).

    III. *La mort dans l'âme* (Paris: Gallimard, 1947); translated by Gerard Hopkins as *Troubled Sleep* (New York: Knopf, 1950), and as *Iron in the Soul* (London: Hamish Hamilton, 1950).

The fourth volume, *La Dernière Chance,* has never been completed. Extracts appeared under the title "Drôle d'Amitié" in *Les Temps Modernes,* November and December, 1949.


### SHORT STORIES

*Le mur* (Paris: Gallimard, 1939); translated by Lloyd Alexander as *Intimacy and Other Stories* (New York: New Directions, 1948).


### PLAYS

*Les mouches* (Paris: Gallimard, 1943); translated by Stuart Gilbert as *The Flies* (New York: Knopf, 1948). [235-241]

*Huis clos* (Paris: Gallimard, 1947); translated by Stuart Gilbert as
*No Exit* (New York: Knopf, 1948). [185-187]

*Morts sans sépulture* (Paris: Gallimard, 1947); translated by Lionel
Abel as *The Victors* (New York: Knopf, 1949).

*La putain respectueuse* (Paris: Gallimard, 1947); translated by Lionel
Abel as *The Respectful Prostitute* (New York: Knopf, 1949).

*Les mains sales* (Paris: Gallimard, 1948); translated by Lionel Abel
as *Dirty Hands* (New York: Knopf, 1949), and by Kitty Black
as *Crime Passionnel* (London: Hamish Hamilton, 1949).

*Le diable et le bon dieu* (Paris: Gallimard, 1951); translated by Kitty
Black as *The Devil and the Good Lord* (New York: Knopf,
1960), and as *Lucifer and the Lord* (London: Hamish Hamilton, 1953).

*Kean, ou désordre et génie* (Paris: Gallimard, 1954); translated by
Kitty Black as *Kean, or Disorder and Genius* (New York:
Knopf, 1960).

*Nekrassov* (Paris: Gallimard, 1956); translated by Sylvia and George
Leeson (New York: Knopf, 1960).

*Les séquestrés d'Altona* (Paris: Gallimard, 1960); translated by Sylvia
and George Leeson as *The Condemned of Altona* (New York:
Knopf, 1961), and as *Loser Wins* (London: Hamish Hamilton,
1960). [484]

Les mouches, Huis clos, Morts sans sépulture, and La putain respectueuse were published in 1947 as a single volume, *Theatre*, by
Gallimard. *The Flies* and *No Exit* were published in America in one
volume, as were *The Victors, The Respectful Prostitute*, and *Dirty
Hands*. The American edition of *The Devil and the Good Lord* also
includes translations of *Kean* and *Nekrassov*.

## FILM SCRIPTS

*Les jeux sont faits* (Paris: Nagel, 1946); translated by Louise Varèse
as *The Chips Are Down* (New York: Lear, 1948; London:
Rider, 1948).

*L'engrenage* (Paris: Nagel, 1948); translated by Mervyn Savill as
*In the Mesh* (London: Dakers, 1954).

## LITERARY AND POLITICAL ESSAYS

*Situations* (6 vols. Paris: Gallimard, 1947, 1948, 1949, 1964, 1965).
First volume, translated by Benita Eisler (New York: Braziller,
1965). Some essays from the first and second volumes have

been translated by Annette Michelson under the title *Literary and Philosophical Essays* (New York: Criterion Books, 1955); the essay *Qu'est-ce que c'est la littérature?* has been translated by Bernard Frechtman as *What Is Literature?* [*Literature and Existentialism*] (New York: Philosophical Library, 1949). [369-377]

Other essays have been translated by Wade Baskin in *Essays in Aesthetics* (New York: Citadel Press and Philosophical Library, 1963).

Sartre's analysis of the Cuban situation has been translated under the title *Sartre on Cuba* (New York: Ballantine Books, 1961).


## AUTOBIOGRAPHY

*Les mots* (Paris: Gallimard, 1964); translated by Bernard Frechtman as *The Words* (New York: Braziller, 1964).


A list of articles, reviews, and interviews can be found in Philip Thody, *Jean-Paul Sartre: A Literary and Political Study* (New York: Macmillan, 1961), pp. 244-46.

For philosophical background, *The Phenomenological Movement*, by Herbert Spiegelberg, can be consulted ("Phænomenologica" series, Vols. V and VI; The Hague: Nijhoff, 1959-60); the first volume covers the German phase of the movement; the second, the French phase. The best philosophical interpretation in English of Sartre himself is *Sartre, Romantic Rationalist* by Iris Murdoch (New Haven: Yale University Press, 1953). The best survey of his philosophical and literary writings is *Jean-Paul Sartre,* by Maurice Cranston (New York: Grove Press, 1962). I have discussed the relation between Sartre's philosophical and literary writings in *Aesthetics Today,* edited by Morris Philipson (New York: Meridian Books, 1961).

The best study of a single philosophical topic is *Emotion in the Thought of Sartre* by Joseph Fell (New York: Columbia University Press, 1965).

Sartre's *Les mots,* translated as *The Words* by Bernard Frechtman (New York: Braziller, 1964), discusses only his childhood and youth; additional biographical information can be found in *Sartre par lui-même,* by Francis Jeanson (Paris: Éditions du Seuil, 1955), and in the volumes of Simone de Beauvoir's autobiography: *Mémoires d'une jeune fille rangée* (Paris: Gallimard, 1958), translated by James Kirkup as *Memoirs of a Dutiful Daughter* (New York and Cleveland: World Publishing Company, 1959); *La force de l'âge* (Paris: Gallimard, 1960), translated by Peter Green as *The Prime of Life* (Cleveland: World Publishing Company, 1962); and *La force des choses* (Paris: Gallimard, 1963), translated by Richard Howard as *Force of Circumstance* (New York: Putnam, 1965).

*Excerpts from Sartre's statement to the Swedish press representatives in Paris the day after he had been awarded the 1964 Nobel Prize for Literature*

". . . My reasons for refusing the prize are both personal and objective.

"These are my personal reasons. My refusal is not a sudden decision. I have always declined official honors. After the war, in 1945, I was proposed for the Legion of Honor. I turned it down, though I had friends in the government. Likewise I never wished to enter the *College de France* as some of my friends suggested.

"This attitude is based on my conception of the role of the writer. A writer who takes a position on political, social, or literary questions should rely only on the means which are his —the written word. Any honors he might receive expose his readers to a pressure which I consider undesirable. The signature 'Jean-Paul Sartre' is one thing; the signature 'Jean-Paul Sartre, Nobel Prize winner,' is something else.

". . . The writer should then refuse to allow himself to be transformed into an institution, even under the most honorable circumstances, as on the present occasion. . . .

"These are my objective reasons for refusing the prize. The only struggle at present possible on the cultural front is for the peaceful coexistence of the two cultures, East and West. I do not mean that reconciliation is in order. I fully realize that their confrontation must necessarily take the form of a conflict, but it should be between men and cultures, without the intervention of institutions.

". . . This is why I cannot accept any honor awarded by the cultural authorities, whether of the East or of the West, even though I appreciate the justification for their existence. Although all my sympathies are socialist, I would be just as unable to accept, for example, the Lenin Prize, should it be offered, which has not happened.

". . . In the present situation the Nobel Prize appears objectively as an honor restricted to writers from the West or to rebels from the East. For example, it has not been awarded to Nerunda, one of the greatest South American poets. Louis Aragon has never been seriously considered, but he deserves it. Unfortunately it was awarded to Pasternak before Sholokhov, so that the only Soviet work to receive the award has been a work published abroad and prohibited in its own country. It should have been possible to maintain the balance by some compensating gesture. During the Algerian war, when we signed the 'Declaration of the 121,' I would have gratefully accepted the prize, for it would have honored not only me but also the freedom for which we were fighting. But that did not happen, and it is only after the end of the struggle that the prize is bestowed on me.

"In the citation of the Swedish Academy, freedom is spoken of. This is a word that lends itself to numerous interpretations. In the West it is taken to mean abstract freedom. But to me it means a more concrete freedom—the right to have more than one pair of shoes and to eat when hungry. There seems to me less danger in declining the prize than in accepting it. To accept it would be to lend myself to what I would describe as an 'objective salvage operation.' I read in the *Figaro Littéraire* that my controversial political past should not be held too much against me. I realize that this article does not express the opinion of the Academy, but it clearly indicates the interpretations that would have been put upon my acceptance in certain right-wing circles. I regard this 'controversial political past' as still valid, even though I am entirely ready to admit to my comrades past mistakes I have made.

"I am not implying that the Nobel Prize is a 'bourgeois prize,' but there you have the bourgeois interpretation that will inevitably be offered by circles I know well."

JEAN-PAUL SARTRE *was born in Paris in 1905. After being graduated from the Ecole Normale Supérieure in 1929 with a doctorate in philosophy, he taught for a while at Le Havre, Laon, and Paris. Taken prisoner in 1940, he was released after nine months and returned to Paris and teaching. His first play,* The Flies, *was produced in Paris during the German Occupation. His second play,* No Exit, *was the first to be performed in Paris after the liberation. From then on Sartre gave up teaching to devote all of his time to writing. Sartre declined the Nobel Prize for Literature. Excerpts from his statement at that time are reprinted at the end of this volume.*

ROBERT DENOON CUMMING *was born in Sydney, Nova Scotia, in 1917, and educated at Harvard, the University of Chicago, the* Ecole practique des hautes études *in Paris, and New College, Oxford, where he was a Rhodes Scholar. He served with the 2nd French Armored Division during World War II, receiving the* Croix de guerre avec étoile, *the Legion of Merit, and a Purple Heart. Since 1948, he has taught in the Philosophy and Political Science Departments at Columbia University. He was Chairman of the Philosophy Department from 1961 to 1964 and an editor of* The Journal of Philosophy *from 1959-1964. He has been awarded Fulbright, Guggenheim, and National Endowment for the Humanities Fellowships. He has edited Plato's* Apology, Euthyphro, *and* Crito, *and is the author of* Human Nature and History: A Study of the Development of Liberal Political Thought.

# VINTAGE BELLES—LETTRES